FRESHMEN ™

Conception
Adolescence
Childhood trauma
Social Condition
Pre School
High School
College
Long distance relationship
Detention
Summer School
Mother/Father
Love/Divorce
Skinny/Fat
Calculus
Foreign
Music
Science
Engineering

Cast out of the main dorms and forced to live in temporary housing in the Boughl Science Buidling, 14 members of the freshmen class of Freese College have been imbued with miraculous superpowers by the explosion of a mysterious device called the Ax-Cell-Erator!

With powers based on whatever they were thinking at that pivotal moment, some of the kids are blessed with fantastic abilities, like the power to seduce others, or tandem telekinesis. But others are cursed: A die-hard vegan can communicate with plants and vegetables, leaving him nothing to eat. A math whiz must become drunk or stoned in order to inebriate his enemies. One kid woke up with a major boost to his... personal equipment. And then there's a talking Beaver with a major attitude.

Led by a lifelong comic book fan who missed the life-changing event, the kids have to deal with the everyday trials of college while learning to become superheroes and delving into the mystery of their superpowered rival fraternity.

Kegger
Freak Superpower inducing accident
Good vs. Evil
Secret Headquaters   Henchmen
Mask vs. No Mask
Cape vs Cape and Cowl
Social Responsibility
Time Travel   Grades
Vigilante
Public service announcements
Licensing   Codename
Graduate
Diploma
Career

MAD... SIMPLY MAD.

FRESHMEN ™

Date Due

APR 10
3/1

Freshmen

co-created by
Seth Green
and **Hugh Sterbakov**

written by
Hugh Sterbakov
pencils by
Leonard Kirk
inks by
Andrew Pepoy
colors by
Tyson Wengler
letters by
Troy Peteri

for even more info than that check out
www.freshmencomic.com
and
www.fatboughl.com

for Top Cow Productions
Marc Silvestri_chief executive officer
Matt Hawkins_president / chief operating officer
Jim McLauchlin_editor in chief
Renae Geerlings_vp of publishing / managing editor
Scott Tucker_editor
Chaz Riggs_production manager
Annie Pham_marketing director
Peter Lam_webmaster
Phil Smith_trades and submissions
Rob Levin_production assistant
Scott Newman_intern

Hi3515

for this edition
Book Design and Layout by:
Phil Smith

BK. 3

What did you think of this book?
We love to hear from our readers.

write us at:
Freshmen Letters
c/o Top Cow Productions, Inc.
10350 Santa Monica Blvd., Suite #100
Los Angeles, CA 90025

To find the comics shop nearest you call 1-888-COMICBOOK

COMIC SHOP LOCATOR SERVICE
1-888-COMIC-BOOK
888-266-4226

image ®

for Image Comics
publisher **Erik Larsen**

Freshmen™ vol. 1 trade paperback, March 2006. FIRST PRINTING. ISBN# 1-58240-593-X
Published by Image Comics Inc. Office of Publication: 1942 University Ave., Suite 305 Berkeley, CA 94704. $16.99 US, $19.60 CAN. Originally published as
Freshmen issues #1-#6 and The *Freshmen* Yearbook. Freshmen is © 2006 Seth Green, Hugh Sterbakov and Top Cow Productions, Inc. "Freshmen," the Freshmen
logos, and the likeness of all featured characters are trademarks of Seth Green, Hugh Sterbakov, and Top Cow Productions, Inc. All rights reserved. The characters,
events and stories in this publication are entirely fictional. With the exception of artwork used for review purposes, none of the contents of this book may be reprint-
ed in any form without the express written consent of Top Cow Productions, Inc.
PRINTED IN CANADA.

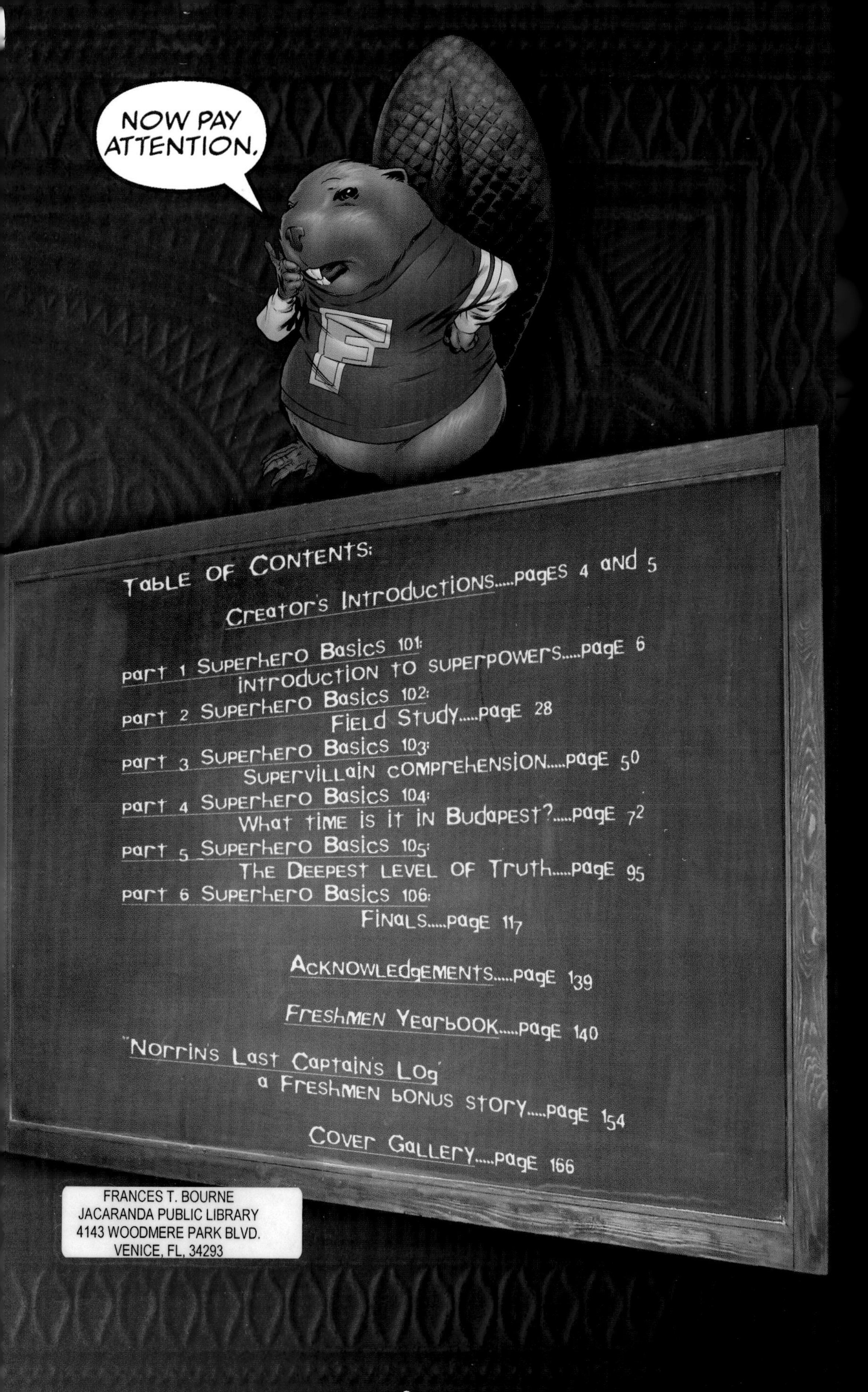
NOW PAY ATTENTION.

Table OF CONTENTS:

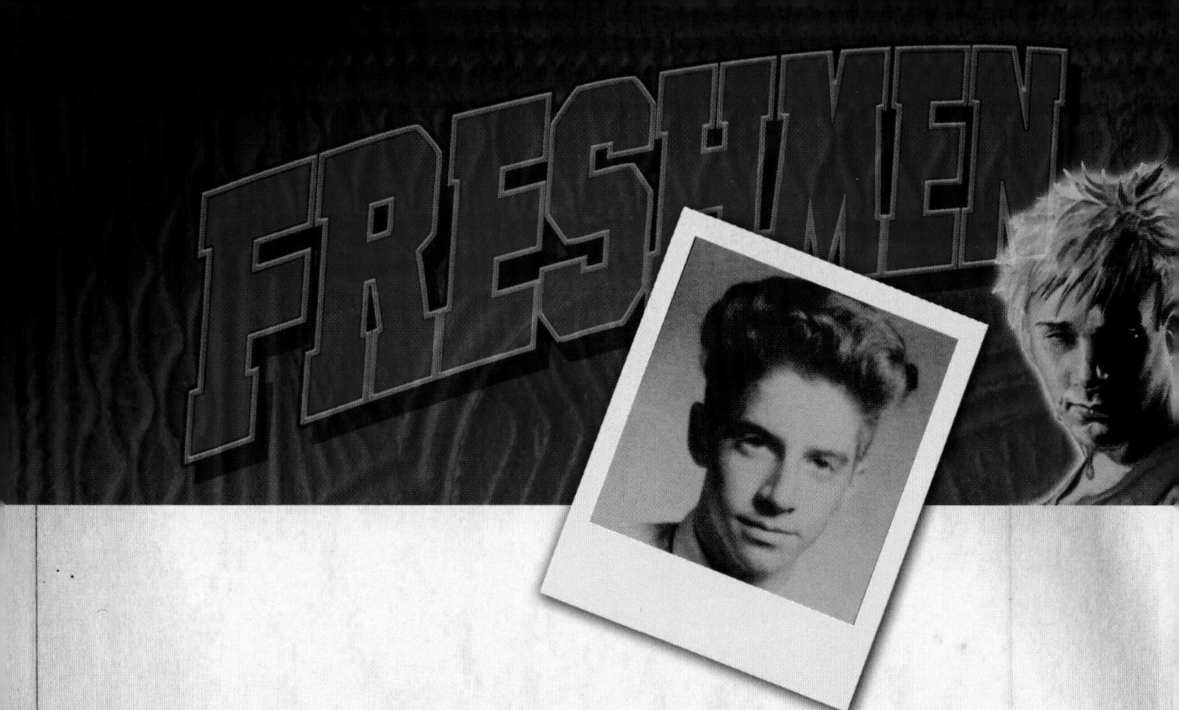
FRESHMEN

Well, here it is, kids! The wait is over. You can read it all in one sitting and you don't have to extract the individual issues from their UV protective clamshell cases, locked deep in the temperature controlled basement in your folks' home.

When Hugh and I first set out to make this comic, I never expected people to have such intense reactions. Thank you so much to everyone that's read and supported this book- it means a lot to us.

A special thanks is owed to Jim and Matt for your enormous support and enthusiasm. You really let us do what we wanted, and gave us the best ingredients available. Big ups to Leonard Kirk, who deserves credit for helping to define the look of the characters. Leonard, the subtleties of your drawings really capture the complexities of our kids' personality. To Andrew, Joe Linsner, and of course, Rodolfo- we're nothing without you. This has been an incredible experience, and we're thrilled to share it with you.

The story is a simple one, of young kids on their own for the first time in their lives. Meant to discover themselves and cement the identities that they will embody for the rest of their lives...with super powers. It's a story about whom you choose to befriend, whom you trust to love, how you define yourself and where your loyalties lay.

So what are you waiting for? Turn the page and get to know our kids! Great adventures await...

Seth Green

February 2006

You've never heard of me before Freshmen. That's okay. I'm the guy who just took the most fulfilling crap in history.

I grew up with an unquenchable thirst for comics. I learned to read on Gerry Conway's Spider-Man run and I came of age under the thrall of Stan Lee, Roger Stern, Matt Wagner, Chris Claremont, Peter David, Alan Moore, Frank Miller and Denny O'Neil. I was that little punk 13 year-old that terrorized every comic convention and store near Philadelphia, and soon enough I started creating my own comics. I was thrown out of so many high school classes for doodling that I nearly didn't graduate.

Then I spent 10 grueling years in the Hollywood development grind. It took away my dignity, my self-esteem, my sense of justice and my hair. But in comics, there's no soulwrenching bottleneck between your imagination and your audience. You write it, they draw it, somebody eventually reads it. And so, having real people read this story was my laxative for the world's wickedest bout of constipation. Yep, I just took a giant metaphoric crap all over the comic book industry and you're holding it in your hands. Unless I've talked you out of it, you're about to read it.

Not that these comics are crap—I couldn't be more pleased than offering Freshmen as my breakout work. It represents me well, since I am every one of these characters at different times of the day. They're confused, unsure, angry, overburdened and neurotic. They're prone to flights of fancy or brutal self-loathing. They're desperate to speak their minds, but terrified of not fitting in. They've become so familiar to me that they write themselves now—I almost feel guilty taking credit for them. But, like I said, I've been hard up. So I will.

When I finished writing this series, I felt like I'd made a bunch of new friends in these characters. I hope you feel the same. Thanks for sharing this crap with me, folks. Read on—it can only get better from here.

Hugh Sterbakov
February 1, 2006

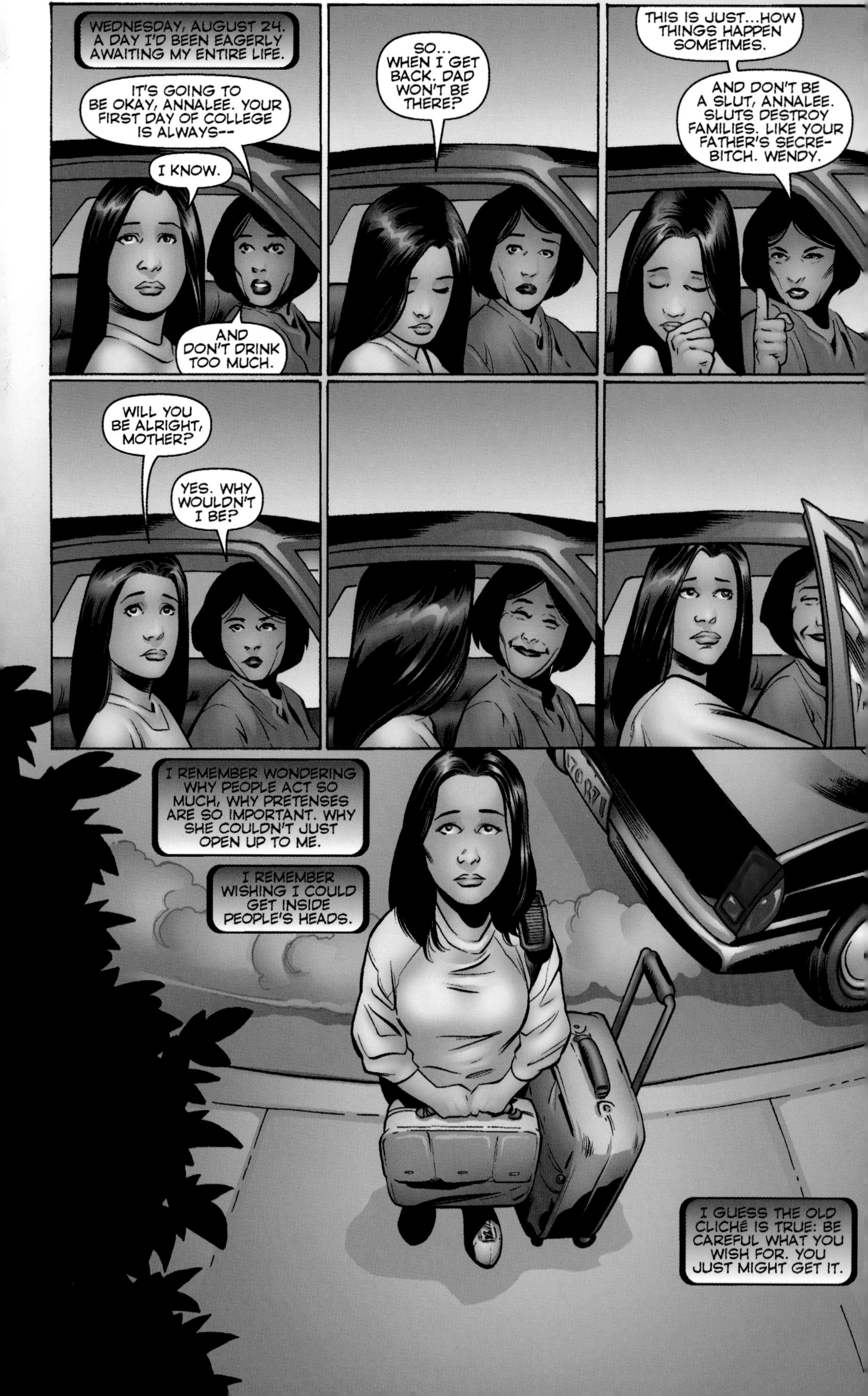
WEDNESDAY, AUGUST 24. A DAY I'D BEEN EAGERLY AWAITING MY ENTIRE LIFE.
IT'S GOING TO BE OKAY, ANNALEE. YOUR FIRST DAY OF COLLEGE IS ALWAYS--
I KNOW.
AND DON'T DRINK TOO MUCH.
SO... WHEN I GET BACK. DAD WON'T BE THERE?
THIS IS JUST...HOW THINGS HAPPEN SOMETIMES.
AND DON'T BE A SLUT, ANNALEE. SLUTS DESTROY FAMILIES. LIKE YOUR FATHER'S SECRE-BITCH. WENDY.
WILL YOU BE ALRIGHT, MOTHER?
YES. WHY WOULDN'T I BE?
I REMEMBER WONDERING WHY PEOPLE ACT SO MUCH, WHY PRETENSES ARE SO IMPORTANT. WHY SHE COULDN'T JUST OPEN UP TO ME.
I REMEMBER WISHING I COULD GET INSIDE PEOPLE'S HEADS.
I GUESS THE OLD CLICHÉ IS TRUE: BE CAREFUL WHAT YOU WISH FOR. YOU JUST MIGHT GET IT.

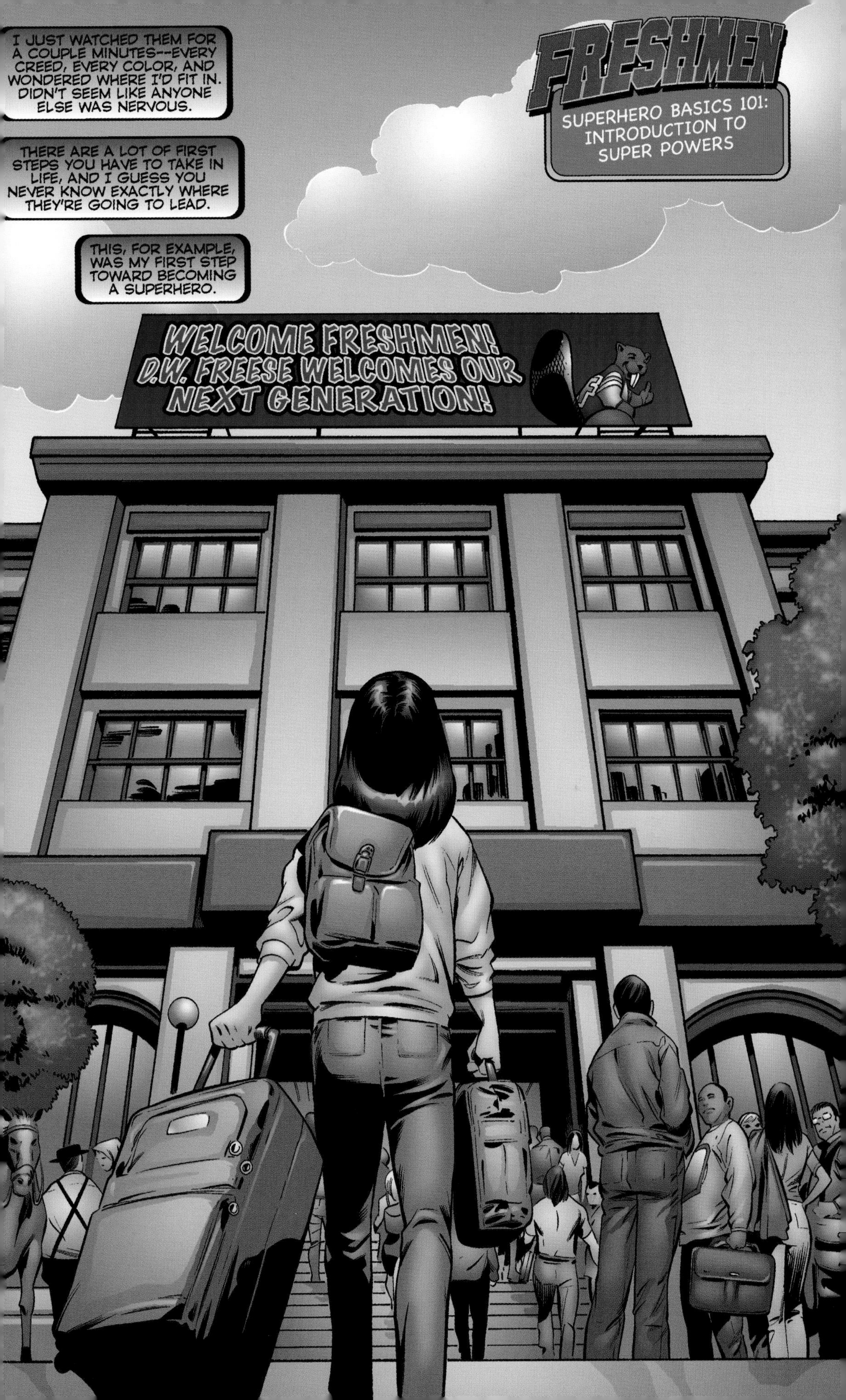
FRESHMEN
SUPERHERO BASICS 101: INTRODUCTION TO SUPER POWERS
I JUST WATCHED THEM FOR A COUPLE MINUTES--EVERY CREED, EVERY COLOR, AND WONDERED WHERE I'D FIT IN. DIDN'T SEEM LIKE ANYONE ELSE WAS NERVOUS.
THERE ARE A LOT OF FIRST STEPS YOU HAVE TO TAKE IN LIFE, AND I GUESS YOU NEVER KNOW EXACTLY WHERE THEY'RE GOING TO LEAD.
THIS, FOR EXAMPLE, WAS MY FIRST STEP TOWARD BECOMING A SUPERHERO.
WELCOME FRESHMEN! D.W. FREESE WELCOMES OUR NEXT GENERATION!

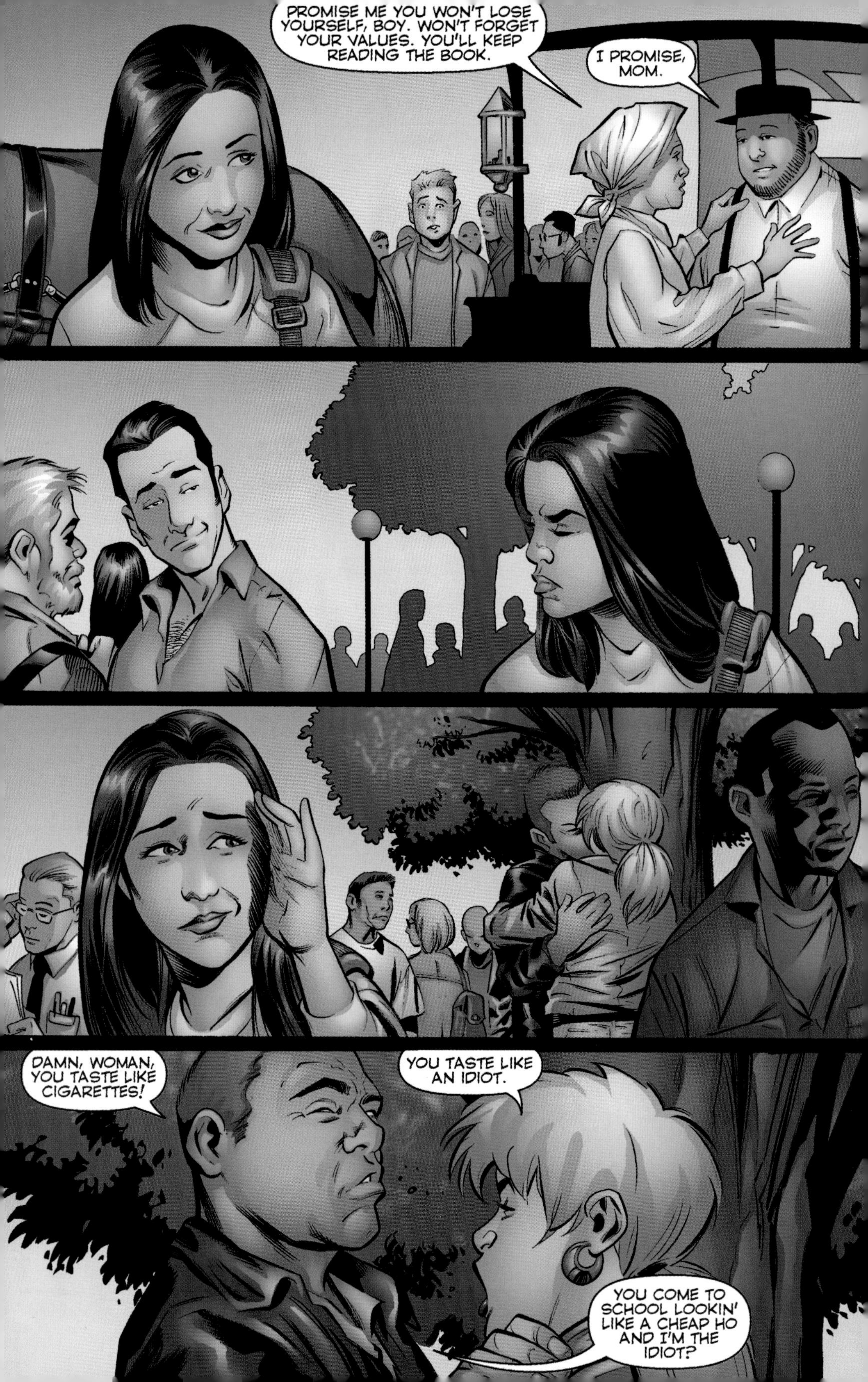
PROMISE ME YOU WON'T LOSE YOURSELF, BOY. WON'T FORGET YOUR VALUES. YOU'LL KEEP READING THE BOOK.
I PROMISE, MOM.
DAMN, WOMAN, YOU TASTE LIKE CIGARETTES!
YOU TASTE LIKE AN IDIOT.
YOU COME TO SCHOOL LOOKIN' LIKE A CHEAP HO AND I'M THE IDIOT?

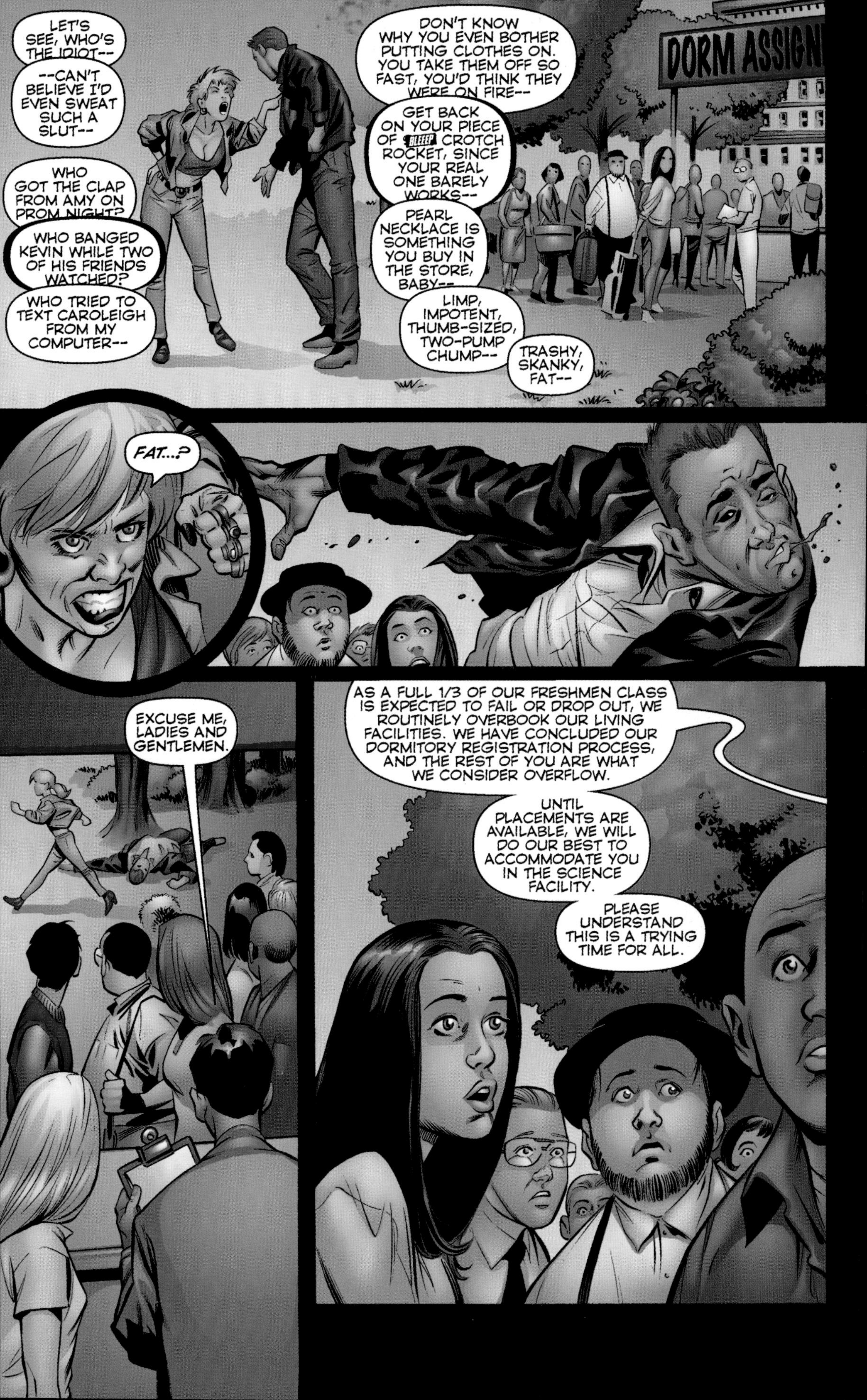
DORM ASSIGN
LET'S SEE, WHO'S THE IDIOT--
DON'T KNOW WHY YOU EVEN BOTHER PUTTING CLOTHES ON. YOU TAKE THEM OFF SO FAST, YOU'D THINK THEY WERE ON FIRE--
--CAN'T BELIEVE I'D EVEN SWEAT SUCH A SLUT--
GET BACK ON YOUR PIECE OF BLEEEP CROTCH ROCKET, SINCE YOUR REAL ONE BARELY WORKS--
WHO GOT THE CLAP FROM AMY ON PROM NIGHT?
PEARL NECKLACE IS SOMETHING YOU BUY IN THE STORE, BABY--
WHO BANGED KEVIN WHILE TWO OF HIS FRIENDS WATCHED?
LIMP, IMPOTENT, THUMB-SIZED, TWO-PUMP CHUMP--
WHO TRIED TO TEXT CAROLEIGH FROM MY COMPUTER--
TRASHY, SKANKY, FAT--
FAT...?
EXCUSE ME, LADIES AND GENTLEMEN.
AS A FULL 1/3 OF OUR FRESHMEN CLASS IS EXPECTED TO FAIL OR DROP OUT, WE ROUTINELY OVERBOOK OUR LIVING FACILITIES. WE HAVE CONCLUDED OUR DORMITORY REGISTRATION PROCESS, AND THE REST OF YOU ARE WHAT WE CONSIDER OVERFLOW.
UNTIL PLACEMENTS ARE AVAILABLE, WE WILL DO OUR BEST TO ACCOMMODATE YOU IN THE SCIENCE FACILITY.
PLEASE UNDERSTAND THIS IS A TRYING TIME FOR ALL.

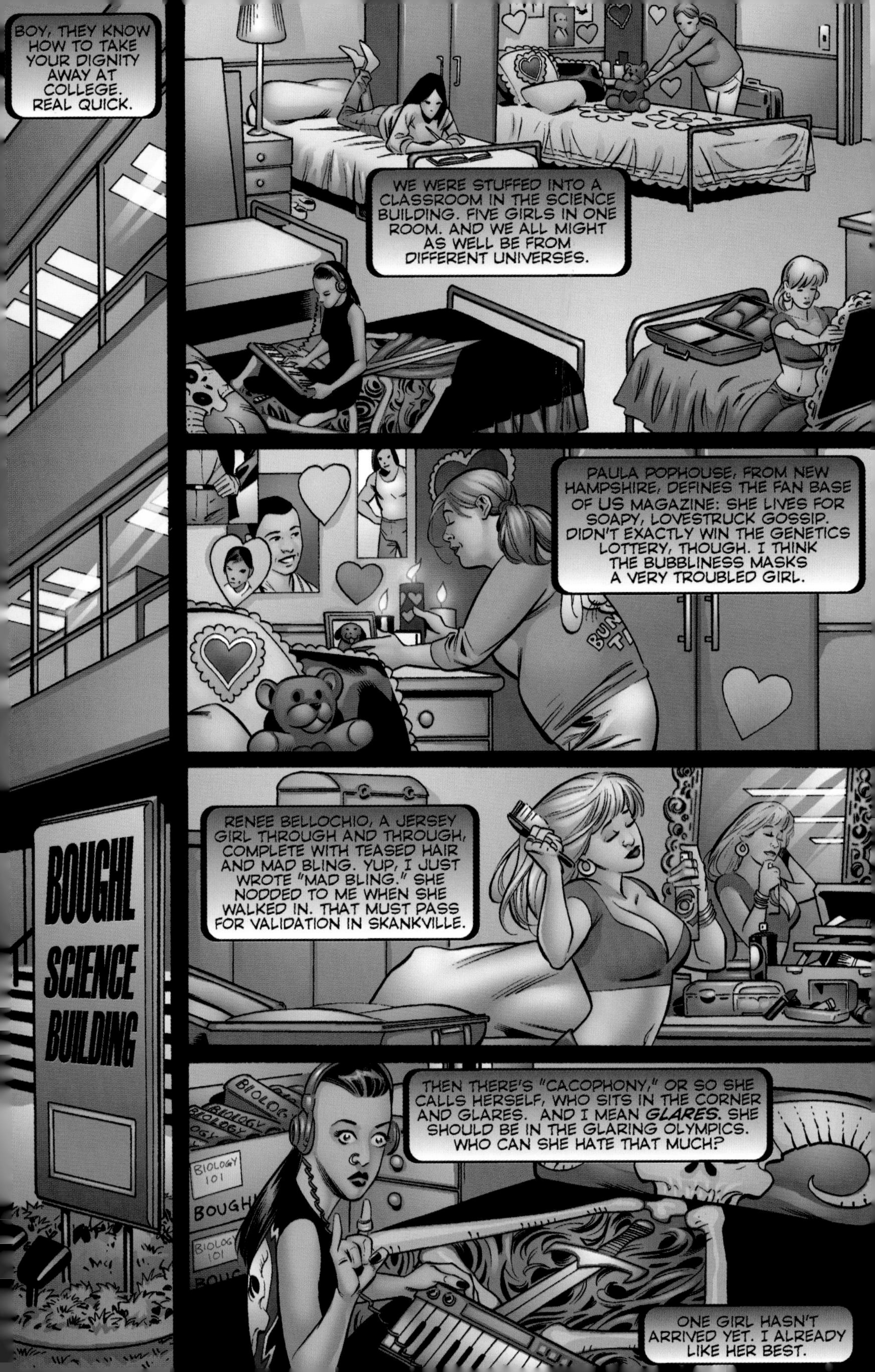

BOY, THEY KNOW HOW TO TAKE YOUR DIGNITY AWAY AT COLLEGE. REAL QUICK.
WE WERE STUFFED INTO A CLASSROOM IN THE SCIENCE BUILDING. FIVE GIRLS IN ONE ROOM. AND WE ALL MIGHT AS WELL BE FROM DIFFERENT UNIVERSES.
PAULA POPHOUSE, FROM NEW HAMPSHIRE, DEFINES THE FAN BASE OF US MAGAZINE: SHE LIVES FOR SOAPY, LOVESTRUCK GOSSIP. DIDN'T EXACTLY WIN THE GENETICS LOTTERY, THOUGH. I THINK THE BUBBLINESS MASKS A VERY TROUBLED GIRL.
BOUGHL SCIENCE BUILDING
RENEE BELLOCHIO, A JERSEY GIRL THROUGH AND THROUGH, COMPLETE WITH TEASED HAIR AND MAD BLING. YUP, I JUST WROTE "MAD BLING." SHE NODDED TO ME WHEN SHE WALKED IN. THAT MUST PASS FOR VALIDATION IN SKANKVILLE.
BIOLOGY
BIOLOGY 101
THEN THERE'S "CACOPHONY," OR SO SHE CALLS HERSELF, WHO SITS IN THE CORNER AND GLARES. AND I MEAN *GLARES*. SHE SHOULD BE IN THE GLARING OLYMPICS. WHO CAN SHE HATE THAT MUCH?
ONE GIRL HASN'T ARRIVED YET. I ALREADY LIKE HER BEST.

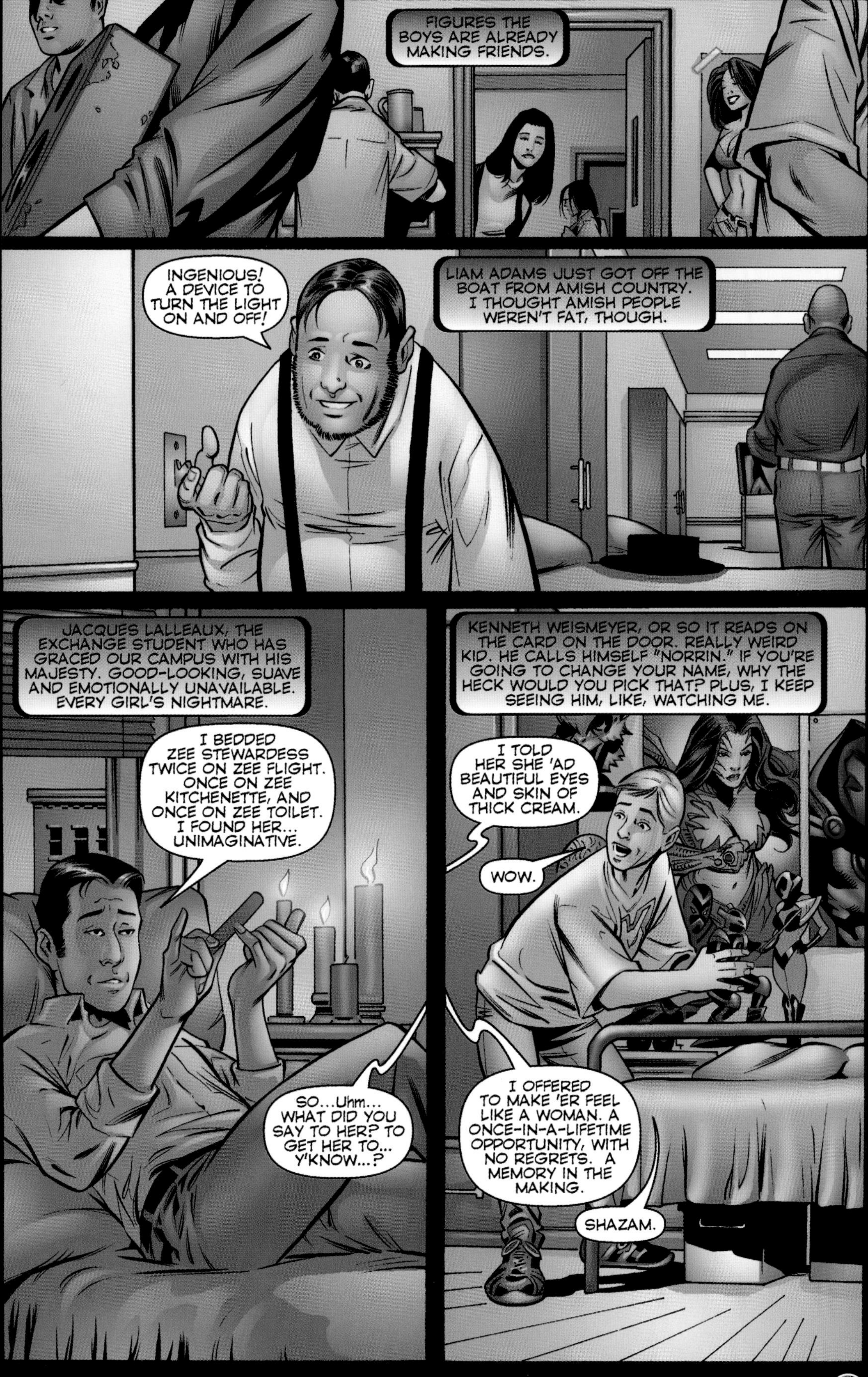
FIGURES THE BOYS ARE ALREADY MAKING FRIENDS.
INGENIOUS! A DEVICE TO TURN THE LIGHT ON AND OFF!
LIAM ADAMS JUST GOT OFF THE BOAT FROM AMISH COUNTRY. I THOUGHT AMISH PEOPLE WEREN'T FAT, THOUGH.
JACQUES LALLEAUX, THE EXCHANGE STUDENT WHO HAS GRACED OUR CAMPUS WITH HIS MAJESTY. GOOD-LOOKING, SUAVE AND EMOTIONALLY UNAVAILABLE. EVERY GIRL'S NIGHTMARE.
I BEDDED ZEE STEWARDESS TWICE ON ZEE FLIGHT. ONCE ON ZEE KITCHENETTE, AND ONCE ON ZEE TOILET. I FOUND HER... UNIMAGINATIVE.
SO...Uhm... WHAT DID YOU SAY TO HER? TO GET HER TO... Y'KNOW...?
KENNETH WEISMEYER, OR SO IT READS ON THE CARD ON THE DOOR. REALLY WEIRD KID. HE CALLS HIMSELF "NORRIN." IF YOU'RE GOING TO CHANGE YOUR NAME, WHY THE HECK WOULD YOU PICK THAT? PLUS, I KEEP SEEING HIM, LIKE, WATCHING ME.
I TOLD HER SHE 'AD BEAUTIFUL EYES AND SKIN OF THICK CREAM.
WOW.
I OFFERED TO MAKE 'ER FEEL LIKE A WOMAN. A ONCE-IN-A-LIFETIME OPPORTUNITY, WITH NO REGRETS. A MEMORY IN THE MAKING.
SHAZAM.

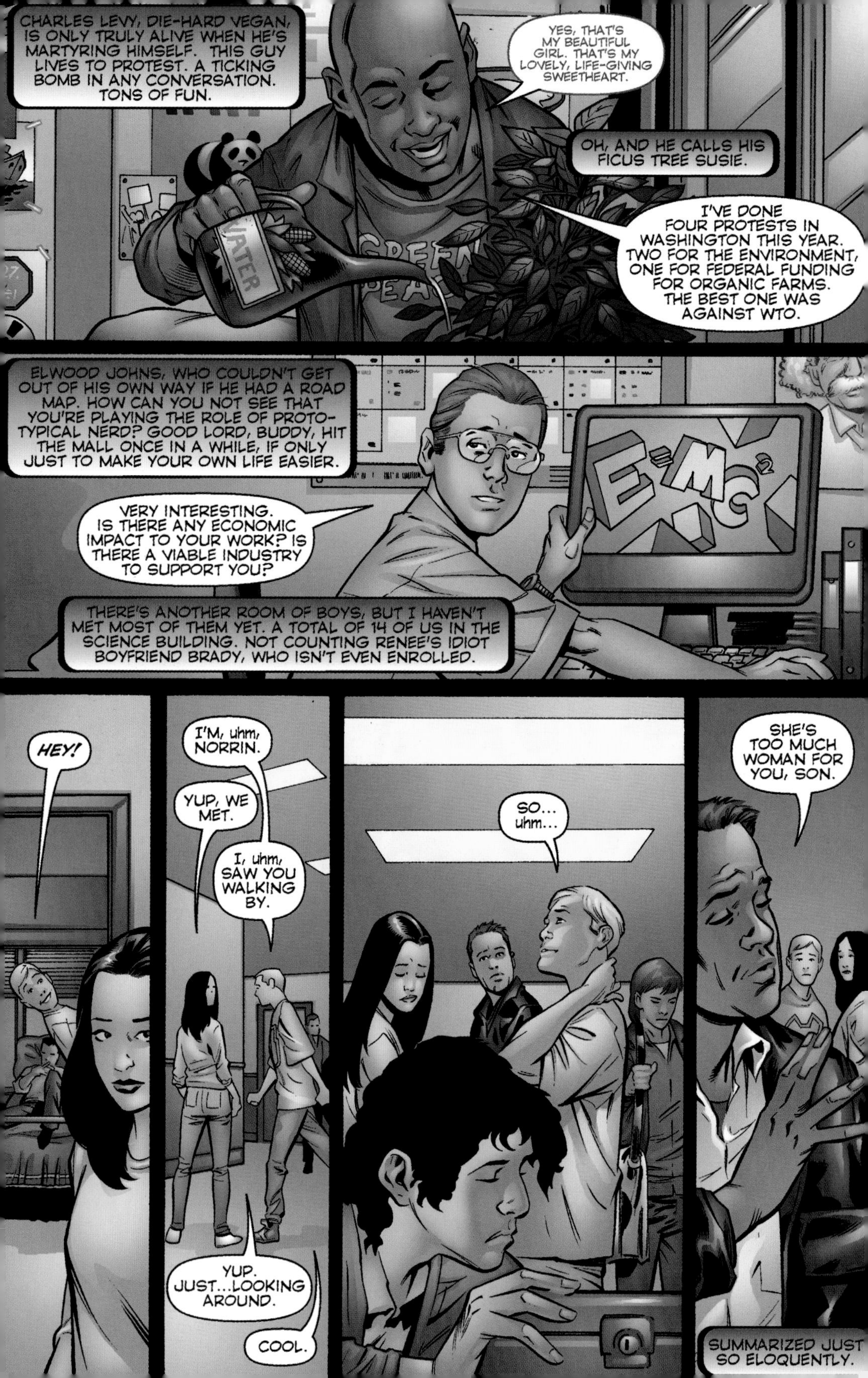
CHARLES LEVY, DIE-HARD VEGAN, IS ONLY TRULY ALIVE WHEN HE'S MARTYRING HIMSELF. THIS GUY LIVES TO PROTEST. A TICKING BOMB IN ANY CONVERSATION. TONS OF FUN.
YES, THAT'S MY BEAUTIFUL GIRL. THAT'S MY LOVELY, LIFE-GIVING SWEETHEART.
OH, AND HE CALLS HIS FICUS TREE SUSIE.
I'VE DONE FOUR PROTESTS IN WASHINGTON THIS YEAR. TWO FOR THE ENVIRONMENT, ONE FOR FEDERAL FUNDING FOR ORGANIC FARMS. THE BEST ONE WAS AGAINST WTO.
WATER
ELWOOD JOHNS, WHO COULDN'T GET OUT OF HIS OWN WAY IF HE HAD A ROAD MAP. HOW CAN YOU NOT SEE THAT YOU'RE PLAYING THE ROLE OF PROTO-TYPICAL NERD? GOOD LORD, BUDDY, HIT THE MALL ONCE IN A WHILE, IF ONLY JUST TO MAKE YOUR OWN LIFE EASIER.
E=MC2
VERY INTERESTING. IS THERE ANY ECONOMIC IMPACT TO YOUR WORK? IS THERE A VIABLE INDUSTRY TO SUPPORT YOU?
THERE'S ANOTHER ROOM OF BOYS, BUT I HAVEN'T MET MOST OF THEM YET. A TOTAL OF 14 OF US IN THE SCIENCE BUILDING. NOT COUNTING RENEE'S IDIOT BOYFRIEND BRADY, WHO ISN'T EVEN ENROLLED.
HEY!
I'M, uhm, NORRIN.
YUP, WE MET.
I, uhm, SAW YOU WALKING BY.
YUP. JUST...LOOKING AROUND.
COOL.
SO... uhm...
SHE'S TOO MUCH WOMAN FOR YOU, SON.
SUMMARIZED JUST SO ELOQUENTLY.

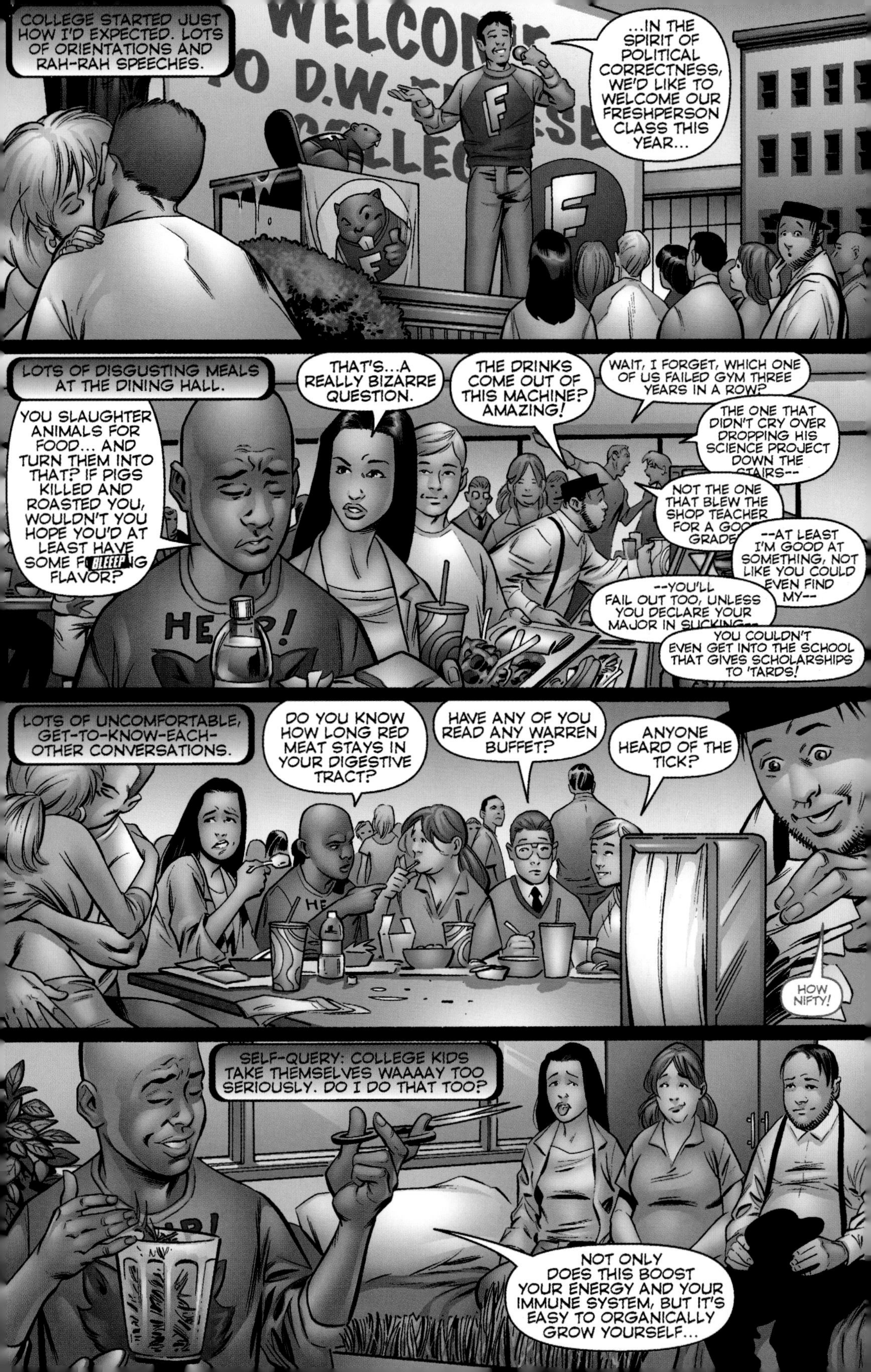
COLLEGE STARTED JUST HOW I'D EXPECTED. LOTS OF ORIENTATIONS AND RAH-RAH SPEECHES.
WELCOME TO D.W. COLLEGE
...IN THE SPIRIT OF POLITICAL CORRECTNESS, WE'D LIKE TO WELCOME OUR FRESHPERSON CLASS THIS YEAR...
LOTS OF DISGUSTING MEALS AT THE DINING HALL.
YOU SLAUGHTER ANIMALS FOR FOOD... AND TURN THEM INTO THAT? IF PIGS KILLED AND ROASTED YOU, WOULDN'T YOU HOPE YOU'D AT LEAST HAVE SOME F BLEEEP NG FLAVOR?
THAT'S...A REALLY BIZARRE QUESTION.
THE DRINKS COME OUT OF THIS MACHINE? AMAZING!
WAIT, I FORGET, WHICH ONE OF US FAILED GYM THREE YEARS IN A ROW?
THE ONE THAT DIDN'T CRY OVER DROPPING HIS SCIENCE PROJECT DOWN THE STAIRS--
NOT THE ONE THAT BLEW THE SHOP TEACHER FOR A GOOD GRADE
--AT LEAST I'M GOOD AT SOMETHING, NOT LIKE YOU COULD EVEN FIND MY--
--YOU'LL FAIL OUT TOO, UNLESS YOU DECLARE YOUR MAJOR IN SUCKING--
YOU COULDN'T EVEN GET INTO THE SCHOOL THAT GIVES SCHOLARSHIPS TO 'TARDS!
LOTS OF UNCOMFORTABLE, GET-TO-KNOW-EACH-OTHER CONVERSATIONS.
DO YOU KNOW HOW LONG RED MEAT STAYS IN YOUR DIGESTIVE TRACT?
HAVE ANY OF YOU READ ANY WARREN BUFFET?
ANYONE HEARD OF THE TICK?
HOW NIFTY!
SELF-QUERY: COLLEGE KIDS TAKE THEMSELVES WAAAAY TOO SERIOUSLY. DO I DO THAT TOO?
NOT ONLY DOES THIS BOOST YOUR ENERGY AND YOUR IMMUNE SYSTEM, BUT IT'S EASY TO ORGANICALLY GROW YOURSELF...

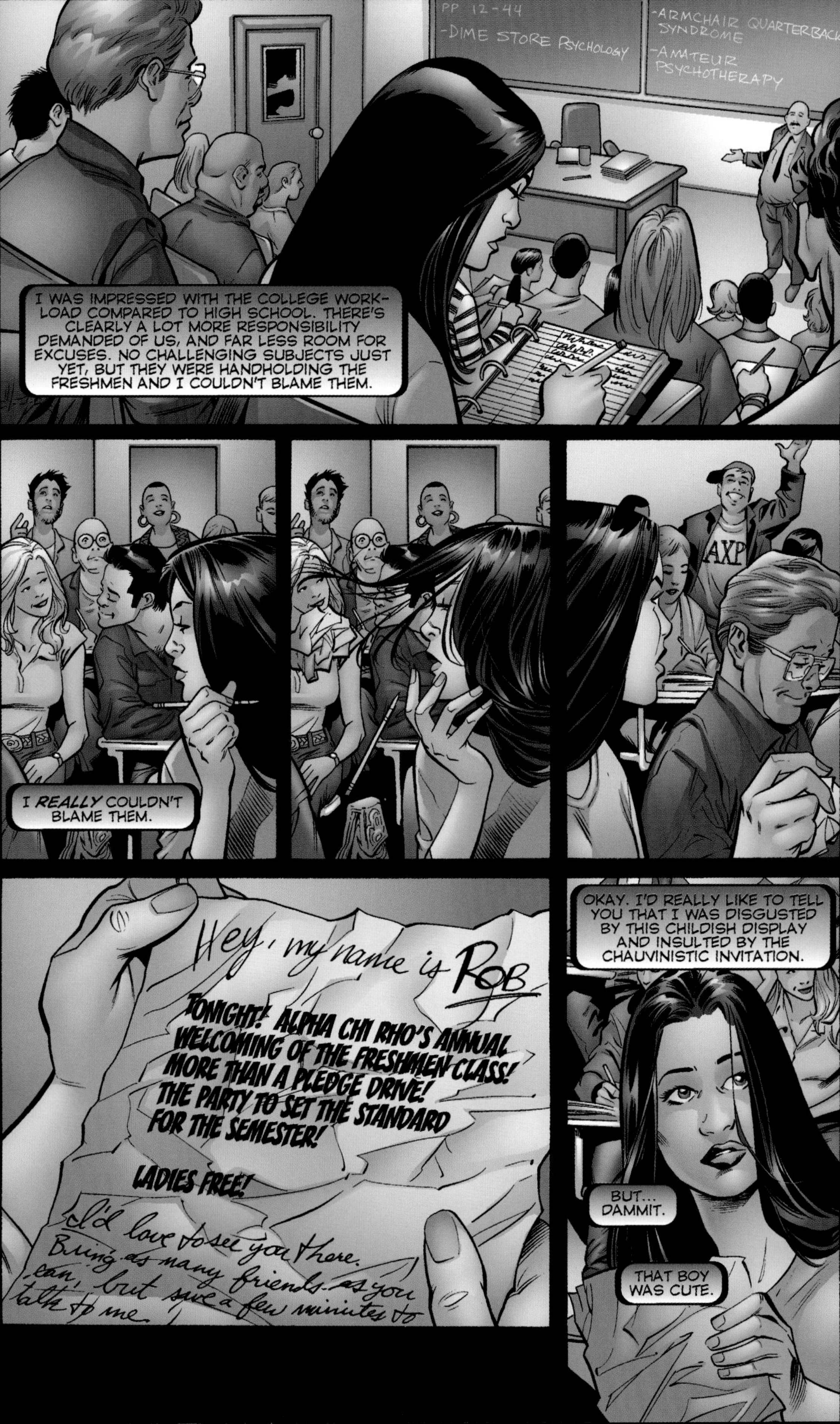
PP 12-44
-DIME STORE PSYCHOLOGY
-ARMCHAIR QUARTERBACK SYNDROME
-AMATEUR PSYCHOTHERAPY
I WAS IMPRESSED WITH THE COLLEGE WORK-LOAD COMPARED TO HIGH SCHOOL. THERE'S CLEARLY A LOT MORE RESPONSIBILITY DEMANDED OF US, AND FAR LESS ROOM FOR EXCUSES. NO CHALLENGING SUBJECTS JUST YET, BUT THEY WERE HANDHOLDING THE FRESHMEN AND I COULDN'T BLAME THEM.
I *REALLY* COULDN'T BLAME THEM.
AXP
Hey, my name is ROB
TONIGHT! ALPHA CHI RHO'S ANNUAL WELCOMING OF THE FRESHMEN CLASS! MORE THAN A PLEDGE DRIVE! THE PARTY TO SET THE STANDARD FOR THE SEMESTER!
LADIES FREE!
I'd love to see you there. Bring as many friends as you can, but save a few minutes to talk to me.
OKAY. I'D REALLY LIKE TO TELL YOU THAT I WAS DISGUSTED BY THIS CHILDISH DISPLAY AND INSULTED BY THE CHAUVINISTIC INVITATION.
BUT... DAMMIT.
THAT BOY WAS CUTE.

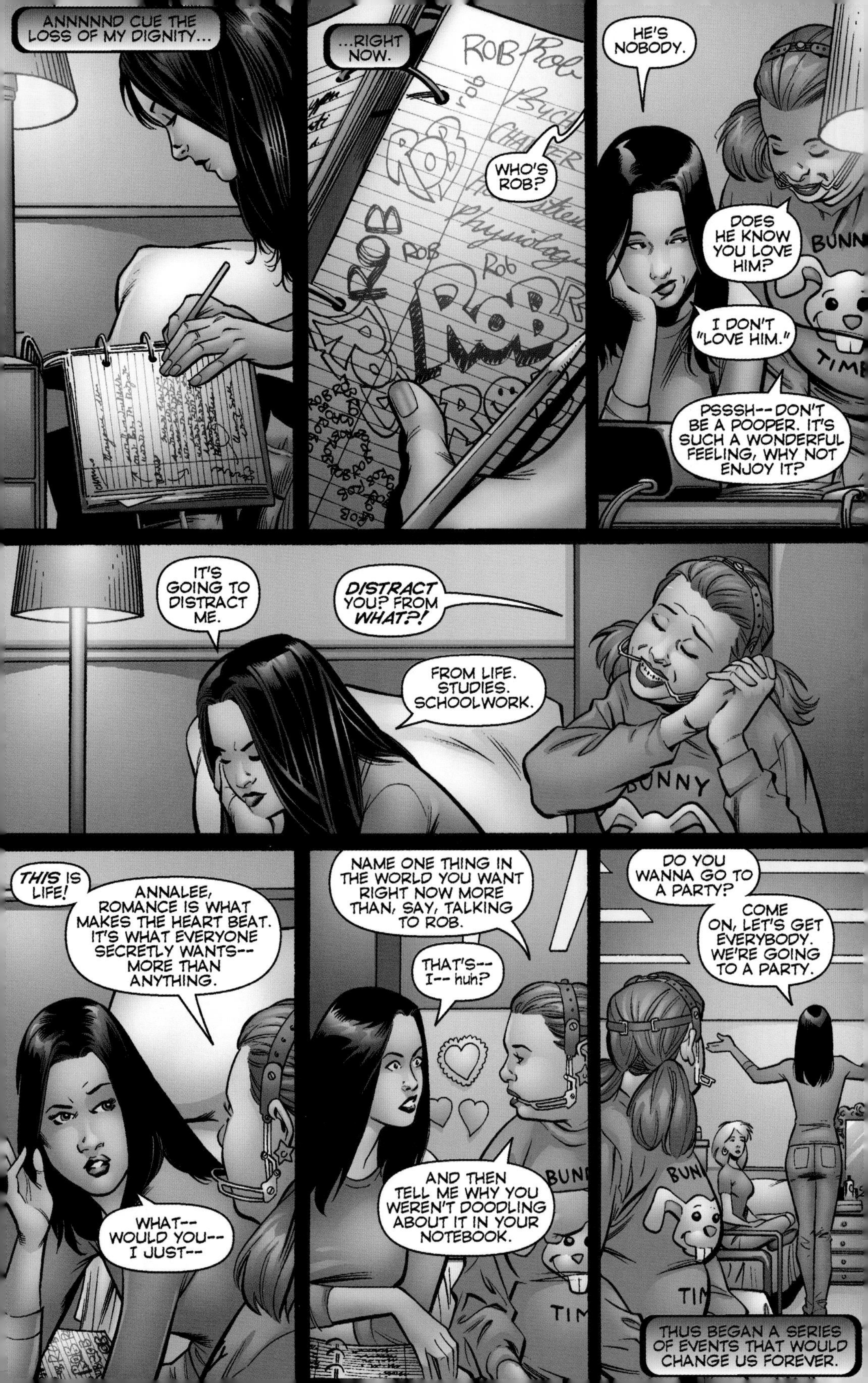
ANNNNND CUE THE LOSS OF MY DIGNITY...
...RIGHT NOW.
WHO'S ROB?
HE'S NOBODY.
DOES HE KNOW YOU LOVE HIM?
I DON'T "LOVE HIM."
PSSSH--DON'T BE A POOPER. IT'S SUCH A WONDERFUL FEELING, WHY NOT ENJOY IT?
IT'S GOING TO DISTRACT ME.
DISTRACT YOU? FROM *WHAT?!*
FROM LIFE. STUDIES. SCHOOLWORK.
THIS IS LIFE!
ANNALEE, ROMANCE IS WHAT MAKES THE HEART BEAT. IT'S WHAT EVERYONE SECRETLY WANTS-- MORE THAN ANYTHING.
WHAT-- WOULD YOU-- I JUST--
NAME ONE THING IN THE WORLD YOU WANT RIGHT NOW MORE THAN, SAY, TALKING TO ROB.
THAT'S-- I-- huh?
AND THEN TELL ME WHY YOU WEREN'T DOODLING ABOUT IT IN YOUR NOTEBOOK.
DO YOU WANNA GO TO A PARTY?
COME ON, LET'S GET EVERYBODY. WE'RE GOING TO A PARTY.
THUS BEGAN A SERIES OF EVENTS THAT WOULD CHANGE US FOREVER.

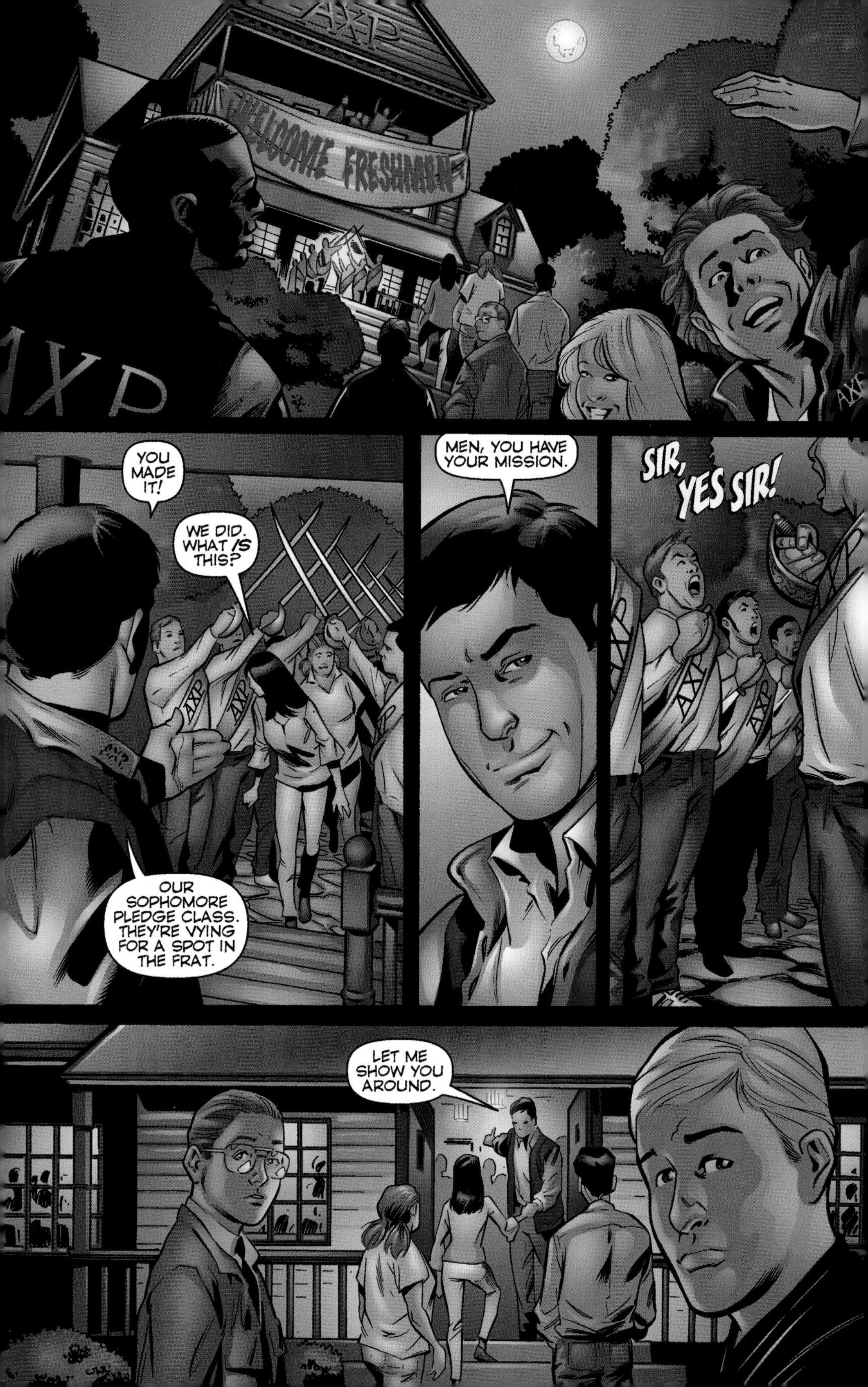
WELCOME FRESHMEN
YOU MADE IT!
WE DID. WHAT IS THIS?
OUR SOPHOMORE PLEDGE CLASS. THEY'RE VYING FOR A SPOT IN THE FRAT.
MEN, YOU HAVE YOUR MISSION.
SIR, YES SIR!
LET ME SHOW YOU AROUND.

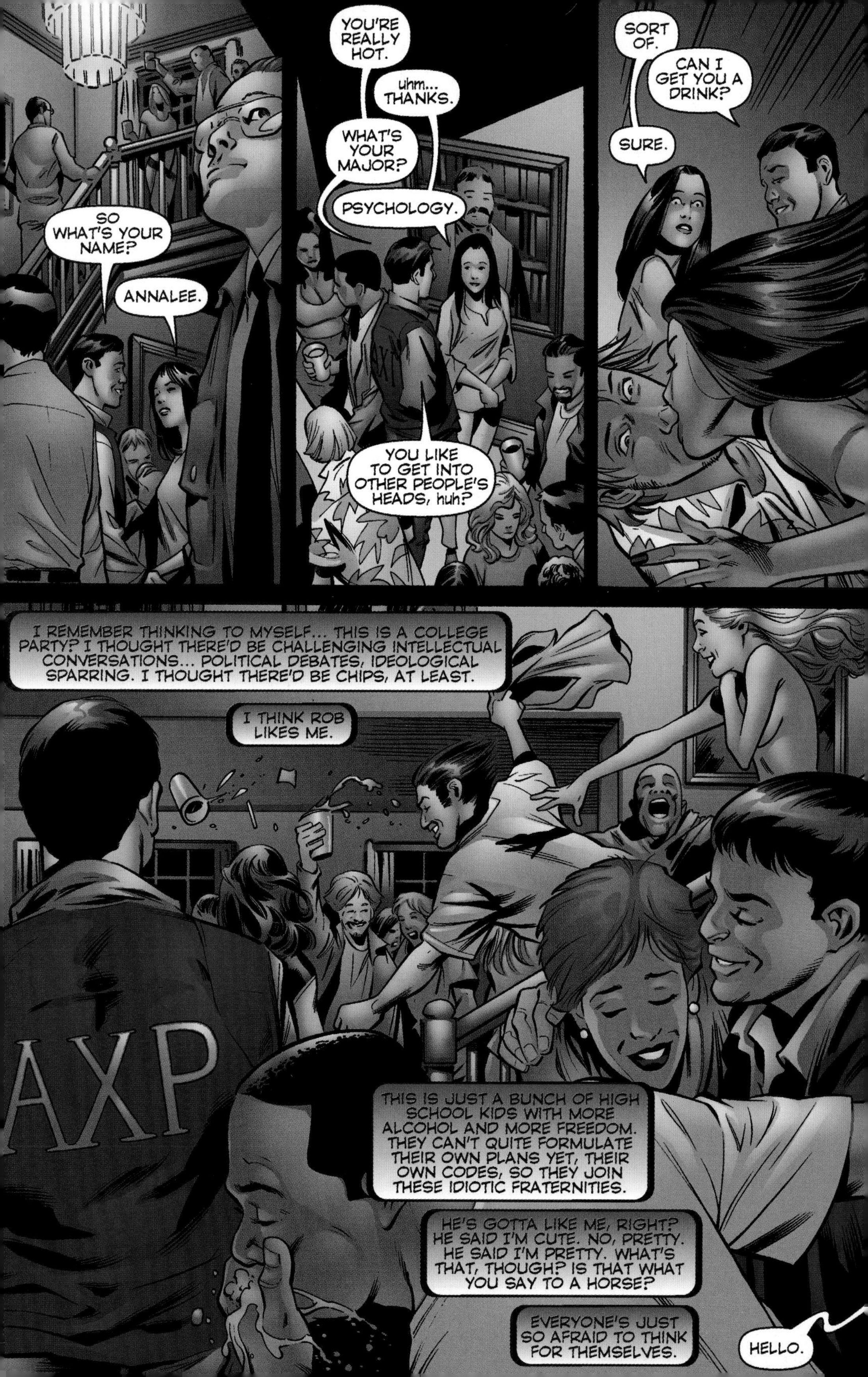
SO WHAT'S YOUR NAME?
ANNALEE.
YOU'RE REALLY HOT.
uhm... THANKS.
WHAT'S YOUR MAJOR?
PSYCHOLOGY.
YOU LIKE TO GET INTO OTHER PEOPLE'S HEADS, huh?
SORT OF.
CAN I GET YOU A DRINK?
SURE.
I REMEMBER THINKING TO MYSELF... THIS IS A COLLEGE PARTY? I THOUGHT THERE'D BE CHALLENGING INTELLECTUAL CONVERSATIONS... POLITICAL DEBATES, IDEOLOGICAL SPARRING. I THOUGHT THERE'D BE CHIPS, AT LEAST.
I THINK ROB LIKES ME.
AXP
THIS IS JUST A BUNCH OF HIGH SCHOOL KIDS WITH MORE ALCOHOL AND MORE FREEDOM. THEY CAN'T QUITE FORMULATE THEIR OWN PLANS YET, THEIR OWN CODES, SO THEY JOIN THESE IDIOTIC FRATERNITIES.
HE'S GOTTA LIKE ME, RIGHT? HE SAID I'M CUTE. NO, PRETTY. HE SAID I'M PRETTY. WHAT'S THAT, THOUGH? IS THAT WHAT YOU SAY TO A HORSE?
EVERYONE'S JUST SO AFRAID TO THINK FOR THEMSELVES.
HELLO.

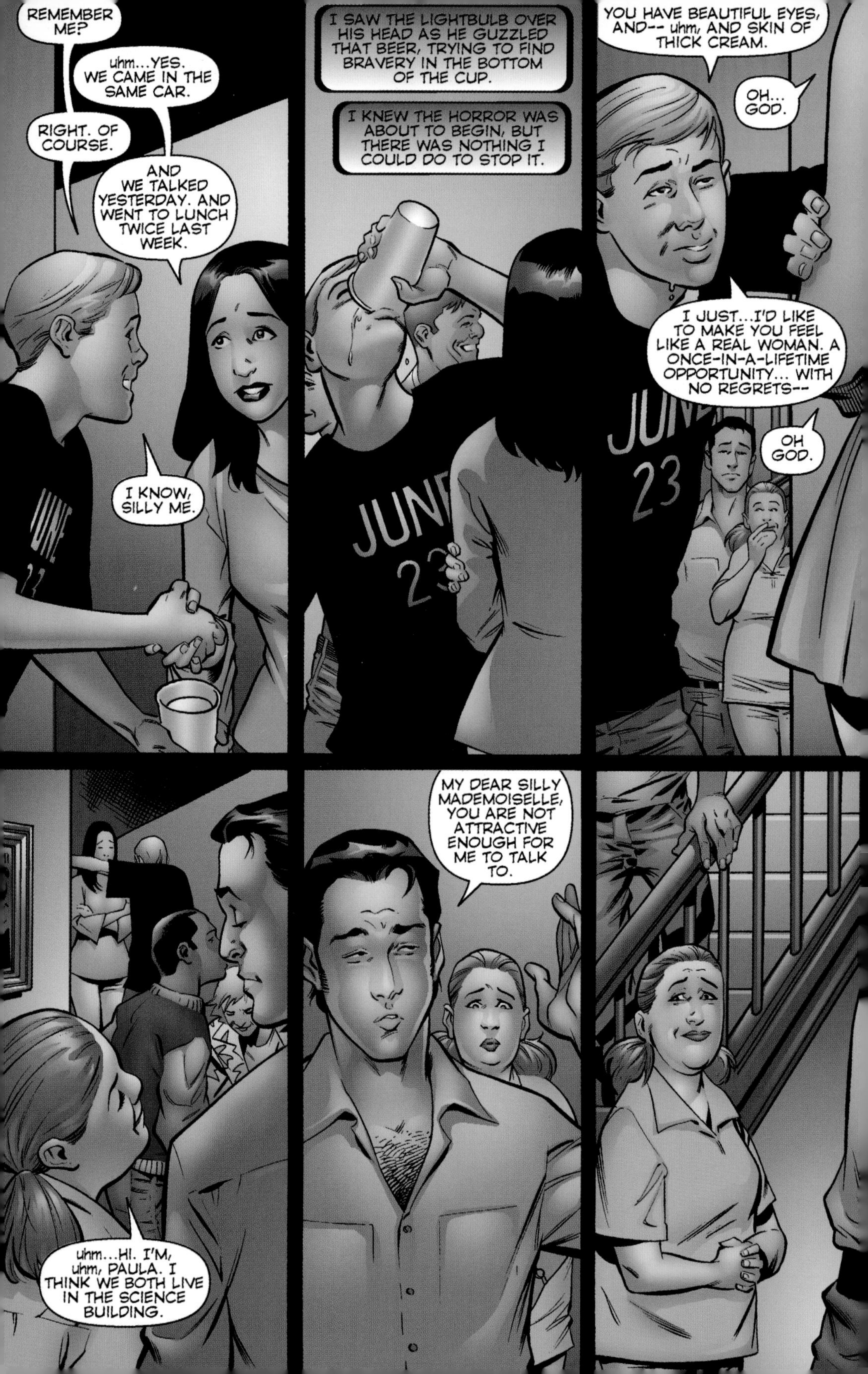

REMEMBER ME?
uhm...YES. WE CAME IN THE SAME CAR.
RIGHT. OF COURSE.
AND WE TALKED YESTERDAY. AND WENT TO LUNCH TWICE LAST WEEK.
I KNOW, SILLY ME.
I SAW THE LIGHTBULB OVER HIS HEAD AS HE GUZZLED THAT BEER, TRYING TO FIND BRAVERY IN THE BOTTOM OF THE CUP.
I KNEW THE HORROR WAS ABOUT TO BEGIN, BUT THERE WAS NOTHING I COULD DO TO STOP IT.
JUNE 23
YOU HAVE BEAUTIFUL EYES, AND-- uhm, AND SKIN OF THICK CREAM.
OH... GOD.
I JUST...I'D LIKE TO MAKE YOU FEEL LIKE A REAL WOMAN. A ONCE-IN-A-LIFETIME OPPORTUNITY... WITH NO REGRETS--
OH GOD.
uhm...HI. I'M, uhm, PAULA. I THINK WE BOTH LIVE IN THE SCIENCE BUILDING.
MY DEAR SILLY MADEMOISELLE, YOU ARE NOT ATTRACTIVE ENOUGH FOR ME TO TALK TO.

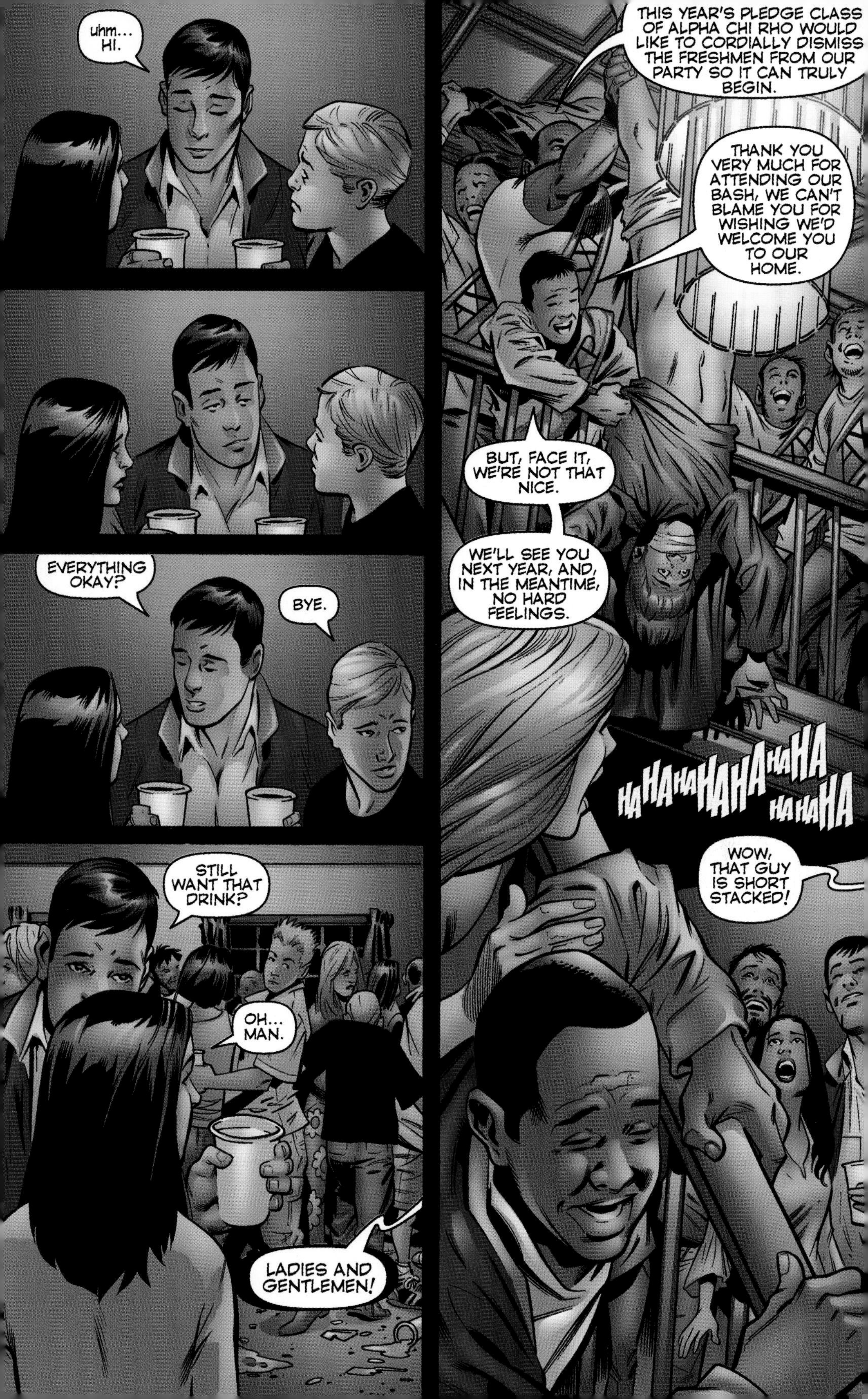
uhm... HI.
EVERYTHING OKAY?
BYE.
STILL WANT THAT DRINK?
OH... MAN.
LADIES AND GENTLEMEN!
THIS YEAR'S PLEDGE CLASS OF ALPHA CHI RHO WOULD LIKE TO CORDIALLY DISMISS THE FRESHMEN FROM OUR PARTY SO IT CAN TRULY BEGIN.
THANK YOU VERY MUCH FOR ATTENDING OUR BASH, WE CAN'T BLAME YOU FOR WISHING WE'D WELCOME YOU TO OUR HOME.
BUT, FACE IT, WE'RE NOT THAT NICE.
WE'LL SEE YOU NEXT YEAR, AND, IN THE MEANTIME, NO HARD FEELINGS.
HAHAHAHAHAHAHAHA
HAHAHA
WOW, THAT GUY IS SHORT STACKED!

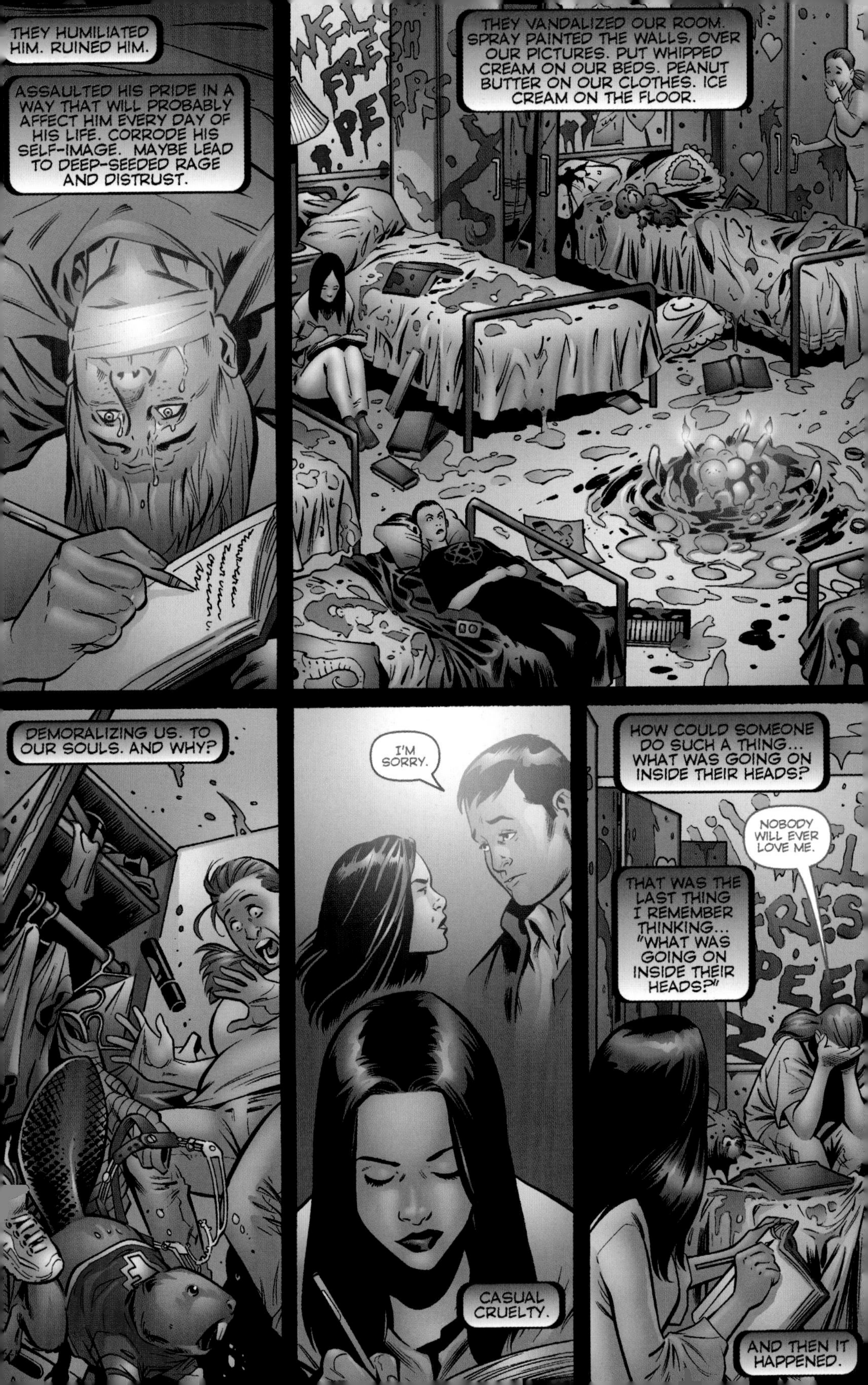
THEY HUMILIATED HIM. RUINED HIM.
ASSAULTED HIS PRIDE IN A WAY THAT WILL PROBABLY AFFECT HIM EVERY DAY OF HIS LIFE. CORRODE HIS SELF-IMAGE. MAYBE LEAD TO DEEP-SEEDED RAGE AND DISTRUST.
THEY VANDALIZED OUR ROOM. SPRAY PAINTED THE WALLS, OVER OUR PICTURES. PUT WHIPPED CREAM ON OUR BEDS. PEANUT BUTTER ON OUR CLOTHES. ICE CREAM ON THE FLOOR.
FRESH PEEPS
DEMORALIZING US. TO OUR SOULS. AND WHY?
I'M SORRY.
CASUAL CRUELTY.
HOW COULD SOMEONE DO SUCH A THING... WHAT WAS GOING ON INSIDE THEIR HEADS?
NOBODY WILL EVER LOVE ME.
THAT WAS THE LAST THING I REMEMBER THINKING... "WHAT WAS GOING ON INSIDE THEIR HEADS?"
AND THEN IT HAPPENED.

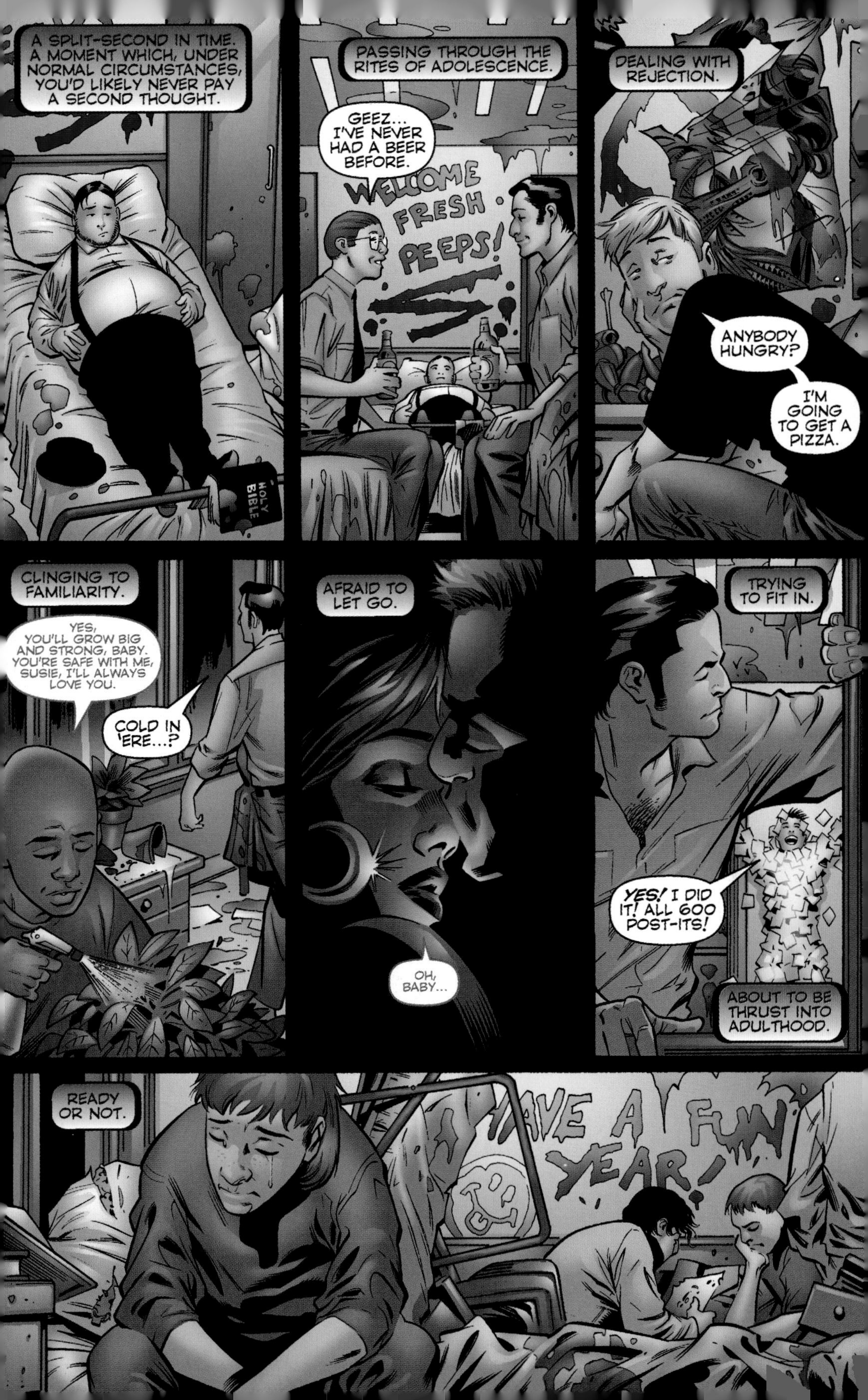

A SPLIT-SECOND IN TIME. A MOMENT WHICH, UNDER NORMAL CIRCUMSTANCES, YOU'D LIKELY NEVER PAY A SECOND THOUGHT.
HOLY BIBLE
PASSING THROUGH THE RITES OF ADOLESCENCE.
GEEZ... I'VE NEVER HAD A BEER BEFORE.
WELCOME FRESH PEEPS!
DEALING WITH REJECTION.
ANYBODY HUNGRY?
I'M GOING TO GET A PIZZA.
CLINGING TO FAMILIARITY.
YES, YOU'LL GROW BIG AND STRONG, BABY. YOU'RE SAFE WITH ME, SUSIE, I'LL ALWAYS LOVE YOU.
COLD IN 'ERE...?
AFRAID TO LET GO.
OH, BABY...
TRYING TO FIT IN.
YES! I DID IT! ALL 600 POST-ITS!
ABOUT TO BE THRUST INTO ADULTHOOD.
READY OR NOT.
HAVE A FUN YEAR!

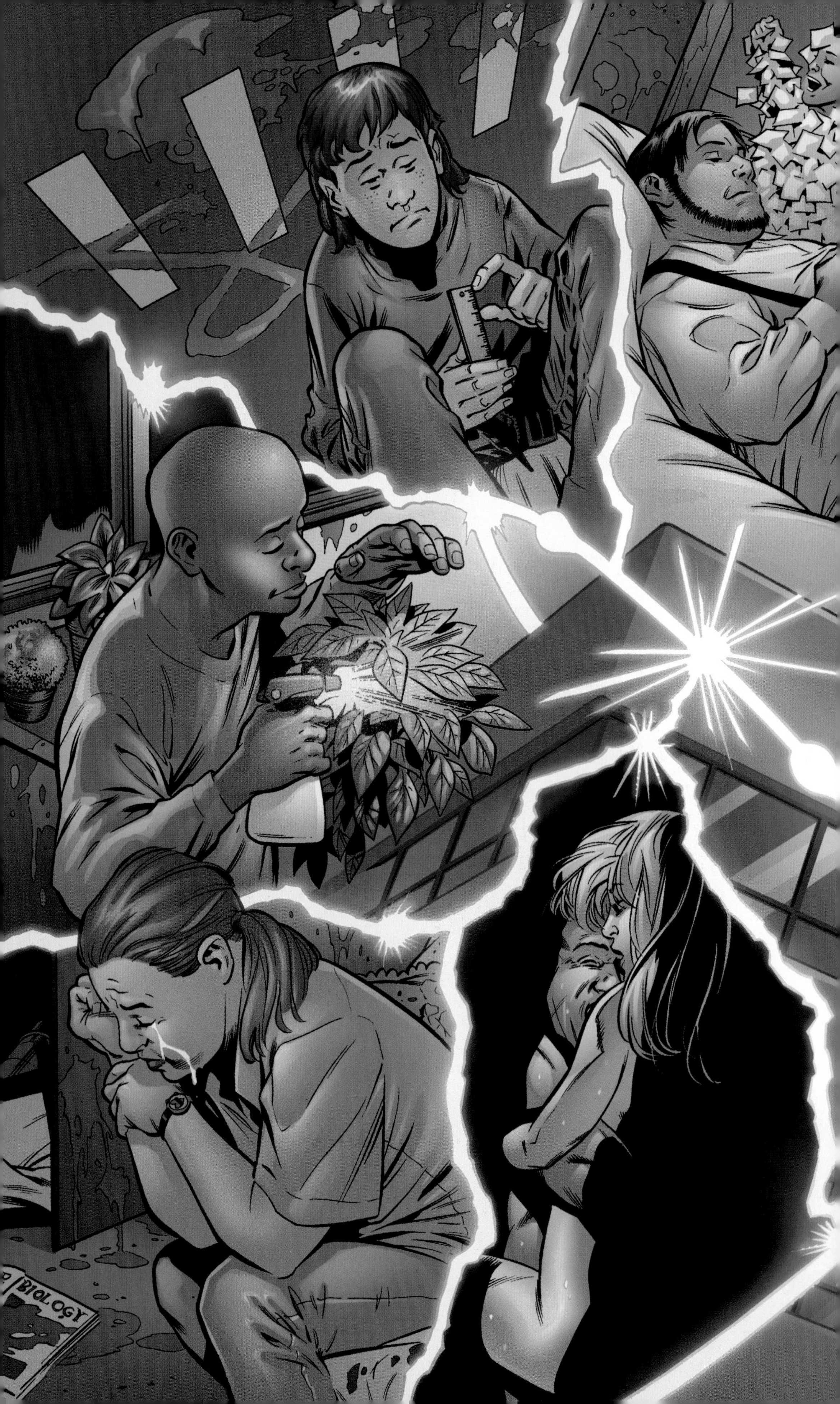
BIOLOGY

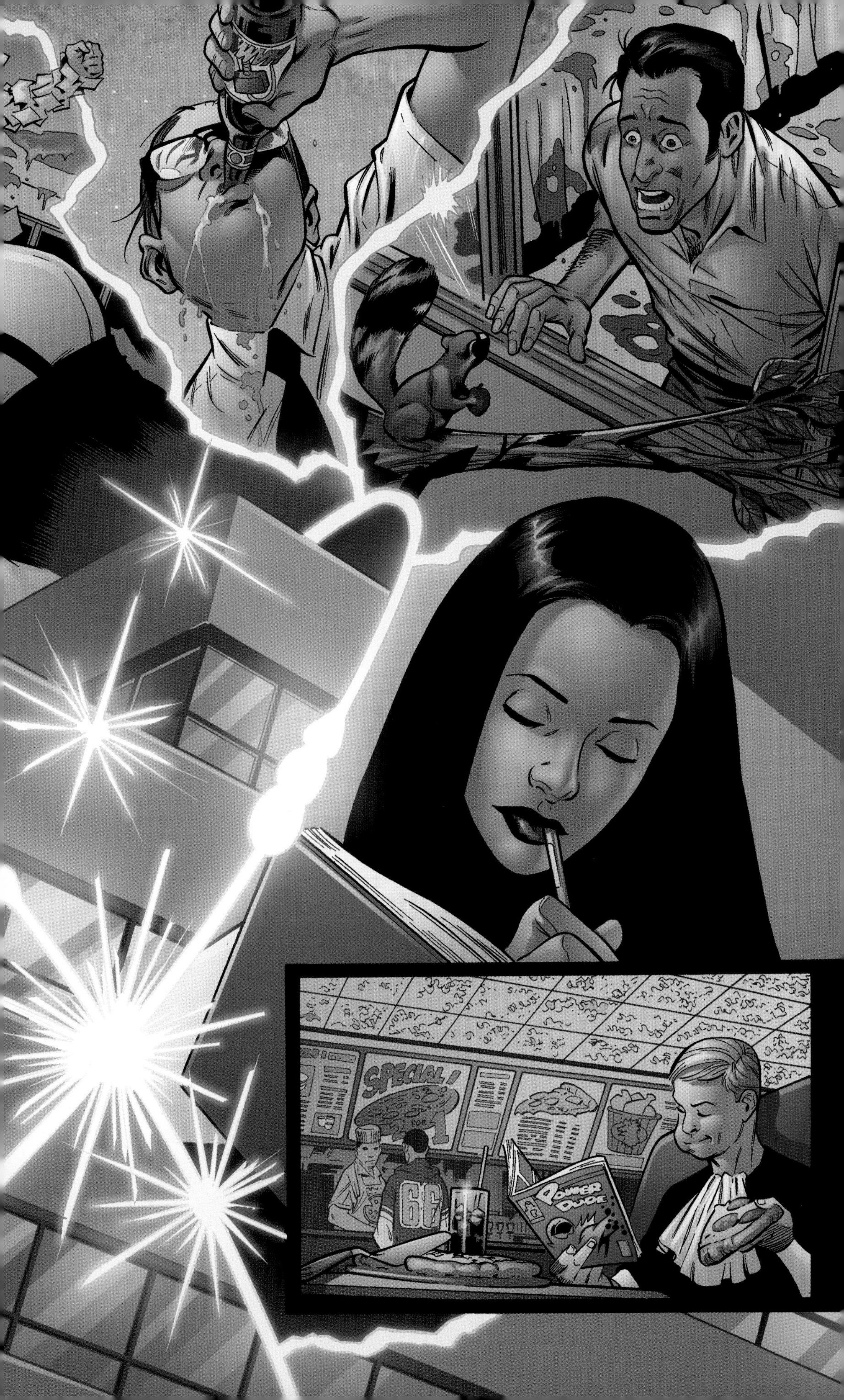
SPECIAL!
FOR 1
66
POWER DUDE

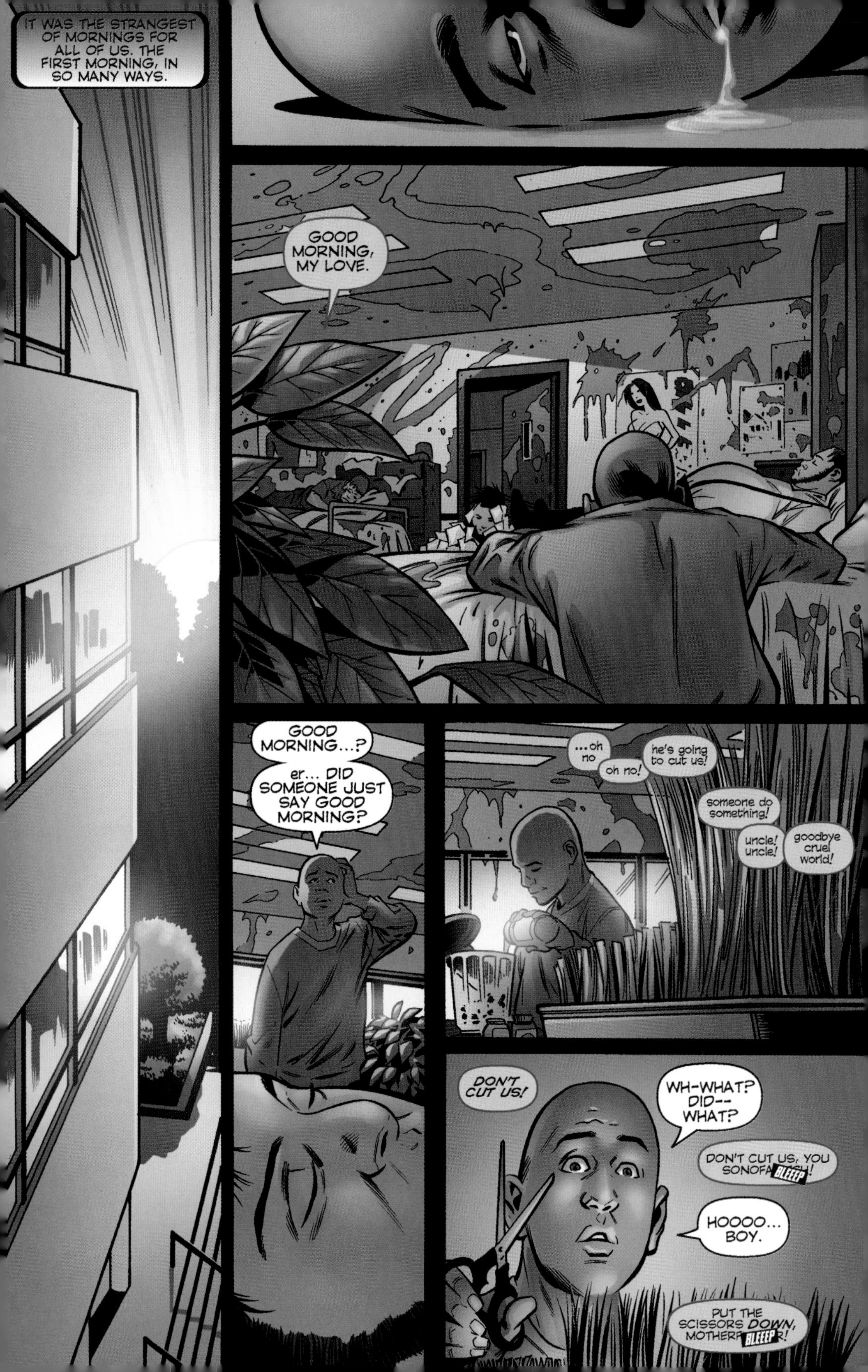
IT WAS THE STRANGEST OF MORNINGS FOR ALL OF US. THE FIRST MORNING, IN SO MANY WAYS.
GOOD MORNING, MY LOVE.
GOOD MORNING...?
er... DID SOMEONE JUST SAY GOOD MORNING?
...oh no
oh no!
he's going to cut us!
someone do something!
uncle! uncle!
goodbye cruel world!
DON'T CUT US!
WH-WHAT? DID-- WHAT?
DON'T CUT US, YOU SONOFA BLEEP!
HOOOO... BOY.
PUT THE SCISSORS DOWN, MOTHER BLEEP R!

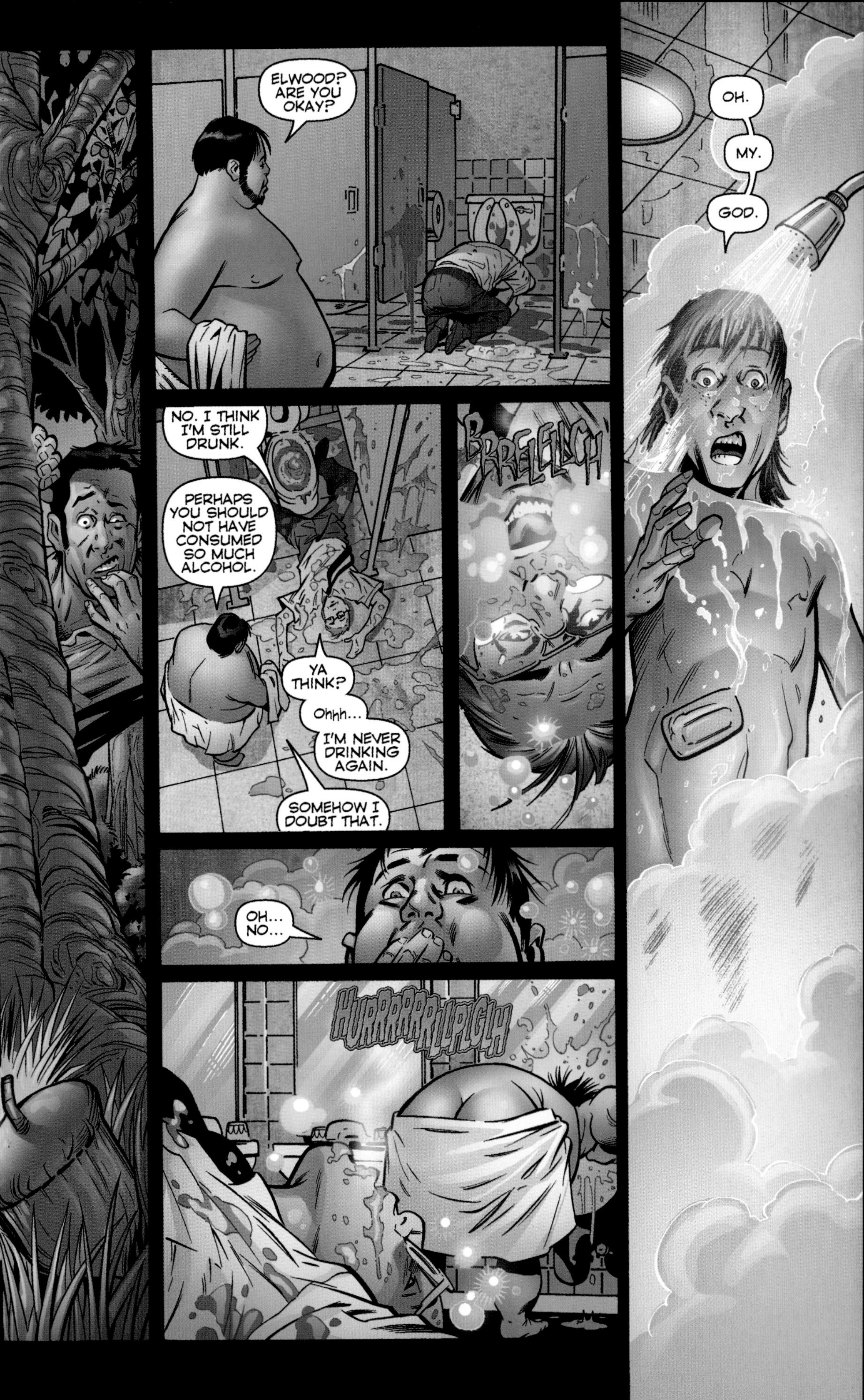
ELWOOD? ARE YOU OKAY?
NO. I THINK I'M STILL DRUNK.
PERHAPS YOU SHOULD NOT HAVE CONSUMED SO MUCH ALCOHOL.
YA THINK?
Ohhh...
I'M NEVER DRINKING AGAIN.
SOMEHOW I DOUBT THAT.
BRRELELLGH
OH... NO...
HURRRRRRLLPLGLH
OH.
MY.
GOD.

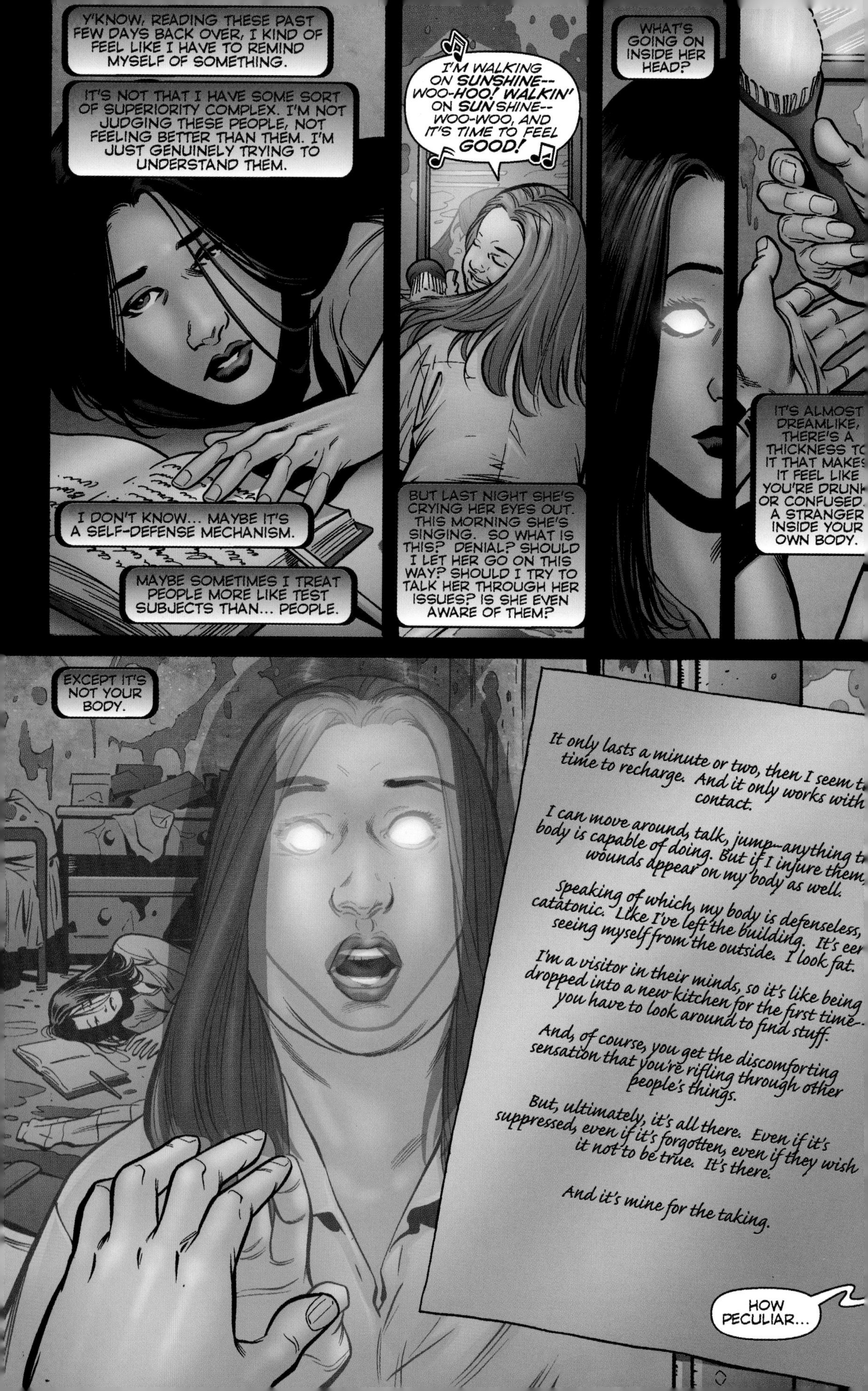
Y'KNOW, READING THESE PAST FEW DAYS BACK OVER, I KIND OF FEEL LIKE I HAVE TO REMIND MYSELF OF SOMETHING.
IT'S NOT THAT I HAVE SOME SORT OF SUPERIORITY COMPLEX. I'M NOT JUDGING THESE PEOPLE, NOT FEELING BETTER THAN THEM. I'M JUST GENUINELY TRYING TO UNDERSTAND THEM.
I DON'T KNOW... MAYBE IT'S A SELF-DEFENSE MECHANISM.
MAYBE SOMETIMES I TREAT PEOPLE MORE LIKE TEST SUBJECTS THAN... PEOPLE.
I'M WALKING ON SUNSHINE-- WOO-HOO! WALKIN' ON SUNSHINE-- WOO-WOO, AND IT'S TIME TO FEEL GOOD!
BUT LAST NIGHT SHE'S CRYING HER EYES OUT. THIS MORNING SHE'S SINGING. SO WHAT IS THIS? DENIAL? SHOULD I LET HER GO ON THIS WAY? SHOULD I TRY TO TALK HER THROUGH HER ISSUES? IS SHE EVEN AWARE OF THEM?
WHAT'S GOING ON INSIDE HER HEAD?
IT'S ALMOST DREAMLIKE. THERE'S A THICKNESS TO IT THAT MAKES IT FEEL LIKE YOU'RE DRUNK OR CONFUSED. A STRANGER INSIDE YOUR OWN BODY.
EXCEPT IT'S NOT YOUR BODY.
It only lasts a minute or two, then I seem t... time to recharge. And it only works with contact.
I can move around, talk, jump--anything t... body is capable of doing. But if I injure them, wounds appear on my body as well.
Speaking of which, my body is defenseless, catatonic. Like I've left the building. It's ee... seeing myself from the outside. I look fat.
I'm a visitor in their minds, so it's like being dropped into a new kitchen for the first time-- you have to look around to find stuff.
And, of course, you get the discomforting sensation that you're rifling through other people's things.
But, ultimately, it's all there. Even if it's suppressed, even if it's forgotten, even if they wish it not to be true. It's there.
And it's mine for the taking.
HOW PECULIAR...

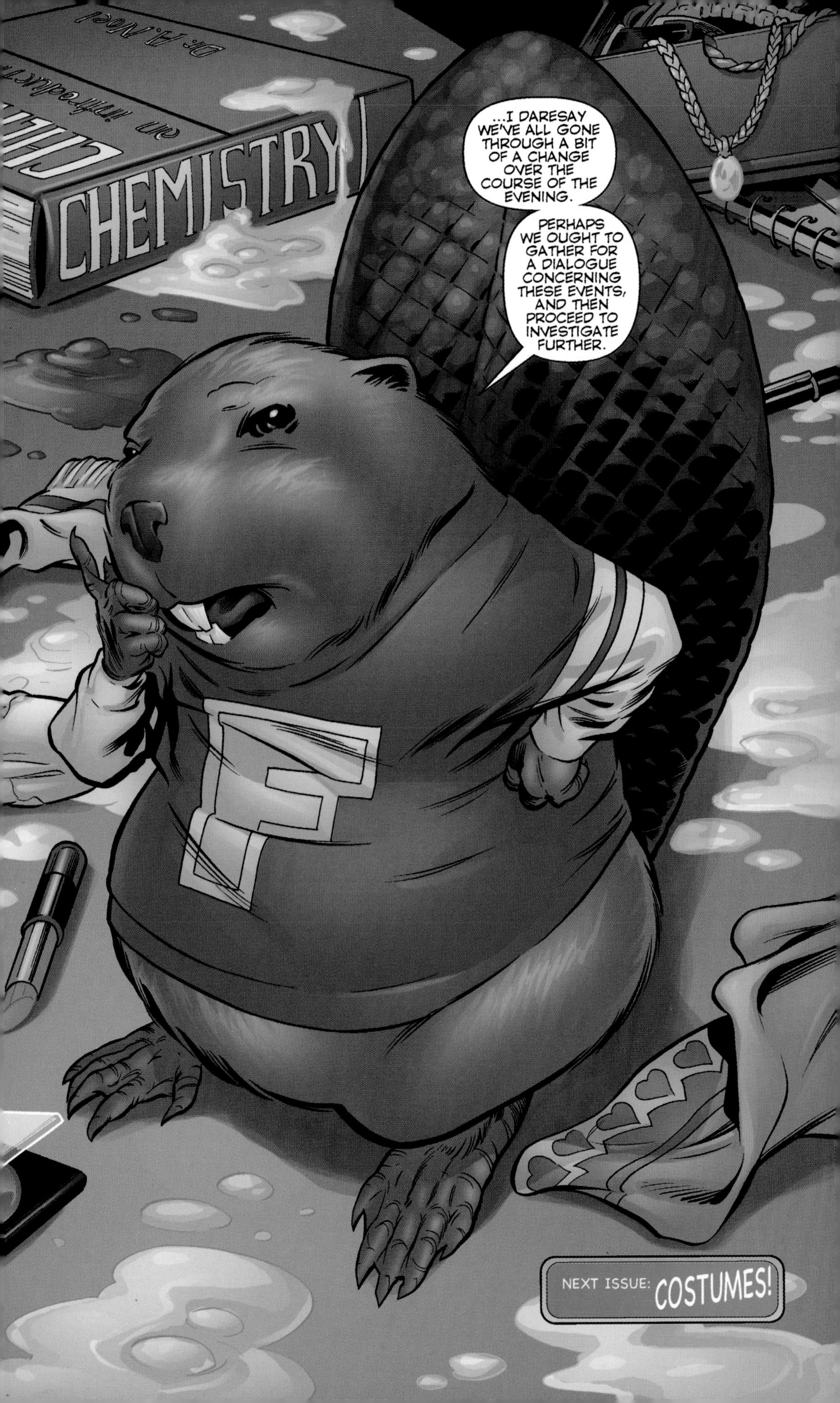
...I DARESAY WE'VE ALL GONE THROUGH A BIT OF A CHANGE OVER THE COURSE OF THE EVENING.
PERHAPS WE OUGHT TO GATHER FOR A DIALOGUE CONCERNING THESE EVENTS, AND THEN PROCEED TO INVESTIGATE FURTHER.
NEXT ISSUE: COSTUMES!
CHEMISTRY
an introduct
Dr. H. Noel

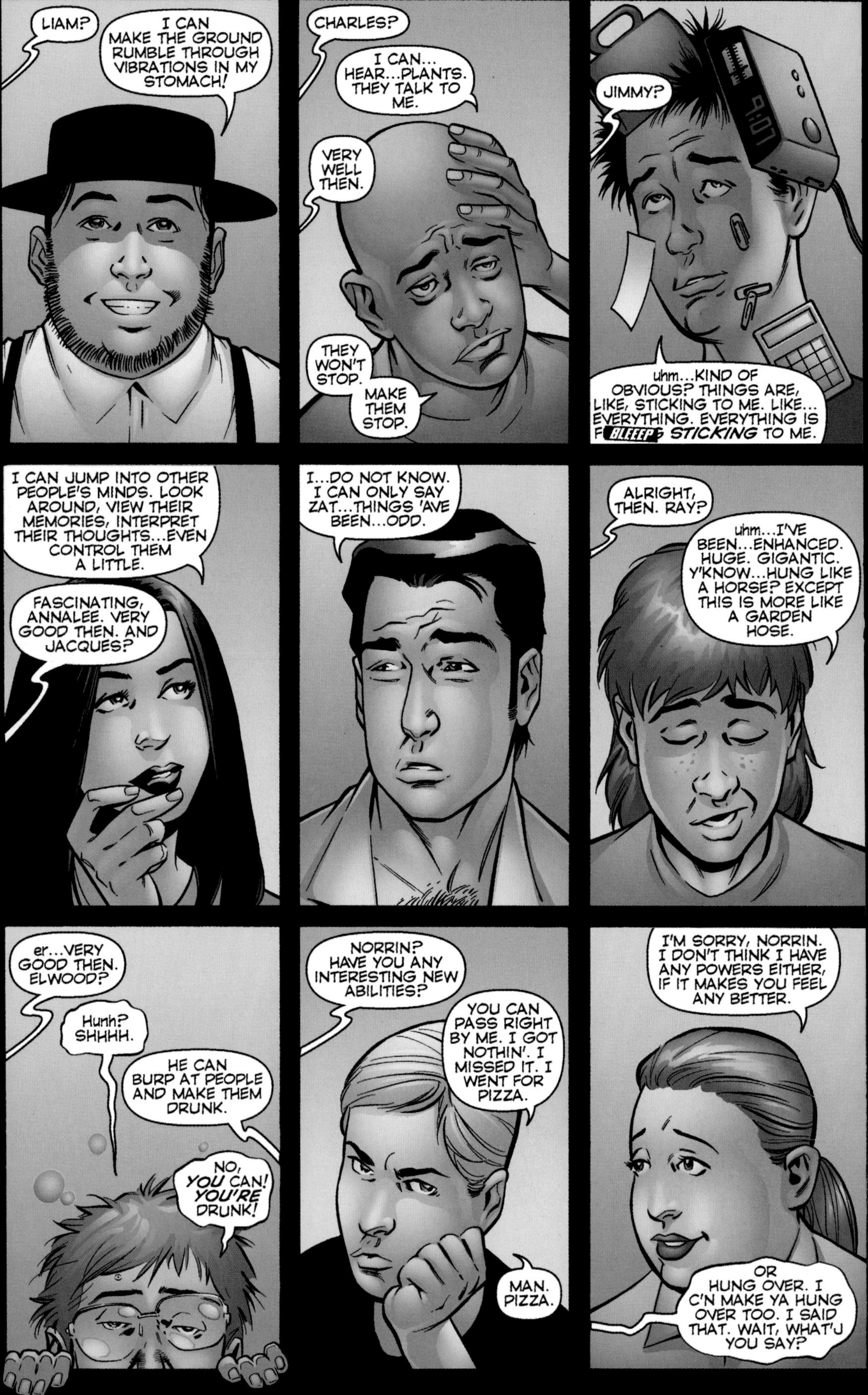
LIAM?
I CAN MAKE THE GROUND RUMBLE THROUGH VIBRATIONS IN MY STOMACH!
CHARLES?
I CAN... HEAR...PLANTS. THEY TALK TO ME.
VERY WELL THEN.
THEY WON'T STOP.
MAKE THEM STOP.
JIMMY?
uhm...KIND OF OBVIOUS? THINGS ARE, LIKE, STICKING TO ME. LIKE... EVERYTHING. EVERYTHING IS F BLEEEP G STICKING TO ME.
I CAN JUMP INTO OTHER PEOPLE'S MINDS. LOOK AROUND, VIEW THEIR MEMORIES, INTERPRET THEIR THOUGHTS...EVEN CONTROL THEM A LITTLE.
FASCINATING, ANNALEE. VERY GOOD THEN. AND JACQUES?
I...DO NOT KNOW. I CAN ONLY SAY ZAT...THINGS 'AVE BEEN...ODD.
ALRIGHT, THEN. RAY?
uhm...I'VE BEEN...ENHANCED. HUGE. GIGANTIC. Y'KNOW...HUNG LIKE A HORSE? EXCEPT THIS IS MORE LIKE A GARDEN HOSE.
er...VERY GOOD THEN. ELWOOD?
Hunh? SHHHH.
HE CAN BURP AT PEOPLE AND MAKE THEM DRUNK.
NO, YOU CAN! YOU'RE DRUNK!
NORRIN? HAVE YOU ANY INTERESTING NEW ABILITIES?
YOU CAN PASS RIGHT BY ME. I GOT NOTHIN'. I MISSED IT. I WENT FOR PIZZA.
MAN. PIZZA.
I'M SORRY, NORRIN. I DON'T THINK I HAVE ANY POWERS EITHER, IF IT MAKES YOU FEEL ANY BETTER.
OR HUNG OVER. I C'N MAKE YA HUNG OVER TOO. I SAID THAT. WAIT, WHAT'J YOU SAY?

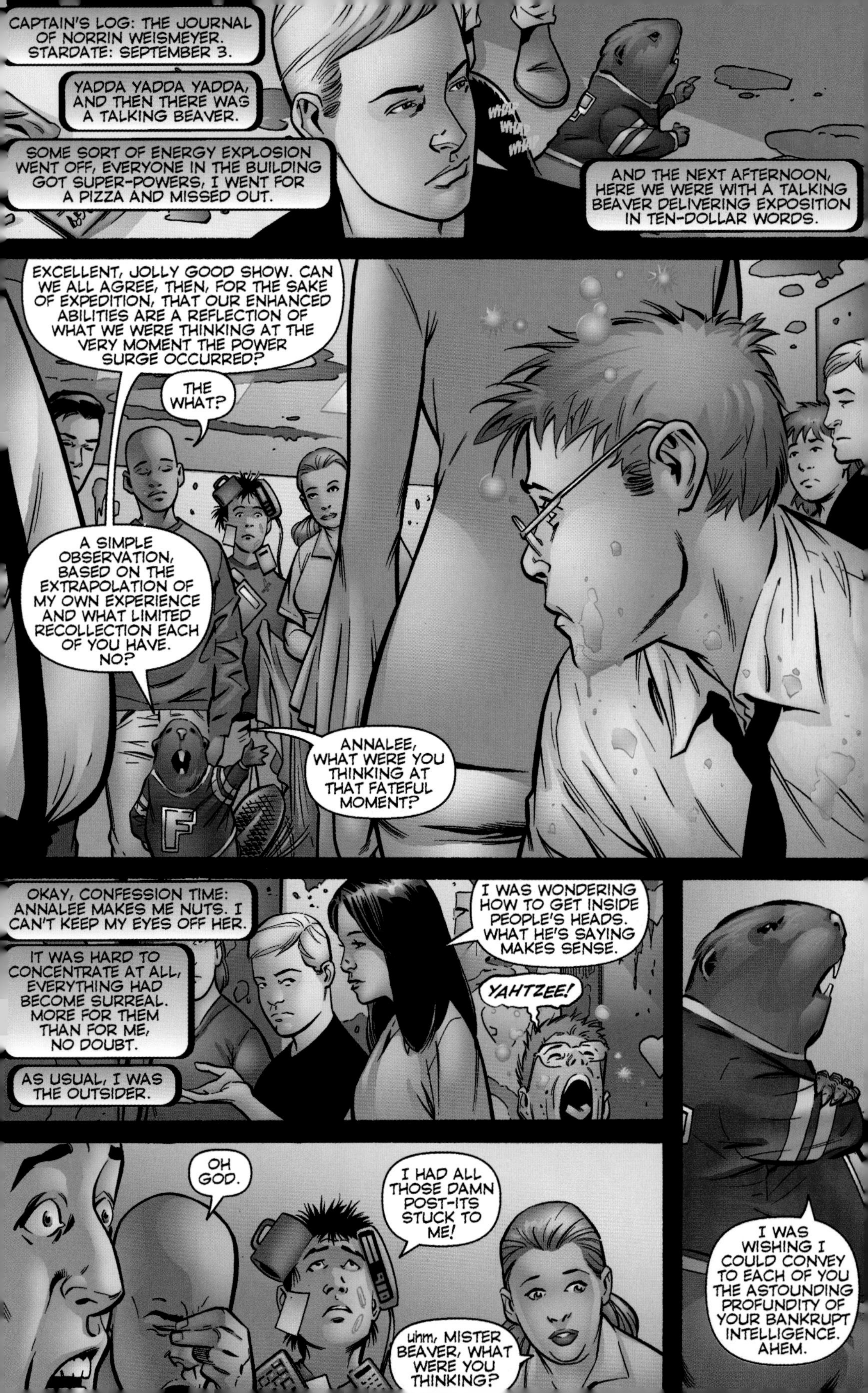
CAPTAIN'S LOG: THE JOURNAL OF NORRIN WEISMEYER. STARDATE: SEPTEMBER 3.
YADDA YADDA YADDA, AND THEN THERE WAS A TALKING BEAVER.
SOME SORT OF ENERGY EXPLOSION WENT OFF, EVERYONE IN THE BUILDING GOT SUPER-POWERS, I WENT FOR A PIZZA AND MISSED OUT.
WHAP WHAP WHAP
AND THE NEXT AFTERNOON, HERE WE WERE WITH A TALKING BEAVER DELIVERING EXPOSITION IN TEN-DOLLAR WORDS.
EXCELLENT, JOLLY GOOD SHOW. CAN WE ALL AGREE, THEN, FOR THE SAKE OF EXPEDITION, THAT OUR ENHANCED ABILITIES ARE A REFLECTION OF WHAT WE WERE THINKING AT THE VERY MOMENT THE POWER SURGE OCCURRED?
THE WHAT?
A SIMPLE OBSERVATION, BASED ON THE EXTRAPOLATION OF MY OWN EXPERIENCE AND WHAT LIMITED RECOLLECTION EACH OF YOU HAVE. NO?
ANNALEE, WHAT WERE YOU THINKING AT THAT FATEFUL MOMENT?
OKAY, CONFESSION TIME: ANNALEE MAKES ME NUTS. I CAN'T KEEP MY EYES OFF HER.
IT WAS HARD TO CONCENTRATE AT ALL, EVERYTHING HAD BECOME SURREAL. MORE FOR THEM THAN FOR ME, NO DOUBT.
AS USUAL, I WAS THE OUTSIDER.
I WAS WONDERING HOW TO GET INSIDE PEOPLE'S HEADS. WHAT HE'S SAYING MAKES SENSE.
YAHTZEE!
OH GOD.
I HAD ALL THOSE DAMN POST-ITS STUCK TO ME!
uhm, MISTER BEAVER, WHAT WERE YOU THINKING?
I WAS WISHING I COULD CONVEY TO EACH OF YOU THE ASTOUNDING PROFUNDITY OF YOUR BANKRUPT INTELLIGENCE. AHEM.

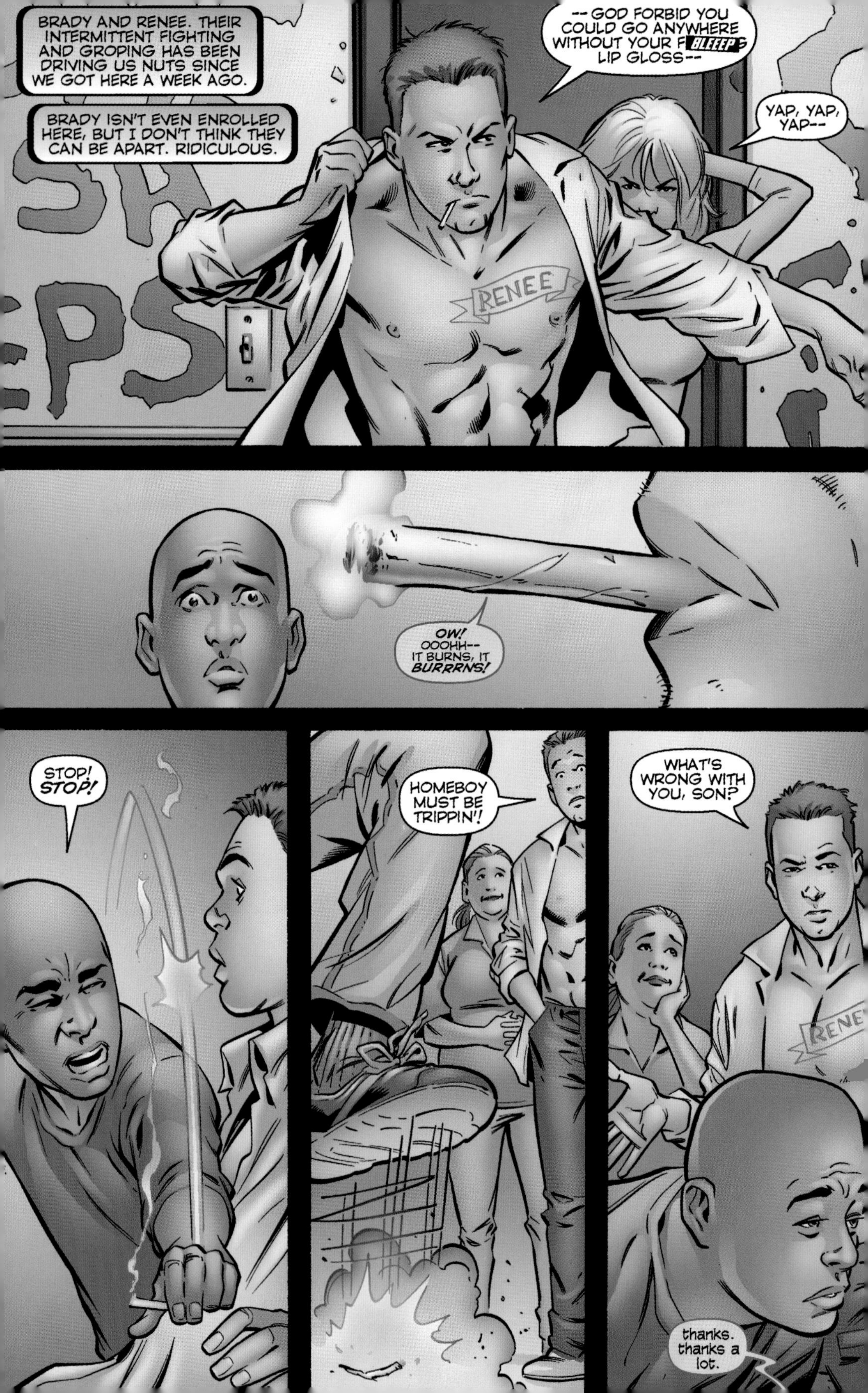
BRADY AND RENEE. THEIR INTERMITTENT FIGHTING AND GROPING HAS BEEN DRIVING US NUTS SINCE WE GOT HERE A WEEK AGO.
BRADY ISN'T EVEN ENROLLED HERE, BUT I DON'T THINK THEY CAN BE APART. RIDICULOUS.
--GOD FORBID YOU COULD GO ANYWHERE WITHOUT YOUR F BLEEEP G LIP GLOSS--
YAP, YAP, YAP--
RENEE
OW! OOOHH-- IT BURNS, IT BURRRNS!
STOP! STOP!
HOMEBOY MUST BE TRIPPIN'!
WHAT'S WRONG WITH YOU, SON?
RENEE
thanks. thanks a lot.

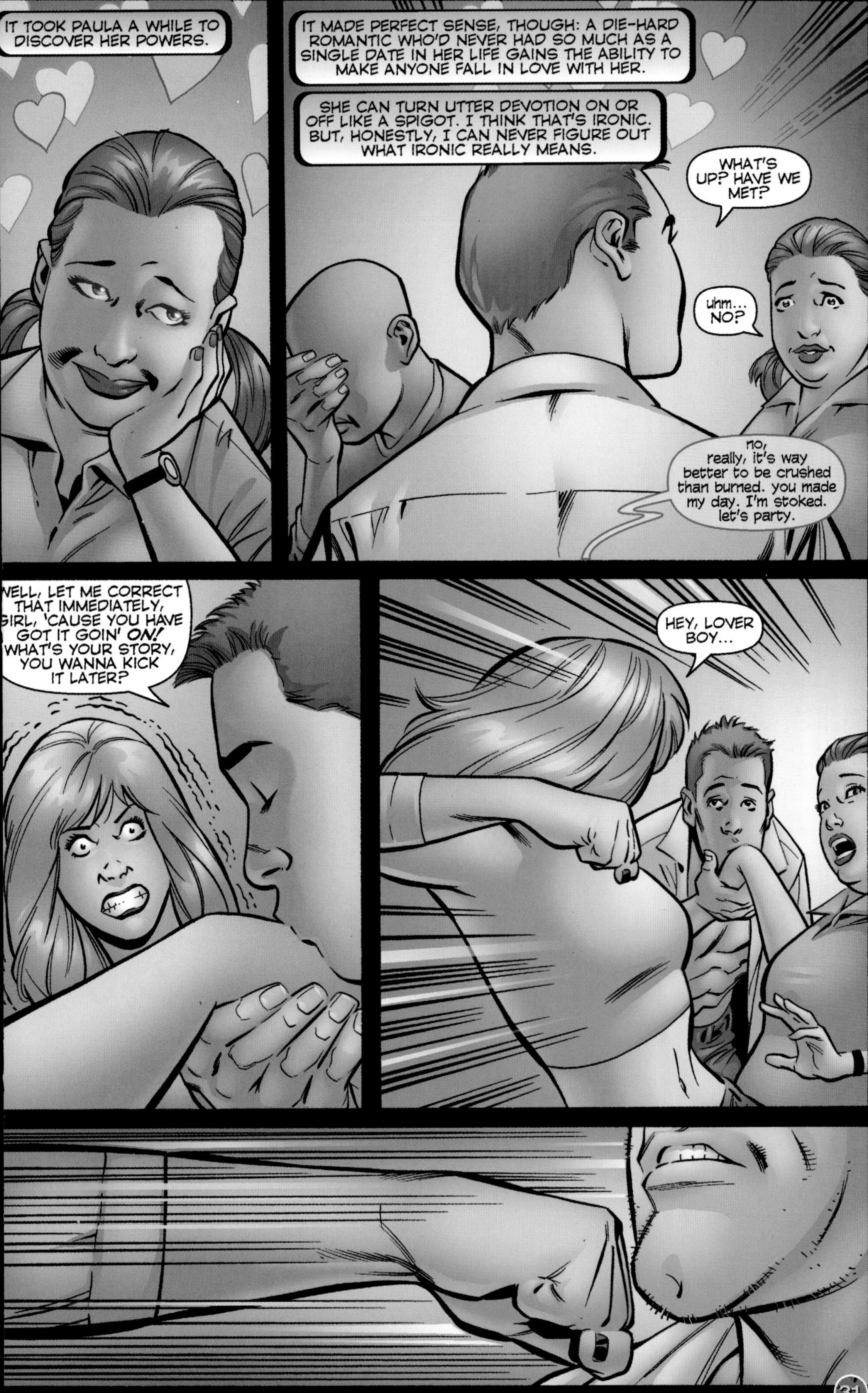
IT TOOK PAULA A WHILE TO DISCOVER HER POWERS.
IT MADE PERFECT SENSE, THOUGH: A DIE-HARD ROMANTIC WHO'D NEVER HAD SO MUCH AS A SINGLE DATE IN HER LIFE GAINS THE ABILITY TO MAKE ANYONE FALL IN LOVE WITH HER.
SHE CAN TURN UTTER DEVOTION ON OR OFF LIKE A SPIGOT. I THINK THAT'S IRONIC. BUT, HONESTLY, I CAN NEVER FIGURE OUT WHAT IRONIC REALLY MEANS.
WHAT'S UP? HAVE WE MET?
uhm... NO?
no, really, it's way better to be crushed than burned. you made my day. I'm stoked. let's party.
WELL, LET ME CORRECT THAT IMMEDIATELY, GIRL, 'CAUSE YOU HAVE GOT IT GOIN' ON! WHAT'S YOUR STORY, YOU WANNA KICK IT LATER?
HEY, LOVER BOY...

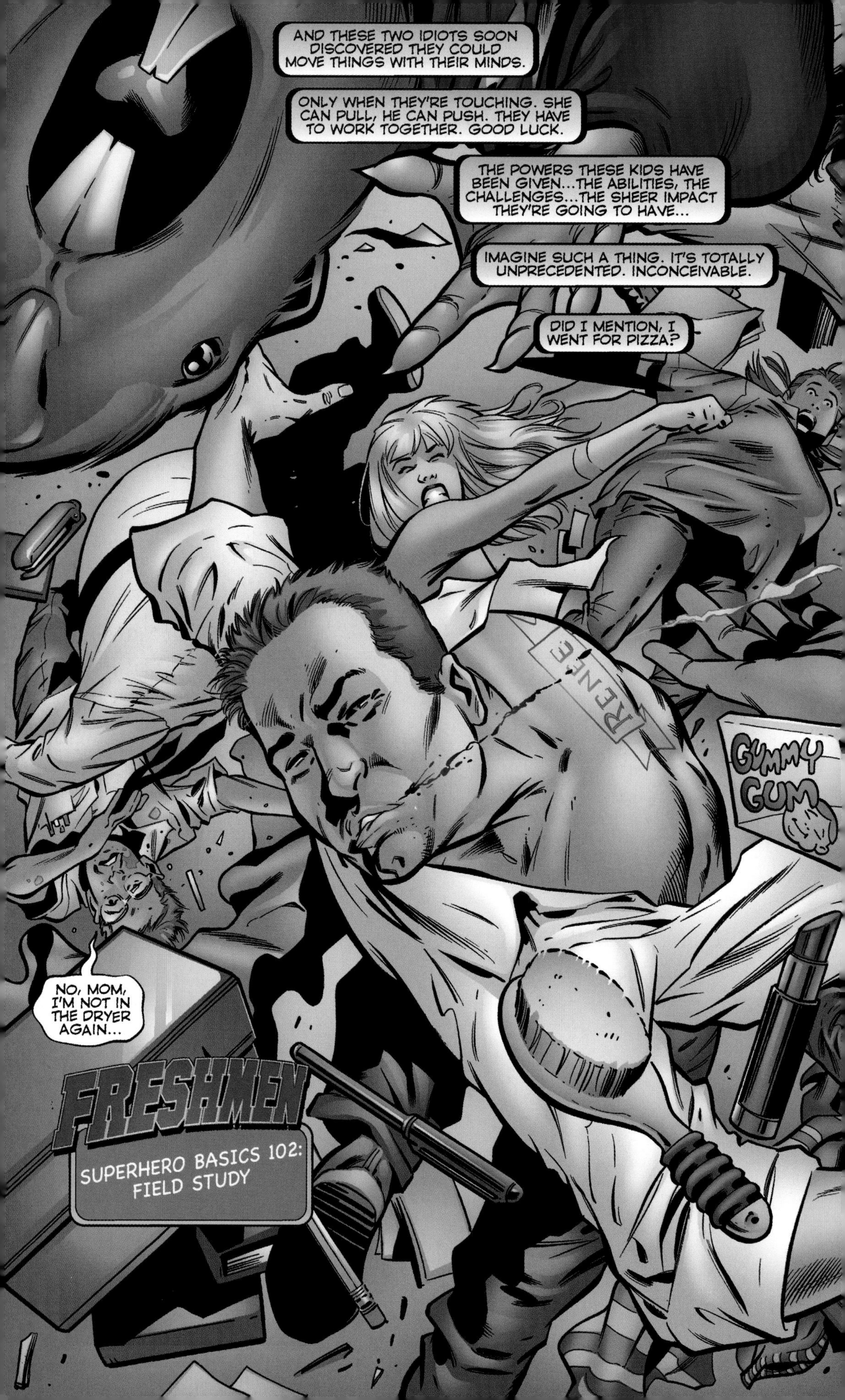
AND THESE TWO IDIOTS SOON DISCOVERED THEY COULD MOVE THINGS WITH THEIR MINDS.
ONLY WHEN THEY'RE TOUCHING. SHE CAN PULL, HE CAN PUSH. THEY HAVE TO WORK TOGETHER. GOOD LUCK.
THE POWERS THESE KIDS HAVE BEEN GIVEN...THE ABILITIES, THE CHALLENGES...THE SHEER IMPACT THEY'RE GOING TO HAVE...
IMAGINE SUCH A THING. IT'S TOTALLY UNPRECEDENTED. INCONCEIVABLE.
DID I MENTION, I WENT FOR PIZZA?
RENEE
GUMMY GUM
NO, MOM, I'M NOT IN THE DRYER AGAIN...
FRESHMEN
SUPERHERO BASICS 102: FIELD STUDY

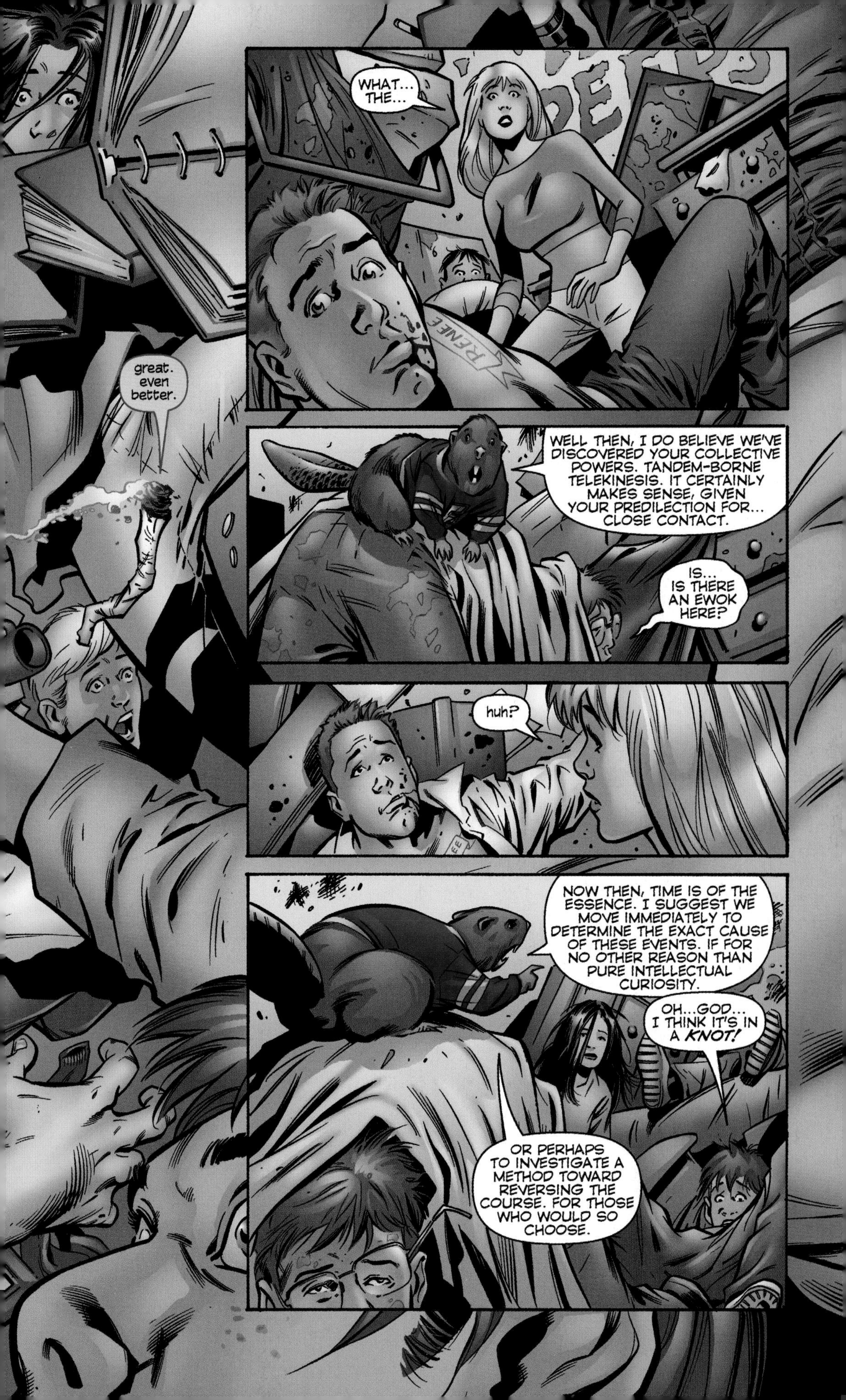
WHAT... THE...
great. even better.
WELL THEN, I DO BELIEVE WE'VE DISCOVERED YOUR COLLECTIVE POWERS. TANDEM-BORNE TELEKINESIS. IT CERTAINLY MAKES SENSE, GIVEN YOUR PREDILECTION FOR... CLOSE CONTACT.
IS... IS THERE AN EWOK HERE?
huh?
NOW THEN, TIME IS OF THE ESSENCE. I SUGGEST WE MOVE IMMEDIATELY TO DETERMINE THE EXACT CAUSE OF THESE EVENTS. IF FOR NO OTHER REASON THAN PURE INTELLECTUAL CURIOSITY.
OH...GOD... I THINK IT'S IN A KNOT!
OR PERHAPS TO INVESTIGATE A METHOD TOWARD REVERSING THE COURSE. FOR THOSE WHO WOULD SO CHOOSE.

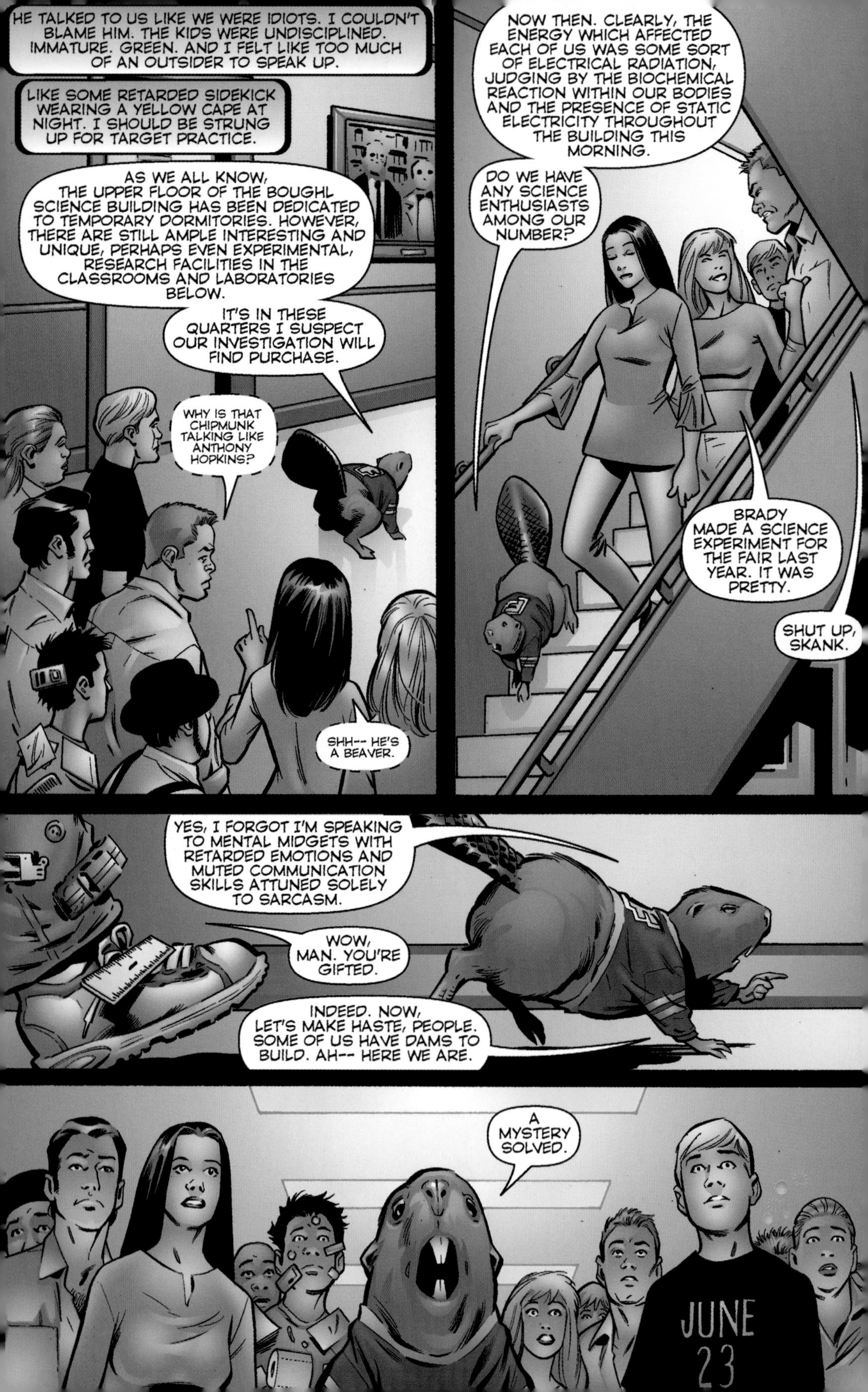
HE TALKED TO US LIKE WE WERE IDIOTS. I COULDN'T BLAME HIM. THE KIDS WERE UNDISCIPLINED. IMMATURE. GREEN. AND I FELT LIKE TOO MUCH OF AN OUTSIDER TO SPEAK UP.
LIKE SOME RETARDED SIDEKICK WEARING A YELLOW CAPE AT NIGHT. I SHOULD BE STRUNG UP FOR TARGET PRACTICE.
AS WE ALL KNOW, THE UPPER FLOOR OF THE BOUGHL SCIENCE BUILDING HAS BEEN DEDICATED TO TEMPORARY DORMITORIES. HOWEVER, THERE ARE STILL AMPLE INTERESTING AND UNIQUE, PERHAPS EVEN EXPERIMENTAL, RESEARCH FACILITIES IN THE CLASSROOMS AND LABORATORIES BELOW.
IT'S IN THESE QUARTERS I SUSPECT OUR INVESTIGATION WILL FIND PURCHASE.
WHY IS THAT CHIPMUNK TALKING LIKE ANTHONY HOPKINS?
SHH-- HE'S A BEAVER.
NOW THEN. CLEARLY, THE ENERGY WHICH AFFECTED EACH OF US WAS SOME SORT OF ELECTRICAL RADIATION, JUDGING BY THE BIOCHEMICAL REACTION WITHIN OUR BODIES AND THE PRESENCE OF STATIC ELECTRICITY THROUGHOUT THE BUILDING THIS MORNING.
DO WE HAVE ANY SCIENCE ENTHUSIASTS AMONG OUR NUMBER?
BRADY MADE A SCIENCE EXPERIMENT FOR THE FAIR LAST YEAR. IT WAS PRETTY.
SHUT UP, SKANK.
YES, I FORGOT I'M SPEAKING TO MENTAL MIDGETS WITH RETARDED EMOTIONS AND MUTED COMMUNICATION SKILLS ATTUNED SOLELY TO SARCASM.
WOW, MAN. YOU'RE GIFTED.
INDEED. NOW, LET'S MAKE HASTE, PEOPLE. SOME OF US HAVE DAMS TO BUILD. AH-- HERE WE ARE.
A MYSTERY SOLVED.
JUNE 23

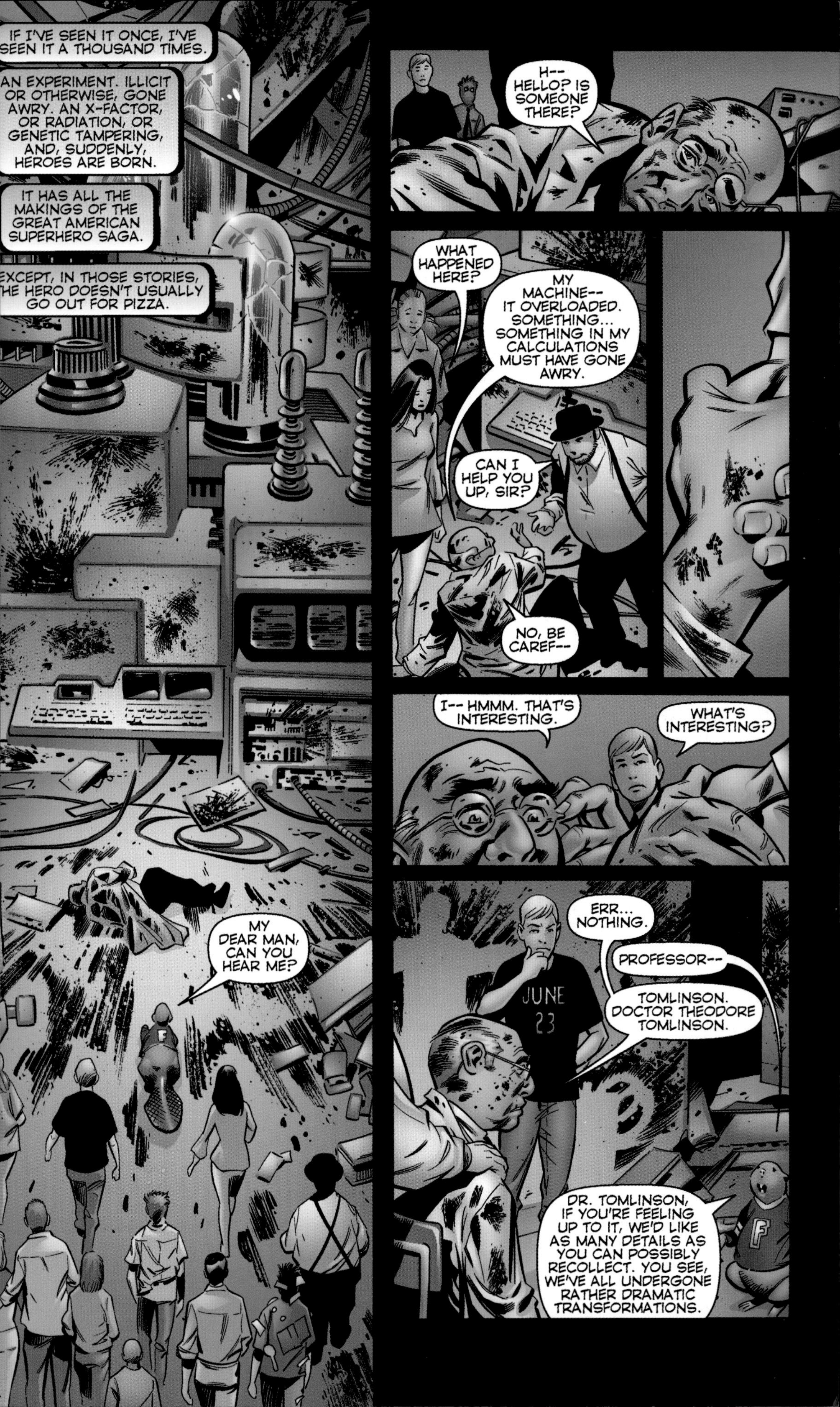
IF I'VE SEEN IT ONCE, I'VE SEEN IT A THOUSAND TIMES.
AN EXPERIMENT. ILLICIT OR OTHERWISE, GONE AWRY. AN X-FACTOR, OR RADIATION, OR GENETIC TAMPERING, AND, SUDDENLY, HEROES ARE BORN.
IT HAS ALL THE MAKINGS OF THE GREAT AMERICAN SUPERHERO SAGA.
EXCEPT, IN THOSE STORIES, THE HERO DOESN'T USUALLY GO OUT FOR PIZZA.
MY DEAR MAN, CAN YOU HEAR ME?
H-- HELLO? IS SOMEONE THERE?
WHAT HAPPENED HERE?
MY MACHINE-- IT OVERLOADED. SOMETHING... SOMETHING IN MY CALCULATIONS MUST HAVE GONE AWRY.
CAN I HELP YOU UP, SIR?
NO, BE CAREF--
I-- HMMM. THAT'S INTERESTING.
WHAT'S INTERESTING?
ERR... NOTHING.
PROFESSOR--
TOMLINSON. DOCTOR THEODORE TOMLINSON.
JUNE 23
DR. TOMLINSON, IF YOU'RE FEELING UP TO IT, WE'D LIKE AS MANY DETAILS AS YOU CAN POSSIBLY RECOLLECT. YOU SEE, WE'VE ALL UNDERGONE RATHER DRAMATIC TRANSFORMATIONS.

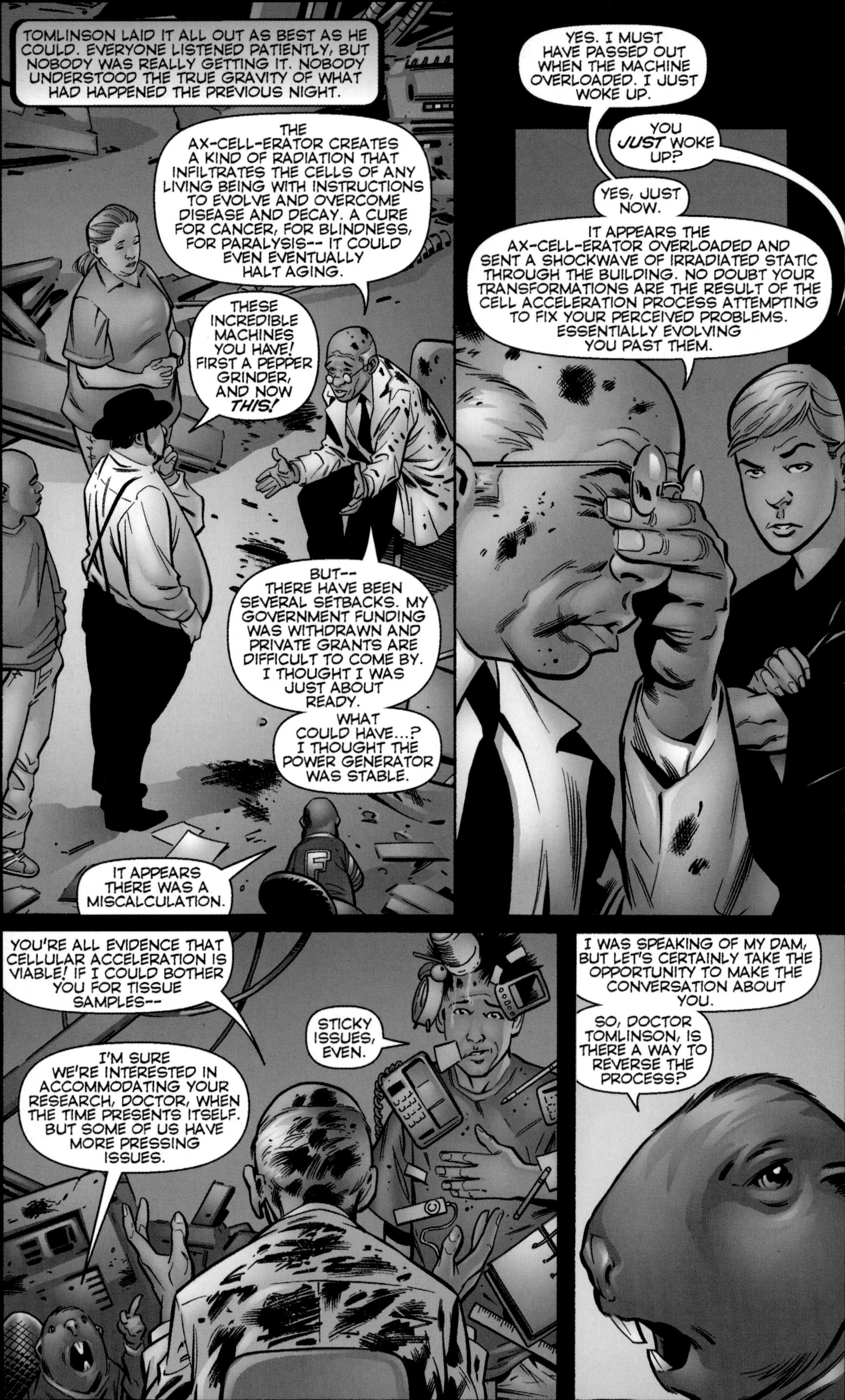
TOMLINSON LAID IT ALL OUT AS BEST AS HE COULD. EVERYONE LISTENED PATIENTLY, BUT NOBODY WAS REALLY GETTING IT. NOBODY UNDERSTOOD THE TRUE GRAVITY OF WHAT HAD HAPPENED THE PREVIOUS NIGHT.
THE AX-CELL-ERATOR CREATES A KIND OF RADIATION THAT INFILTRATES THE CELLS OF ANY LIVING BEING WITH INSTRUCTIONS TO EVOLVE AND OVERCOME DISEASE AND DECAY. A CURE FOR CANCER, FOR BLINDNESS, FOR PARALYSIS-- IT COULD EVEN EVENTUALLY HALT AGING.
THESE INCREDIBLE MACHINES YOU HAVE! FIRST A PEPPER GRINDER, AND NOW *THIS!*
BUT-- THERE HAVE BEEN SEVERAL SETBACKS. MY GOVERNMENT FUNDING WAS WITHDRAWN AND PRIVATE GRANTS ARE DIFFICULT TO COME BY. I THOUGHT I WAS JUST ABOUT READY.
WHAT COULD HAVE...? I THOUGHT THE POWER GENERATOR WAS STABLE.
IT APPEARS THERE WAS A MISCALCULATION.
YES. I MUST HAVE PASSED OUT WHEN THE MACHINE OVERLOADED. I JUST WOKE UP.
YOU *JUST* WOKE UP?
YES, JUST NOW.
IT APPEARS THE AX-CELL-ERATOR OVERLOADED AND SENT A SHOCKWAVE OF IRRADIATED STATIC THROUGH THE BUILDING. NO DOUBT YOUR TRANSFORMATIONS ARE THE RESULT OF THE CELL ACCELERATION PROCESS ATTEMPTING TO FIX YOUR PERCEIVED PROBLEMS. ESSENTIALLY EVOLVING YOU PAST THEM.
YOU'RE ALL EVIDENCE THAT CELLULAR ACCELERATION IS VIABLE! IF I COULD BOTHER YOU FOR TISSUE SAMPLES--
STICKY ISSUES, EVEN.
I'M SURE WE'RE INTERESTED IN ACCOMMODATING YOUR RESEARCH, DOCTOR, WHEN THE TIME PRESENTS ITSELF. BUT SOME OF US HAVE MORE PRESSING ISSUES.
I WAS SPEAKING OF MY DAM, BUT LET'S CERTAINLY TAKE THE OPPORTUNITY TO MAKE THE CONVERSATION ABOUT YOU.
SO, DOCTOR TOMLINSON, IS THERE A WAY TO REVERSE THE PROCESS?

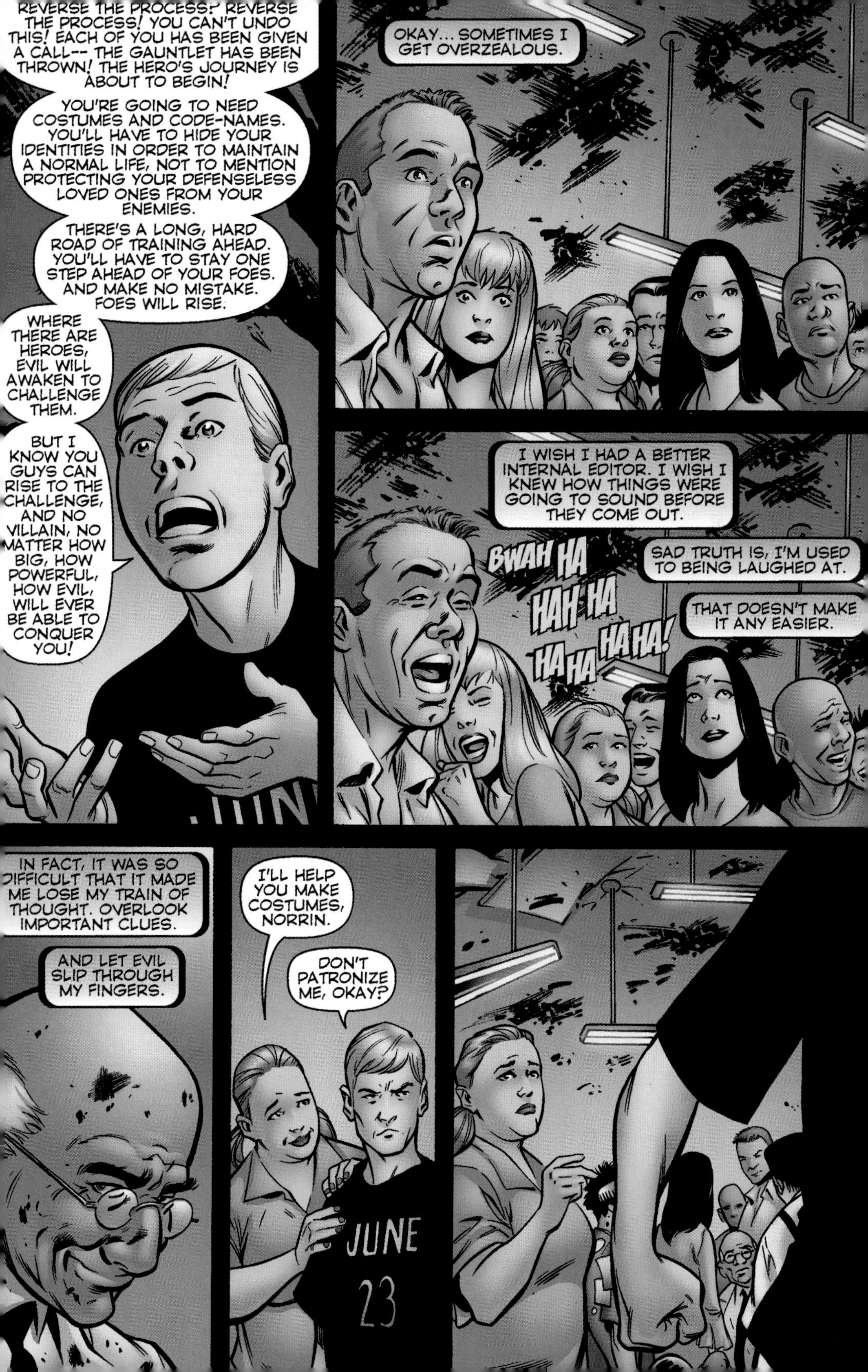
REVERSE THE PROCESS? REVERSE THE PROCESS! YOU CAN'T UNDO THIS! EACH OF YOU HAS BEEN GIVEN A CALL-- THE GAUNTLET HAS BEEN THROWN! THE HERO'S JOURNEY IS ABOUT TO BEGIN!
YOU'RE GOING TO NEED COSTUMES AND CODE-NAMES. YOU'LL HAVE TO HIDE YOUR IDENTITIES IN ORDER TO MAINTAIN A NORMAL LIFE, NOT TO MENTION PROTECTING YOUR DEFENSELESS LOVED ONES FROM YOUR ENEMIES.
THERE'S A LONG, HARD ROAD OF TRAINING AHEAD. YOU'LL HAVE TO STAY ONE STEP AHEAD OF YOUR FOES. AND MAKE NO MISTAKE. FOES WILL RISE.
WHERE THERE ARE HEROES, EVIL WILL AWAKEN TO CHALLENGE THEM.
BUT I KNOW YOU GUYS CAN RISE TO THE CHALLENGE, AND NO VILLAIN, NO MATTER HOW BIG, HOW POWERFUL, HOW EVIL, WILL EVER BE ABLE TO CONQUER YOU!
OKAY... SOMETIMES I GET OVERZEALOUS.
I WISH I HAD A BETTER INTERNAL EDITOR. I WISH I KNEW HOW THINGS WERE GOING TO SOUND BEFORE THEY COME OUT.
BWAH HA HAH HA HA HA HA HA!
SAD TRUTH IS, I'M USED TO BEING LAUGHED AT.
THAT DOESN'T MAKE IT ANY EASIER.
IN FACT, IT WAS SO DIFFICULT THAT IT MADE ME LOSE MY TRAIN OF THOUGHT. OVERLOOK IMPORTANT CLUES.
AND LET EVIL SLIP THROUGH MY FINGERS.
I'LL HELP YOU MAKE COSTUMES, NORRIN.
DON'T PATRONIZE ME, OKAY?
JUNE 23

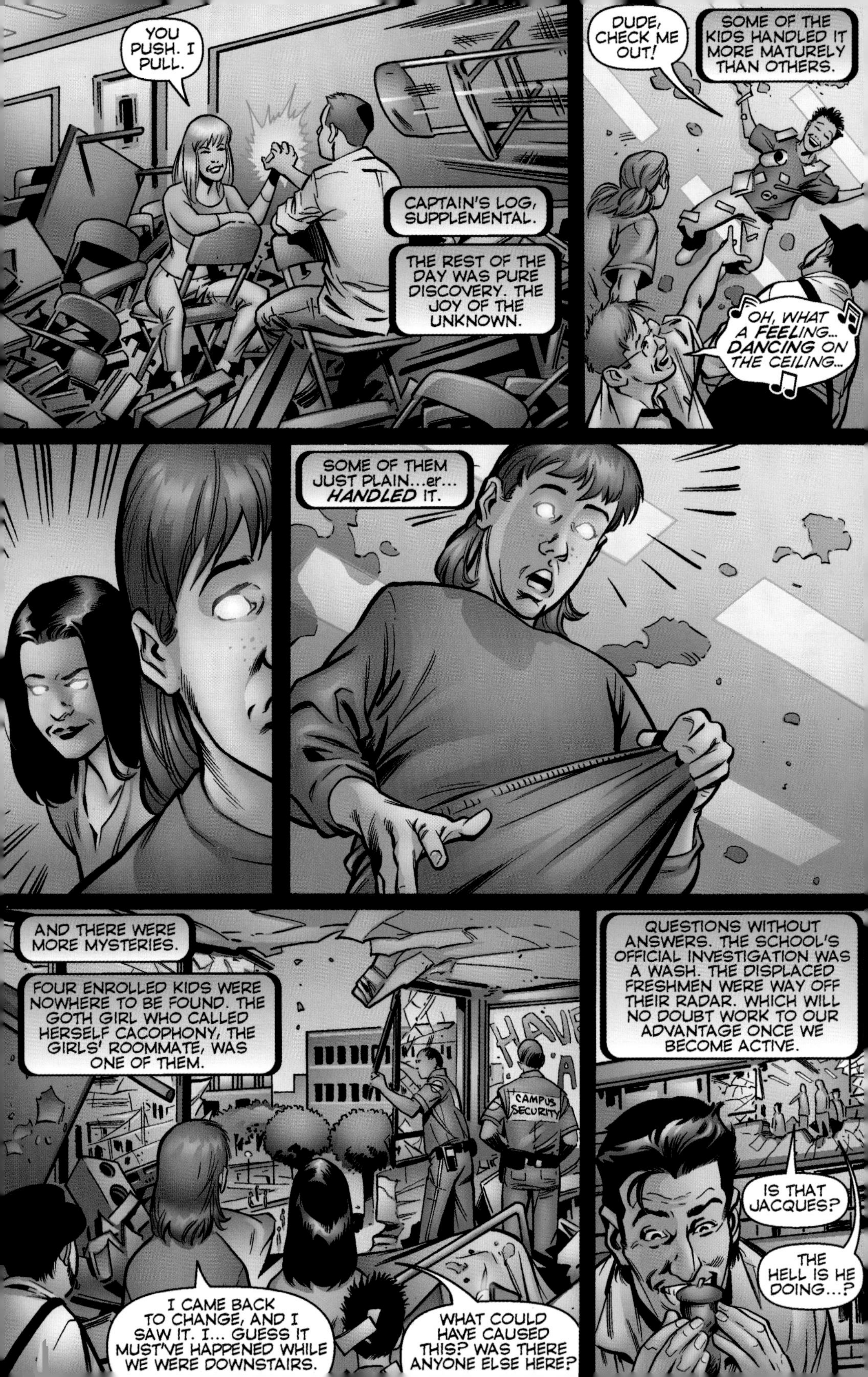
YOU PUSH. I PULL.
CAPTAIN'S LOG, SUPPLEMENTAL.
THE REST OF THE DAY WAS PURE DISCOVERY. THE JOY OF THE UNKNOWN.
DUDE, CHECK ME OUT!
SOME OF THE KIDS HANDLED IT MORE MATURELY THAN OTHERS.
OH, WHAT A FEELING... DANCING ON THE CEILING...
SOME OF THEM JUST PLAIN...er... HANDLED IT.
AND THERE WERE MORE MYSTERIES.
FOUR ENROLLED KIDS WERE NOWHERE TO BE FOUND. THE GOTH GIRL WHO CALLED HERSELF CACOPHONY, THE GIRLS' ROOMMATE, WAS ONE OF THEM.
CAMPUS SECURITY
I CAME BACK TO CHANGE, AND I SAW IT. I... GUESS IT MUST'VE HAPPENED WHILE WE WERE DOWNSTAIRS.
WHAT COULD HAVE CAUSED THIS? WAS THERE ANYONE ELSE HERE?
QUESTIONS WITHOUT ANSWERS. THE SCHOOL'S OFFICIAL INVESTIGATION WAS A WASH. THE DISPLACED FRESHMEN WERE WAY OFF THEIR RADAR. WHICH WILL NO DOUBT WORK TO OUR ADVANTAGE ONCE WE BECOME ACTIVE.
IS THAT JACQUES?
THE HELL IS HE DOING...?

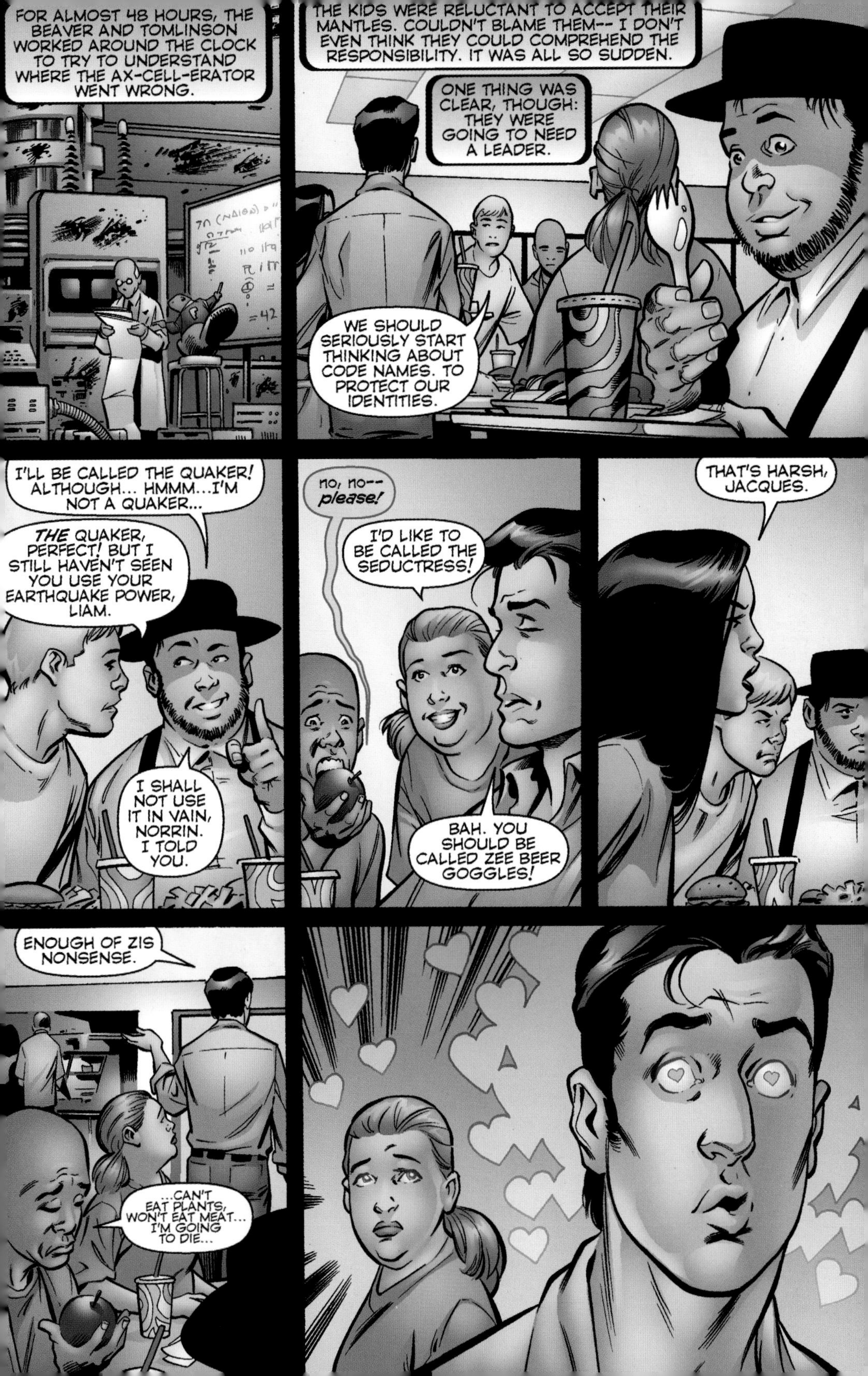
FOR ALMOST 48 HOURS, THE BEAVER AND TOMLINSON WORKED AROUND THE CLOCK TO TRY TO UNDERSTAND WHERE THE AX-CELL-ERATOR WENT WRONG.
THE KIDS WERE RELUCTANT TO ACCEPT THEIR MANTLES. COULDN'T BLAME THEM-- I DON'T EVEN THINK THEY COULD COMPREHEND THE RESPONSIBILITY. IT WAS ALL SO SUDDEN.
ONE THING WAS CLEAR, THOUGH: THEY WERE GOING TO NEED A LEADER.
WE SHOULD SERIOUSLY START THINKING ABOUT CODE NAMES. TO PROTECT OUR IDENTITIES.
I'LL BE CALLED THE QUAKER! ALTHOUGH... HMMM...I'M NOT A QUAKER...
THE QUAKER, PERFECT! BUT I STILL HAVEN'T SEEN YOU USE YOUR EARTHQUAKE POWER, LIAM.
I SHALL NOT USE IT IN VAIN, NORRIN. I TOLD YOU.
no, no-- please!
I'D LIKE TO BE CALLED THE SEDUCTRESS!
BAH. YOU SHOULD BE CALLED ZEE BEER GOGGLES!
THAT'S HARSH, JACQUES.
ENOUGH OF ZIS NONSENSE.
...CAN'T EAT PLANTS, WON'T EAT MEAT... I'M GOING TO DIE...

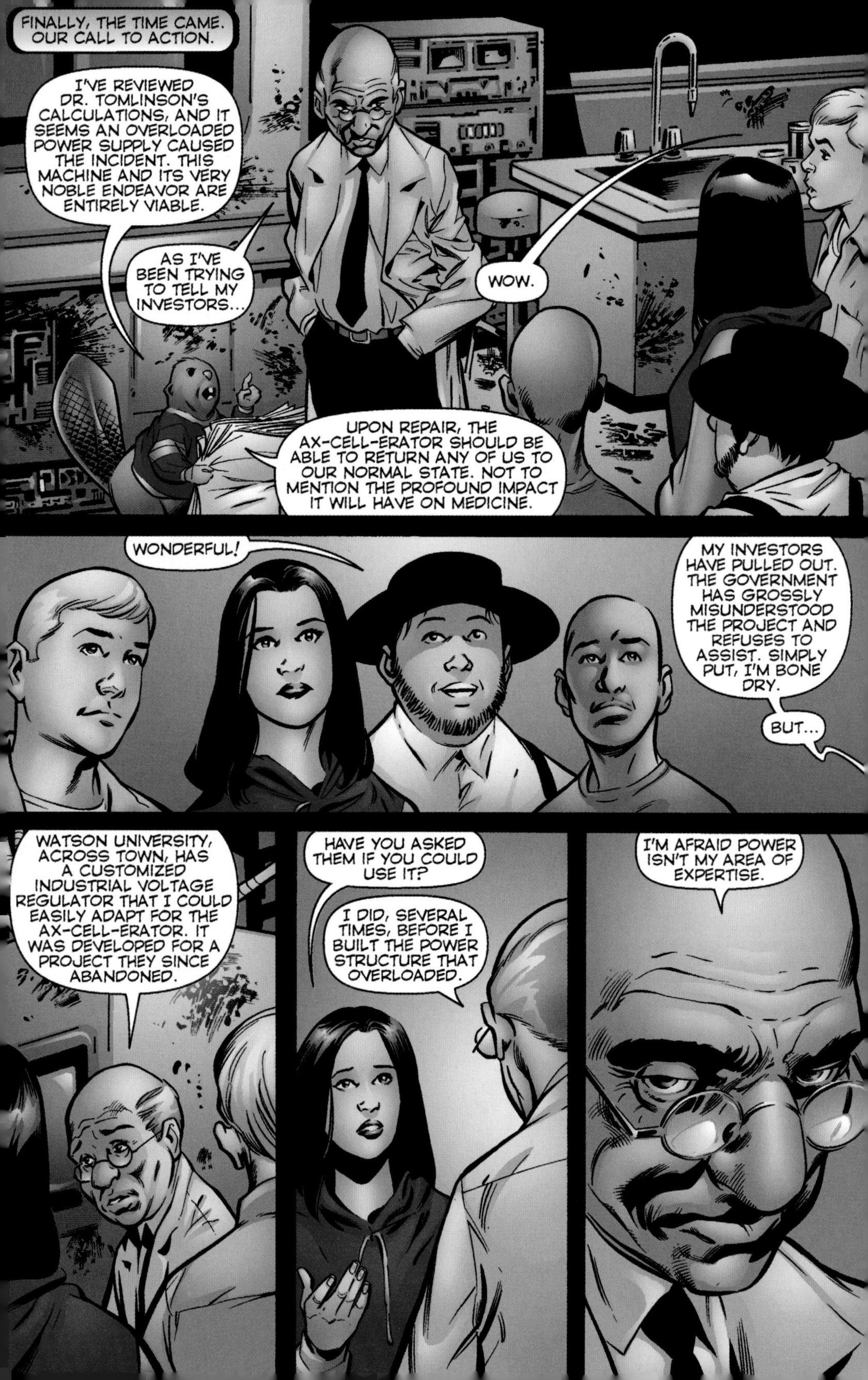
FINALLY, THE TIME CAME. OUR CALL TO ACTION.
I'VE REVIEWED DR. TOMLINSON'S CALCULATIONS, AND IT SEEMS AN OVERLOADED POWER SUPPLY CAUSED THE INCIDENT. THIS MACHINE AND ITS VERY NOBLE ENDEAVOR ARE ENTIRELY VIABLE.
AS I'VE BEEN TRYING TO TELL MY INVESTORS...
WOW.
UPON REPAIR, THE AX-CELL-ERATOR SHOULD BE ABLE TO RETURN ANY OF US TO OUR NORMAL STATE. NOT TO MENTION THE PROFOUND IMPACT IT WILL HAVE ON MEDICINE.
WONDERFUL!
MY INVESTORS HAVE PULLED OUT. THE GOVERNMENT HAS GROSSLY MISUNDERSTOOD THE PROJECT AND REFUSES TO ASSIST. SIMPLY PUT, I'M BONE DRY.
BUT...
WATSON UNIVERSITY, ACROSS TOWN, HAS A CUSTOMIZED INDUSTRIAL VOLTAGE REGULATOR THAT I COULD EASILY ADAPT FOR THE AX-CELL-ERATOR. IT WAS DEVELOPED FOR A PROJECT THEY SINCE ABANDONED.
HAVE YOU ASKED THEM IF YOU COULD USE IT?
I DID, SEVERAL TIMES, BEFORE I BUILT THE POWER STRUCTURE THAT OVERLOADED.
I'M AFRAID POWER ISN'T MY AREA OF EXPERTISE.

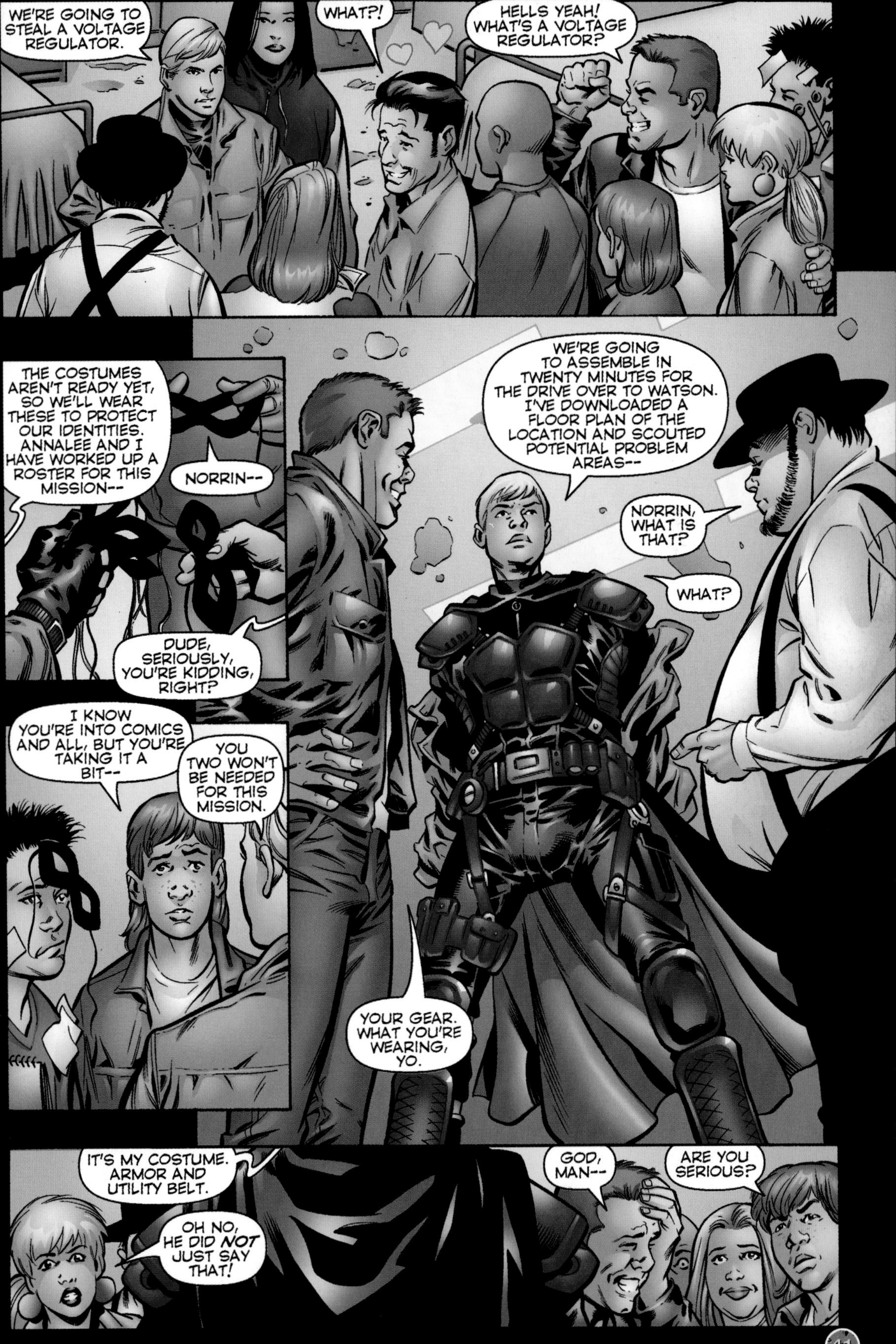
WE'RE GOING TO STEAL A VOLTAGE REGULATOR.
WHAT?!
HELLS YEAH! WHAT'S A VOLTAGE REGULATOR?
THE COSTUMES AREN'T READY YET, SO WE'LL WEAR THESE TO PROTECT OUR IDENTITIES. ANNALEE AND I HAVE WORKED UP A ROSTER FOR THIS MISSION--
NORRIN--
DUDE, SERIOUSLY, YOU'RE KIDDING, RIGHT?
I KNOW YOU'RE INTO COMICS AND ALL, BUT YOU'RE TAKING IT A BIT--
YOU TWO WON'T BE NEEDED FOR THIS MISSION.
WE'RE GOING TO ASSEMBLE IN TWENTY MINUTES FOR THE DRIVE OVER TO WATSON. I'VE DOWNLOADED A FLOOR PLAN OF THE LOCATION AND SCOUTED POTENTIAL PROBLEM AREAS--
NORRIN, WHAT IS THAT?
WHAT?
YOUR GEAR. WHAT YOU'RE WEARING, YO.
IT'S MY COSTUME. ARMOR AND UTILITY BELT.
OH NO, HE DID NOT JUST SAY THAT!
GOD, MAN--
ARE YOU SERIOUS?

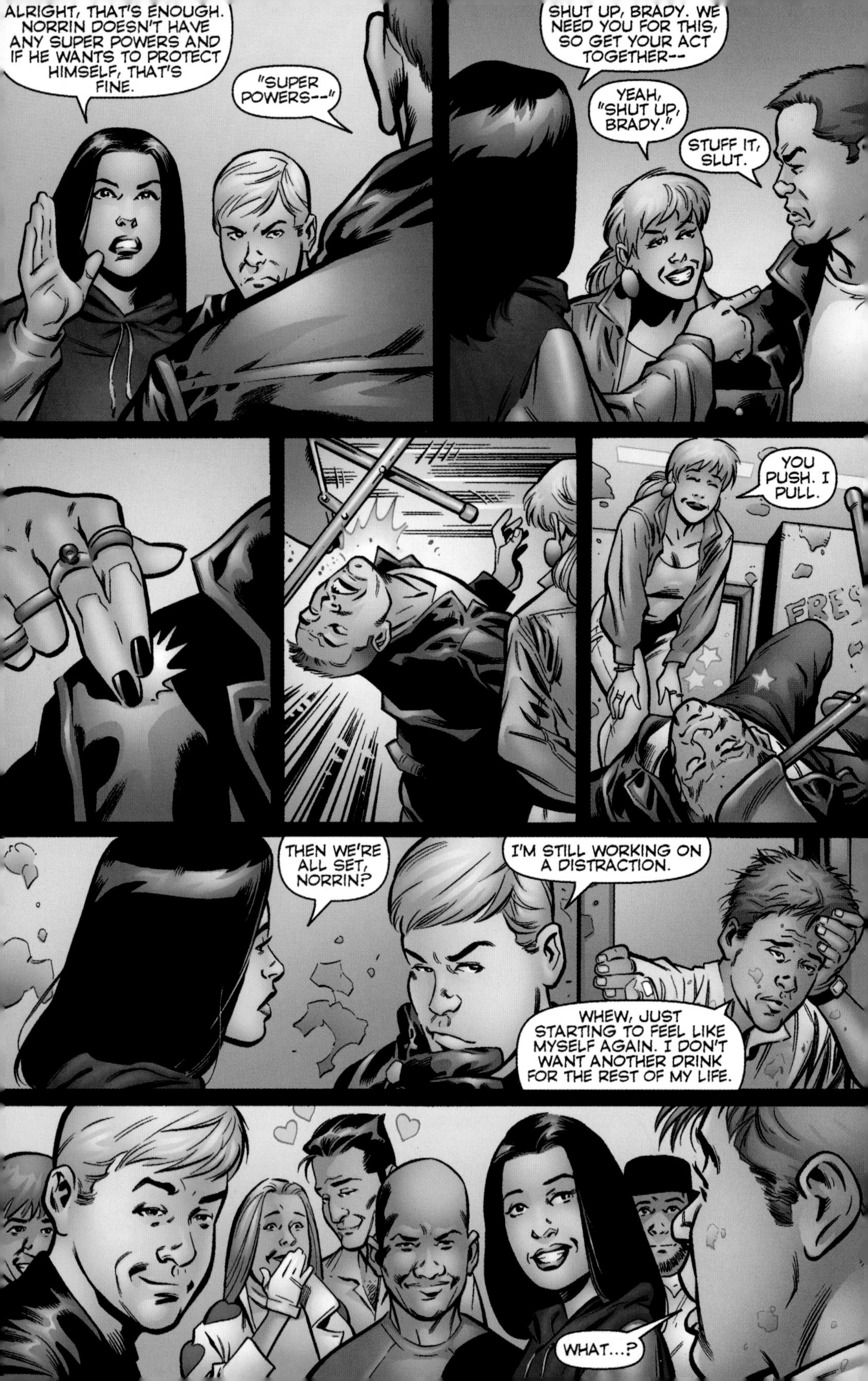
ALRIGHT, THAT'S ENOUGH. NORRIN DOESN'T HAVE ANY SUPER POWERS AND IF HE WANTS TO PROTECT HIMSELF, THAT'S FINE.
"SUPER POWERS--"
SHUT UP, BRADY. WE NEED YOU FOR THIS, SO GET YOUR ACT TOGETHER--
YEAH, "SHUT UP, BRADY."
STUFF IT, SLUT.
YOU PUSH. I PULL.
FRES
THEN WE'RE ALL SET, NORRIN?
I'M STILL WORKING ON A DISTRACTION.
WHEW, JUST STARTING TO FEEL LIKE MYSELF AGAIN. I DON'T WANT ANOTHER DRINK FOR THE REST OF MY LIFE.
WHAT...?

STARDATE: SEPTEMBER 5. THE TEAM HAS INFILTRATED JOMITA STADIUM AT WATSON UNIVERSITY. IT'S THEIR HOMECOMING FOOTBALL GAME, AGAINST OUR OWN FREESE BEAVERS.

ONE BOTTLE DOWN.

NEXT ONE'S UP. HOW YA FEELIN', ELWOOD?

WEEE.

BUUUUURP!

WHAT THE--

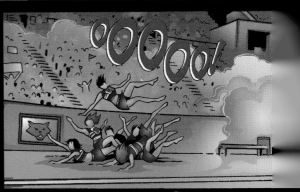

OOOOOO!

OKAY, PAULA, YOU STAY HERE, TAKE CARE OF HIM. ANYBODY ASKS YOU TO MOVE, THEY FALL IN LOVE WITH YOU.

YES SIR!

EVERYONE ELSE, FOLLOW NORRIN.

HOO-BOY... I GOT A BEAUT BREWIN'.

LET ME 'ELP YOU.

YOUR COSTUME IS VERY BECOMING, MY DEAR. VERY SEXY.

BAREEELLLUGH!

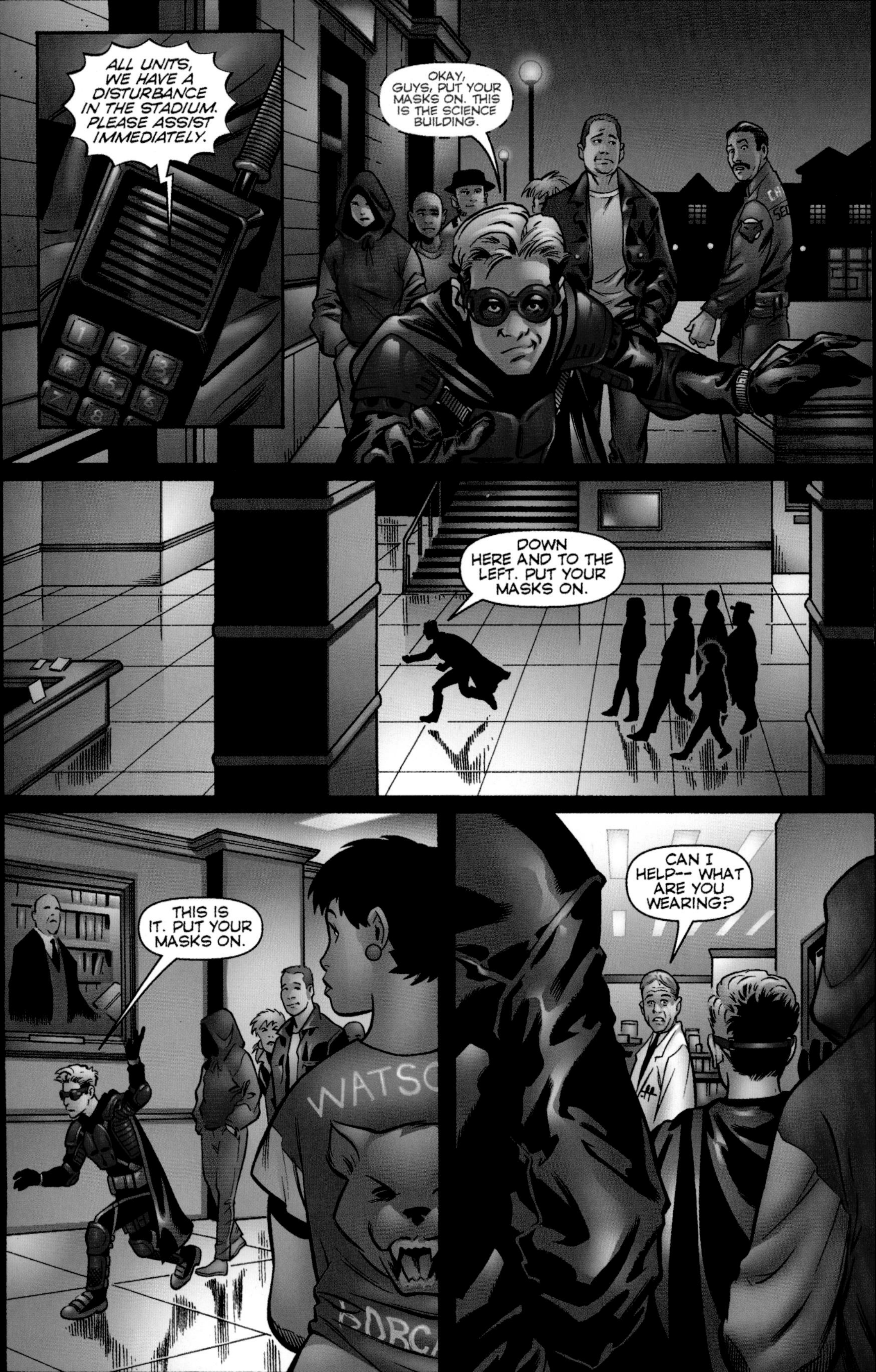
ALL UNITS, WE HAVE A DISTURBANCE IN THE STADIUM. PLEASE ASSIST IMMEDIATELY.
OKAY, GUYS, PUT YOUR MASKS ON. THIS IS THE SCIENCE BUILDING.
DOWN HERE AND TO THE LEFT. PUT YOUR MASKS ON.
THIS IS IT. PUT YOUR MASKS ON.
CAN I HELP-- WHAT ARE YOU WEARING?

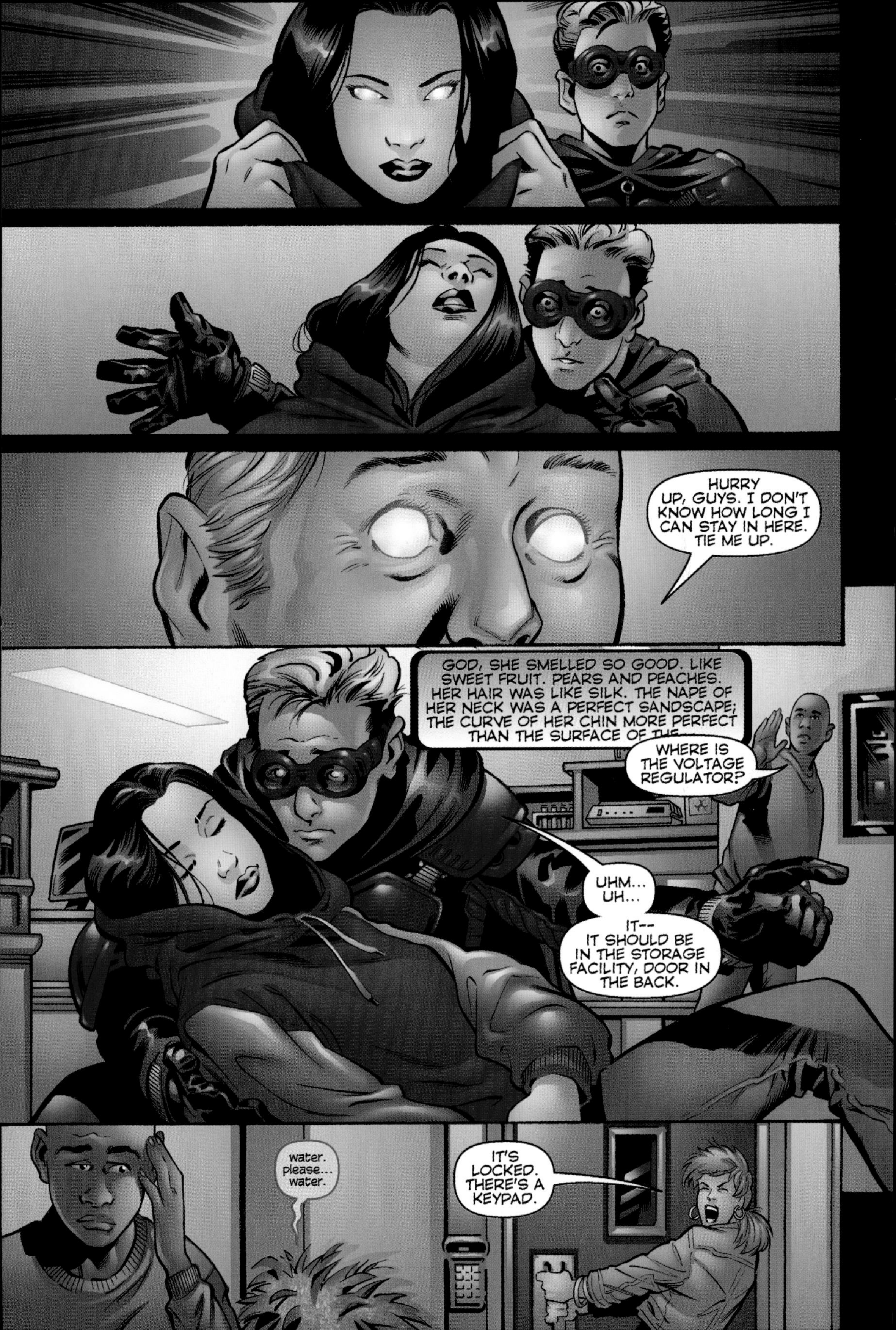
HURRY UP, GUYS. I DON'T KNOW HOW LONG I CAN STAY IN HERE. TIE ME UP.
GOD, SHE SMELLED SO GOOD. LIKE SWEET FRUIT. PEARS AND PEACHES. HER HAIR WAS LIKE SILK. THE NAPE OF HER NECK WAS A PERFECT SANDSCAPE; THE CURVE OF HER CHIN MORE PERFECT THAN THE SURFACE OF THE--
WHERE IS THE VOLTAGE REGULATOR?
UHM... UH...
IT-- IT SHOULD BE IN THE STORAGE FACILITY, DOOR IN THE BACK.
water. please... water.
IT'S LOCKED. THERE'S A KEYPAD.

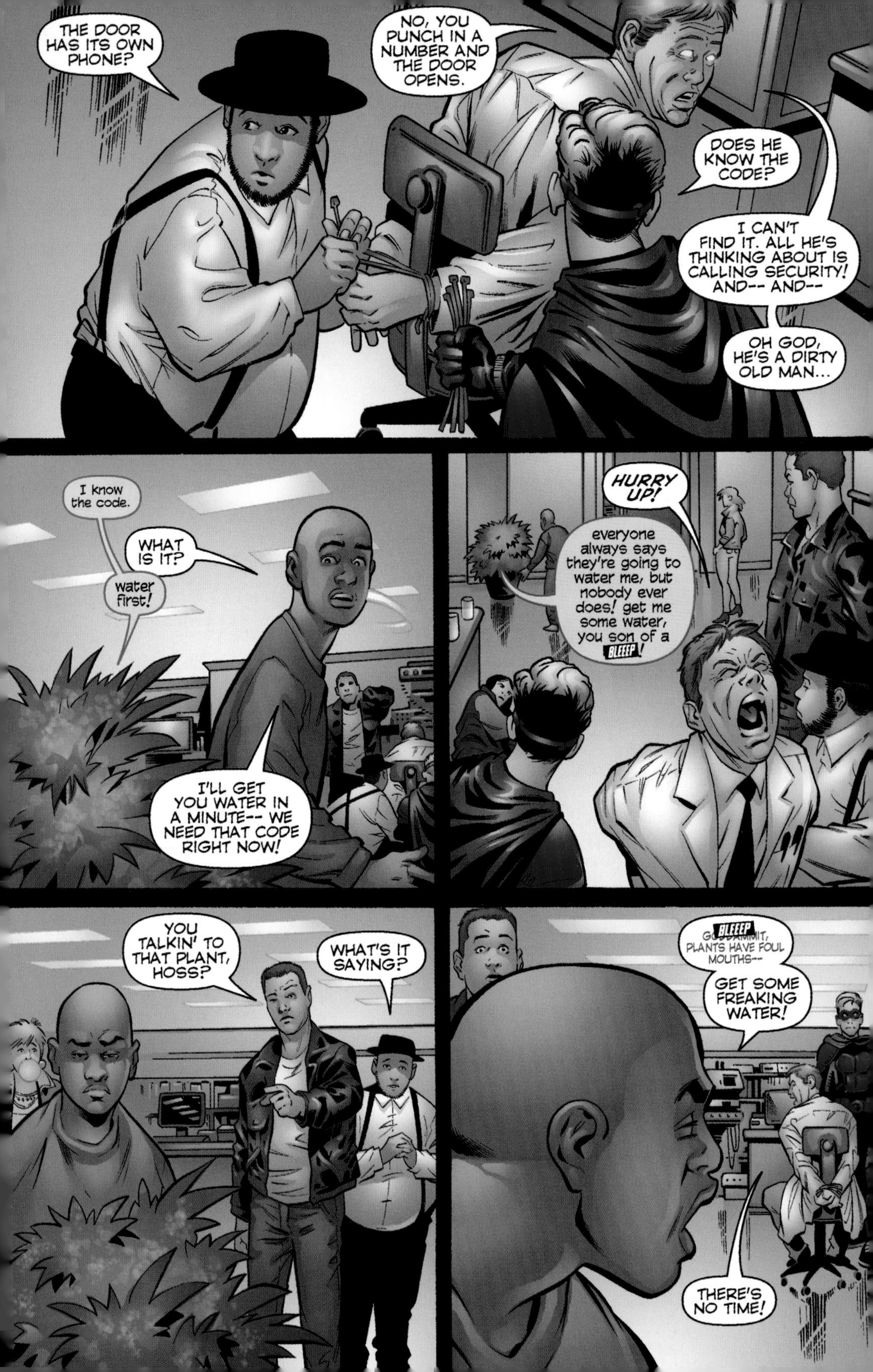
THE DOOR HAS ITS OWN PHONE?
NO, YOU PUNCH IN A NUMBER AND THE DOOR OPENS.
DOES HE KNOW THE CODE?
I CAN'T FIND IT. ALL HE'S THINKING ABOUT IS CALLING SECURITY! AND-- AND--
OH GOD, HE'S A DIRTY OLD MAN...
I know the code.
WHAT IS IT?
water first!
I'LL GET YOU WATER IN A MINUTE-- WE NEED THAT CODE RIGHT NOW!
HURRY UP!
everyone always says they're going to water me, but nobody ever does! get me some water, you son of a BLEEEP!
YOU TALKIN' TO THAT PLANT, HOSS?
WHAT'S IT SAYING?
BLEEEP GODDAMMIT, PLANTS HAVE FOUL MOUTHS--
GET SOME FREAKING WATER!
THERE'S NO TIME!

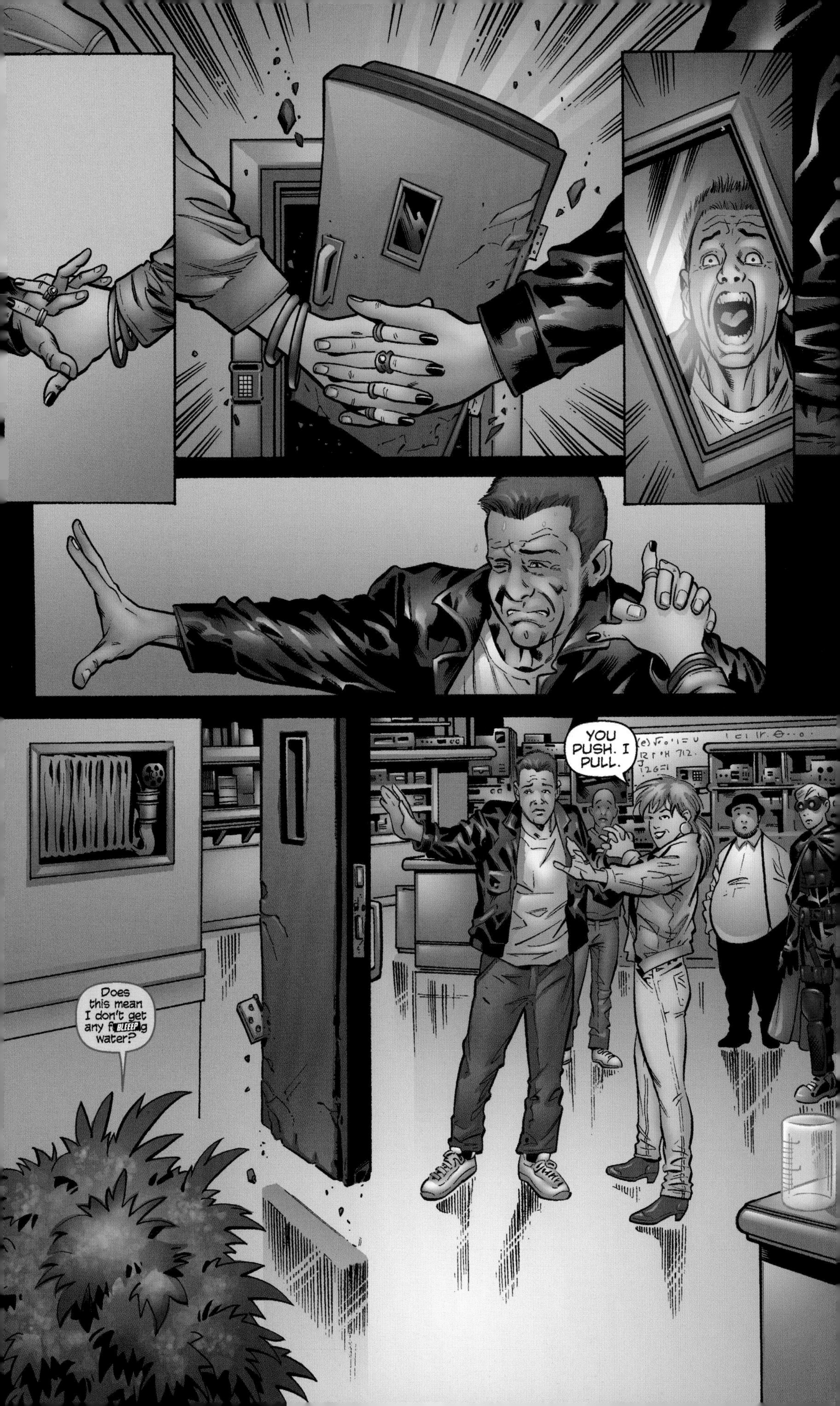
YOU PUSH. I PULL.
Does this mean I don't get any f BLEEEP g water?

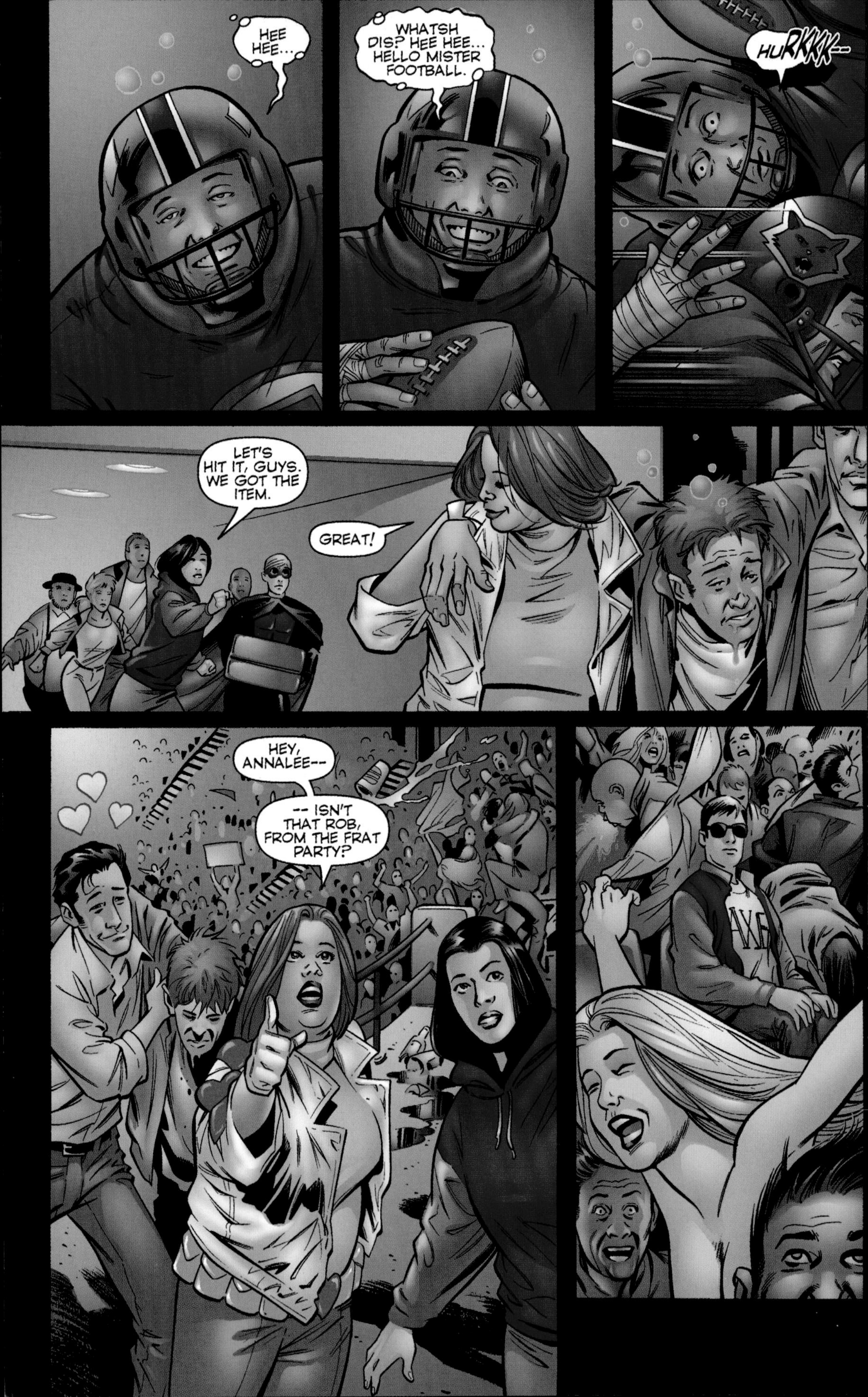
HEE HEE...
WHATSH DIS? HEE HEE... HELLO MISTER FOOTBALL.
HURKKK--
LET'S HIT IT, GUYS. WE GOT THE ITEM.
GREAT!
HEY, ANNALEE--
-- ISN'T THAT ROB, FROM THE FRAT PARTY?

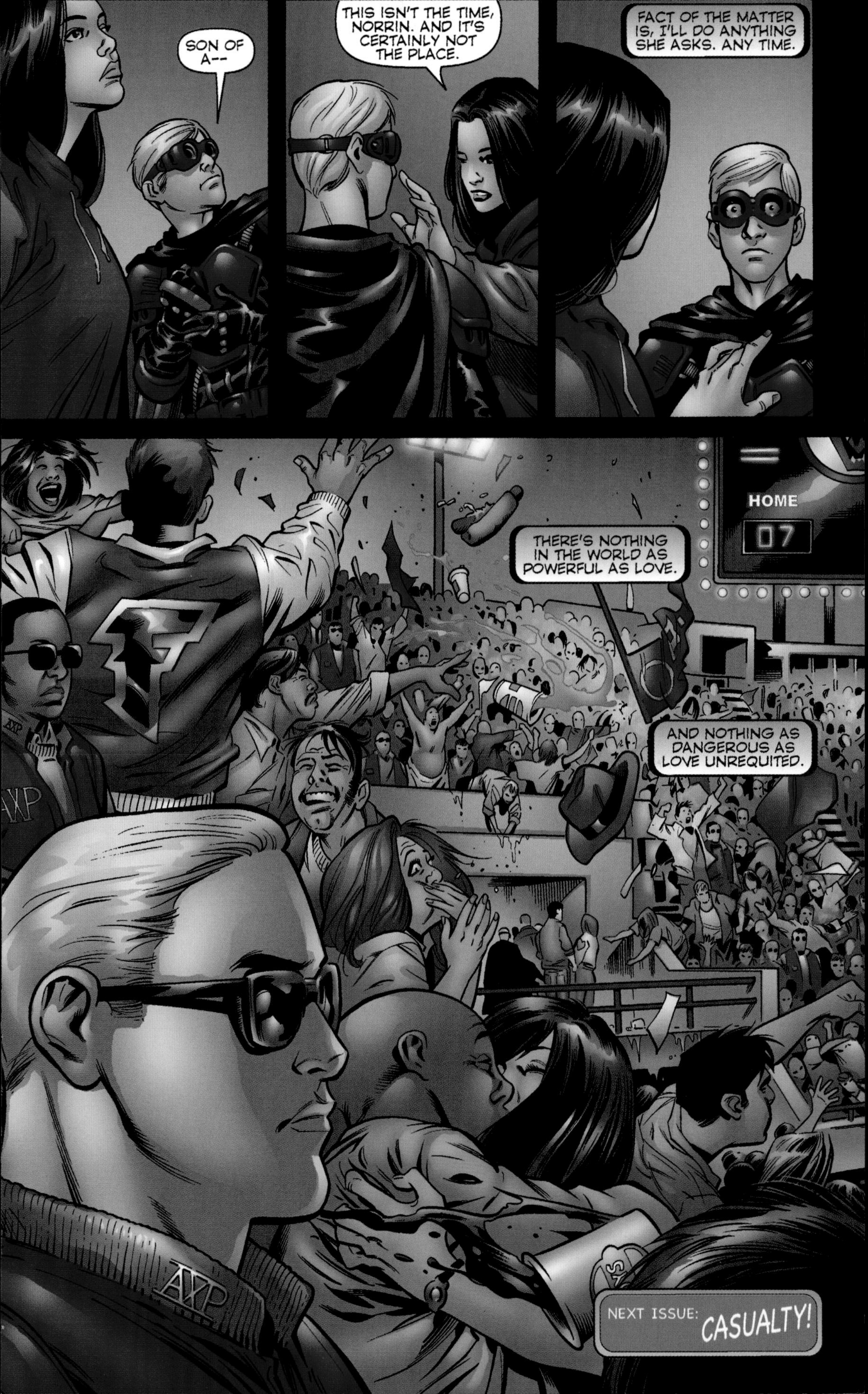
SON OF A--
THIS ISN'T THE TIME, NORRIN. AND IT'S CERTAINLY NOT THE PLACE.
FACT OF THE MATTER IS, I'LL DO ANYTHING SHE ASKS. ANY TIME.
HOME
07
THERE'S NOTHING IN THE WORLD AS POWERFUL AS LOVE.
AND NOTHING AS DANGEROUS AS LOVE UNREQUITED.
NEXT ISSUE: CASUALTY!

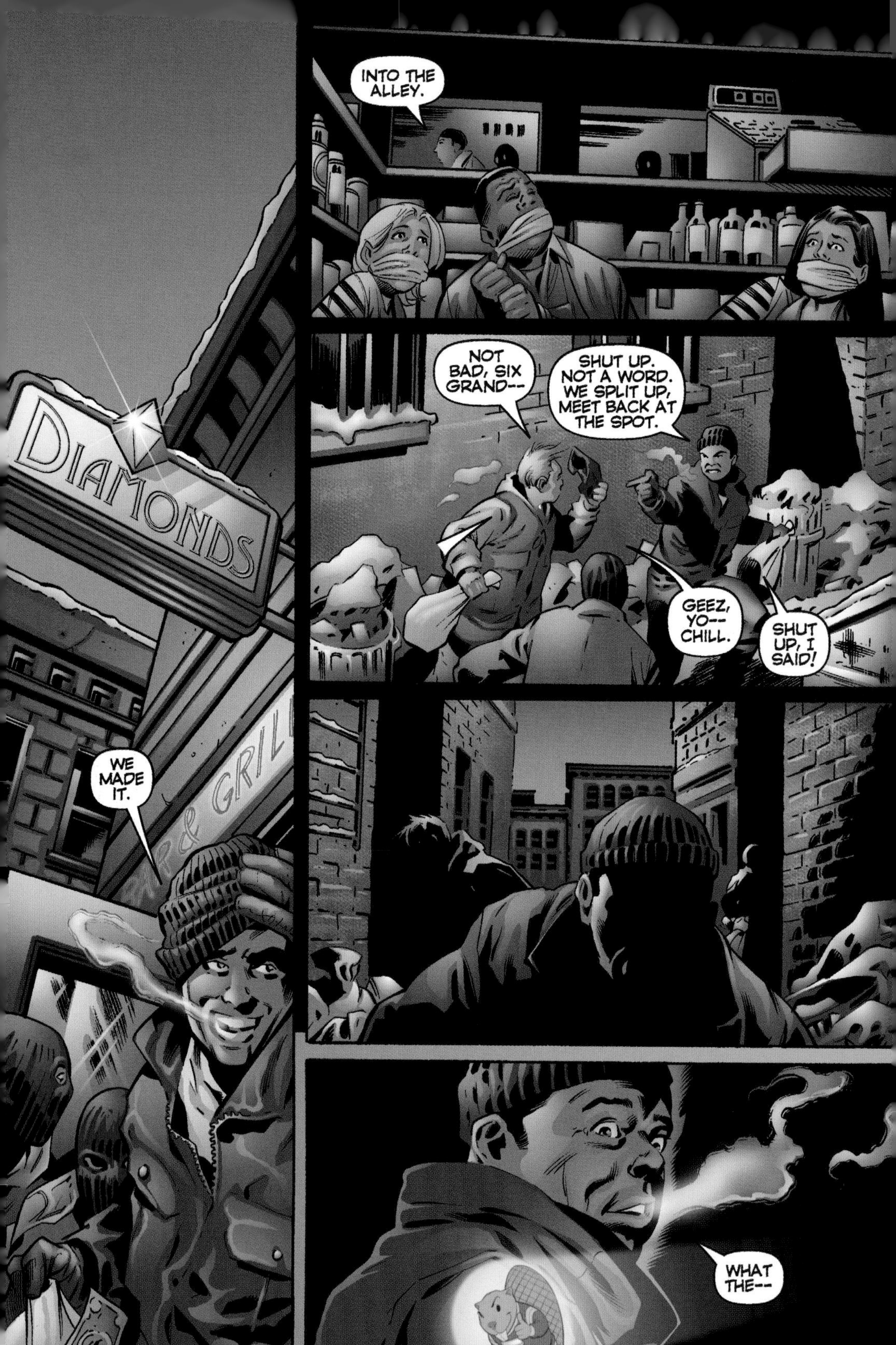
DIAMONDS
WE MADE IT.
INTO THE ALLEY.
NOT BAD, SIX GRAND--
SHUT UP. NOT A WORD. WE SPLIT UP, MEET BACK AT THE SPOT.
GEEZ, YO--CHILL.
SHUT UP, I SAID!
WHAT THE--

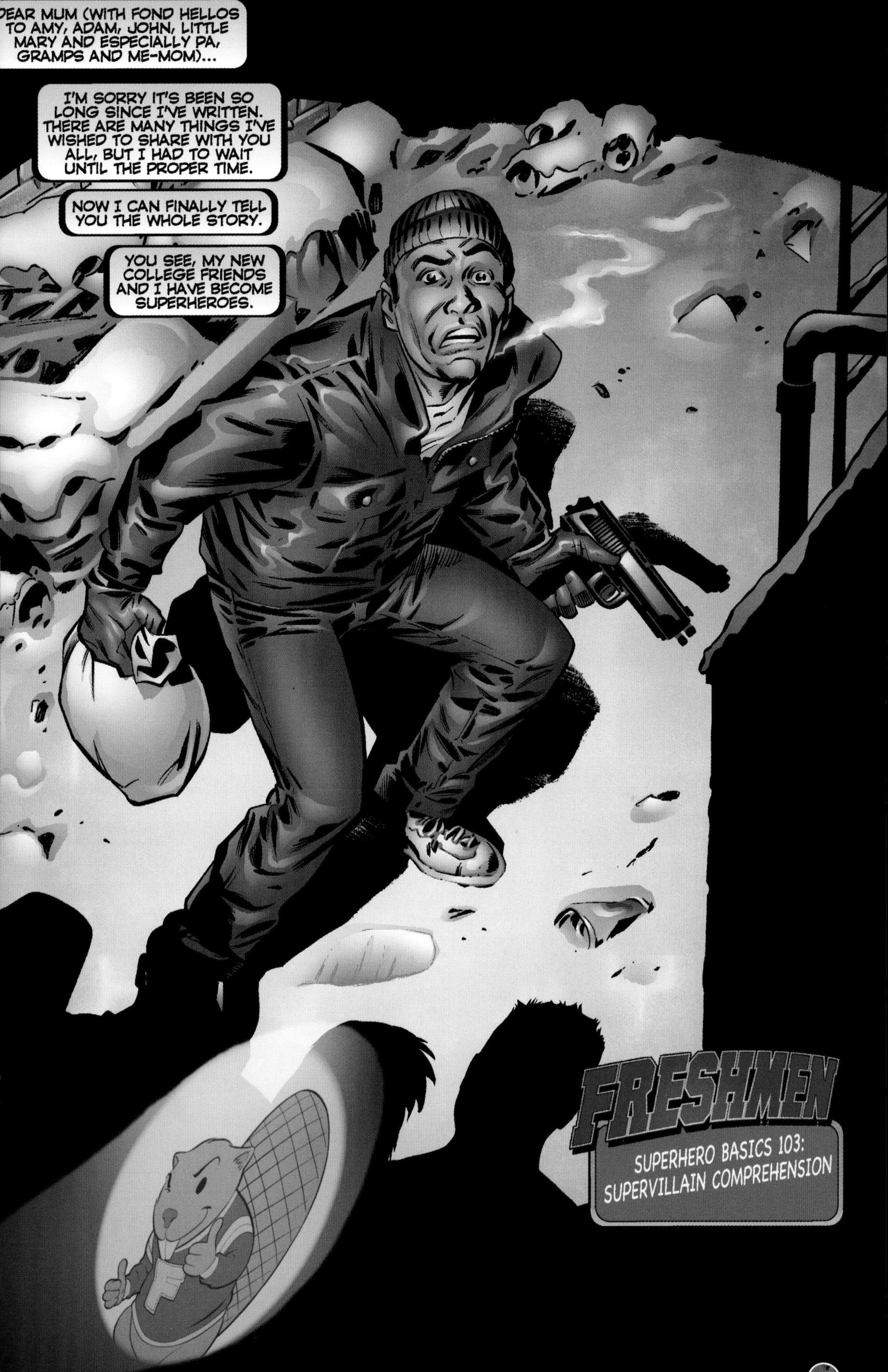
DEAR MUM (WITH FOND HELLOS TO AMY, ADAM, JOHN, LITTLE MARY AND ESPECIALLY PA, GRAMPS AND ME-MOM)...
I'M SORRY IT'S BEEN SO LONG SINCE I'VE WRITTEN. THERE ARE MANY THINGS I'VE WISHED TO SHARE WITH YOU ALL, BUT I HAD TO WAIT UNTIL THE PROPER TIME.
NOW I CAN FINALLY TELL YOU THE WHOLE STORY.
YOU SEE, MY NEW COLLEGE FRIENDS AND I HAVE BECOME SUPERHEROES.
FRESHMEN
SUPERHERO BASICS 103: SUPERVILLAIN COMPREHENSION

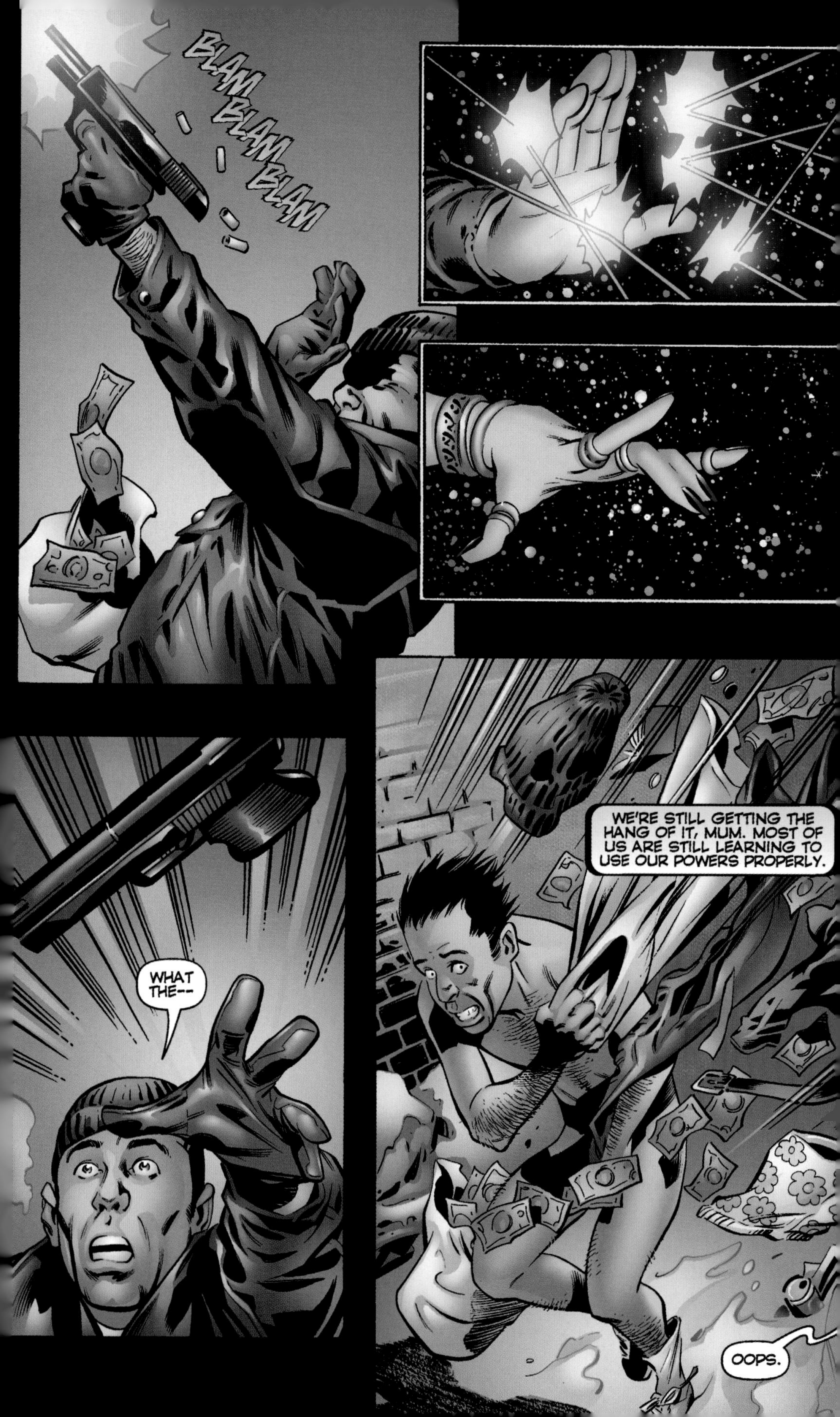
BLAM
BLAM
BLAM
WHAT THE--
WE'RE STILL GETTING THE HANG OF IT, MUM. MOST OF US ARE STILL LEARNING TO USE OUR POWERS PROPERLY.
OOPS.

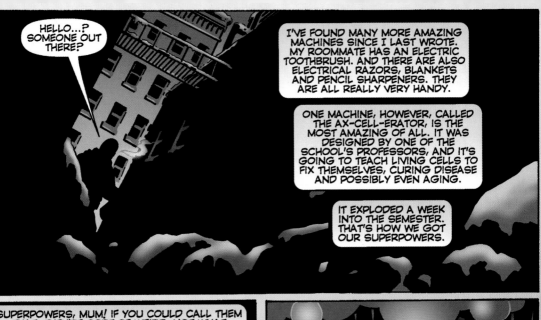

HELLO...? SOMEONE OUT THERE?

I'VE FOUND MANY MORE AMAZING MACHINES SINCE I LAST WROTE. MY ROOMMATE HAS AN ELECTRIC TOOTHBRUSH. AND THERE ARE ALSO ELECTRICAL RAZORS, BLANKETS AND PENCIL SHARPENERS. THEY ARE ALL REALLY VERY HANDY.

ONE MACHINE, HOWEVER, CALLED THE AX-CELL-ERATOR, IS THE MOST AMAZING OF ALL. IT WAS DESIGNED BY ONE OF THE SCHOOL'S PROFESSORS, AND IT'S GOING TO TEACH LIVING CELLS TO FIX THEMSELVES, CURING DISEASE AND POSSIBLY EVEN AGING.

IT EXPLODED A WEEK INTO THE SEMESTER. THAT'S HOW WE GOT OUR SUPERPOWERS.

SUPERPOWERS, MUM! IF YOU COULD CALL THEM THAT. THEY'RE SORT OF WEIRD, NOT WHAT YOU'D USUALLY SEE IN THE MOVING PICTURES.

BELLLLCH

OhGod OhGod OhGod OhGod OhGod...

MY FRIEND ELWOOD, WHO WE CALL THE INTOXICATOR, CAN BURP AT ANYONE AND MAKE THEM DRUNK. OR HUNG OVER. BASICALLY, HOWEVER HE'S FEELING AT THE TIME.

OF COURSE, ALCOHOL IS NOT VIRTUOUS, MUM. HOWEVER, ELWOOD ALWAYS USES HIS POWER FOR THE GOOD OF THE COMMUNITY.

RRREEEKKK HURRRRRRR!

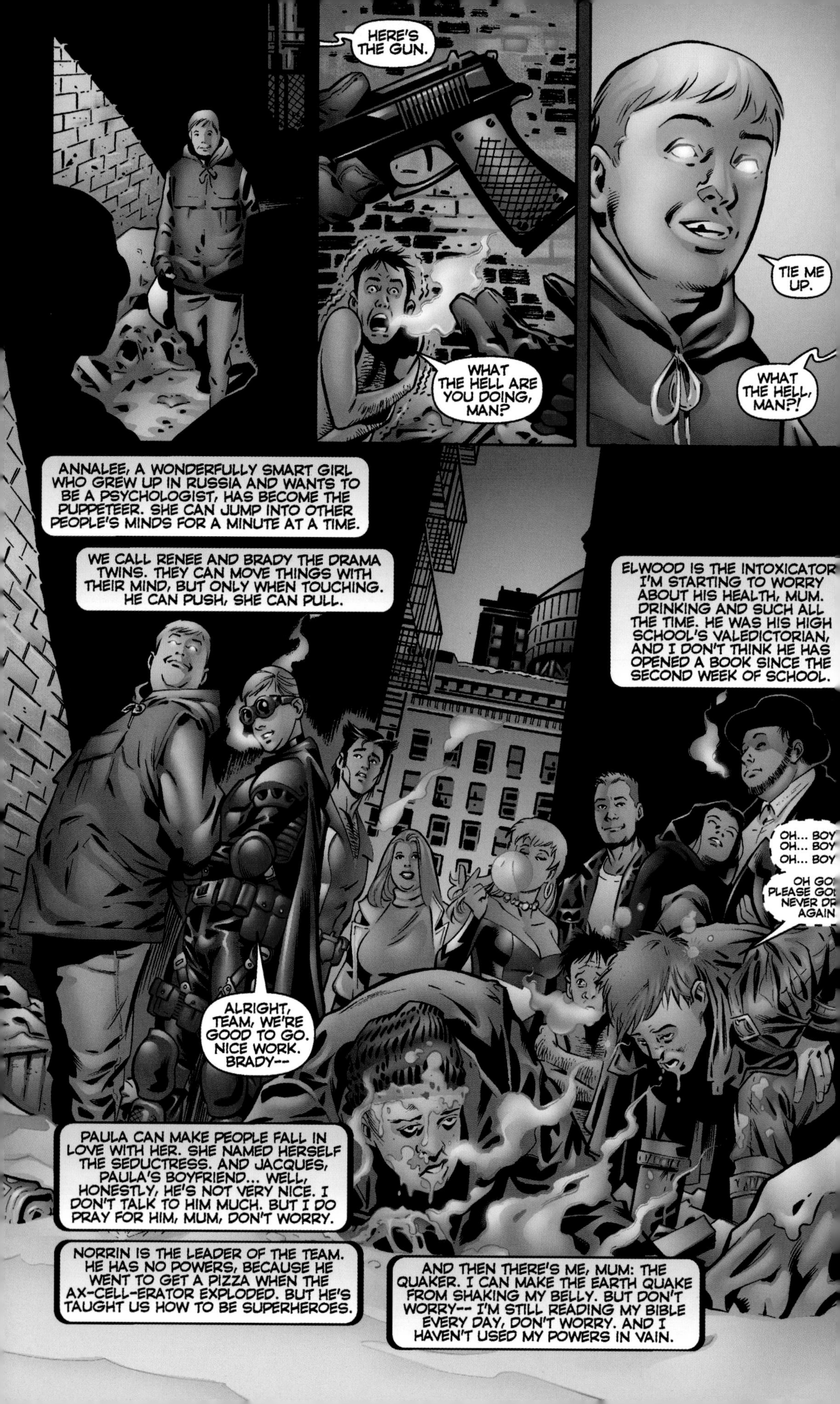

HERE'S THE GUN.
WHAT THE HELL ARE YOU DOING, MAN?
TIE ME UP.
WHAT THE HELL, MAN?!
ANNALEE, A WONDERFULLY SMART GIRL WHO GREW UP IN RUSSIA AND WANTS TO BE A PSYCHOLOGIST, HAS BECOME THE PUPPETEER. SHE CAN JUMP INTO OTHER PEOPLE'S MINDS FOR A MINUTE AT A TIME.
WE CALL RENEE AND BRADY THE DRAMA TWINS. THEY CAN MOVE THINGS WITH THEIR MIND, BUT ONLY WHEN TOUCHING. HE CAN PUSH, SHE CAN PULL.
ELWOOD IS THE INTOXICATOR. I'M STARTING TO WORRY ABOUT HIS HEALTH, MUM. DRINKING AND SUCH ALL THE TIME. HE WAS HIS HIGH SCHOOL'S VALEDICTORIAN, AND I DON'T THINK HE HAS OPENED A BOOK SINCE THE SECOND WEEK OF SCHOOL.
OH... BOY OH... BOY OH... BOY
OH GO PLEASE GO NEVER DR AGAIN
ALRIGHT, TEAM, WE'RE GOOD TO GO. NICE WORK. BRADY--
PAULA CAN MAKE PEOPLE FALL IN LOVE WITH HER. SHE NAMED HERSELF THE SEDUCTRESS. AND JACQUES, PAULA'S BOYFRIEND... WELL, HONESTLY, HE'S NOT VERY NICE. I DON'T TALK TO HIM MUCH. BUT I DO PRAY FOR HIM, MUM, DON'T WORRY.
NORRIN IS THE LEADER OF THE TEAM. HE HAS NO POWERS, BECAUSE HE WENT TO GET A PIZZA WHEN THE AX-CELL-ERATOR EXPLODED. BUT HE'S TAUGHT US HOW TO BE SUPERHEROES.
AND THEN THERE'S ME, MUM: THE QUAKER. I CAN MAKE THE EARTH QUAKE FROM SHAKING MY BELLY. BUT DON'T WORRY-- I'M STILL READING MY BIBLE EVERY DAY, DON'T WORRY. AND I HAVEN'T USED MY POWERS IN VAIN.

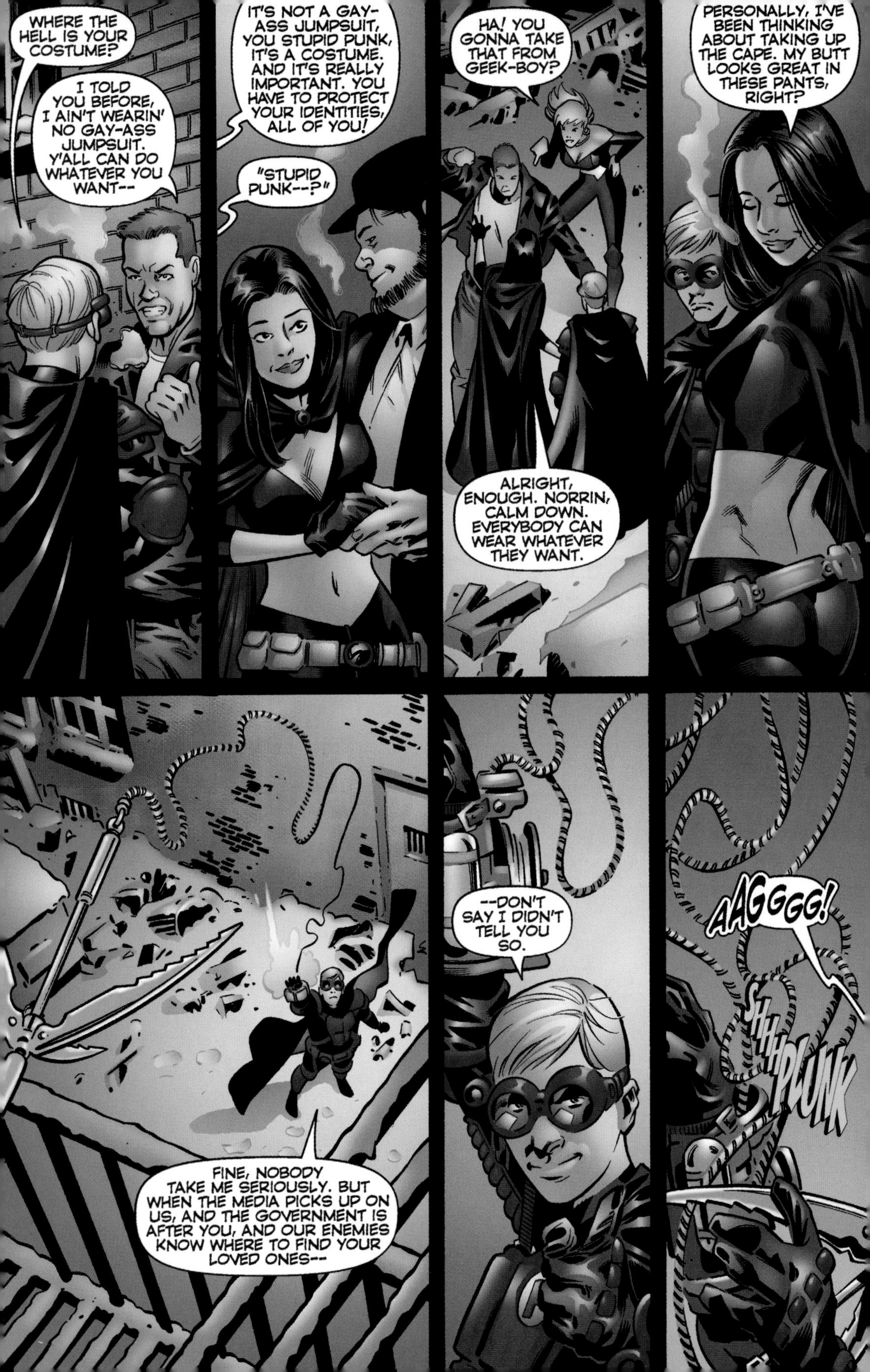
WHERE THE HELL IS YOUR COSTUME?
I TOLD YOU BEFORE, I AIN'T WEARIN' NO GAY-ASS JUMPSUIT. Y'ALL CAN DO WHATEVER YOU WANT--
IT'S NOT A GAY-ASS JUMPSUIT, YOU STUPID PUNK, IT'S A COSTUME. AND IT'S REALLY IMPORTANT. YOU HAVE TO PROTECT YOUR IDENTITIES, ALL OF YOU!
"STUPID PUNK--?"
HA! YOU GONNA TAKE THAT FROM GEEK-BOY?
ALRIGHT, ENOUGH. NORRIN, CALM DOWN. EVERYBODY CAN WEAR WHATEVER THEY WANT.
PERSONALLY, I'VE BEEN THINKING ABOUT TAKING UP THE CAPE. MY BUTT LOOKS GREAT IN THESE PANTS, RIGHT?
FINE, NOBODY TAKE ME SERIOUSLY. BUT WHEN THE MEDIA PICKS UP ON US, AND THE GOVERNMENT IS AFTER YOU, AND OUR ENEMIES KNOW WHERE TO FIND YOUR LOVED ONES--
--DON'T SAY I DIDN'T TELL YOU SO.
AAGGGG!
SHHHPLUNK

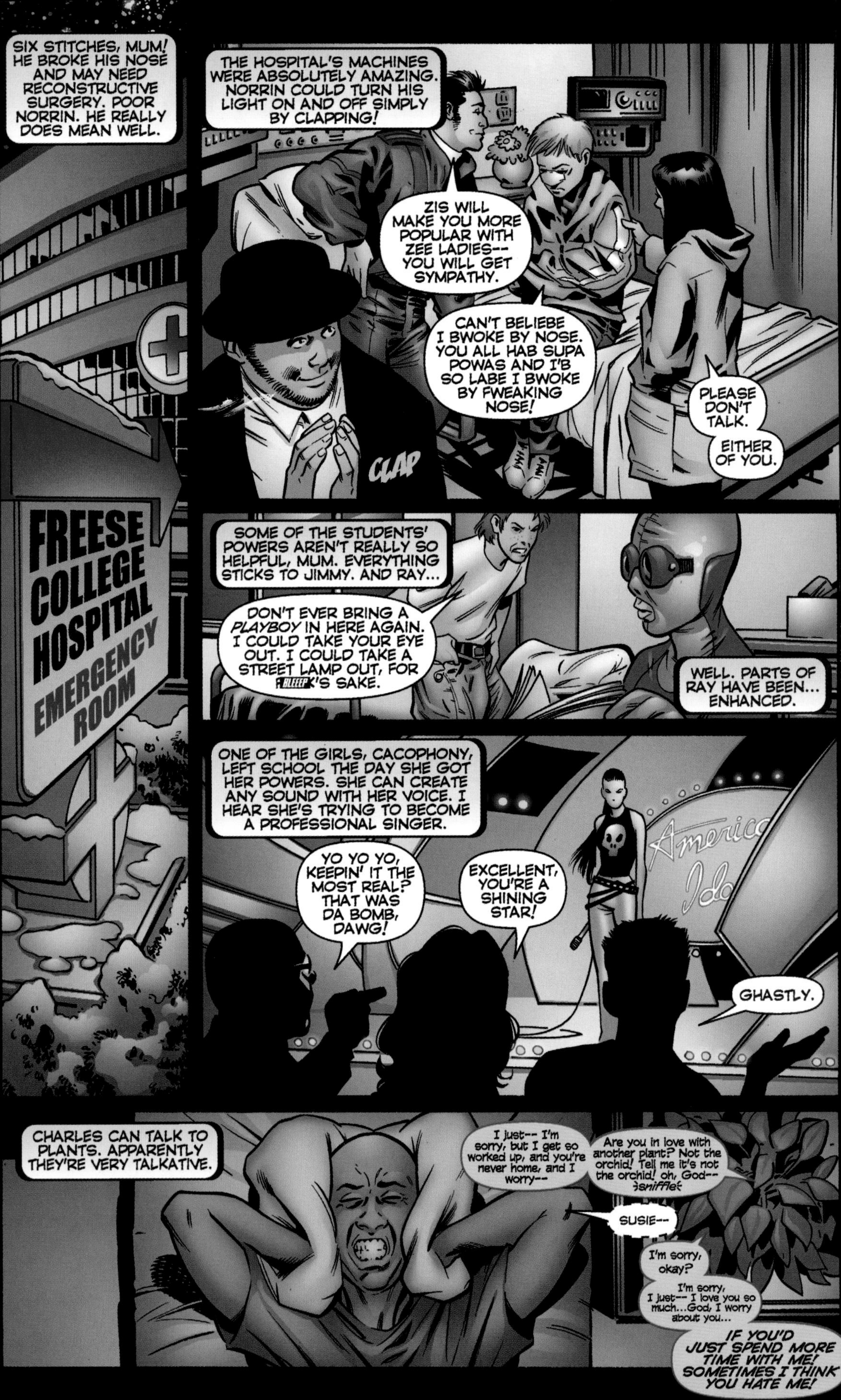
SIX STITCHES, MUM! HE BROKE HIS NOSE AND MAY NEED RECONSTRUCTIVE SURGERY. POOR NORRIN. HE REALLY DOES MEAN WELL.
THE HOSPITAL'S MACHINES WERE ABSOLUTELY AMAZING. NORRIN COULD TURN HIS LIGHT ON AND OFF SIMPLY BY CLAPPING!
ZIS WILL MAKE YOU MORE POPULAR WITH ZEE LADIES-- YOU WILL GET SYMPATHY.
CAN'T BELIEBE I BWOKE BY NOSE. YOU ALL HAB SUPA POWAS AND I'B SO LABE I BWOKE BY FWEAKING NOSE!
PLEASE DON'T TALK.
EITHER OF YOU.
CLAP
FREESE COLLEGE HOSPITAL
EMERGENCY ROOM
SOME OF THE STUDENTS' POWERS AREN'T REALLY SO HELPFUL, MUM. EVERYTHING STICKS TO JIMMY. AND RAY...
DON'T EVER BRING A *PLAYBOY* IN HERE AGAIN. I COULD TAKE YOUR EYE OUT. I COULD TAKE A STREET LAMP OUT, FOR F-BLEEEP-K'S SAKE.
WELL. PARTS OF RAY HAVE BEEN... ENHANCED.
ONE OF THE GIRLS, CACOPHONY, LEFT SCHOOL THE DAY SHE GOT HER POWERS. SHE CAN CREATE ANY SOUND WITH HER VOICE. I HEAR SHE'S TRYING TO BECOME A PROFESSIONAL SINGER.
YO YO YO, KEEPIN' IT THE MOST REAL? THAT WAS DA BOMB, DAWG!
EXCELLENT, YOU'RE A SHINING STAR!
GHASTLY.
CHARLES CAN TALK TO PLANTS. APPARENTLY THEY'RE VERY TALKATIVE.
I just-- I'm sorry, but I get so worked up, and you're never home, and I worry--
Are you in love with another plant? Not the orchid! Tell me it's not the orchid! oh, God-- *sniffle*
SUSIE--
I'm sorry, okay?
I'm sorry, I just-- I love you so much...God, I worry about you...
IF YOU'D JUST SPEND MORE TIME WITH ME! SOMETIMES I THINK YOU HATE ME!

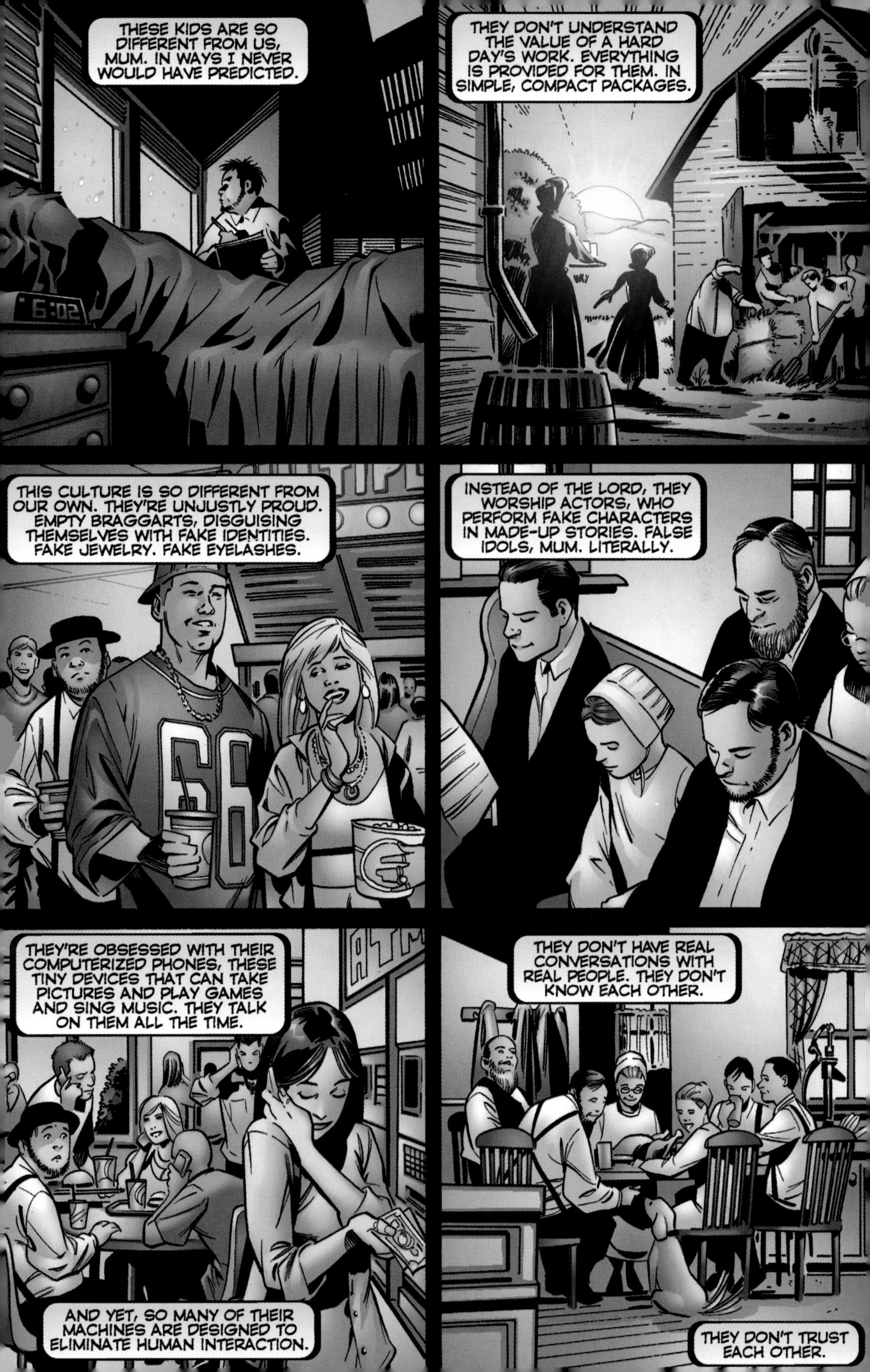
THESE KIDS ARE SO DIFFERENT FROM US, MUM. IN WAYS I NEVER WOULD HAVE PREDICTED.
6:02
THEY DON'T UNDERSTAND THE VALUE OF A HARD DAY'S WORK. EVERYTHING IS PROVIDED FOR THEM. IN SIMPLE, COMPACT PACKAGES.
THIS CULTURE IS SO DIFFERENT FROM OUR OWN. THEY'RE UNJUSTLY PROUD. EMPTY BRAGGARTS, DISGUISING THEMSELVES WITH FAKE IDENTITIES. FAKE JEWELRY. FAKE EYELASHES.
66
INSTEAD OF THE LORD, THEY WORSHIP ACTORS, WHO PERFORM FAKE CHARACTERS IN MADE-UP STORIES. FALSE IDOLS, MUM. LITERALLY.
THEY'RE OBSESSED WITH THEIR COMPUTERIZED PHONES, THESE TINY DEVICES THAT CAN TAKE PICTURES AND PLAY GAMES AND SING MUSIC. THEY TALK ON THEM ALL THE TIME.
AND YET, SO MANY OF THEIR MACHINES ARE DESIGNED TO ELIMINATE HUMAN INTERACTION.
THEY DON'T HAVE REAL CONVERSATIONS WITH REAL PEOPLE. THEY DON'T KNOW EACH OTHER.
THEY DON'T TRUST EACH OTHER.

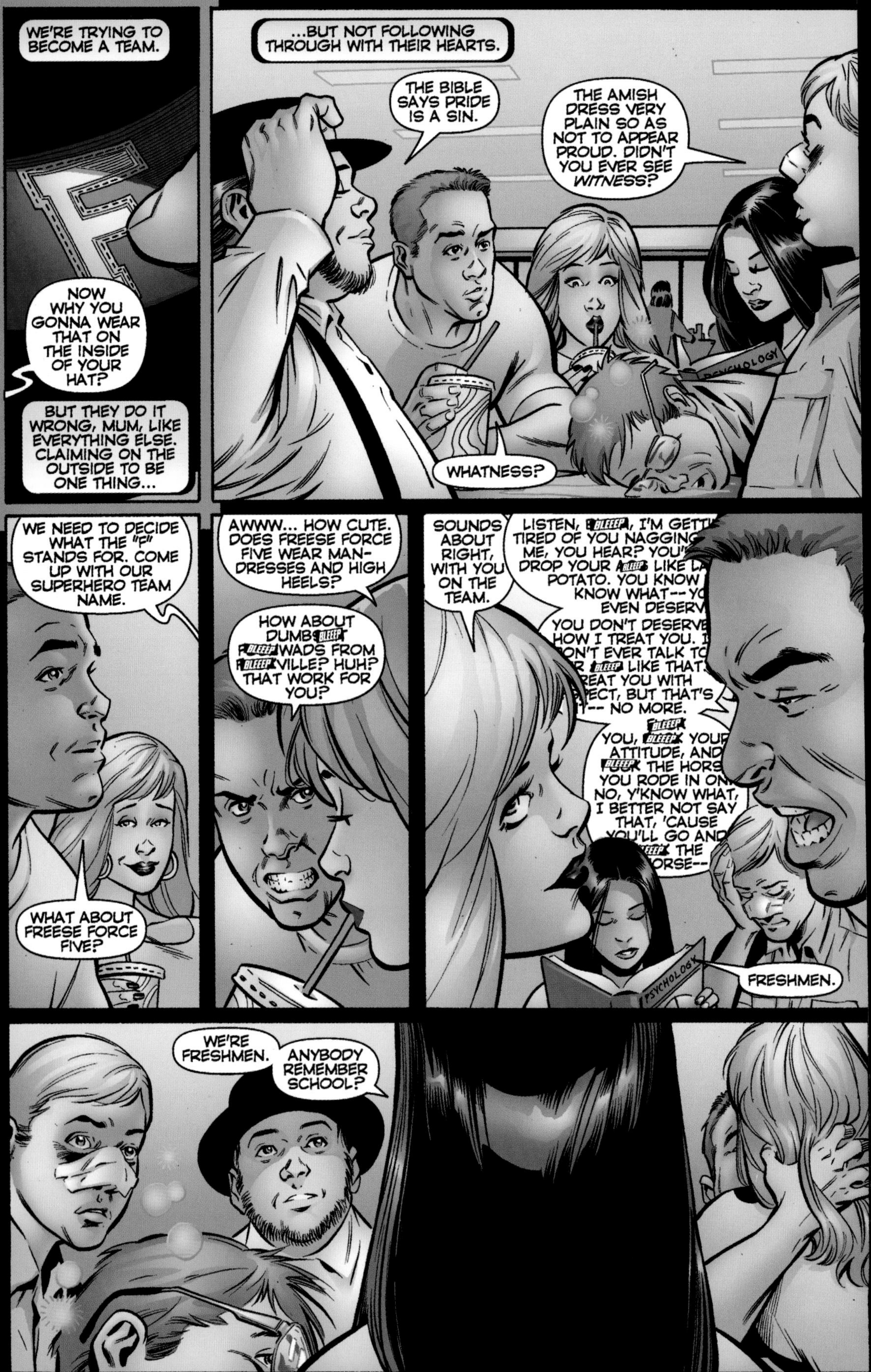
WE'RE TRYING TO BECOME A TEAM.
NOW WHY YOU GONNA WEAR THAT ON THE INSIDE OF YOUR HAT?
BUT THEY DO IT WRONG, MUM, LIKE EVERYTHING ELSE. CLAIMING ON THE OUTSIDE TO BE ONE THING...
...BUT NOT FOLLOWING THROUGH WITH THEIR HEARTS.
THE BIBLE SAYS PRIDE IS A SIN.
THE AMISH DRESS VERY PLAIN SO AS NOT TO APPEAR PROUD. DIDN'T YOU EVER SEE *WITNESS*?
WHATNESS?
PSYCHOLOGY
WE NEED TO DECIDE WHAT THE "F" STANDS FOR. COME UP WITH OUR SUPERHERO TEAM NAME.
WHAT ABOUT FREESE FORCE FIVE?
AWWW... HOW CUTE. DOES FREESE FORCE FIVE WEAR MAN-DRESSES AND HIGH HEELS?
HOW ABOUT DUMB BLEEEP WADS FROM BLEEEP VILLE? HUH? THAT WORK FOR YOU?
SOUNDS ABOUT RIGHT, WITH YOU ON THE TEAM.
LISTEN, BLEEEP, I'M GETT TIRED OF YOU NAGGING ME, YOU HEAR? YOU' DROP YOUR BLEEEP LIKE L POTATO. YOU KNOW KNOW WHAT-- Y EVEN DESERV
YOU DON'T DESERVE HOW I TREAT YOU. ON'T EVER TALK TO R BLEEEP LIKE THAT. REAT YOU WITH ECT, BUT THAT'S -- NO MORE.
YOU, BLEEEP, BLEEEP YOUR ATTITUDE, AND BLEEEP THE HORS YOU RODE IN ON NO, Y'KNOW WHAT, I BETTER NOT SAY THAT, 'CAUSE YOU'LL GO AND BLEEEP THE ORSE--
PSYCHOLOGY
FRESHMEN.
WE'RE FRESHMEN.
ANYBODY REMEMBER SCHOOL?

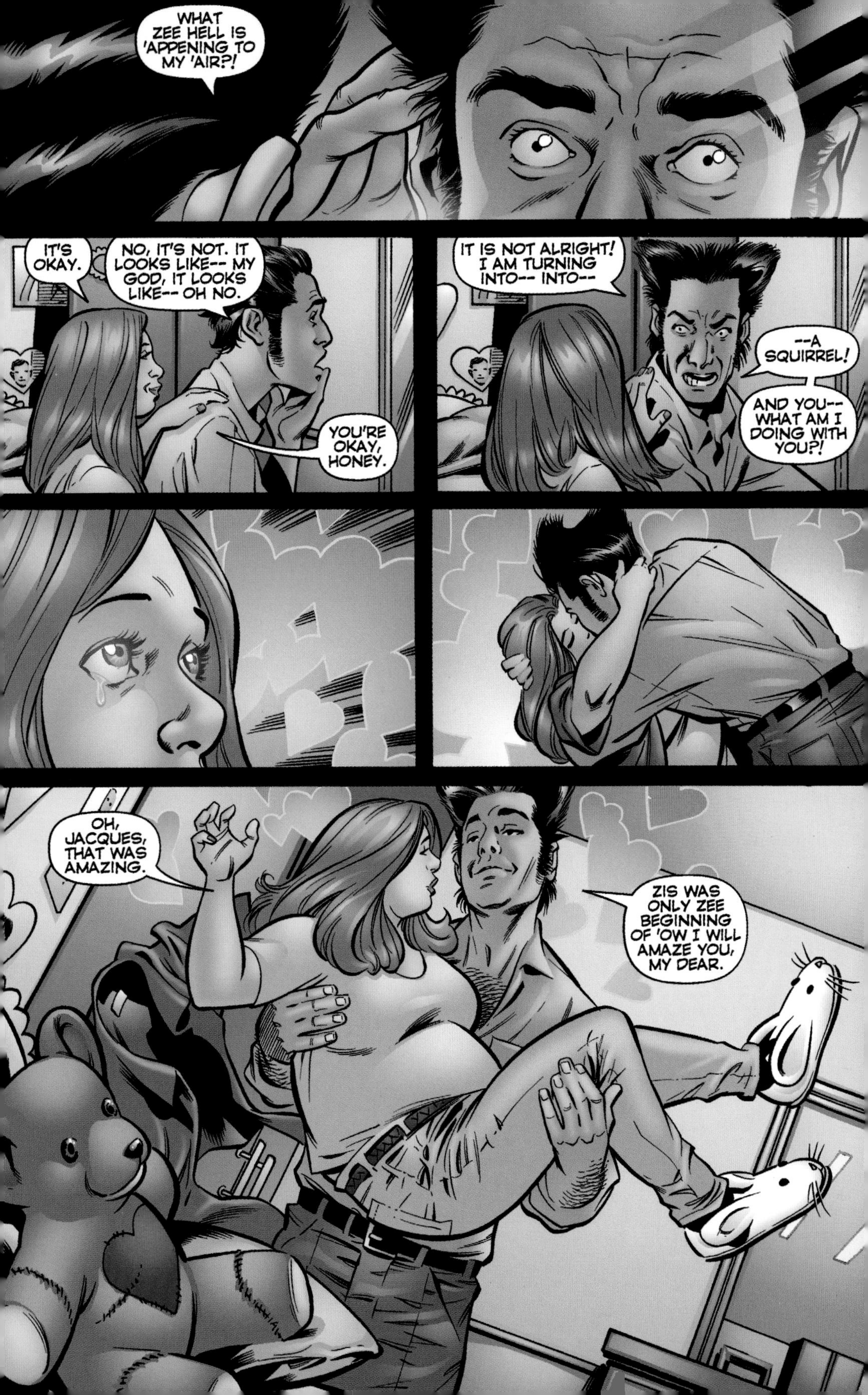
WHAT ZEE HELL IS 'APPENING TO MY 'AIR?!
IT'S OKAY.
NO, IT'S NOT. IT LOOKS LIKE-- MY GOD, IT LOOKS LIKE-- OH NO.
YOU'RE OKAY, HONEY.
IT IS NOT ALRIGHT! I AM TURNING INTO-- INTO--
--A SQUIRREL!
AND YOU-- WHAT AM I DOING WITH YOU?!
OH, JACQUES, THAT WAS AMAZING.
ZIS WAS ONLY ZEE BEGINNING OF 'OW I WILL AMAZE YOU, MY DEAR.

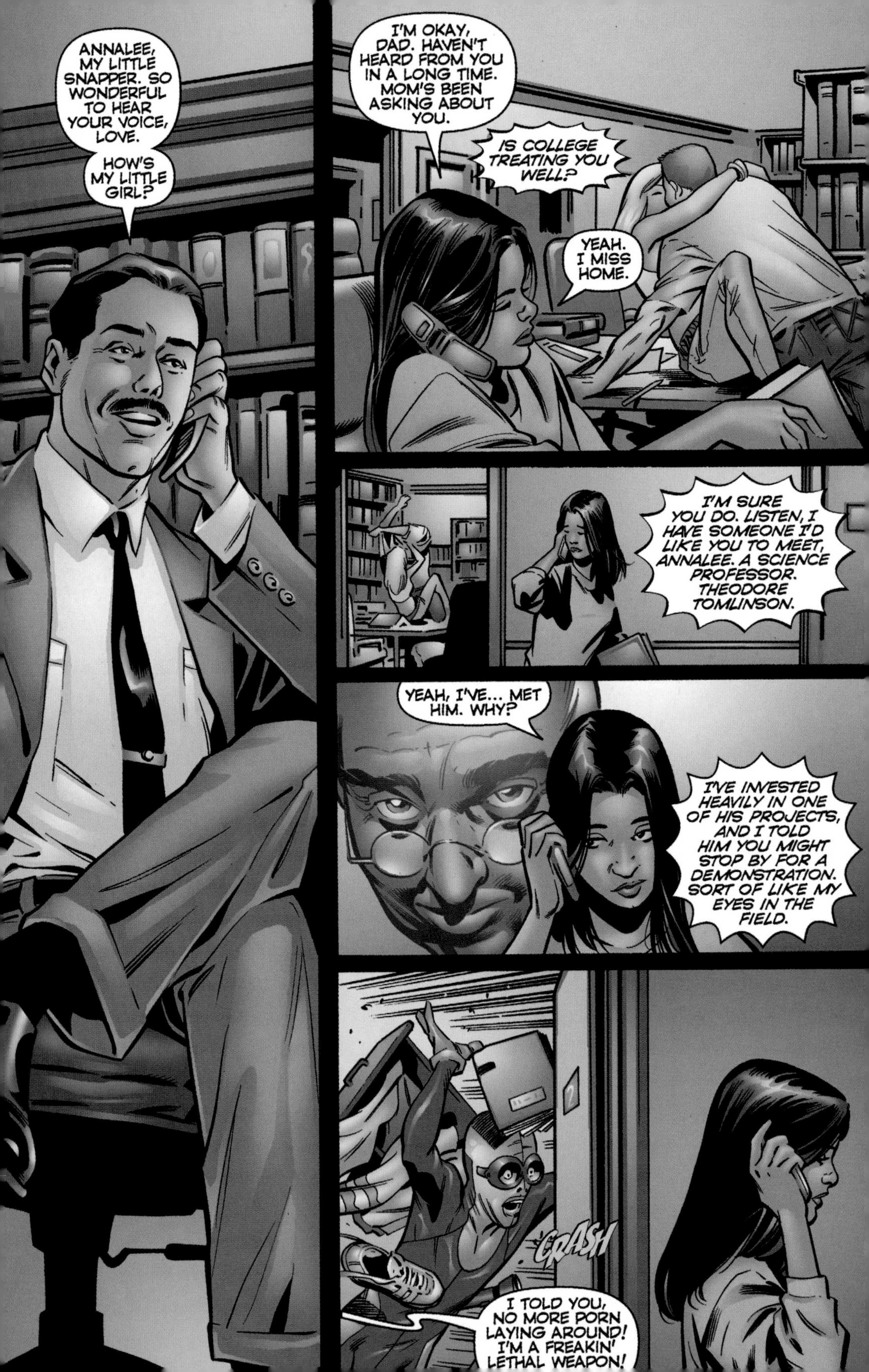
ANNALEE, MY LITTLE SNAPPER. SO WONDERFUL TO HEAR YOUR VOICE, LOVE.
HOW'S MY LITTLE GIRL?
I'M OKAY, DAD. HAVEN'T HEARD FROM YOU IN A LONG TIME. MOM'S BEEN ASKING ABOUT YOU.
IS COLLEGE TREATING YOU WELL?
YEAH. I MISS HOME.
I'M SURE YOU DO. LISTEN, I HAVE SOMEONE I'D LIKE YOU TO MEET, ANNALEE. A SCIENCE PROFESSOR. THEODORE TOMLINSON.
YEAH, I'VE... MET HIM. WHY?
I'VE INVESTED HEAVILY IN ONE OF HIS PROJECTS, AND I TOLD HIM YOU MIGHT STOP BY FOR A DEMONSTRATION. SORT OF LIKE MY EYES IN THE FIELD.
CRASH
I TOLD YOU, NO MORE PORN LAYING AROUND! I'M A FREAKIN' LETHAL WEAPON!

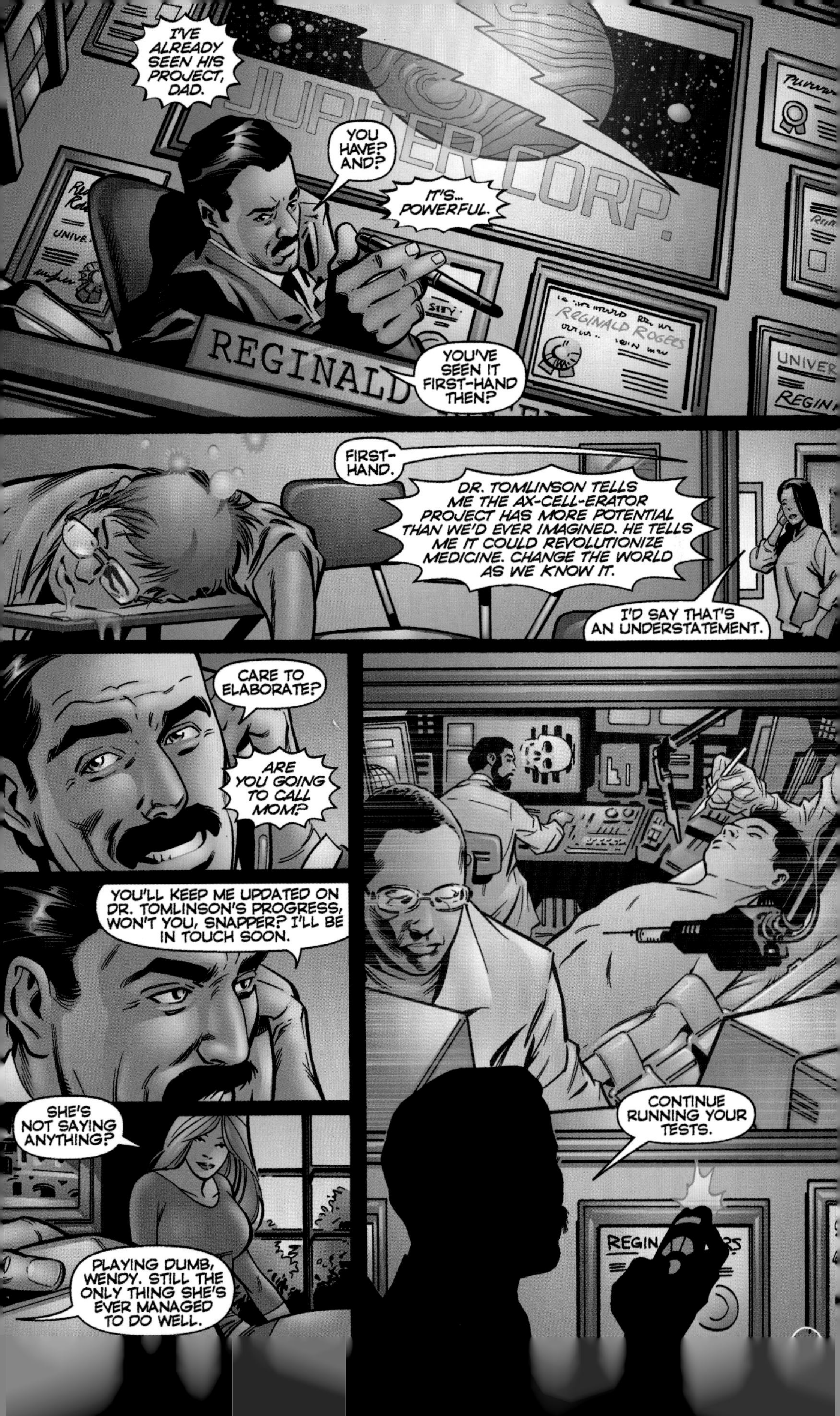

I'VE ALREADY SEEN HIS PROJECT, DAD.
JUPITER CORP.
YOU HAVE? AND?
IT'S... POWERFUL.
REGINALD
REGINALD ROGERS
YOU'VE SEEN IT FIRST-HAND THEN?
FIRST-HAND.
DR. TOMLINSON TELLS ME THE AX-CELL-ERATOR PROJECT HAS MORE POTENTIAL THAN WE'D EVER IMAGINED. HE TELLS ME IT COULD REVOLUTIONIZE MEDICINE. CHANGE THE WORLD AS WE KNOW IT.
I'D SAY THAT'S AN UNDERSTATEMENT.
CARE TO ELABORATE?
ARE YOU GOING TO CALL MOM?
YOU'LL KEEP ME UPDATED ON DR. TOMLINSON'S PROGRESS, WON'T YOU, SNAPPER? I'LL BE IN TOUCH SOON.
SHE'S NOT SAYING ANYTHING?
PLAYING DUMB, WENDY. STILL THE ONLY THING SHE'S EVER MANAGED TO DO WELL.
CONTINUE RUNNING YOUR TESTS.

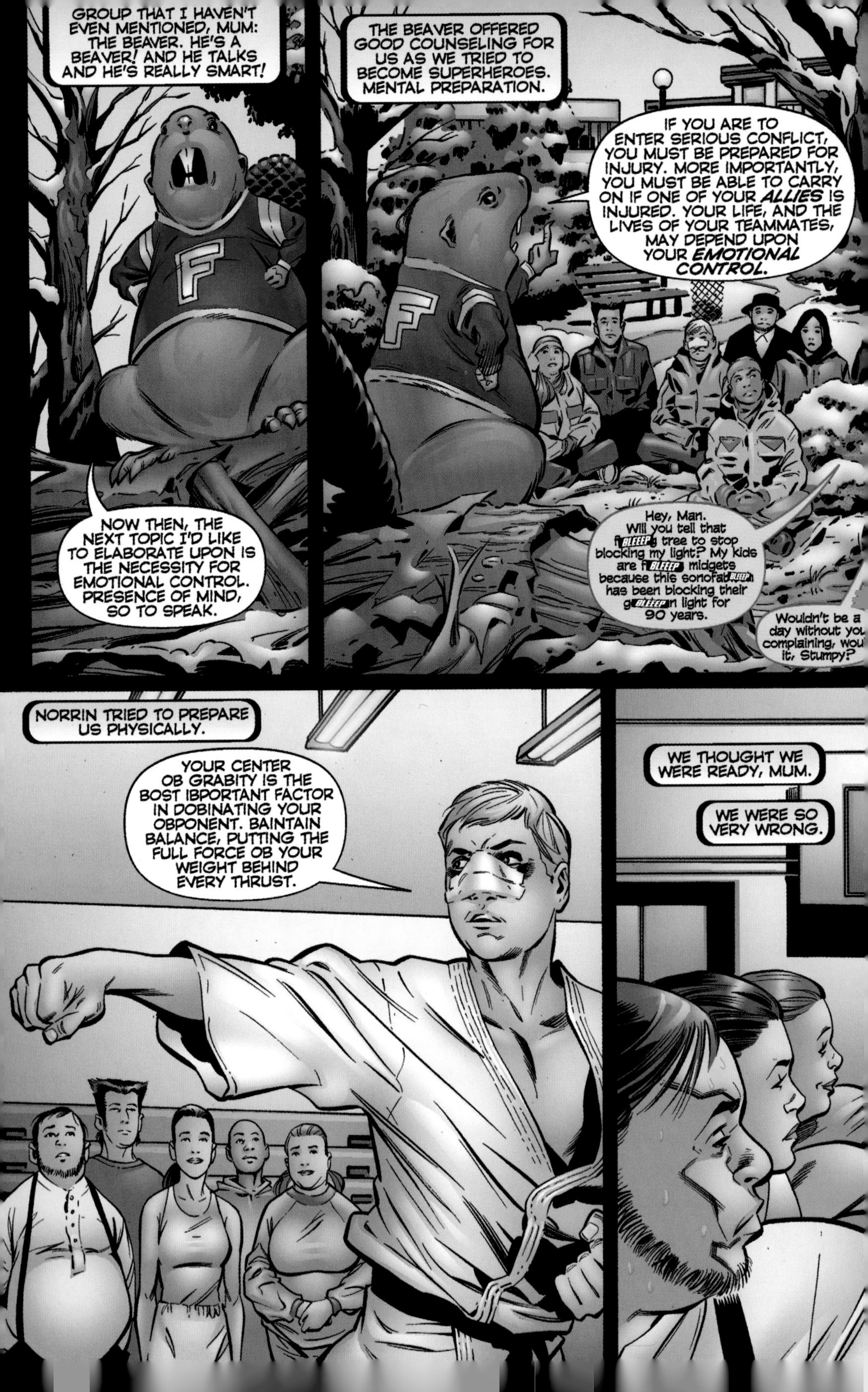
GROUP THAT I HAVEN'T EVEN MENTIONED, MUM: THE BEAVER. HE'S A BEAVER! AND HE TALKS AND HE'S REALLY SMART!
NOW THEN, THE NEXT TOPIC I'D LIKE TO ELABORATE UPON IS THE NECESSITY FOR EMOTIONAL CONTROL. PRESENCE OF MIND, SO TO SPEAK.
THE BEAVER OFFERED GOOD COUNSELING FOR US AS WE TRIED TO BECOME SUPERHEROES. MENTAL PREPARATION.
IF YOU ARE TO ENTER SERIOUS CONFLICT, YOU MUST BE PREPARED FOR INJURY. MORE IMPORTANTLY, YOU MUST BE ABLE TO CARRY ON IF ONE OF YOUR ALLIES IS INJURED. YOUR LIFE, AND THE LIVES OF YOUR TEAMMATES, MAY DEPEND UPON YOUR EMOTIONAL CONTROL.
Hey, Man. Will you tell that f BLEEEP g tree to stop blocking my light? My kids are f BLEEEP midgets because this sonofa BLEEP h has been blocking their g BLEEEP n light for 90 years.
Wouldn't be a day without you complaining, woul it, Stumpy?
NORRIN TRIED TO PREPARE US PHYSICALLY.
YOUR CENTER OB GRABITY IS THE BOST IBPORTANT FACTOR IN DOBINATING YOUR OBPONENT. BAINTAIN BALANCE, PUTTING THE FULL FORCE OB YOUR WEIGHT BEHIND EVERY THRUST.
WE THOUGHT WE WERE READY, MUM.
WE WERE SO VERY WRONG.

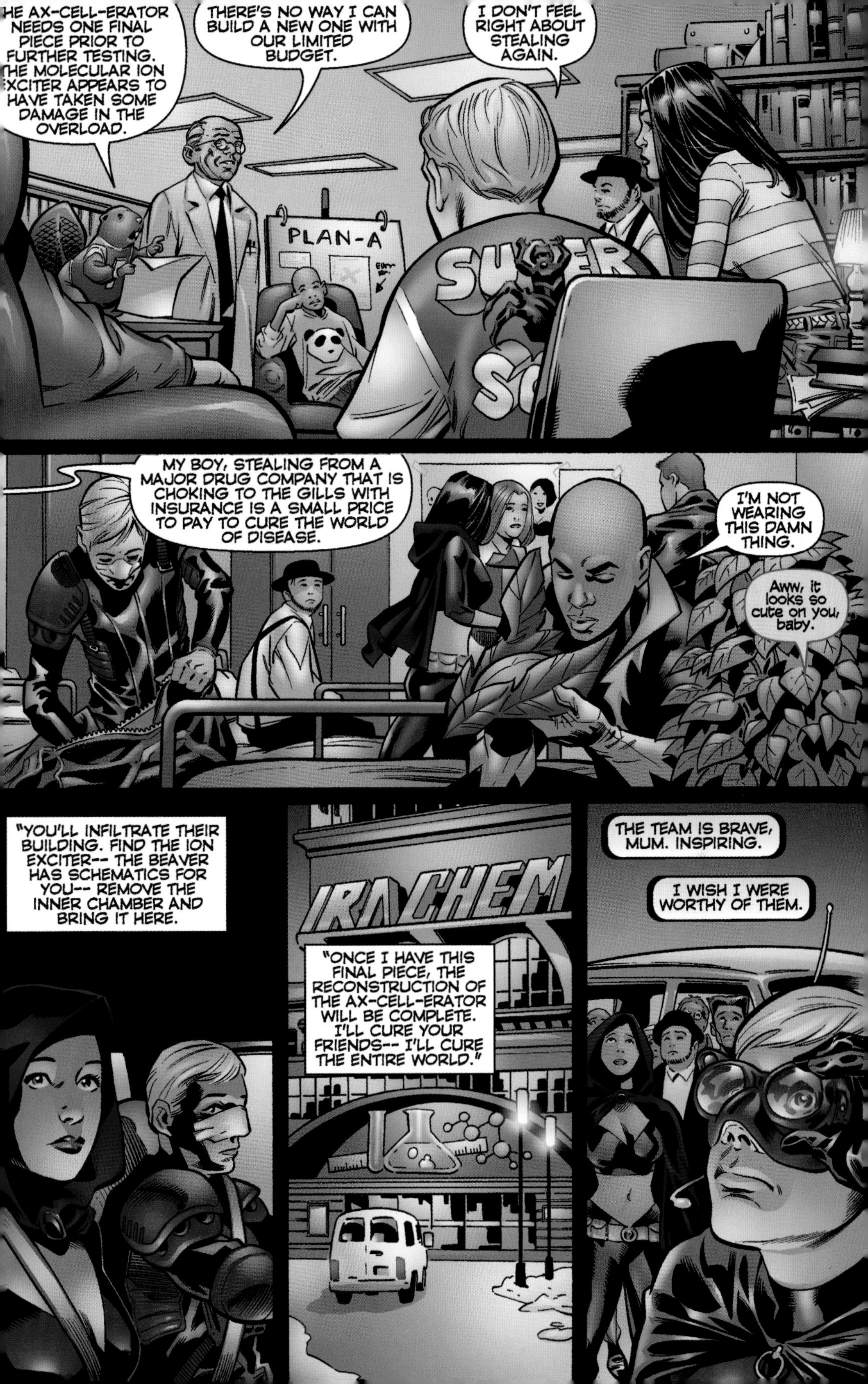

HE AX-CELL-ERATOR NEEDS ONE FINAL PIECE PRIOR TO FURTHER TESTING. THE MOLECULAR ION EXCITER APPEARS TO HAVE TAKEN SOME DAMAGE IN THE OVERLOAD.
THERE'S NO WAY I CAN BUILD A NEW ONE WITH OUR LIMITED BUDGET.
I DON'T FEEL RIGHT ABOUT STEALING AGAIN.
PLAN-A
SUPER SO
MY BOY, STEALING FROM A MAJOR DRUG COMPANY THAT IS CHOKING TO THE GILLS WITH INSURANCE IS A SMALL PRICE TO PAY TO CURE THE WORLD OF DISEASE.
I'M NOT WEARING THIS DAMN THING.
Aww, it looks so cute on you, baby.
"YOU'LL INFILTRATE THEIR BUILDING. FIND THE ION EXCITER-- THE BEAVER HAS SCHEMATICS FOR YOU-- REMOVE THE INNER CHAMBER AND BRING IT HERE.
IRACHEM
"ONCE I HAVE THIS FINAL PIECE, THE RECONSTRUCTION OF THE AX-CELL-ERATOR WILL BE COMPLETE. I'LL CURE YOUR FRIENDS-- I'LL CURE THE ENTIRE WORLD."
THE TEAM IS BRAVE, MUM. INSPIRING.
I WISH I WERE WORTHY OF THEM.

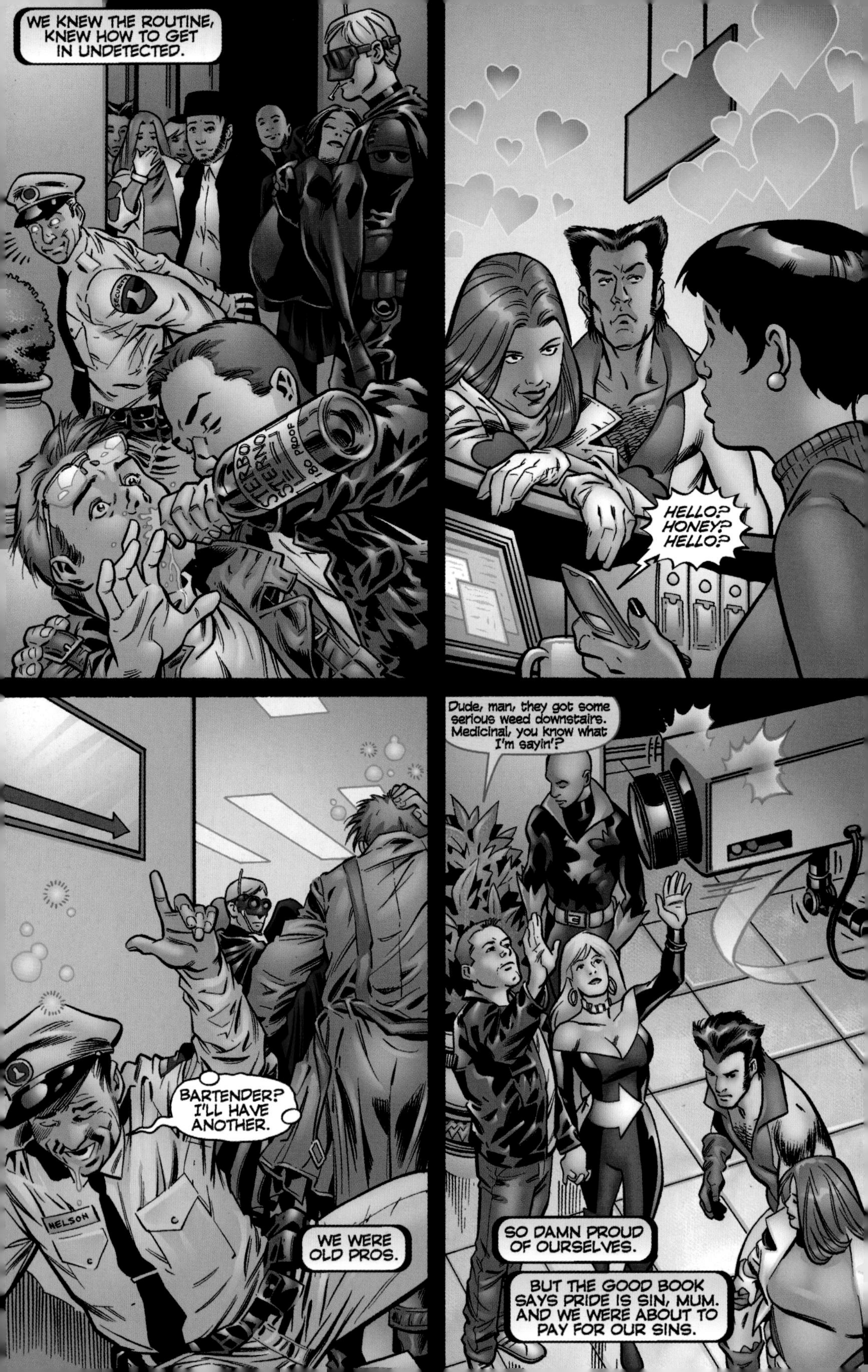
WE KNEW THE ROUTINE, KNEW HOW TO GET IN UNDETECTED.
STERBO STERNO 180 PROOF
HELLO? HONEY? HELLO?
BARTENDER? I'LL HAVE ANOTHER.
NELSON
WE WERE OLD PROS.
Dude, man, they got some serious weed downstairs. Medicinal, you know what I'm sayin'?
SO DAMN PROUD OF OURSELVES.
BUT THE GOOD BOOK SAYS PRIDE IS SIN, MUM. AND WE WERE ABOUT TO PAY FOR OUR SINS.

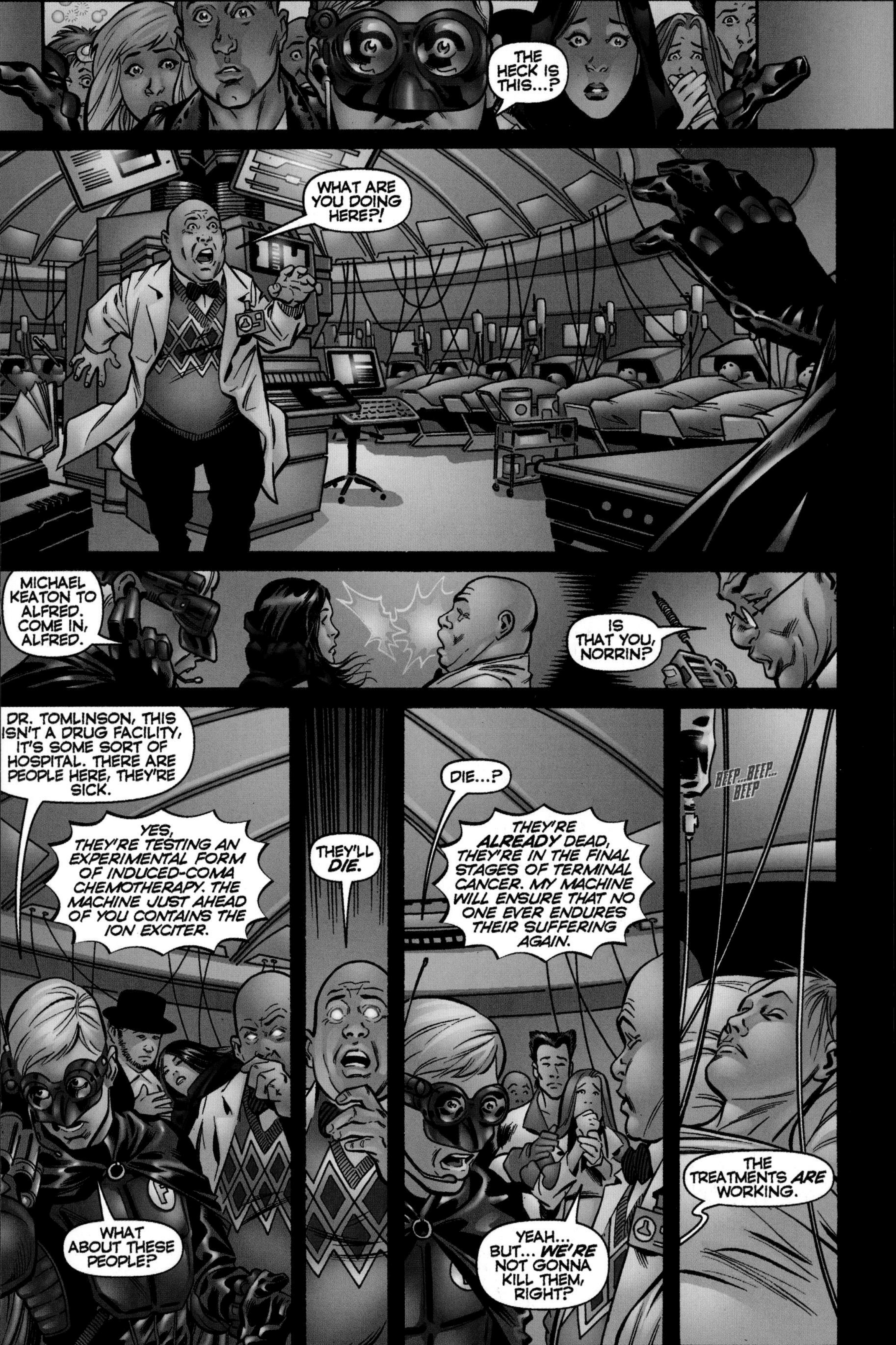
THE HECK IS THIS...?
WHAT ARE YOU DOING HERE?!
MICHAEL KEATON TO ALFRED. COME IN, ALFRED.
IS THAT YOU, NORRIN?
DR. TOMLINSON, THIS ISN'T A DRUG FACILITY, IT'S SOME SORT OF HOSPITAL. THERE ARE PEOPLE HERE, THEY'RE SICK.
YES, THEY'RE TESTING AN EXPERIMENTAL FORM OF INDUCED-COMA CHEMOTHERAPY. THE MACHINE JUST AHEAD OF YOU CONTAINS THE ION EXCITER.
WHAT ABOUT THESE PEOPLE?
THEY'LL DIE.
DIE...?
THEY'RE ALREADY DEAD, THEY'RE IN THE FINAL STAGES OF TERMINAL CANCER. MY MACHINE WILL ENSURE THAT NO ONE EVER ENDURES THEIR SUFFERING AGAIN.
YEAH... BUT... WE'RE NOT GONNA KILL THEM, RIGHT?
BEEP...BEEP... BEEP
THE TREATMENTS ARE WORKING.

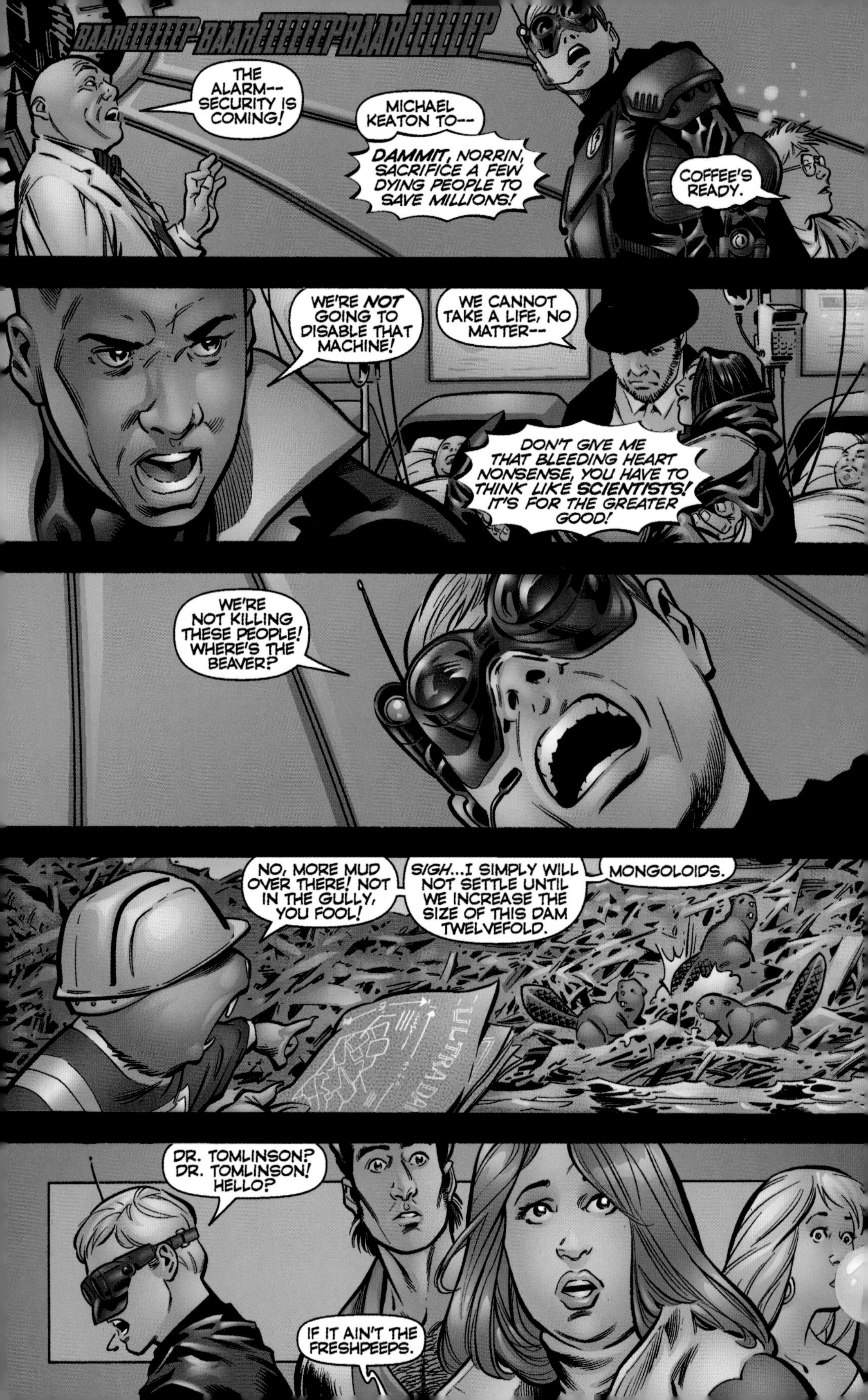
BAAREEEEEP BAAREEEEEP BAAREEEEEP
THE ALARM-- SECURITY IS COMING!
MICHAEL KEATON TO--
DAMMIT, NORRIN, SACRIFICE A FEW DYING PEOPLE TO SAVE MILLIONS!
COFFEE'S READY.
WE'RE NOT GOING TO DISABLE THAT MACHINE!
WE CANNOT TAKE A LIFE, NO MATTER--
DON'T GIVE ME THAT BLEEDING HEART NONSENSE, YOU HAVE TO THINK LIKE SCIENTISTS! IT'S FOR THE GREATER GOOD!
WE'RE NOT KILLING THESE PEOPLE! WHERE'S THE BEAVER?
NO, MORE MUD OVER THERE! NOT IN THE GULLY, YOU FOOL!
SIGH...I SIMPLY WILL NOT SETTLE UNTIL WE INCREASE THE SIZE OF THIS DAM TWELVEFOLD.
MONGOLOIDS.
DR. TOMLINSON? DR. TOMLINSON! HELLO?
IF IT AIN'T THE FRESHPEEPS.

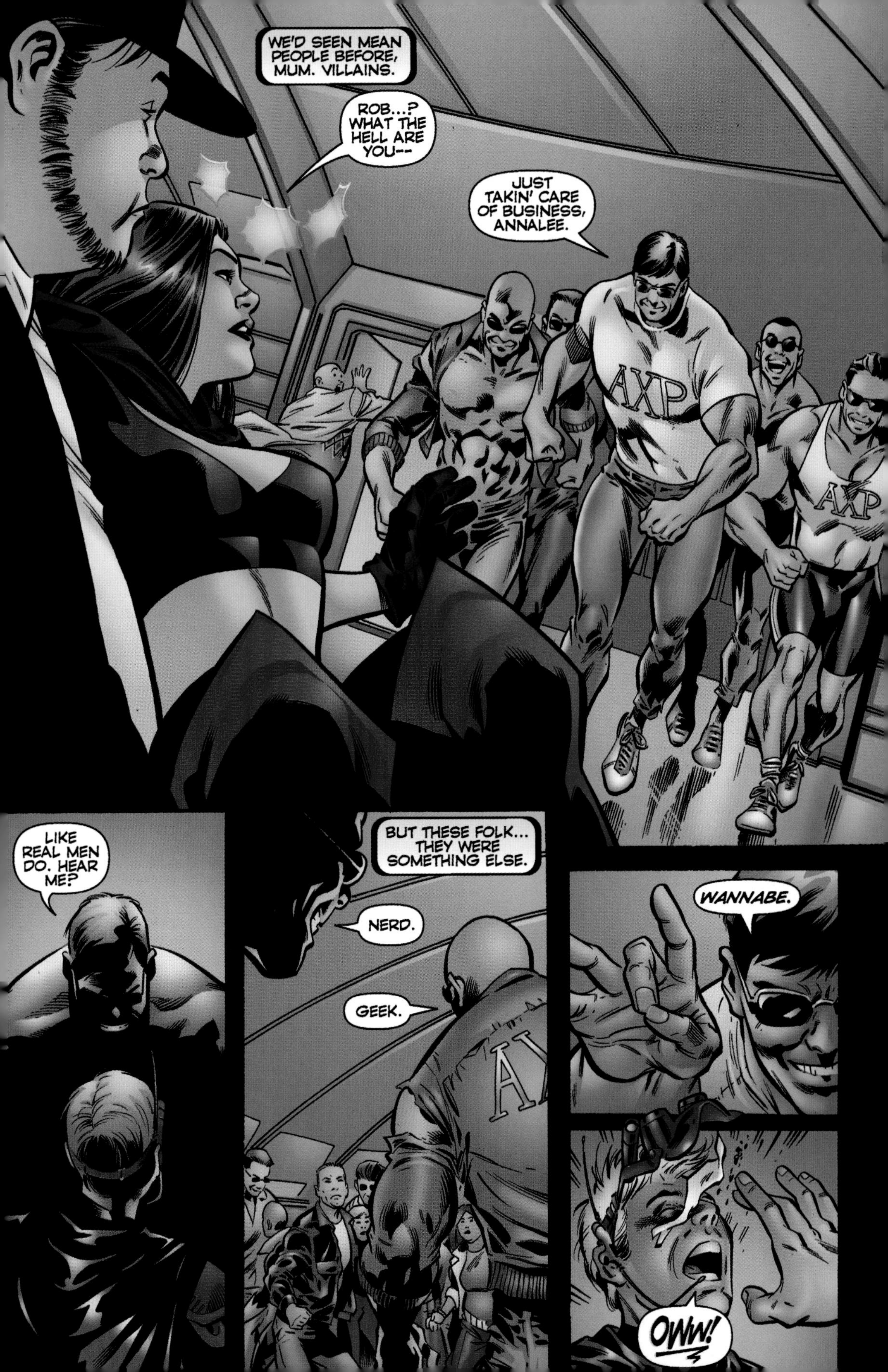
WE'D SEEN MEAN PEOPLE BEFORE, MUM. VILLAINS.
ROB...? WHAT THE HELL ARE YOU--
JUST TAKIN' CARE OF BUSINESS, ANNALEE.
AXP
AXP
LIKE REAL MEN DO. HEAR ME?
BUT THESE FOLK... THEY WERE SOMETHING ELSE.
NERD.
GEEK.
WANNABE.
OWW!

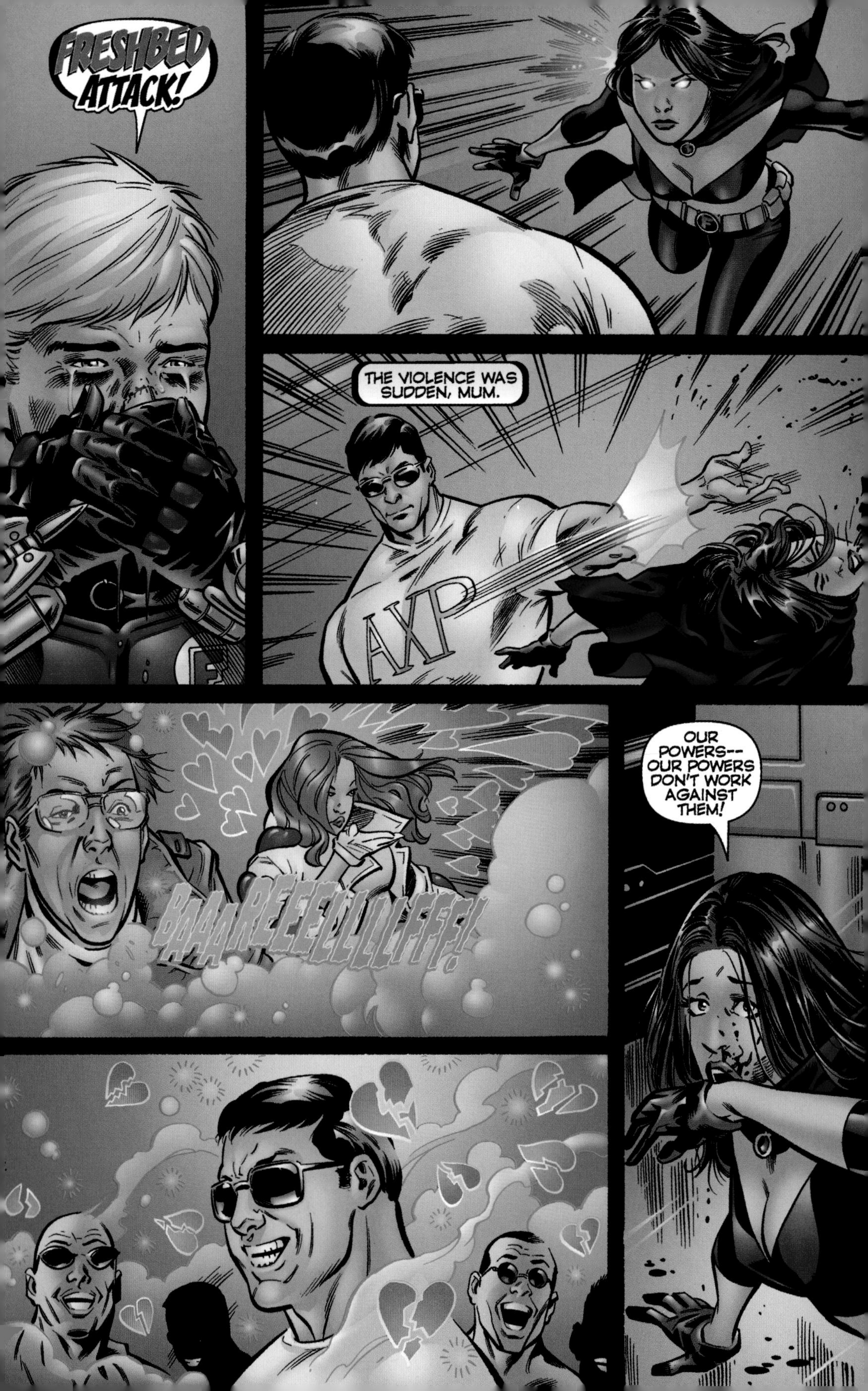
FRESHBED ATTACK!
THE VIOLENCE WAS SUDDEN, MUM.
BAAAREEEELLLLFFF!
OUR POWERS-- OUR POWERS DON'T WORK AGAINST THEM!

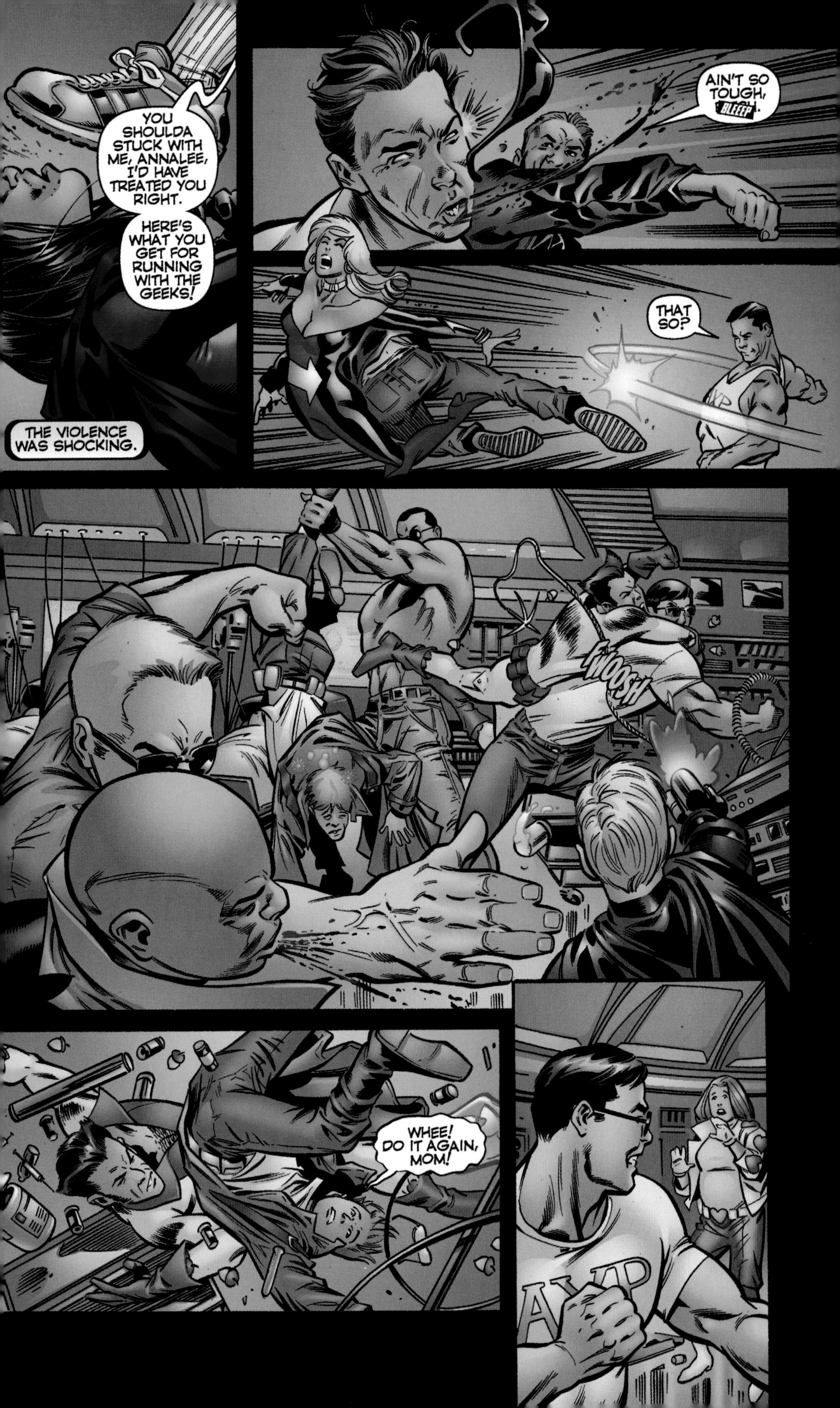
YOU SHOULDA STUCK WITH ME, ANNALEE, I'D HAVE TREATED YOU RIGHT.
HERE'S WHAT YOU GET FOR RUNNING WITH THE GEEKS!
THE VIOLENCE WAS SHOCKING.
AIN'T SO TOUGH, BLEEEP.
THAT SO?
FWOOSH
WHEE! DO IT AGAIN, MOM!

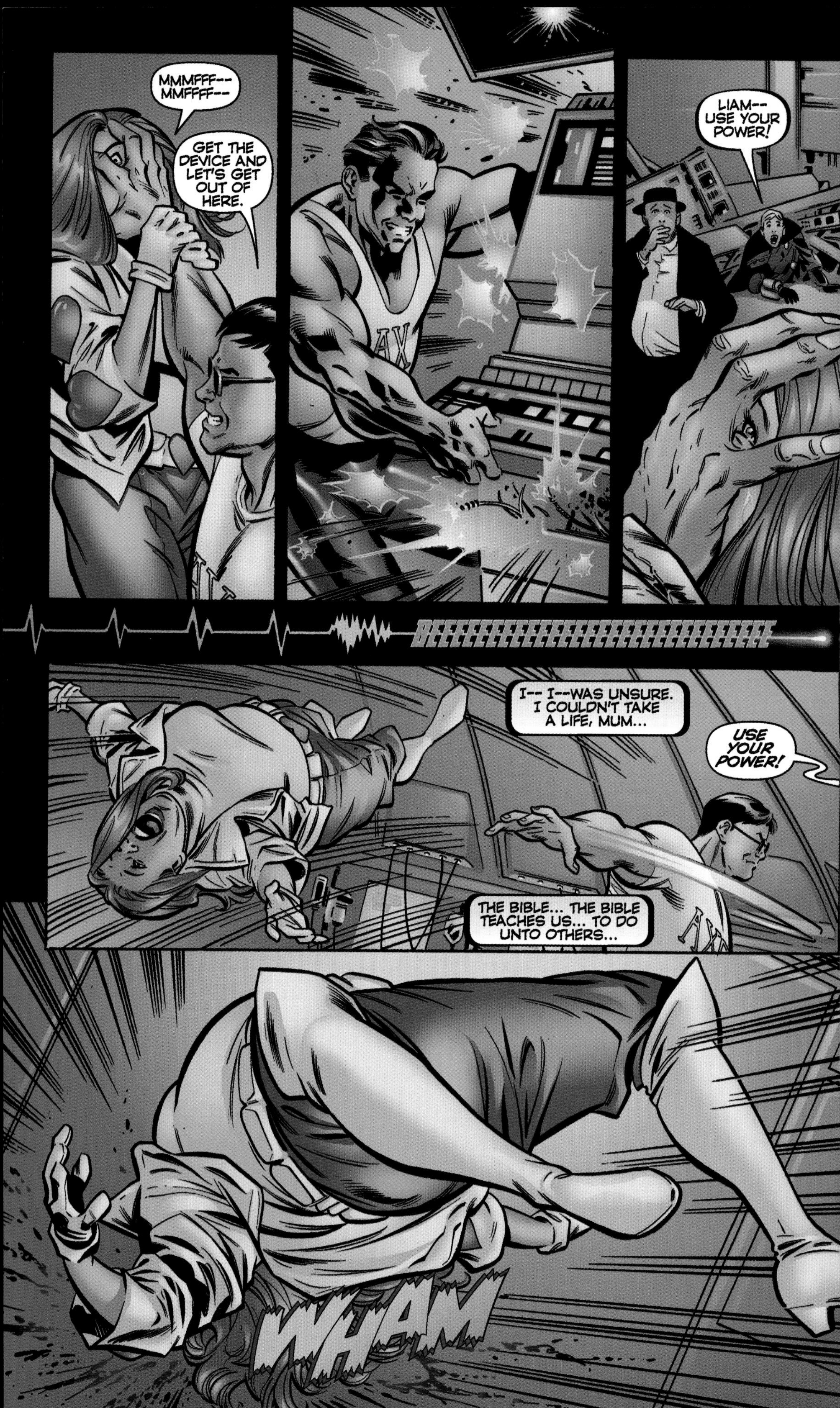
MMMFFF-- MMFFFF--
GET THE DEVICE AND LET'S GET OUT OF HERE.
LIAM-- USE YOUR POWER!
BEEEEEEEEEEEEEEEEEEEEEEEEEEEEEE
I-- I--WAS UNSURE. I COULDN'T TAKE A LIFE, MUM...
USE YOUR POWER!
THE BIBLE... THE BIBLE TEACHES US... TO DO UNTO OTHERS...
WHAM

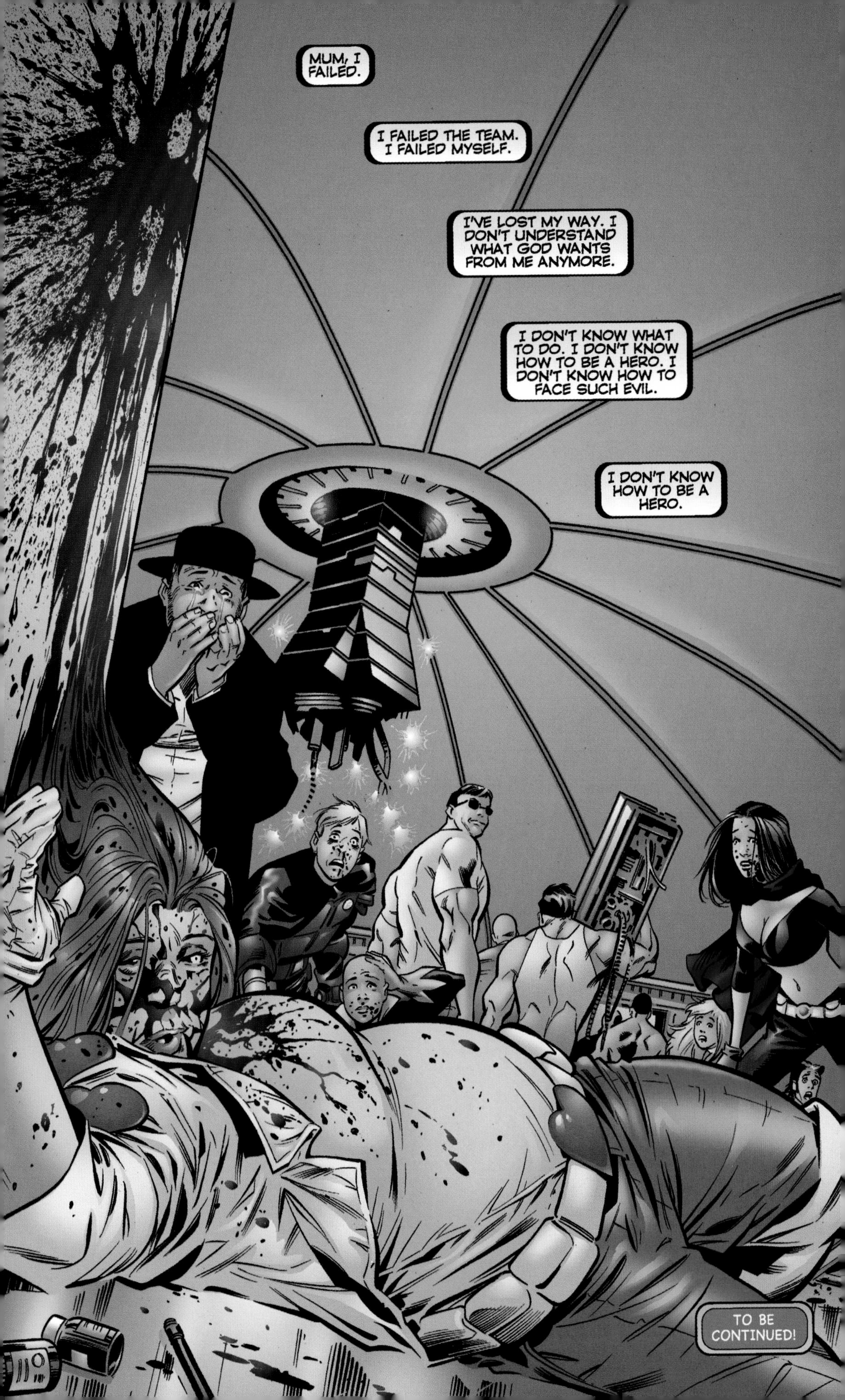
MUM, I FAILED.
I FAILED THE TEAM. I FAILED MYSELF.
I'VE LOST MY WAY. I DON'T UNDERSTAND WHAT GOD WANTS FROM ME ANYMORE.
I DON'T KNOW WHAT TO DO. I DON'T KNOW HOW TO BE A HERO. I DON'T KNOW HOW TO FACE SUCH EVIL.
I DON'T KNOW HOW TO BE A HERO.
TO BE CONTINUED!

CAST OUT OF THE MAIN DORMS AND FORCED TO LIVE IN TEMPORARY HOUSING IN THE BOUGHL SCIENCE BUILDING, THE FRESHMEN CLASS OF FREESE COLLEGE HAS BEEN IMBUED WITH MIRACULOUS SUPERPOWERS BY THE EXPLOSION OF A MYSTERIOUS DEVICE CALLED THE AX-CELL-ERATOR!

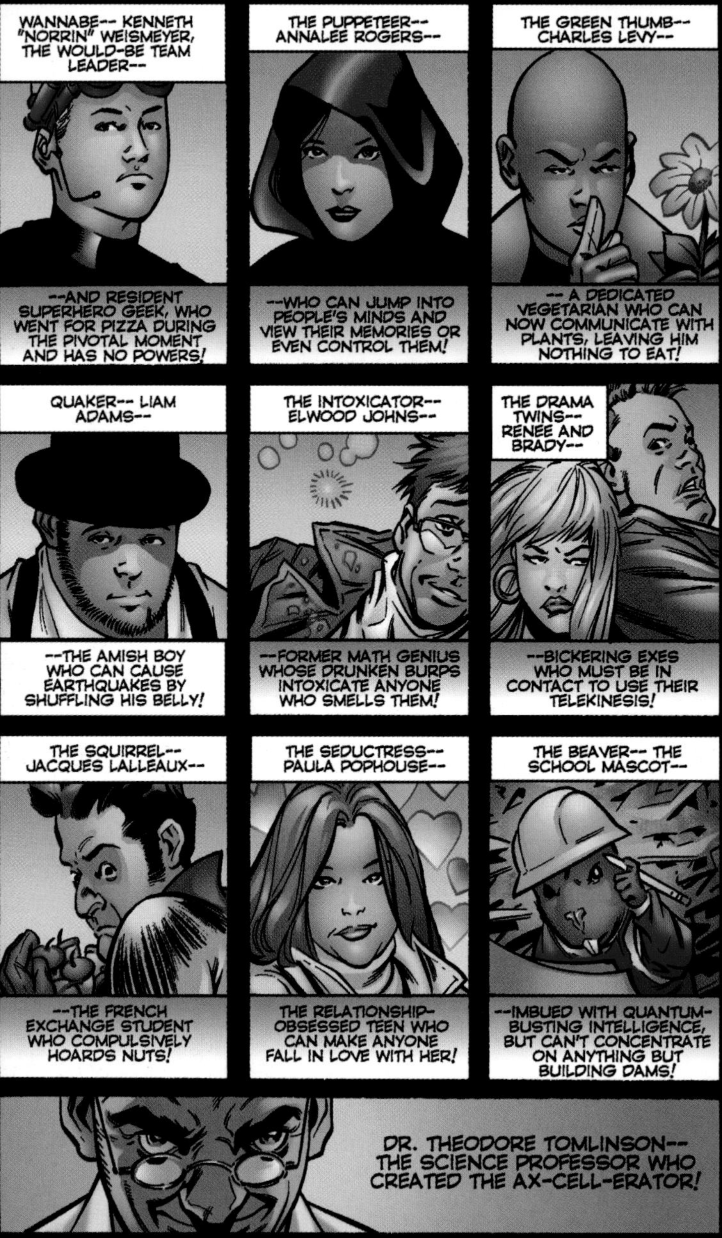
WANNABE-- KENNETH "NORRIN" WEISMEYER, THE WOULD-BE TEAM LEADER--
--AND RESIDENT SUPERHERO GEEK, WHO WENT FOR PIZZA DURING THE PIVOTAL MOMENT AND HAS NO POWERS!
THE PUPPETEER-- ANNALEE ROGERS--
--WHO CAN JUMP INTO PEOPLE'S MINDS AND VIEW THEIR MEMORIES OR EVEN CONTROL THEM!
THE GREEN THUMB-- CHARLES LEVY--
-- A DEDICATED VEGETARIAN WHO CAN NOW COMMUNICATE WITH PLANTS, LEAVING HIM NOTHING TO EAT!
QUAKER-- LIAM ADAMS--
--THE AMISH BOY WHO CAN CAUSE EARTHQUAKES BY SHUFFLING HIS BELLY!
THE INTOXICATOR-- ELWOOD JOHNS--
--FORMER MATH GENIUS WHOSE DRUNKEN BURPS INTOXICATE ANYONE WHO SMELLS THEM!
THE DRAMA TWINS-- RENEE AND BRADY--
--BICKERING EXES WHO MUST BE IN CONTACT TO USE THEIR TELEKINESIS!
THE SQUIRREL-- JACQUES LALLEAUX--
--THE FRENCH EXCHANGE STUDENT WHO COMPULSIVELY HOARDS NUTS!
THE SEDUCTRESS-- PAULA POPHOUSE--
THE RELATIONSHIP-OBSESSED TEEN WHO CAN MAKE ANYONE FALL IN LOVE WITH HER!
THE BEAVER-- THE SCHOOL MASCOT--
--IMBUED WITH QUANTUM-BUSTING INTELLIGENCE, BUT CAN'T CONCENTRATE ON ANYTHING BUT BUILDING DAMS!
DR. THEODORE TOMLINSON-- THE SCIENCE PROFESSOR WHO CREATED THE AX-CELL-ERATOR!

PREVIOUSLY IN FRESHMEN:
AFTER DISCOVERING THEIR BIZARRE AND AMAZING POWERS, OUR YOUNG HEROES WERE EMPLOYED BY THE CREATOR OF THE AX-CELL-ERATOR, DR. TOMLINSON, TO HELP REPAIR THE MACHINE THAT COULD CURE ALL DISEASES AND EVEN PREVENT AGING.

WANNABE, SUPERHERO OBSESSED BUT POWERLESS, HAS TAKEN DUBIOUS LEADERSHIP OF THE TEAM, BUT MOST OF THE KIDS TURN TO HIS UNREQUITED LOVE, THE PUPPETEER, FOR GUIDANCE.

ALTHOUGH THE KIDS' FIRST FIELD ASSIGNMENT WENT WELL, THEIR NEXT ADVENTURE TOOK A DISASTROUS TURN FOR THE DIRE, WHEN THE INEXPLICABLY HULKING FRAT GUYS INTERCEPTED THEIR MISSION AND STOLE A PIECE OF THE AX-CELL-ERATOR FROM UNDER THEM. IN THE MELEE, THE SEDUCTRESS WAS CRITICALLY INJURED...

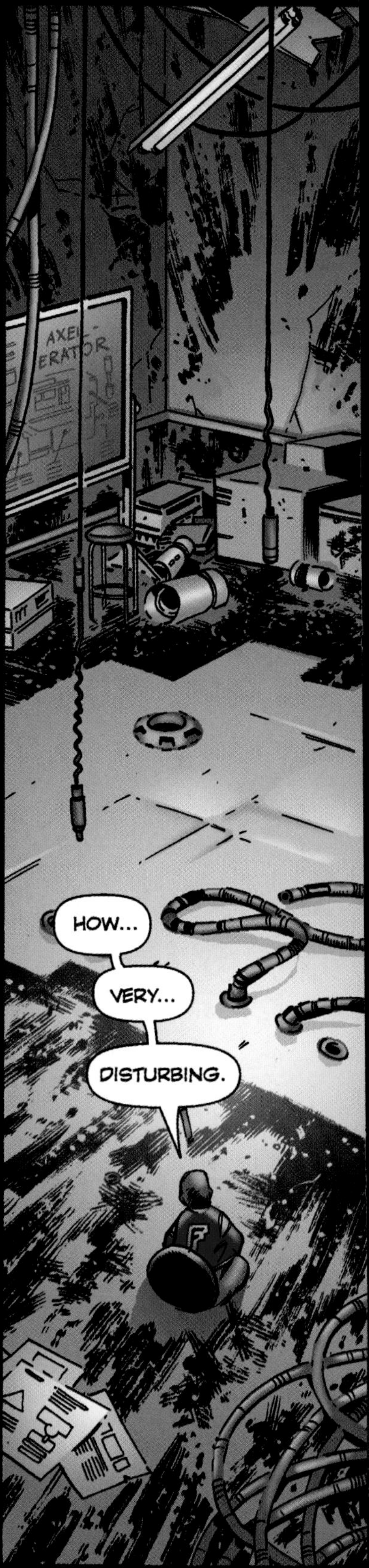
AXEL
ERATOR
HOW...
VERY...
DISTURBING.

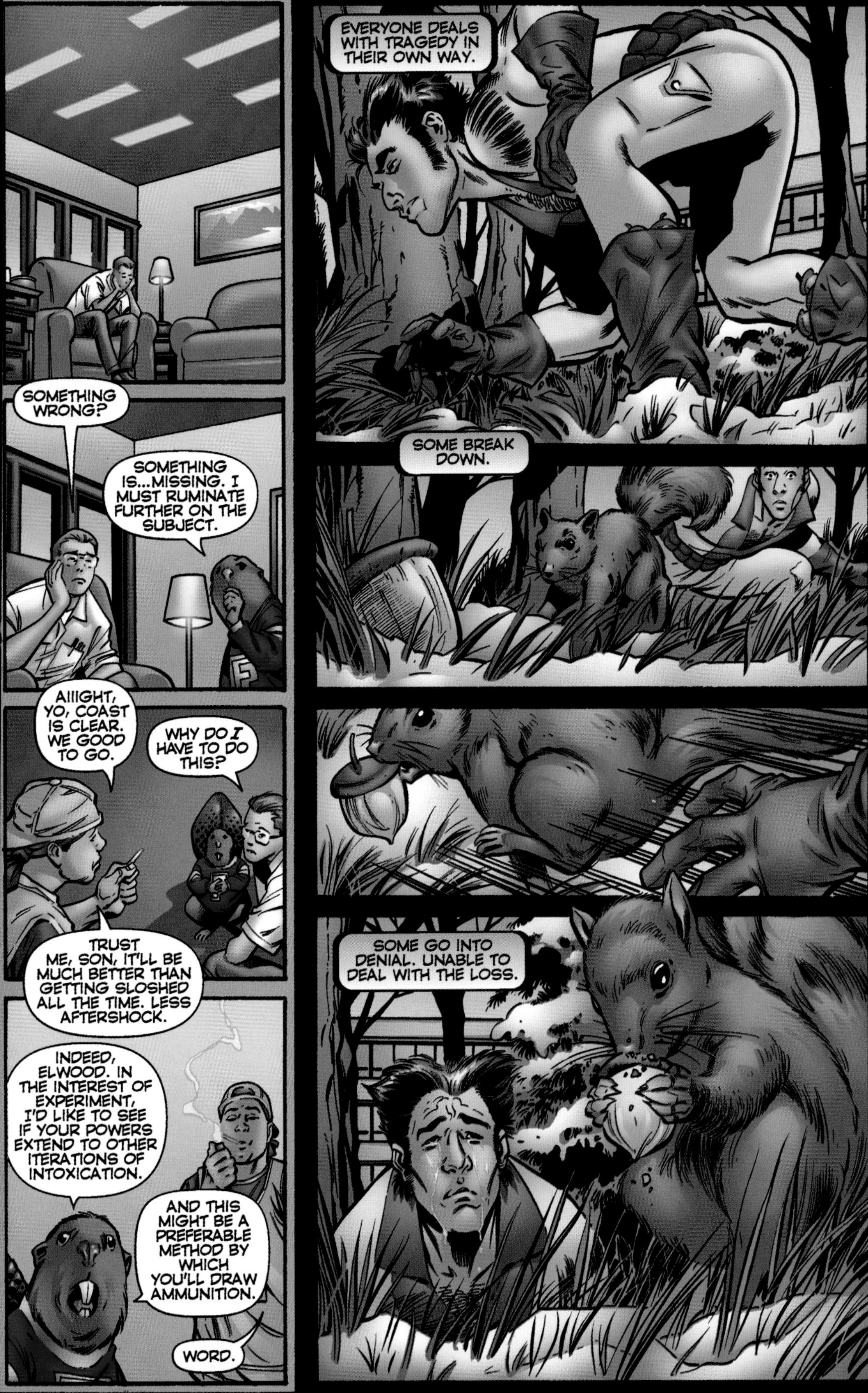
SOMETHING WRONG?
SOMETHING IS...MISSING. I MUST RUMINATE FURTHER ON THE SUBJECT.
AIIIGHT, YO, COAST IS CLEAR. WE GOOD TO GO.
WHY DO I HAVE TO DO THIS?
TRUST ME, SON, IT'LL BE MUCH BETTER THAN GETTING SLOSHED ALL THE TIME. LESS AFTERSHOCK.
INDEED, ELWOOD. IN THE INTEREST OF EXPERIMENT, I'D LIKE TO SEE IF YOUR POWERS EXTEND TO OTHER ITERATIONS OF INTOXICATION.
AND THIS MIGHT BE A PREFERABLE METHOD BY WHICH YOU'LL DRAW AMMUNITION.
WORD.
EVERYONE DEALS WITH TRAGEDY IN THEIR OWN WAY.
SOME BREAK DOWN.
SOME GO INTO DENIAL. UNABLE TO DEAL WITH THE LOSS.

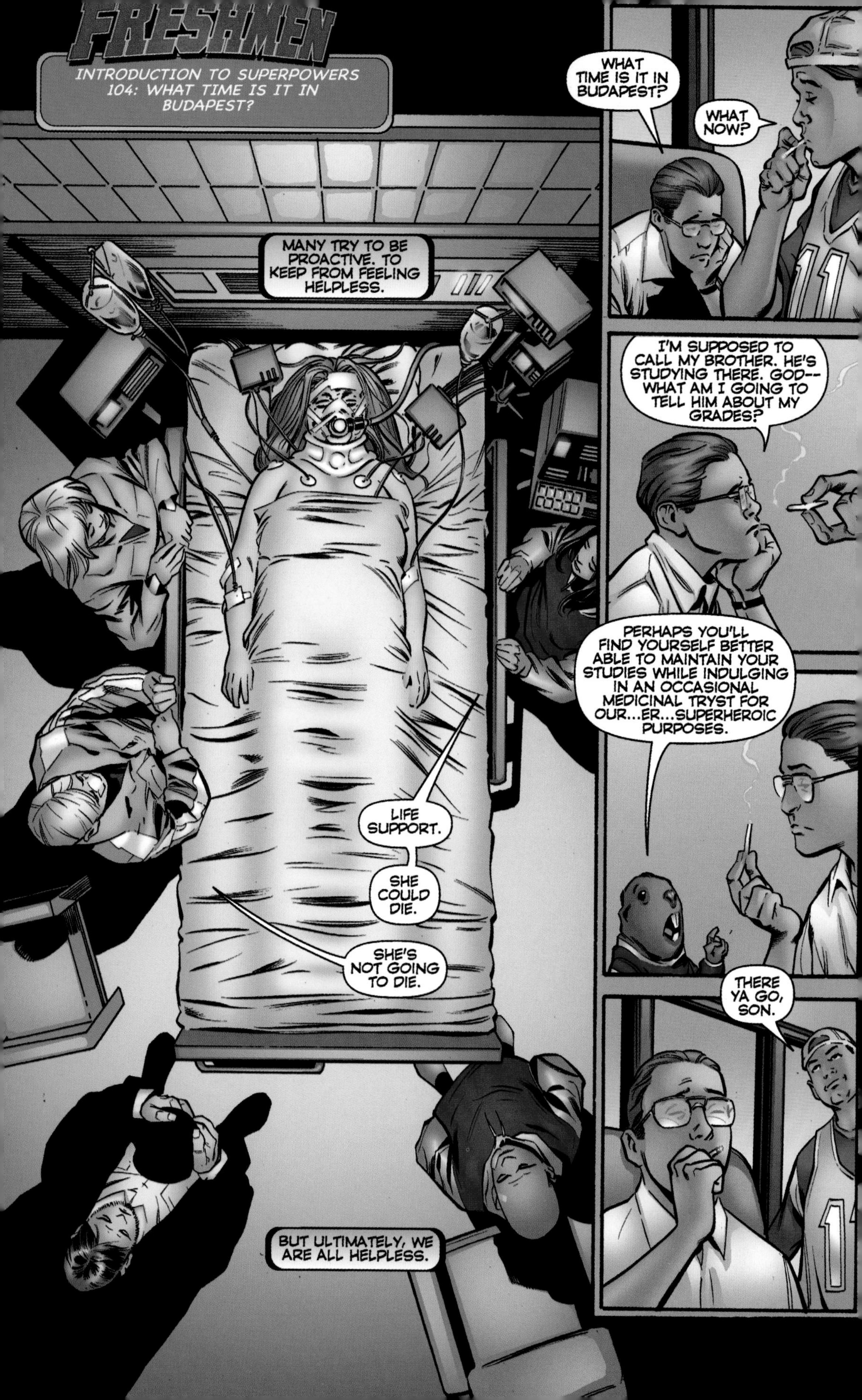
FRESHMEN
INTRODUCTION TO SUPERPOWERS 104: WHAT TIME IS IT IN BUDAPEST?
MANY TRY TO BE PROACTIVE. TO KEEP FROM FEELING HELPLESS.
LIFE SUPPORT.
SHE COULD DIE.
SHE'S NOT GOING TO DIE.
BUT ULTIMATELY, WE ARE ALL HELPLESS.
WHAT TIME IS IT IN BUDAPEST?
WHAT NOW?
I'M SUPPOSED TO CALL MY BROTHER. HE'S STUDYING THERE. GOD-- WHAT AM I GOING TO TELL HIM ABOUT MY GRADES?
PERHAPS YOU'LL FIND YOURSELF BETTER ABLE TO MAINTAIN YOUR STUDIES WHILE INDULGING IN AN OCCASIONAL MEDICINAL TRYST FOR OUR...ER...SUPERHEROIC PURPOSES.
THERE YA GO, SON.

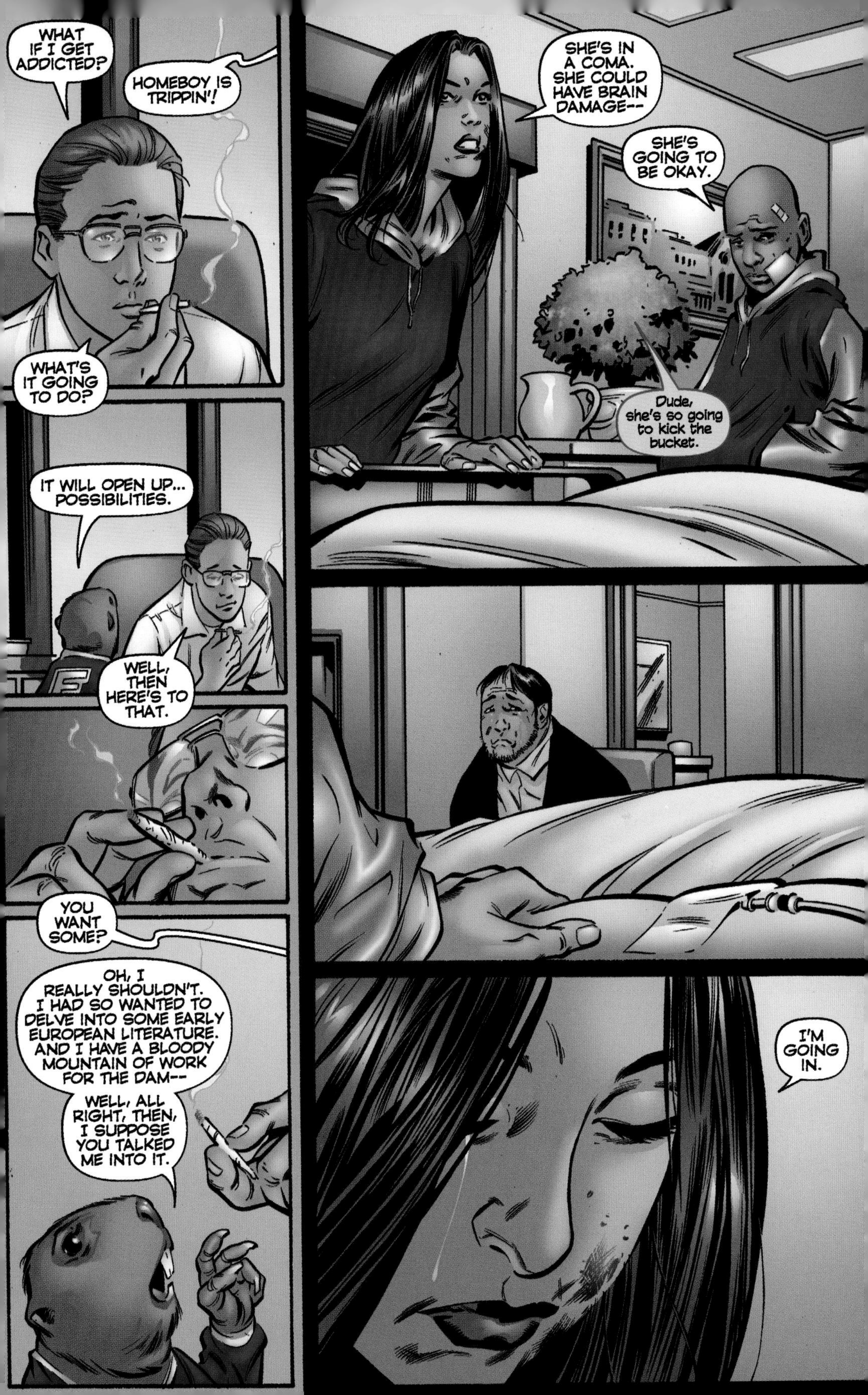
WHAT IF I GET ADDICTED?
HOMEBOY IS TRIPPIN'!
WHAT'S IT GOING TO DO?
IT WILL OPEN UP... POSSIBILITIES.
WELL, THEN HERE'S TO THAT.
YOU WANT SOME?
OH, I REALLY SHOULDN'T. I HAD SO WANTED TO DELVE INTO SOME EARLY EUROPEAN LITERATURE. AND I HAVE A BLOODY MOUNTAIN OF WORK FOR THE DAM--
WELL, ALL RIGHT, THEN, I SUPPOSE YOU TALKED ME INTO IT.
SHE'S IN A COMA. SHE COULD HAVE BRAIN DAMAGE--
SHE'S GOING TO BE OKAY.
Dude, she's so going to kick the bucket.
I'M GOING IN.

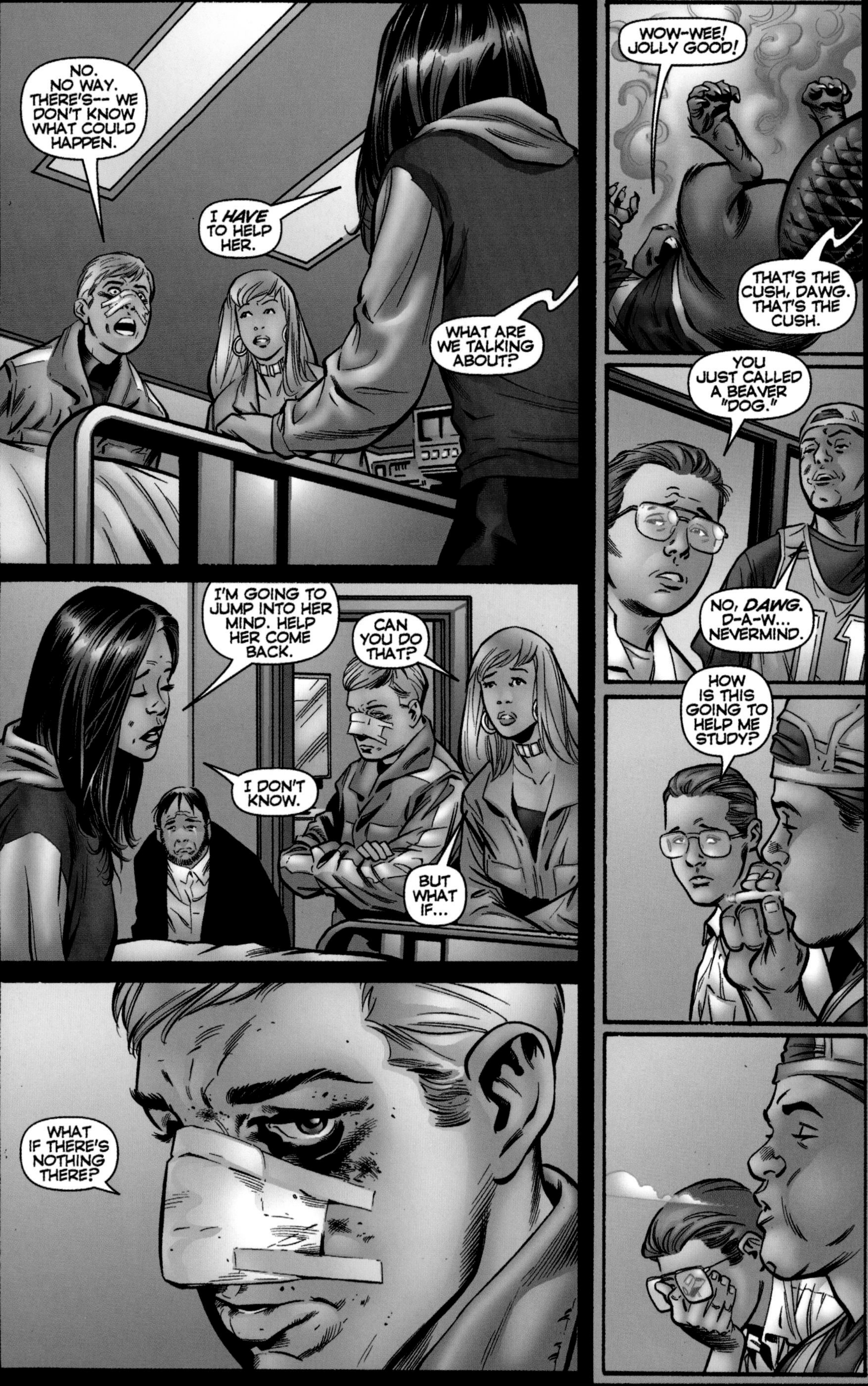
NO. NO WAY. THERE'S-- WE DON'T KNOW WHAT COULD HAPPEN.
I HAVE TO HELP HER.
WHAT ARE WE TALKING ABOUT?
I'M GOING TO JUMP INTO HER MIND. HELP HER COME BACK.
CAN YOU DO THAT?
I DON'T KNOW.
BUT WHAT IF...
WHAT IF THERE'S NOTHING THERE?
WOW-WEE! JOLLY GOOD!
THAT'S THE CUSH, DAWG. THAT'S THE CUSH.
YOU JUST CALLED A BEAVER "DOG."
NO, DAWG. D-A-W... NEVERMIND.
HOW IS THIS GOING TO HELP ME STUDY?

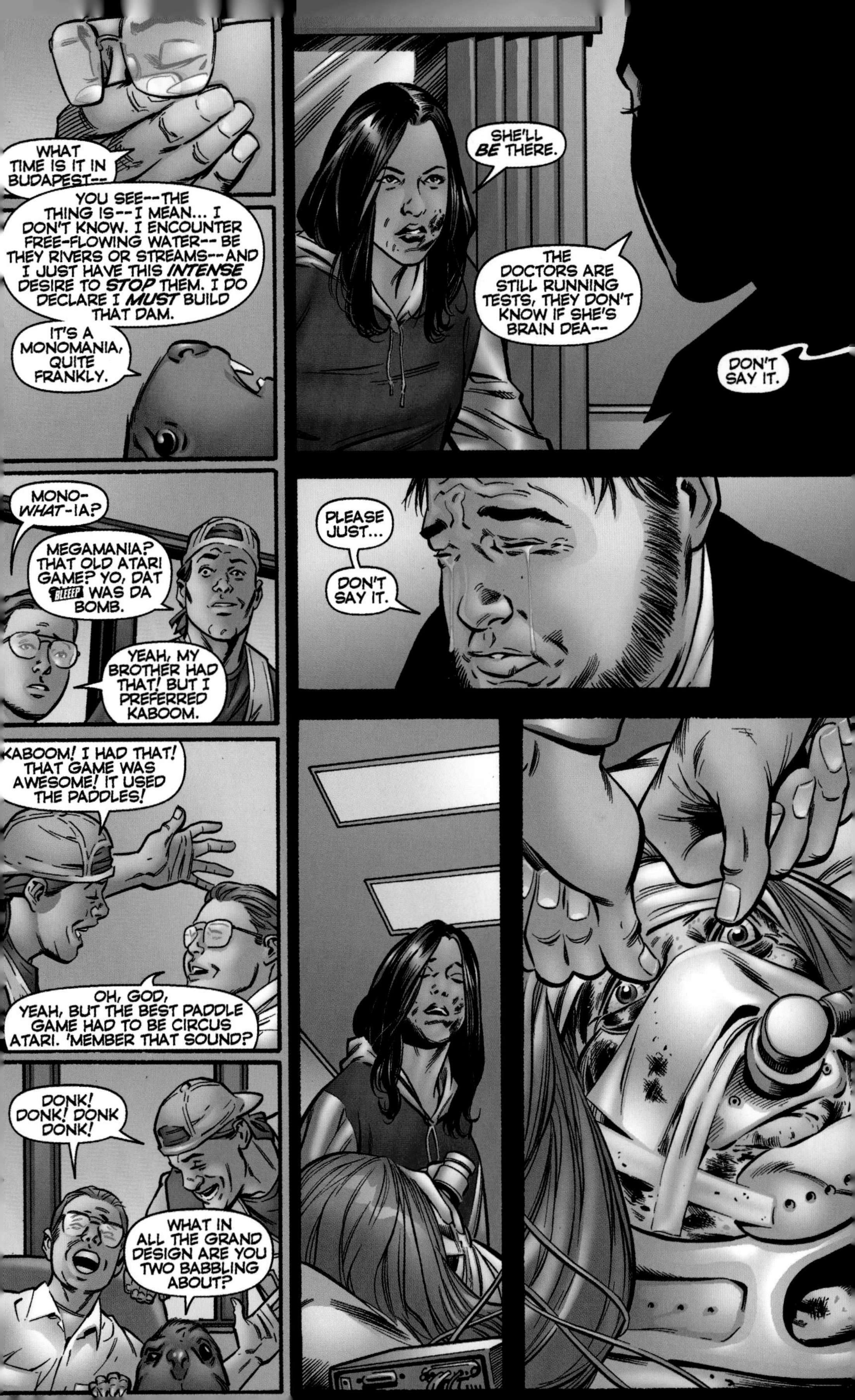
WHAT TIME IS IT IN BUDAPEST--
YOU SEE--THE THING IS--I MEAN... I DON'T KNOW. I ENCOUNTER FREE-FLOWING WATER--BE THEY RIVERS OR STREAMS--AND I JUST HAVE THIS *INTENSE* DESIRE TO *STOP* THEM. I DO DECLARE I *MUST* BUILD THAT DAM.
IT'S A MONOMANIA, QUITE FRANKLY.
MONO-*WHAT*-IA?
MEGAMANIA? THAT OLD ATARI GAME? YO, DAT BLEEEP WAS DA BOMB.
YEAH, MY BROTHER HAD THAT! BUT I PREFERRED KABOOM.
KABOOM! I HAD THAT! THAT GAME WAS AWESOME! IT USED THE PADDLES!
OH, GOD, YEAH, BUT THE BEST PADDLE GAME HAD TO BE CIRCUS ATARI. 'MEMBER THAT SOUND?
DONK! DONK! DONK DONK!
WHAT IN ALL THE GRAND DESIGN ARE YOU TWO BABBLING ABOUT?
SHE'LL *BE* THERE.
THE DOCTORS ARE STILL RUNNING TESTS, THEY DON'T KNOW IF SHE'S BRAIN DEA--
DON'T SAY IT.
PLEASE JUST...
DON'T SAY IT.

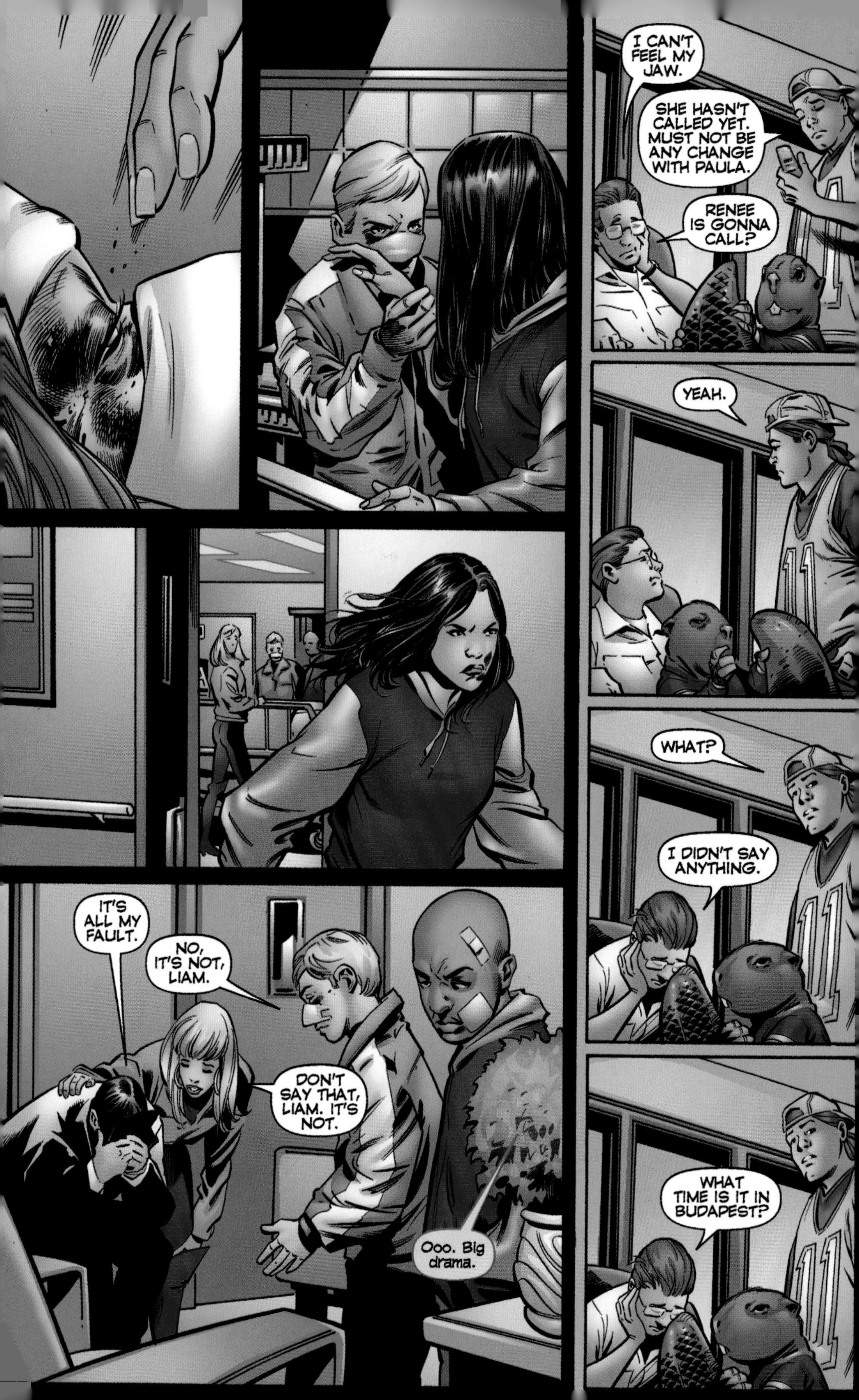
I CAN'T FEEL MY JAW.
SHE HASN'T CALLED YET. MUST NOT BE ANY CHANGE WITH PAULA.
RENEE IS GONNA CALL?
YEAH.
WHAT?
I DIDN'T SAY ANYTHING.
WHAT TIME IS IT IN BUDAPEST?
IT'S ALL MY FAULT.
NO, IT'S NOT, LIAM.
DON'T SAY THAT, LIAM. IT'S NOT.
Ooo. Big drama.

OKAY...I KNOW WHAT YOU'RE THINKING. YOU'RE THINKING WHY THE HELL DO I STAY WITH HER EVEN THOUGH SHE'S AN ABUSIVE *BLEEP*. THE WAY SHE TALKS TO ME AND EVERYTHING.

YOU JUST HAVE TO UNDERSTAND, THOUGH-- THIS IS MY FIRST LOVE. MY FIRST KISS. MY FIRST... EVERYTHING. I'VE BEEN WITH HER SINCE 7TH GRADE, I DON'T KNOW ANY DIFFERENT.

AND YOU GUYS HAVE ONLY SEEN US AT OUR WORST. WE HAVE THESE AMAZING MOMENTS, WHERE SHE UNDERSTANDS ME BETTER THAN ANY ONE EVER HAS.

IT JUST FEELS LIKE... IT FEELS LIKE... LIKE SHE'S HOME, Y'KNOW? IT FEELS LIKE NOTHING WOULD BE THE SAME WITHOUT HER.

WE ALWAYS KEEP FIGHTING. I JUST... I CAN'T GET HER TO TREAT ME RIGHT. I CAN'T GET HER TO RESPECT ME. DON'T MATTER IF I SEND HER FLOWERS OR I CURSE HER OUT... I ALWAYS GET THE SAME.

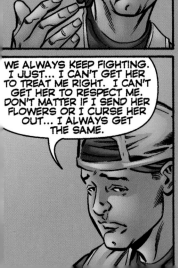

EVERYONE DEALS WITH TRAGEDY IN THEIR OWN WAY.

SOME ARE ASHAMED, FRUSTRATED BY THEIR VULNERABILITIES.

THE STRONGEST NEMESIS OF THE HUMAN PSYCHE IS SHAME. HUMILIATION.

IT LEADS TO INHIBITION. SELF-PROTECTION. RISK AVERSION. FREEZES YOU DEAD MORE THAN ANY PHYSICAL HANDICAP.

JACQUES.

WHAT ARE YOU DOING HERE?

NOS'ZING.

WHY AREN'T YOU AT THE HOSPITAL?

I WEEL GO WHEN I AM READY.

WHAT'S IN YOUR DRESSER, JACQUES?

NOS'ZING.

IT KEEPS YOU FROM OPENING UP TO STRANGERS. ACCEPTING HELP. MAKING FRIENDS.

I COULD *MAKE* YOU OPEN IT.

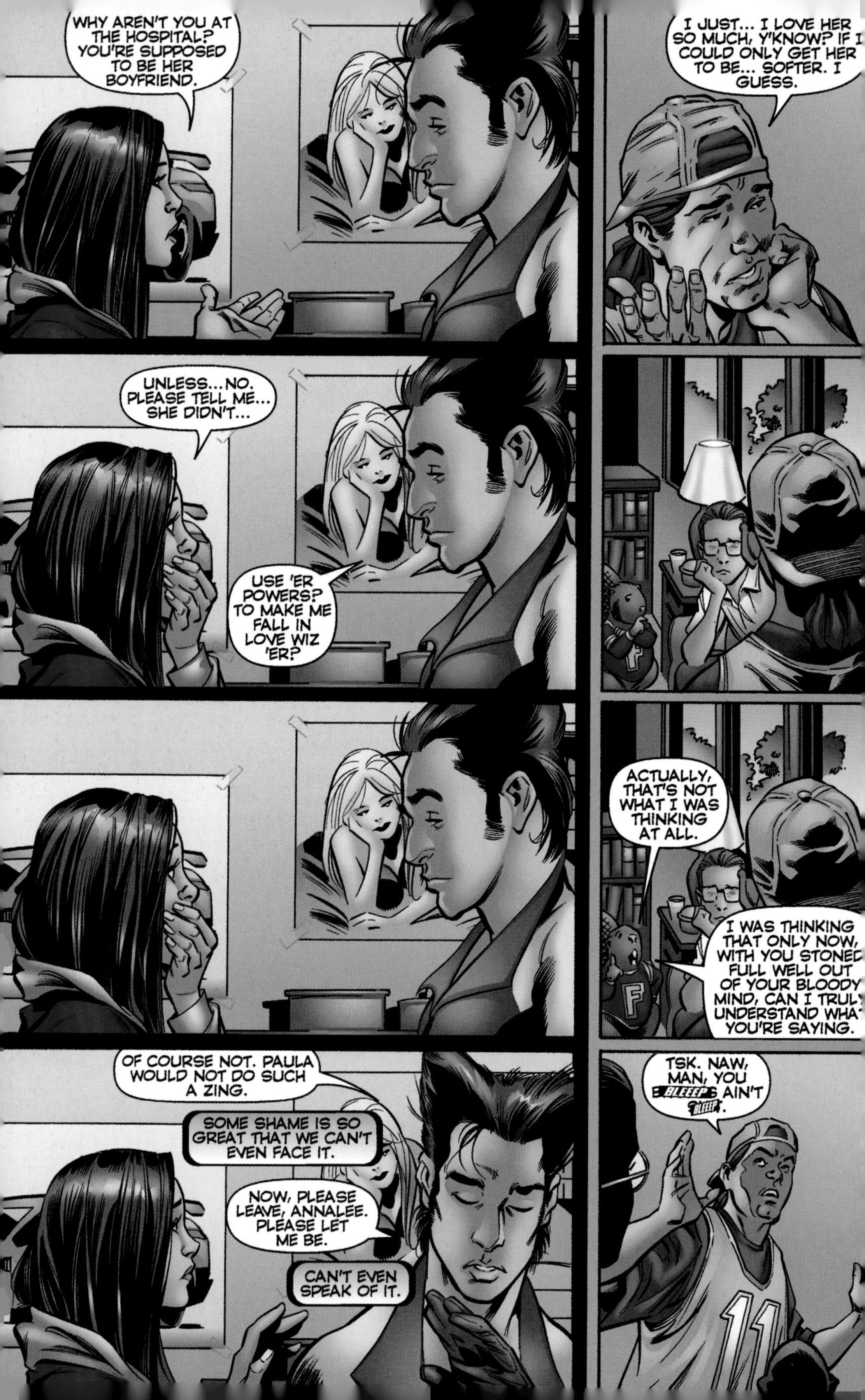
WHY AREN'T YOU AT THE HOSPITAL? YOU'RE SUPPOSED TO BE HER BOYFRIEND.
I JUST... I LOVE HER SO MUCH, Y'KNOW? IF I COULD ONLY GET HER TO BE... SOFTER. I GUESS.
UNLESS...NO. PLEASE TELL ME... SHE DIDN'T...
USE 'ER POWERS? TO MAKE ME FALL IN LOVE WIZ 'ER?
ACTUALLY, THAT'S NOT WHAT I WAS THINKING AT ALL.
I WAS THINKING THAT ONLY NOW, WITH YOU STONED FULL WELL OUT OF YOUR BLOODY MIND, CAN I TRULY UNDERSTAND WHAT YOU'RE SAYING.
OF COURSE NOT. PAULA WOULD NOT DO SUCH A ZING.
SOME SHAME IS SO GREAT THAT WE CAN'T EVEN FACE IT.
NOW, PLEASE LEAVE, ANNALEE. PLEASE LET ME BE.
CAN'T EVEN SPEAK OF IT.
TSK. NAW, MAN, YOU B BLEEEP S AIN'T BLEEEP.

WHOA. I'VE GOT ONE BREWING.

HOO-BOY, THIS IS GOING TO BE--

GARRRUUUUURRUULLGGGHHHF!!

EVERYONE DEALS WITH TRAGEDY IN THEIR OWN WAY.

SOME TRY TO BARGAIN. RAGE AGAINST THAT WHICH THEY CANNOT CONTROL.

WHAT ARE WE GOING TO DO ABOUT THE FRAT GUYS?

WE'RE GOING TO REGROUP.

WE'RE GOING TO GET PREPARED.

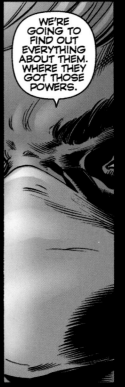

WE'RE GOING TO FIND OUT EVERYTHING ABOUT THEM. WHERE THEY GOT THOSE POWERS.

UNPREPARED TO ADMIT THEIR HELPLESSNESS.

AND THEN WE'RE GOING TO *DESTROY* THEM.

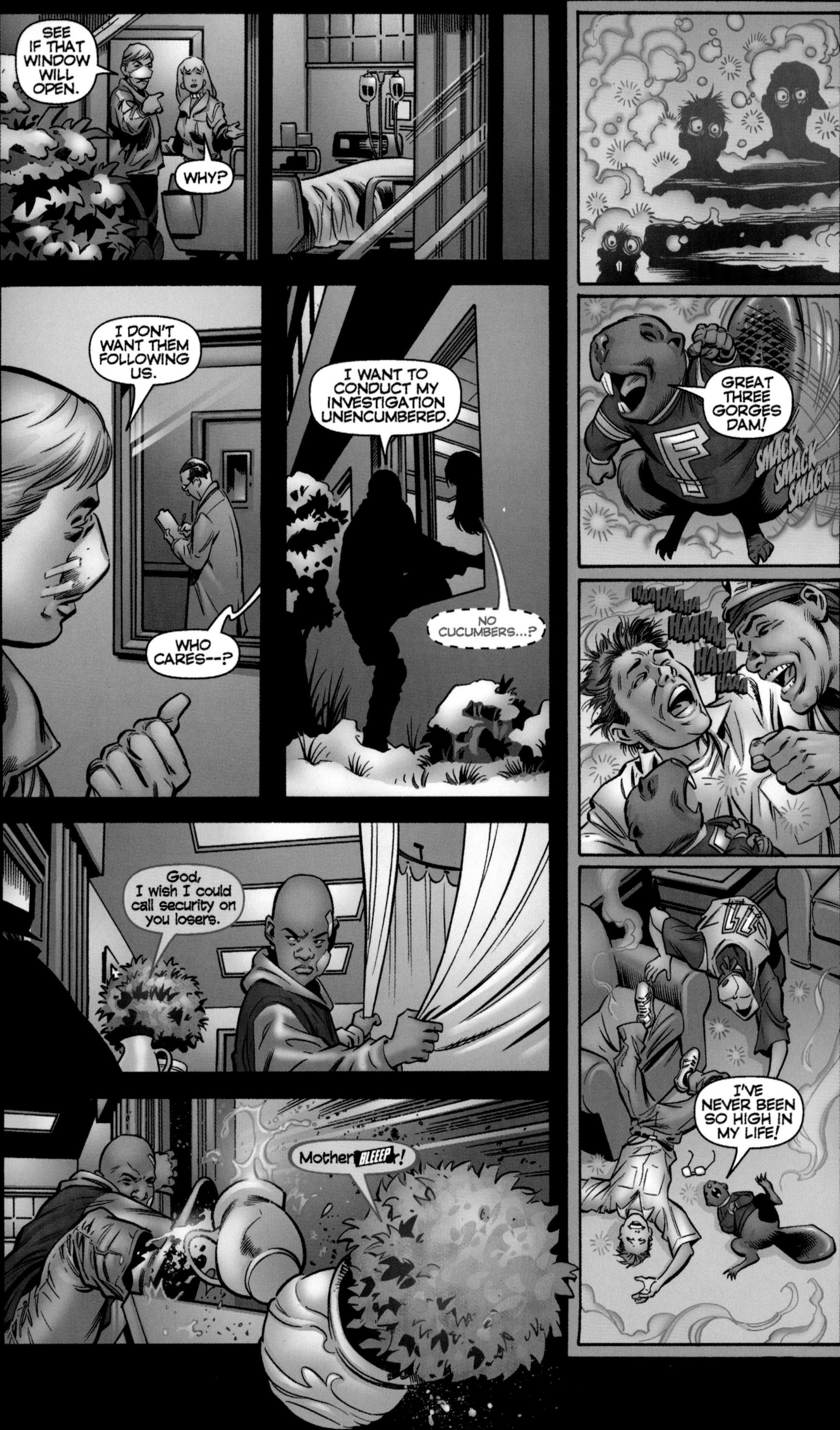
SEE IF THAT WINDOW WILL OPEN.
WHY?
HAAHAHAHAHAHA
GREAT THREE GORGES DAM!
SMACK SMACK SMACK
I DON'T WANT THEM FOLLOWING US.
WHO CARES--?
I WANT TO CONDUCT MY INVESTIGATION UNENCUMBERED.
NO CUCUMBERS...?
HAAHAA HAAHAA HAHA HAAA
God, I wish I could call security on you losers.
Mother BLEEEP!
I'VE NEVER BEEN SO HIGH IN MY LIFE!

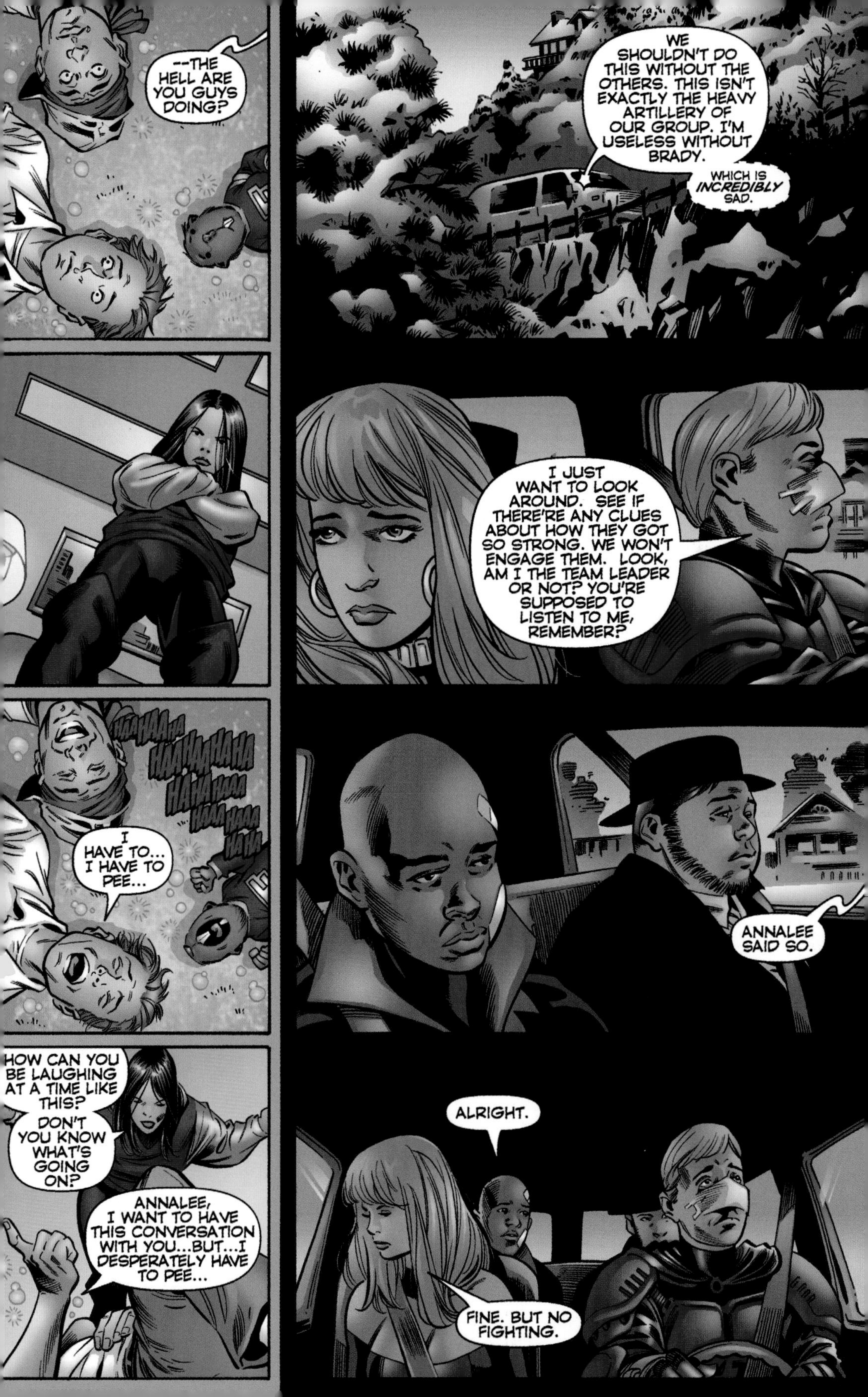
--THE HELL ARE YOU GUYS DOING?
WE SHOULDN'T DO THIS WITHOUT THE OTHERS. THIS ISN'T EXACTLY THE HEAVY ARTILLERY OF OUR GROUP. I'M USELESS WITHOUT BRADY.
WHICH IS *INCREDIBLY* SAD.
I JUST WANT TO LOOK AROUND. SEE IF THERE'RE ANY CLUES ABOUT HOW THEY GOT SO STRONG. WE WON'T ENGAGE THEM. LOOK, AM I THE TEAM LEADER OR NOT? YOU'RE SUPPOSED TO LISTEN TO ME, REMEMBER?
HAAHAAHA HAHAAHAHA HAHAHAAA HAAAHAAA HAHA
I HAVE TO... I HAVE TO PEE...
ANNALEE SAID SO.
HOW CAN YOU BE LAUGHING AT A TIME LIKE THIS?
DON'T YOU KNOW WHAT'S GOING ON?
ANNALEE, I WANT TO HAVE THIS CONVERSATION WITH YOU...BUT...I DESPERATELY HAVE TO PEE...
ALRIGHT.
FINE. BUT NO FIGHTING.

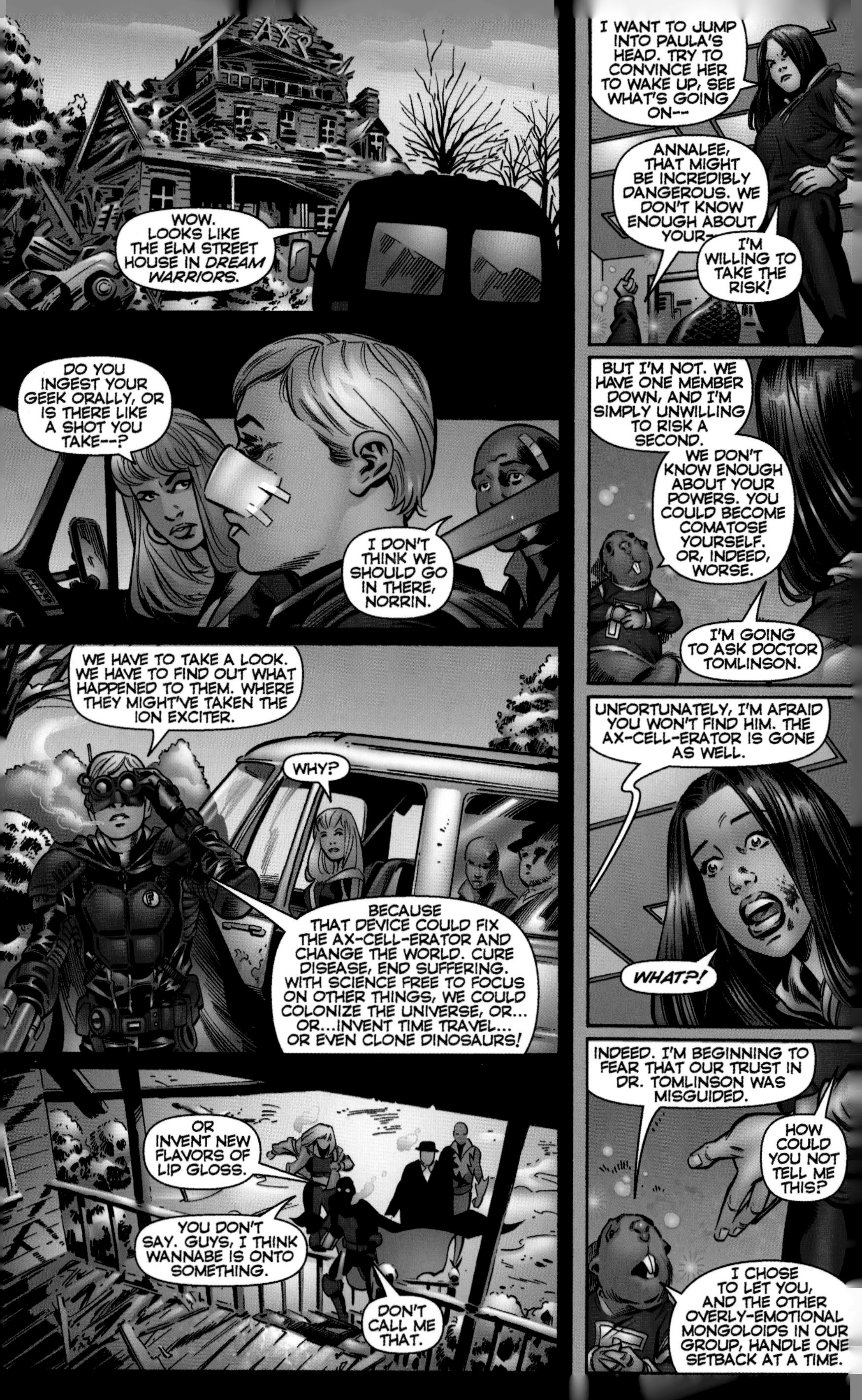
WOW. LOOKS LIKE THE ELM STREET HOUSE IN *DREAM WARRIORS*.
DO YOU INGEST YOUR GEEK ORALLY, OR IS THERE LIKE A SHOT YOU TAKE--?
I DON'T THINK WE SHOULD GO IN THERE, NORRIN.
WE HAVE TO TAKE A LOOK. WE HAVE TO FIND OUT WHAT HAPPENED TO THEM. WHERE THEY MIGHT'VE TAKEN THE ION EXCITER.
WHY?
BECAUSE THAT DEVICE COULD FIX THE AX-CELL-ERATOR AND CHANGE THE WORLD. CURE DISEASE, END SUFFERING. WITH SCIENCE FREE TO FOCUS ON OTHER THINGS, WE COULD COLONIZE THE UNIVERSE, OR... OR...INVENT TIME TRAVEL... OR EVEN CLONE DINOSAURS!
OR INVENT NEW FLAVORS OF LIP GLOSS.
YOU DON'T SAY. GUYS, I THINK WANNABE IS ONTO SOMETHING.
DON'T CALL ME THAT.
I WANT TO JUMP INTO PAULA'S HEAD. TRY TO CONVINCE HER TO WAKE UP, SEE WHAT'S GOING ON--
ANNALEE, THAT MIGHT BE INCREDIBLY DANGEROUS. WE DON'T KNOW ENOUGH ABOUT YOUR--
I'M WILLING TO TAKE THE RISK!
BUT I'M NOT. WE HAVE ONE MEMBER DOWN, AND I'M SIMPLY UNWILLING TO RISK A SECOND.
WE DON'T KNOW ENOUGH ABOUT YOUR POWERS. YOU COULD BECOME COMATOSE YOURSELF. OR, INDEED, WORSE.
I'M GOING TO ASK DOCTOR TOMLINSON.
UNFORTUNATELY, I'M AFRAID YOU WON'T FIND HIM. THE AX-CELL-ERATOR IS GONE AS WELL.
WHAT?!
INDEED. I'M BEGINNING TO FEAR THAT OUR TRUST IN DR. TOMLINSON WAS MISGUIDED.
HOW COULD YOU NOT TELL ME THIS?
I CHOSE TO LET YOU, AND THE OTHER OVERLY-EMOTIONAL MONGOLOIDS IN OUR GROUP, HANDLE ONE SETBACK AT A TIME.

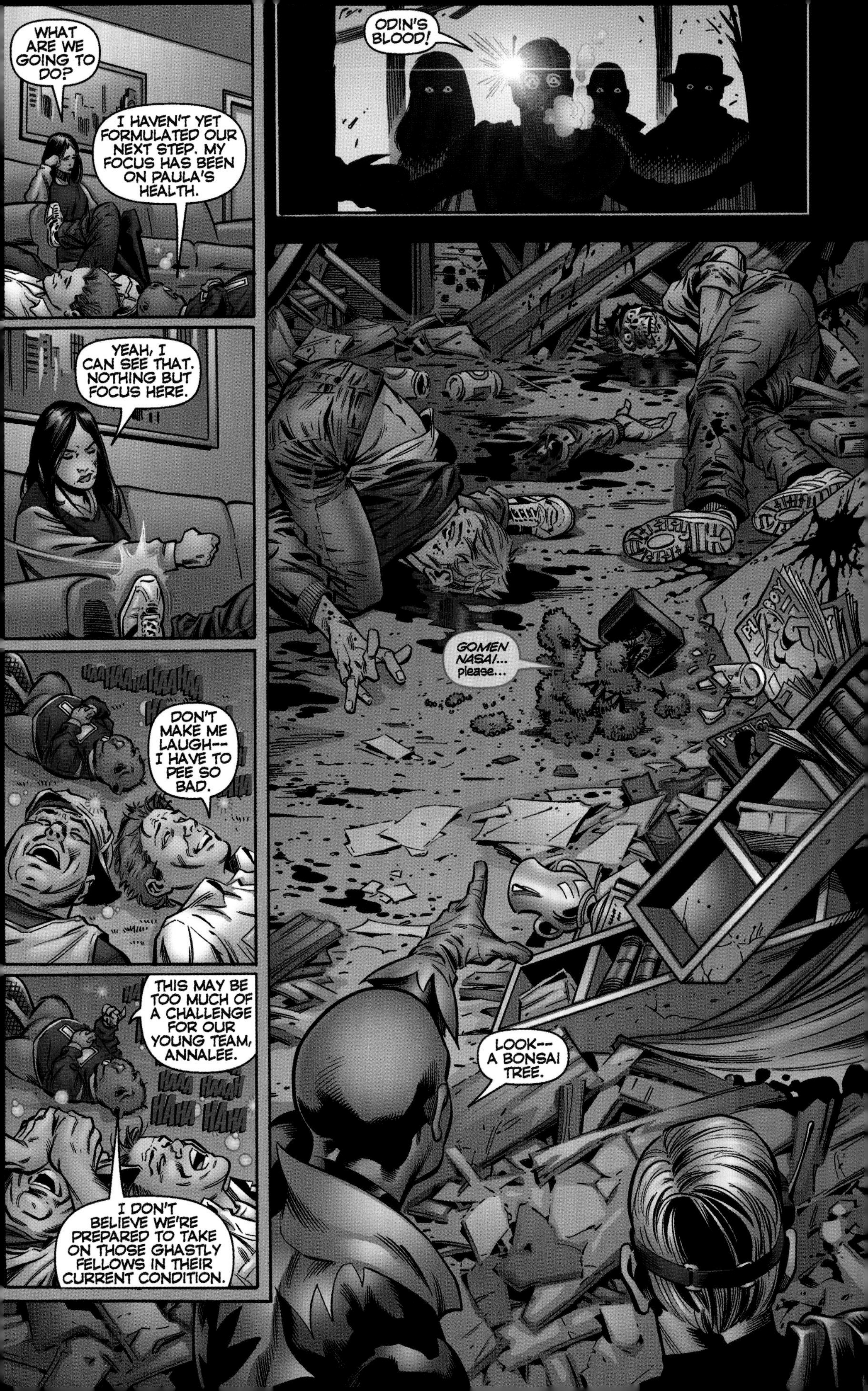
WHAT ARE WE GOING TO DO?
I HAVEN'T YET FORMULATED OUR NEXT STEP. MY FOCUS HAS BEEN ON PAULA'S HEALTH.
YEAH, I CAN SEE THAT. NOTHING BUT FOCUS HERE.
HAHAHAHAHAHAHA
DON'T MAKE ME LAUGH-- I HAVE TO PEE SO BAD.
THIS MAY BE TOO MUCH OF A CHALLENGE FOR OUR YOUNG TEAM, ANNALEE.
HAAHA HAAAH HAHA HAHA
I DON'T BELIEVE WE'RE PREPARED TO TAKE ON THOSE GHASTLY FELLOWS IN THEIR CURRENT CONDITION.
ODIN'S BLOOD!
GOMEN NASAI... please...
PLAYBOY
LOOK-- A BONSAI TREE.

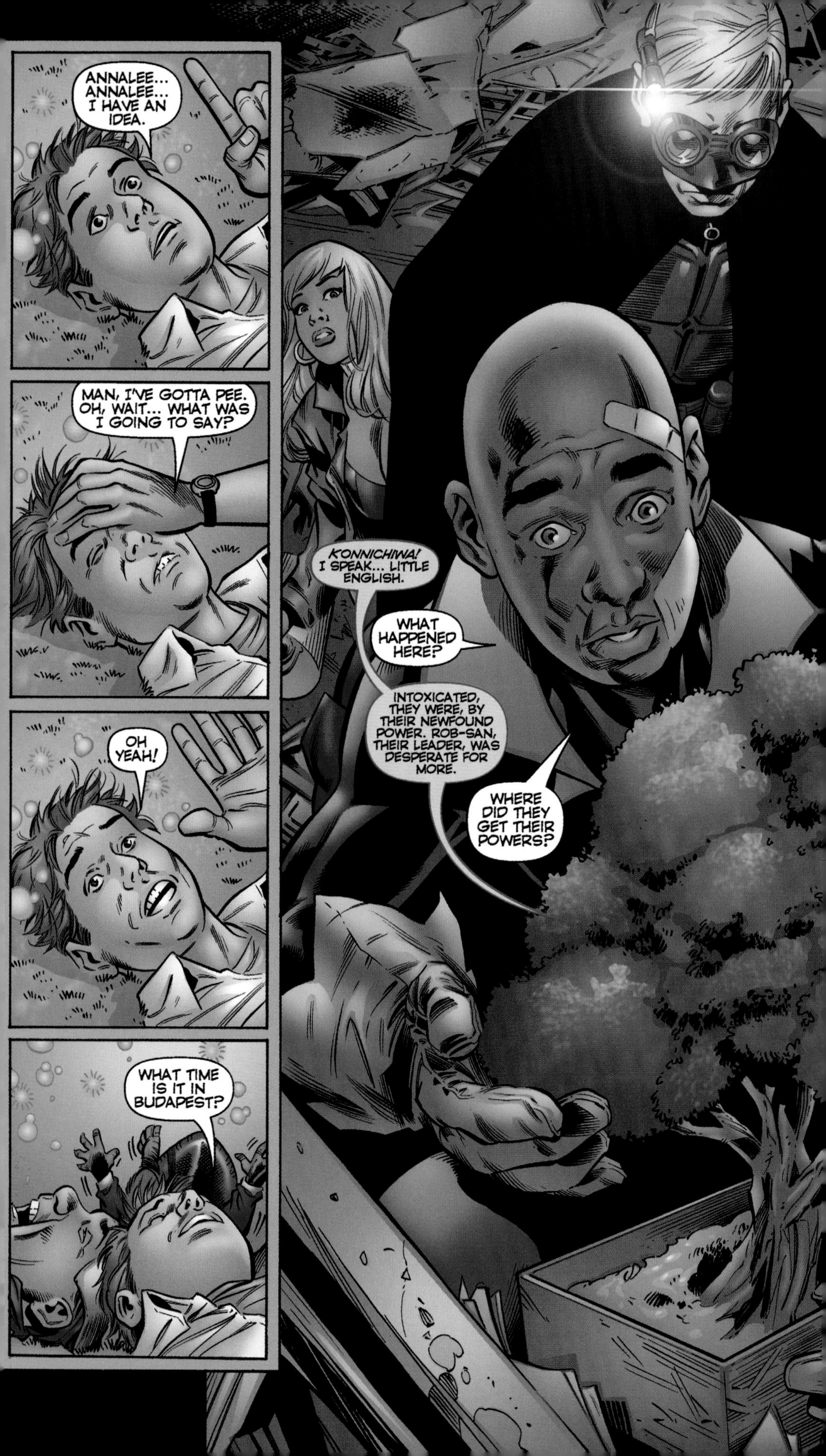
ANNALEE... ANNALEE... I HAVE AN IDEA.
MAN, I'VE GOTTA PEE. OH, WAIT... WHAT WAS I GOING TO SAY?
OH YEAH!
WHAT TIME IS IT IN BUDAPEST?
KONNICHIWA! I SPEAK... LITTLE ENGLISH.
WHAT HAPPENED HERE?
INTOXICATED, THEY WERE, BY THEIR NEWFOUND POWER. ROB-SAN, THEIR LEADER, WAS DESPERATE FOR MORE.
WHERE DID THEY GET THEIR POWERS?

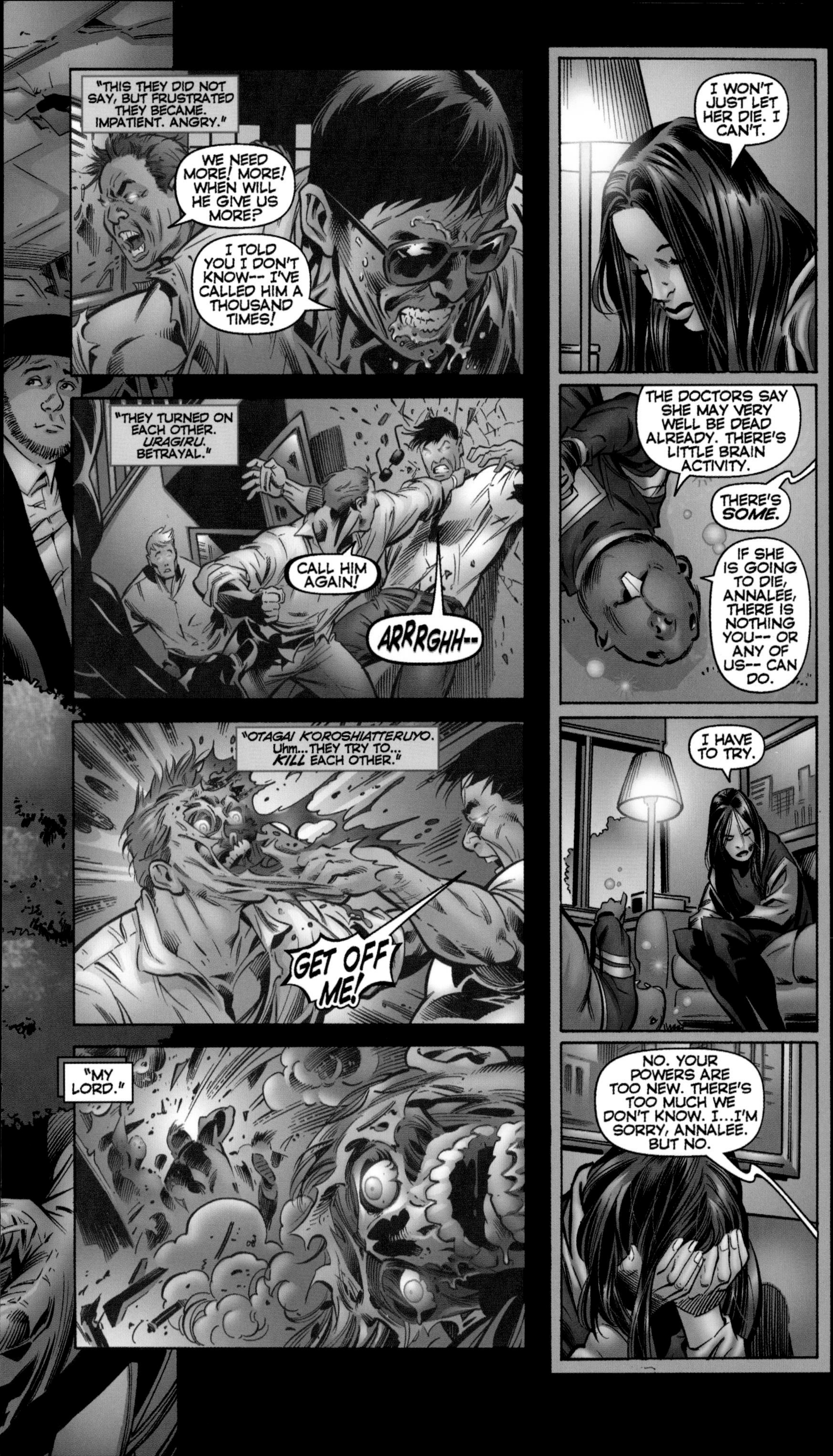
"THIS THEY DID NOT SAY, BUT FRUSTRATED THEY BECAME. IMPATIENT. ANGRY."
WE NEED MORE! MORE! WHEN WILL HE GIVE US MORE?
I TOLD YOU I DON'T KNOW-- I'VE CALLED HIM A THOUSAND TIMES!
"THEY TURNED ON EACH OTHER. URAGIRU. BETRAYAL."
CALL HIM AGAIN!
ARRRGHH--
"OTAGAI KOROSHIATTERUYO. Uhm... THEY TRY TO... KILL EACH OTHER."
GET OFF ME!
"MY LORD."
I WON'T JUST LET HER DIE. I CAN'T.
THE DOCTORS SAY SHE MAY VERY WELL BE DEAD ALREADY. THERE'S LITTLE BRAIN ACTIVITY.
THERE'S SOME.
IF SHE IS GOING TO DIE, ANNALEE, THERE IS NOTHING YOU-- OR ANY OF US-- CAN DO.
I HAVE TO TRY.
NO. YOUR POWERS ARE TOO NEW. THERE'S TOO MUCH WE DON'T KNOW. I...I'M SORRY, ANNALEE. BUT NO.

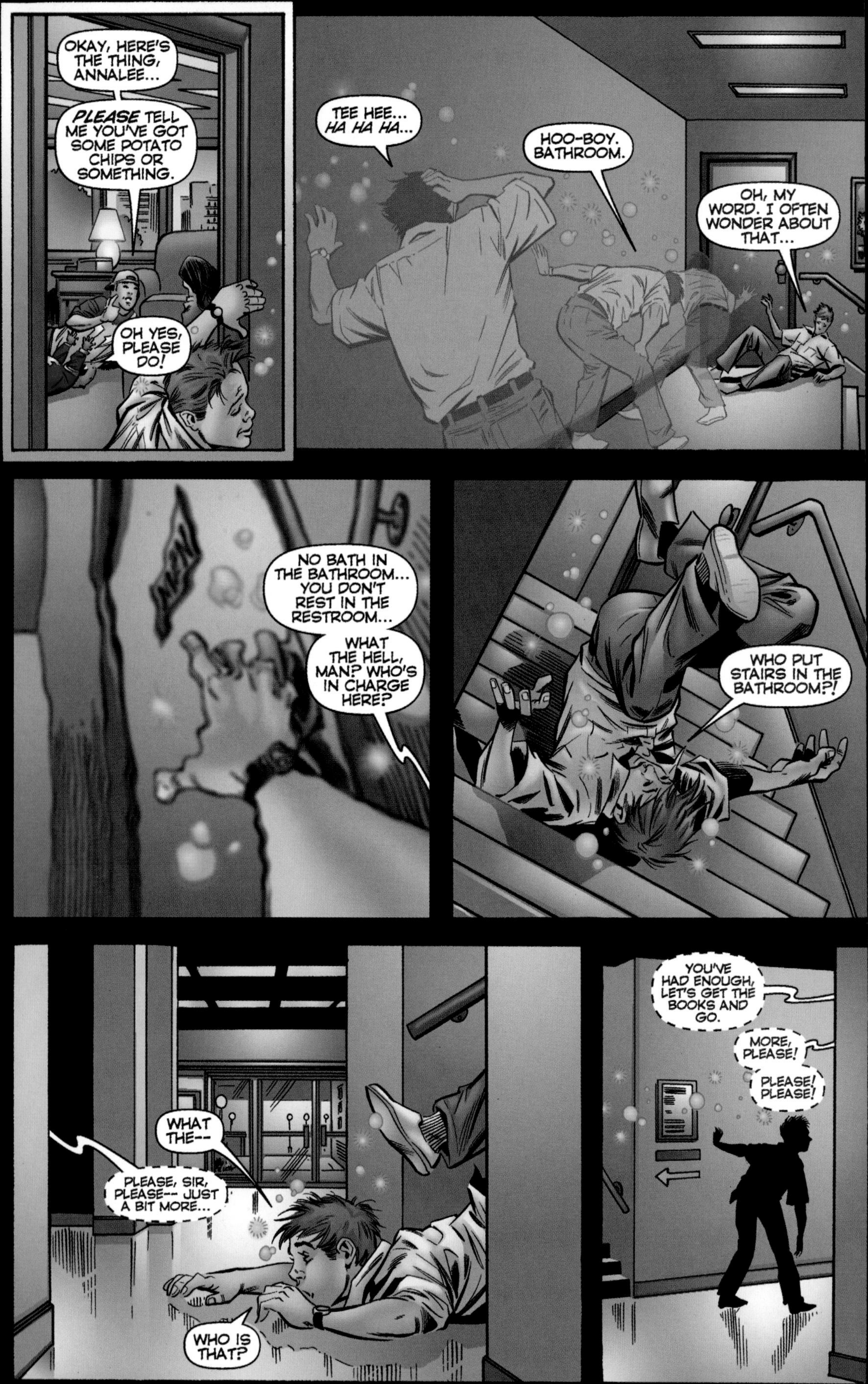
OKAY, HERE'S THE THING, ANNALEE...
PLEASE TELL ME YOU'VE GOT SOME POTATO CHIPS OR SOMETHING.
OH YES, PLEASE DO!
TEE HEE... HA HA HA...
HOO-BOY. BATHROOM.
OH, MY WORD. I OFTEN WONDER ABOUT THAT...
NO BATH IN THE BATHROOM... YOU DON'T REST IN THE RESTROOM...
WHAT THE HELL, MAN? WHO'S IN CHARGE HERE?
WHO PUT STAIRS IN THE BATHROOM?!
WHAT THE--
PLEASE, SIR, PLEASE-- JUST A BIT MORE...
WHO IS THAT?
YOU'VE HAD ENOUGH, LET'S GET THE BOOKS AND GO.
MORE, PLEASE!
PLEASE! PLEASE!

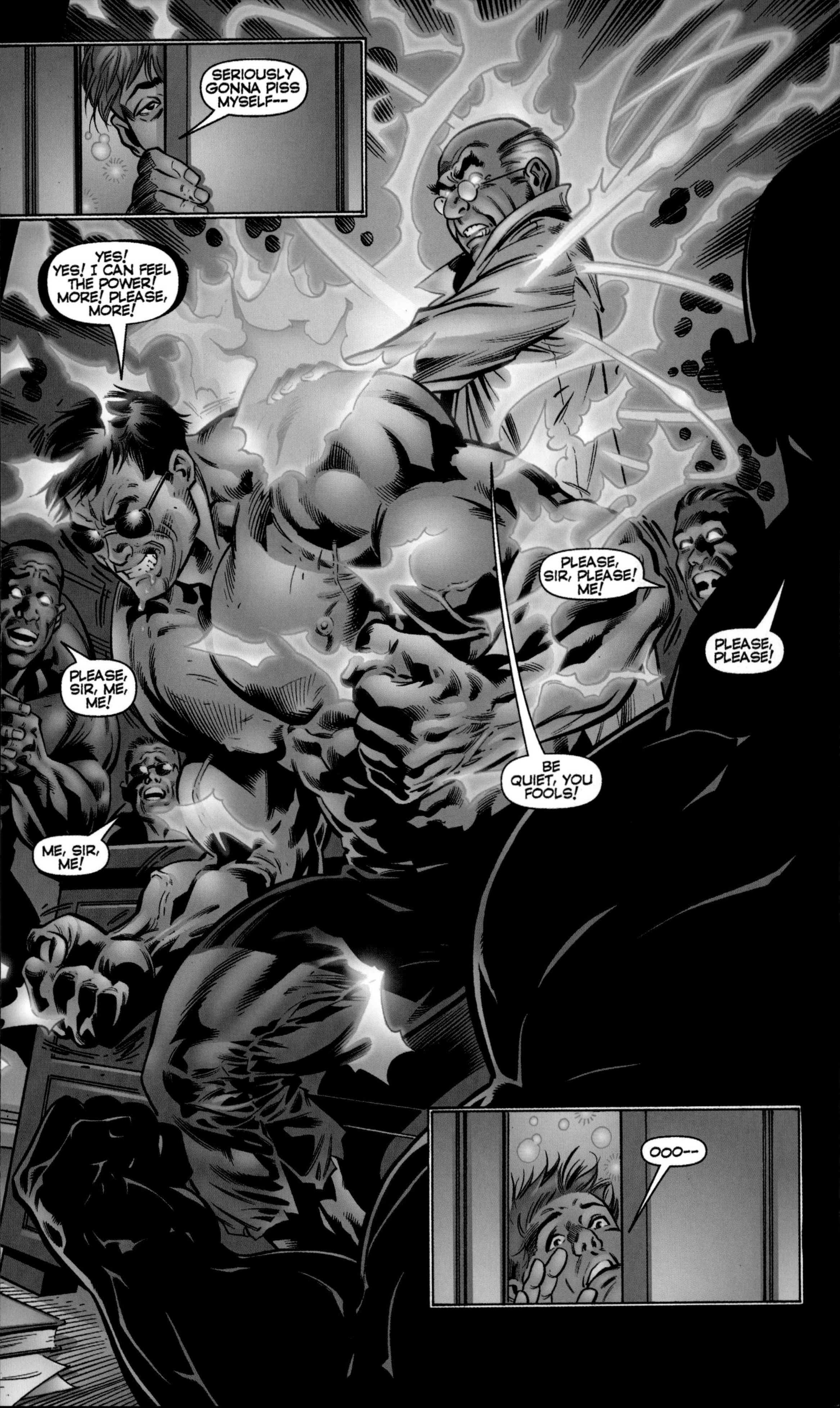
SERIOUSLY GONNA PISS MYSELF--
YES! YES! I CAN FEEL THE POWER! MORE! PLEASE, MORE!
PLEASE, SIR, PLEASE! ME!
PLEASE, PLEASE!
PLEASE, SIR, ME, ME!
BE QUIET, YOU FOOLS!
ME, SIR, ME!
OOO--

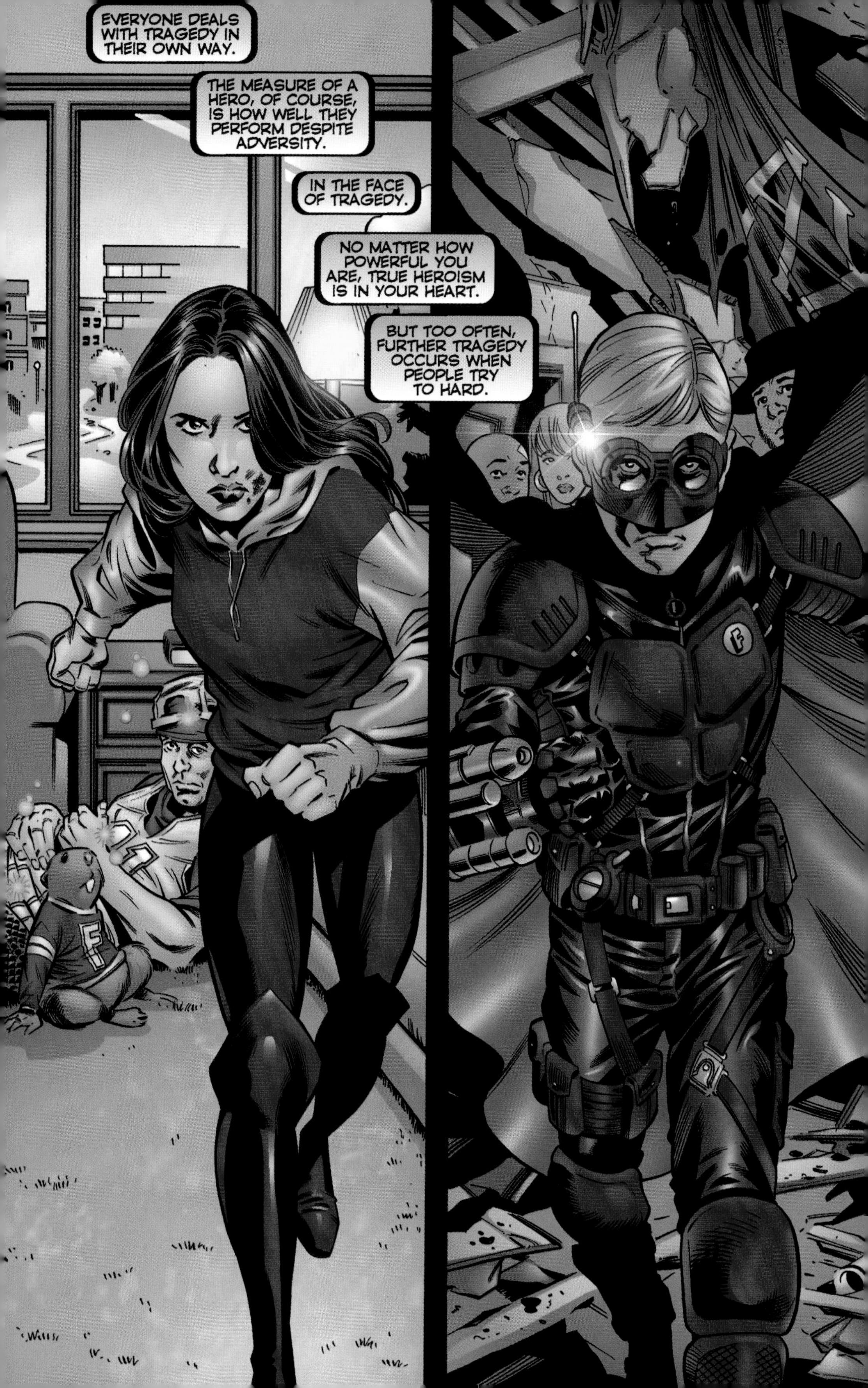
EVERYONE DEALS WITH TRAGEDY IN THEIR OWN WAY.
THE MEASURE OF A HERO, OF COURSE, IS HOW WELL THEY PERFORM DESPITE ADVERSITY.
IN THE FACE OF TRAGEDY.
NO MATTER HOW POWERFUL YOU ARE, TRUE HEROISM IS IN YOUR HEART.
BUT TOO OFTEN, FURTHER TRAGEDY OCCURS WHEN PEOPLE TRY TO HARD.

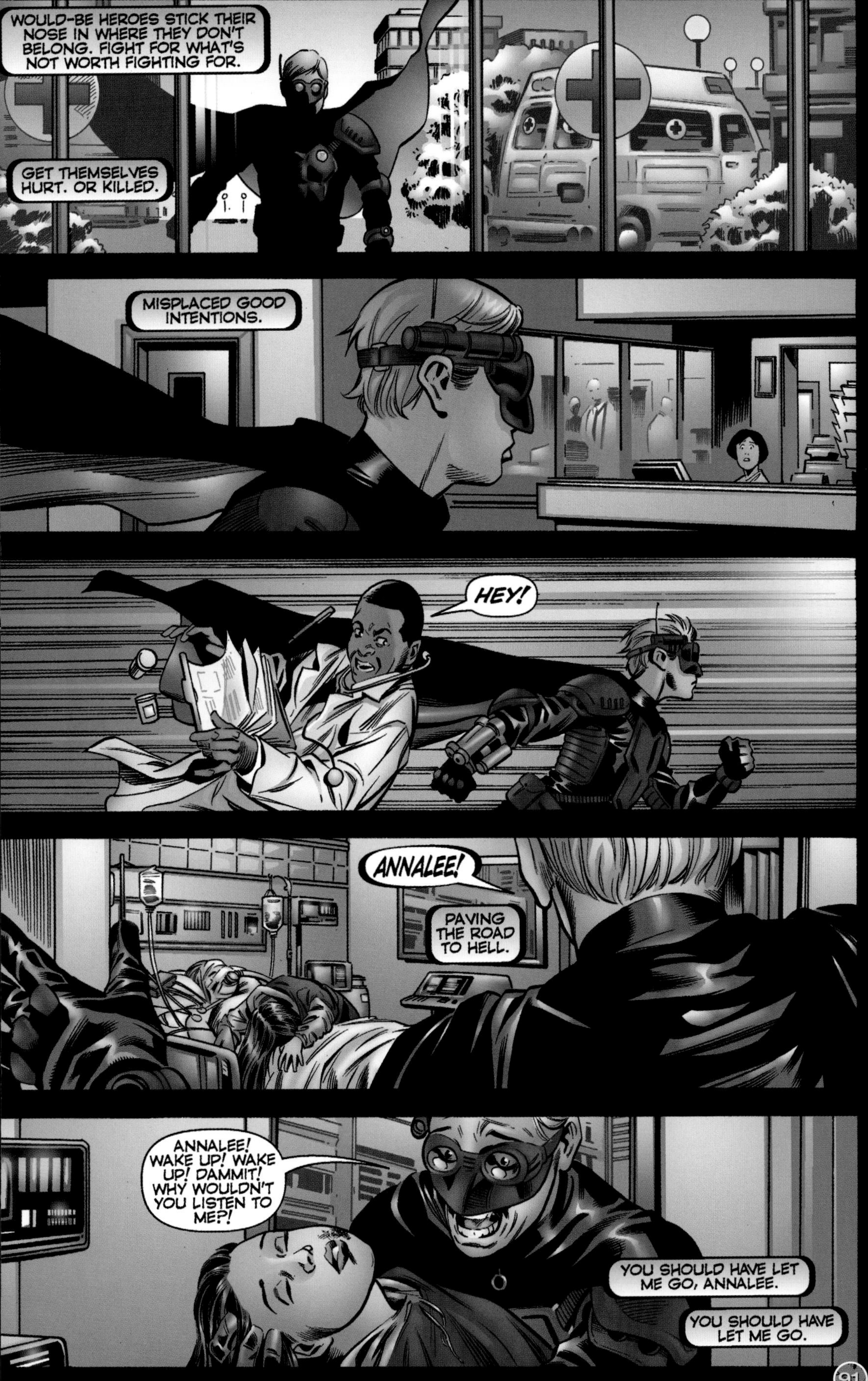
WOULD-BE HEROES STICK THEIR NOSE IN WHERE THEY DON'T BELONG. FIGHT FOR WHAT'S NOT WORTH FIGHTING FOR.
GET THEMSELVES HURT. OR KILLED.
MISPLACED GOOD INTENTIONS.
HEY!
ANNALEE!
PAVING THE ROAD TO HELL.
ANNALEE! WAKE UP! WAKE UP! DAMMIT! WHY WOULDN'T YOU LISTEN TO ME?!
YOU SHOULD HAVE LET ME GO, ANNALEE.
YOU SHOULD HAVE LET ME GO.

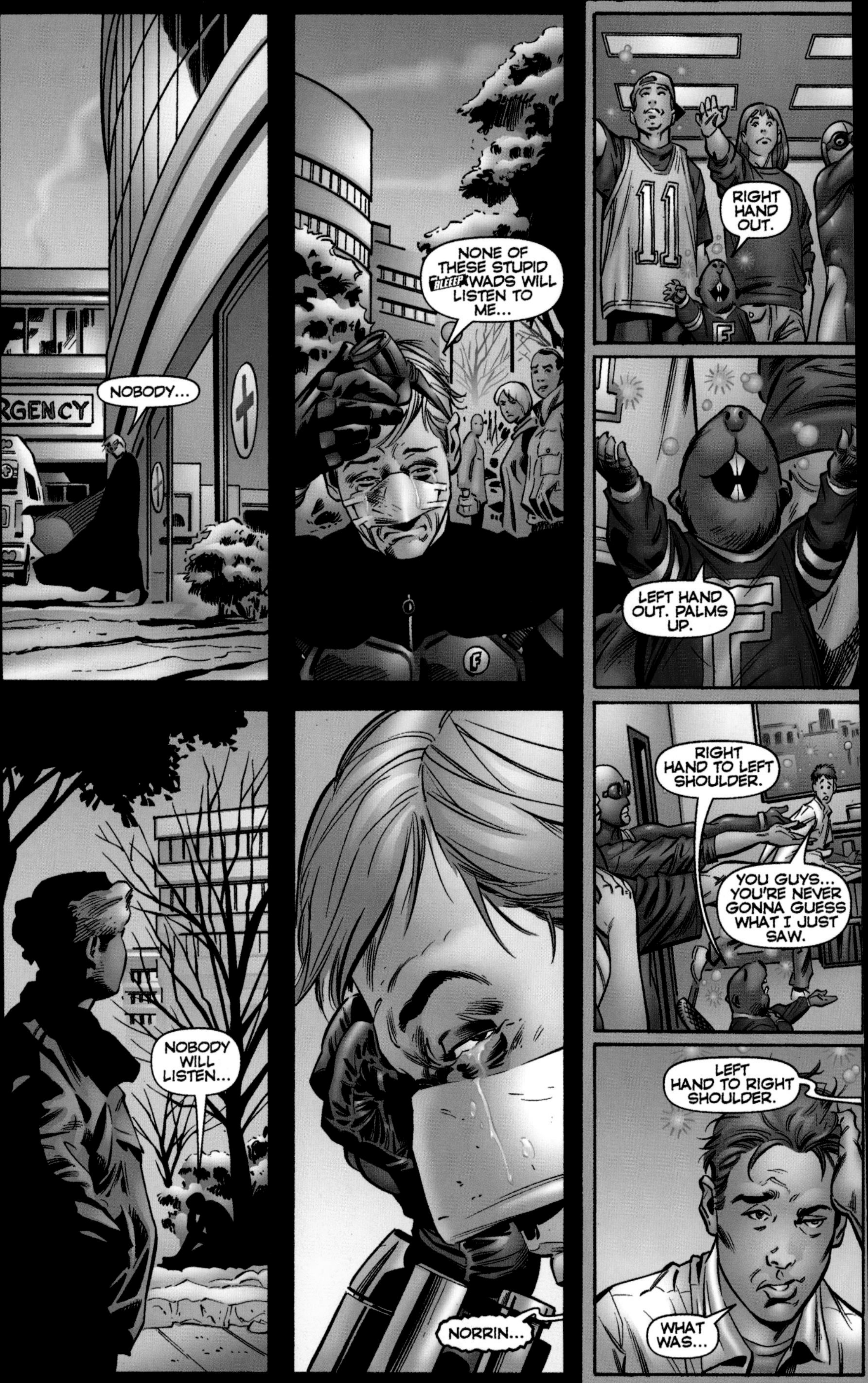
NOBODY...
NONE OF THESE STUPID F BLEEEP WADS WILL LISTEN TO ME...
RIGHT HAND OUT.
LEFT HAND OUT. PALMS UP.
NOBODY WILL LISTEN...
NORRIN...
RIGHT HAND TO LEFT SHOULDER.
YOU GUYS... YOU'RE NEVER GONNA GUESS WHAT I JUST SAW.
LEFT HAND TO RIGHT SHOULDER.
WHAT WAS...

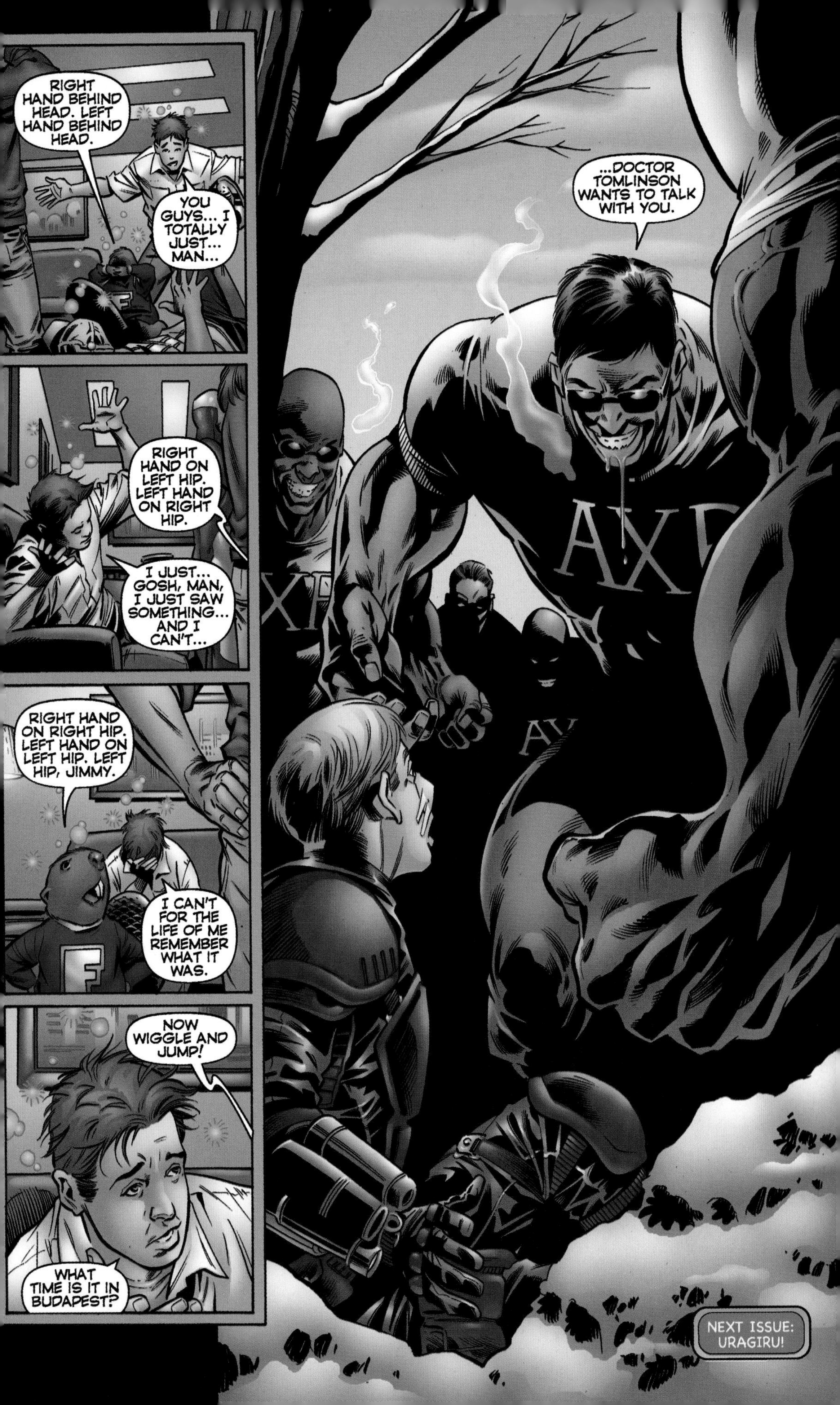
RIGHT HAND BEHIND HEAD. LEFT HAND BEHIND HEAD.
YOU GUYS... I TOTALLY JUST... MAN...
RIGHT HAND ON LEFT HIP. LEFT HAND ON RIGHT HIP.
I JUST... GOSH, MAN, I JUST SAW SOMETHING... AND I CAN'T...
RIGHT HAND ON RIGHT HIP. LEFT HAND ON LEFT HIP. LEFT HIP, JIMMY.
I CAN'T FOR THE LIFE OF ME REMEMBER WHAT IT WAS.
NOW WIGGLE AND JUMP!
WHAT TIME IS IT IN BUDAPEST?
...DOCTOR TOMLINSON WANTS TO TALK WITH YOU.
NEXT ISSUE: URAGIRU!

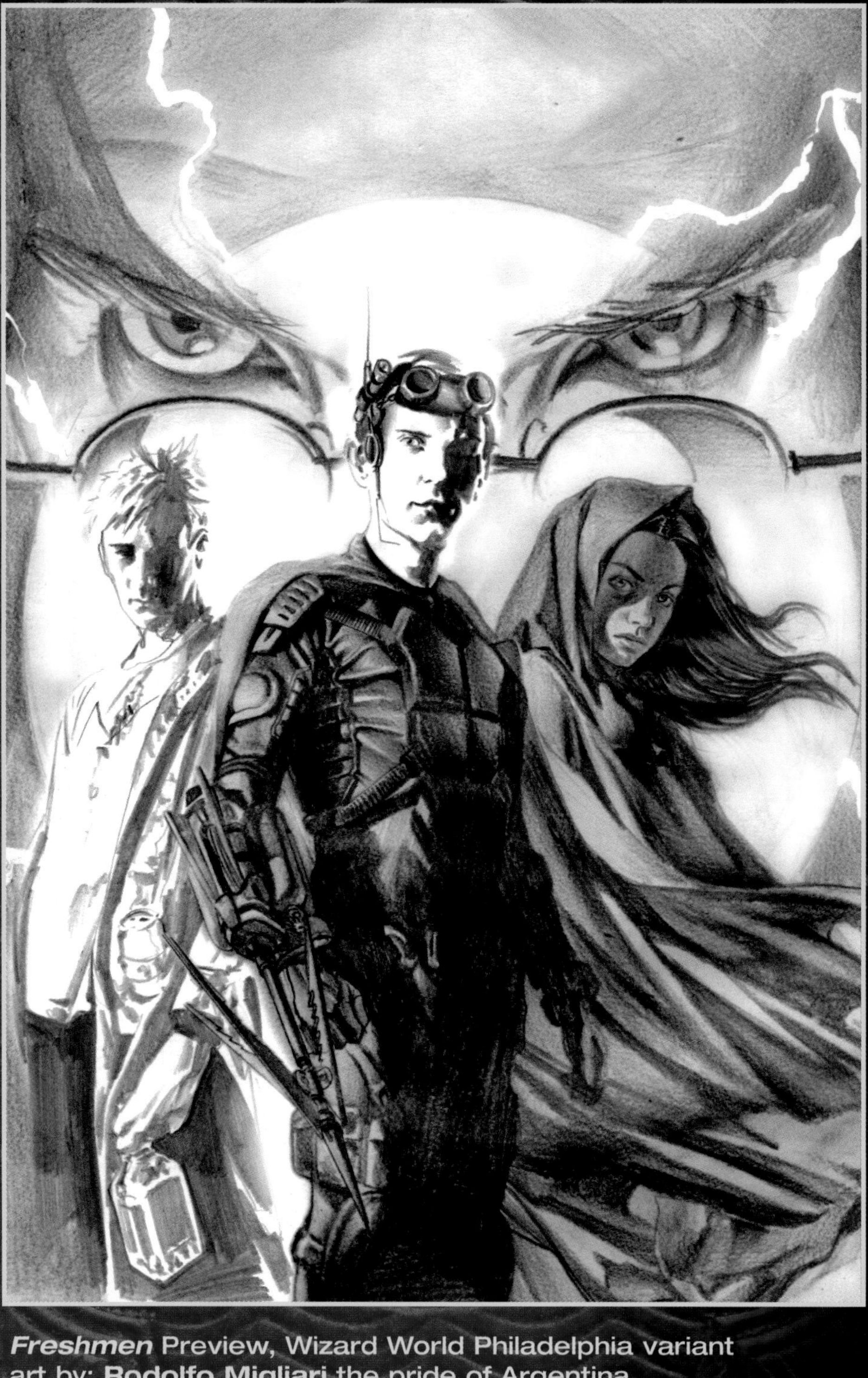

Freshmen Preview, Wizard World Philadelphia variant
art by: **Rodolfo Migliari** the pride of Argentina

WANNABE-- KENNETH "NORRIN" WEISMEYER, THE WOULD-BE TEAM LEADER--

THE PUPPETEER-- ANNALEE ROGERS--

THE GREEN THUMB-- CHARLES LEVY--

QUAKER-- LIAM ADAMS--

THE INTOXICATOR-- ELWOOD JOHNS--

--AND RESIDENT SUPERHERO GEEK, WHO WENT FOR PIZZA DURING THE PIVOTAL MOMENT AND HAS NO POWERS!

--WHO CAN JUMP INTO PEOPLE'S MINDS AND VIEW THEIR MEMORIES OR EVEN CONTROL THEM!

-- A DEDICATED VEGETARIAN WHO CAN NOW COMMUNICATE WITH PLANTS, LEAVING HIM NOTHING TO EAT!

--THE AMISH BOY WHO CAN CAUSE EARTHQUAKES BY SHUFFLING HIS BELLY!

--FORMER MATH GENIUS WHOSE DRUNKEN BURPS INTOXICATE ANYONE WHO SMELLS THEM!

THE DRAMA TWINS-- RENEE AND BRADY--

THE SQUIRREL-- JACQUES LALLEAUX--

THE SEDUCTRESS-- PAULA POPHOUSE--

THE BEAVER-- THE SCHOOL MASCOT--

--BICKERING EXES WHO MUST BE IN CONTACT TO USE THEIR TELEKINESIS!

--THE FRENCH EXCHANGE STUDENT WHO COMPULSIVELY HOARDS NUTS!

THE LOVELORN TEEN WHO CAN MAKE ANYONE FALL IN LOVE WITH HER!

--IMBUED WITH QUANTUM-BUSTING INTELLIGENCE, BUT CAN'T CONCENTRATE ON ANYTHING BUT BUILDING DAMS!

DR. THEODORE TOMLINSON-- THE SCIENCE PROFESSOR WHO CREATED THE AX-CELL-ERATOR!

I FOUND OUT IT'S, LIKE, SUPER, TOO. UPER POWERED. UNBREAKABLE. LIKE SUPERM--

HOW DID YOU...? YOU KNOW...

I RAN IT OVER WITH MY CAR. THAT WAS A TRYING MOMENT.

PREVIOUSLY IN FRESHMEN:

AFTER DISCOVERING THEIR BIZARRE AND AMAZING POWERS, OUR YOUNG HEROES WERE EMPLOYED BY THE CREATOR OF THE AX-CELL-ERATOR, DR. TOMLINSON, TO HELP REPAIR THE MACHINE THAT COULD CURE ALL DISEASES AND EVEN PREVENT AGING.

WANNABE, SUPERHERO OBSESSED BUT POWERLESS, TRIED TO TAKE LEADERSHIP, BUT HE WAS CONSTANTLY DISOBEYED BY HIS REBELLIOUS TEAMMATES.

THE SEDUCTRESS WAS CRITICALLY INJURED IN THE KIDS' FIRST BATTLE WITH THE MYSTERIOUSLY SUPER POWERED FRAT GUYS. AGAINST THE WISHES OF THE BEAVER AND WANNABE, THE PUPPETEER HAS JUMPED INTO HER COMATOSE MIND.

DISTRESSED THAT HIS TEAM DOES NOT RESPECT HIM AND UPSET THAT ANNALEE, HIS UNREQUITED LOVE, DISOBEYED HIM, WANNABE WAS CAPTURED BY THE FRAT GUYS FIVE DAYS AGO...

SUSIE, FOR THE LAST TIME! I CAN'T PROMISE YOU THAT I'LL NEVER WATER ANOTHER PLANT! THAT'S RIDICULOUS! IT'S NOT CHEATING!

How can you say that! You're so *insensitive*! Oh, God, three years! I've wasted three of the best years of my life on you!

WOW, SO THE SUPER POWERS REALLY ADD SOMETHING TO IT, HUH?

WORD, YO.

SO... OKAY. FOLLOW ME HERE.

ASK YOURSELF... WHAT WOULD ALIENS THINK ABOUT THE GAME OF GOLF? YOU WALK UP TO A BALL... HIT IT AS FAR AWAY FROM YOURSELF AS YOU CAN...

AND THEN YOU WALK UP TO IT AGAIN.

WHAT THE *BLEEEP*, MAN?

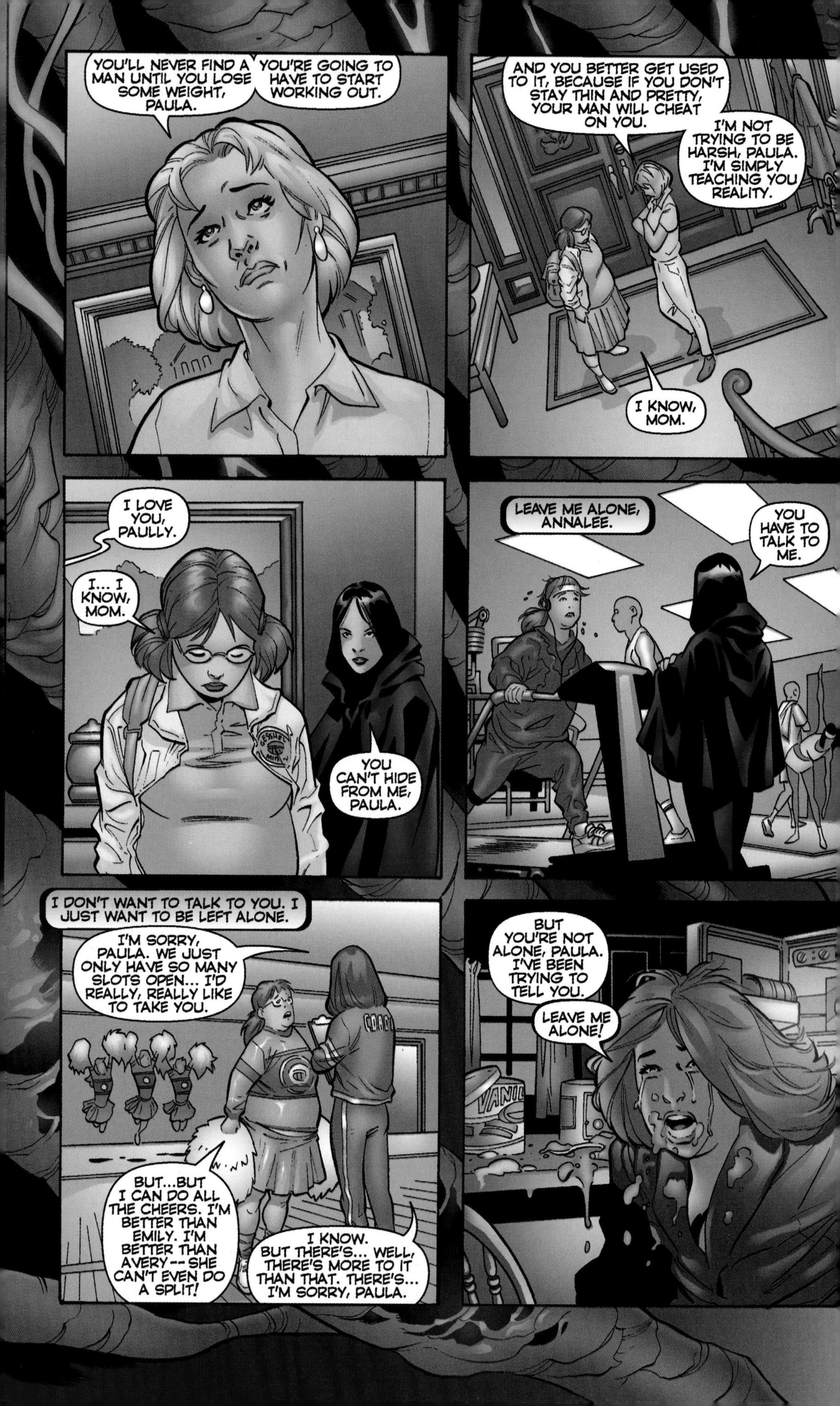
YOU'LL NEVER FIND A MAN UNTIL YOU LOSE SOME WEIGHT, PAULA.
YOU'RE GOING TO HAVE TO START WORKING OUT.
AND YOU BETTER GET USED TO IT, BECAUSE IF YOU DON'T STAY THIN AND PRETTY, YOUR MAN WILL CHEAT ON YOU.
I'M NOT TRYING TO BE HARSH, PAULA. I'M SIMPLY TEACHING YOU REALITY.
I KNOW, MOM.
I LOVE YOU, PAULLY.
I... I KNOW, MOM.
YOU CAN'T HIDE FROM ME, PAULA.
LEAVE ME ALONE, ANNALEE.
YOU HAVE TO TALK TO ME.
I DON'T WANT TO TALK TO YOU. I JUST WANT TO BE LEFT ALONE.
I'M SORRY, PAULA. WE JUST ONLY HAVE SO MANY SLOTS OPEN... I'D REALLY, REALLY LIKE TO TAKE YOU.
BUT...BUT I CAN DO ALL THE CHEERS. I'M BETTER THAN EMILY. I'M BETTER THAN AVERY-- SHE CAN'T EVEN DO A SPLIT!
I KNOW. BUT THERE'S... WELL, THERE'S MORE TO IT THAN THAT. THERE'S... I'M SORRY, PAULA.
BUT YOU'RE NOT ALONE, PAULA. I'VE BEEN TRYING TO TELL YOU.
LEAVE ME ALONE!

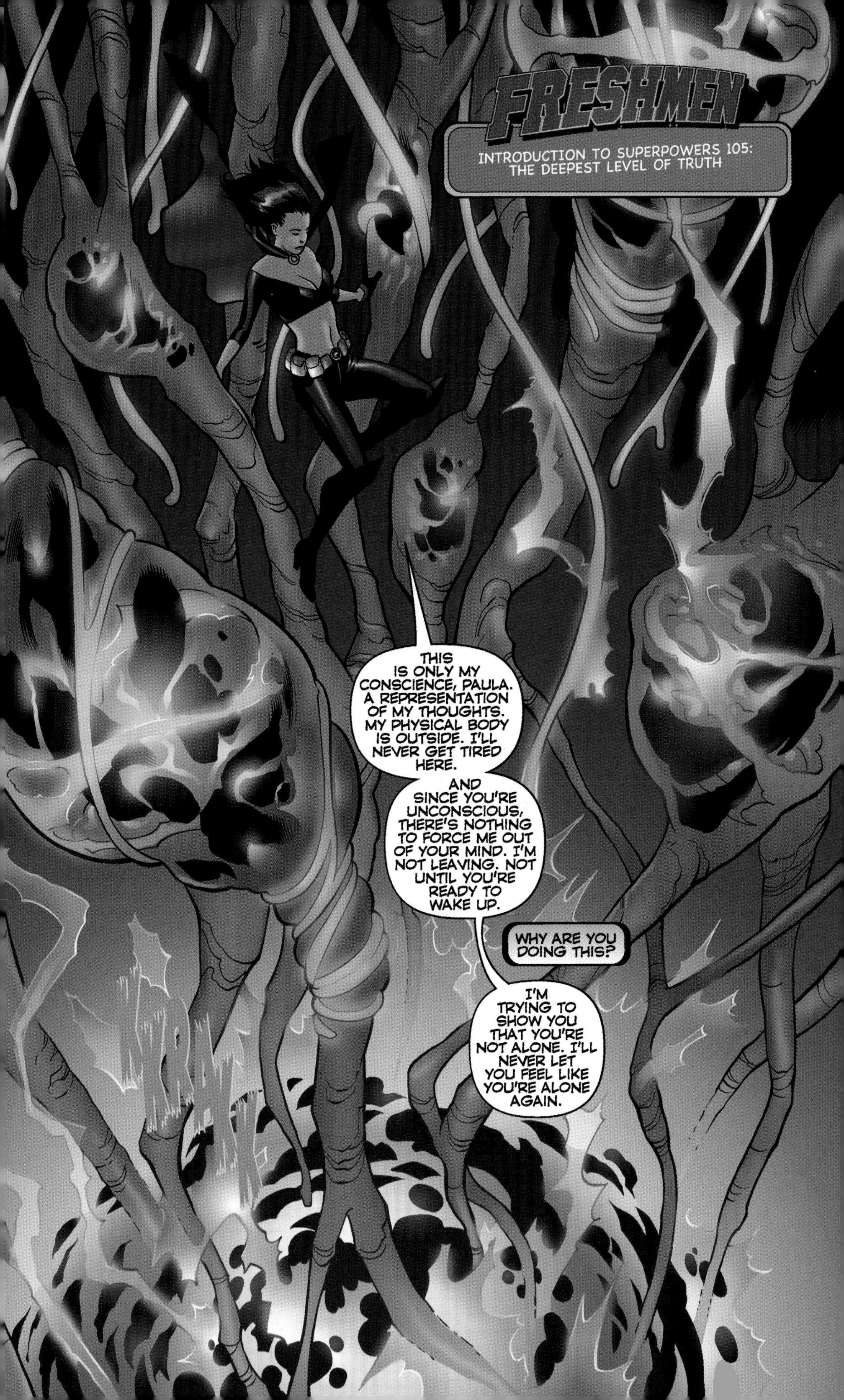
FRESHMEN
INTRODUCTION TO SUPERPOWERS 105: THE DEEPEST LEVEL OF TRUTH
THIS IS ONLY MY CONSCIENCE, PAULA. A REPRESENTATION OF MY THOUGHTS. MY PHYSICAL BODY IS OUTSIDE. I'LL NEVER GET TIRED HERE.
AND SINCE YOU'RE UNCONSCIOUS, THERE'S NOTHING TO FORCE ME OUT OF YOUR MIND. I'M NOT LEAVING. NOT UNTIL YOU'RE READY TO WAKE UP.
WHY ARE YOU DOING THIS?
I'M TRYING TO SHOW YOU THAT YOU'RE NOT ALONE. I'LL NEVER LET YOU FEEL LIKE YOU'RE ALONE AGAIN.
KRAK

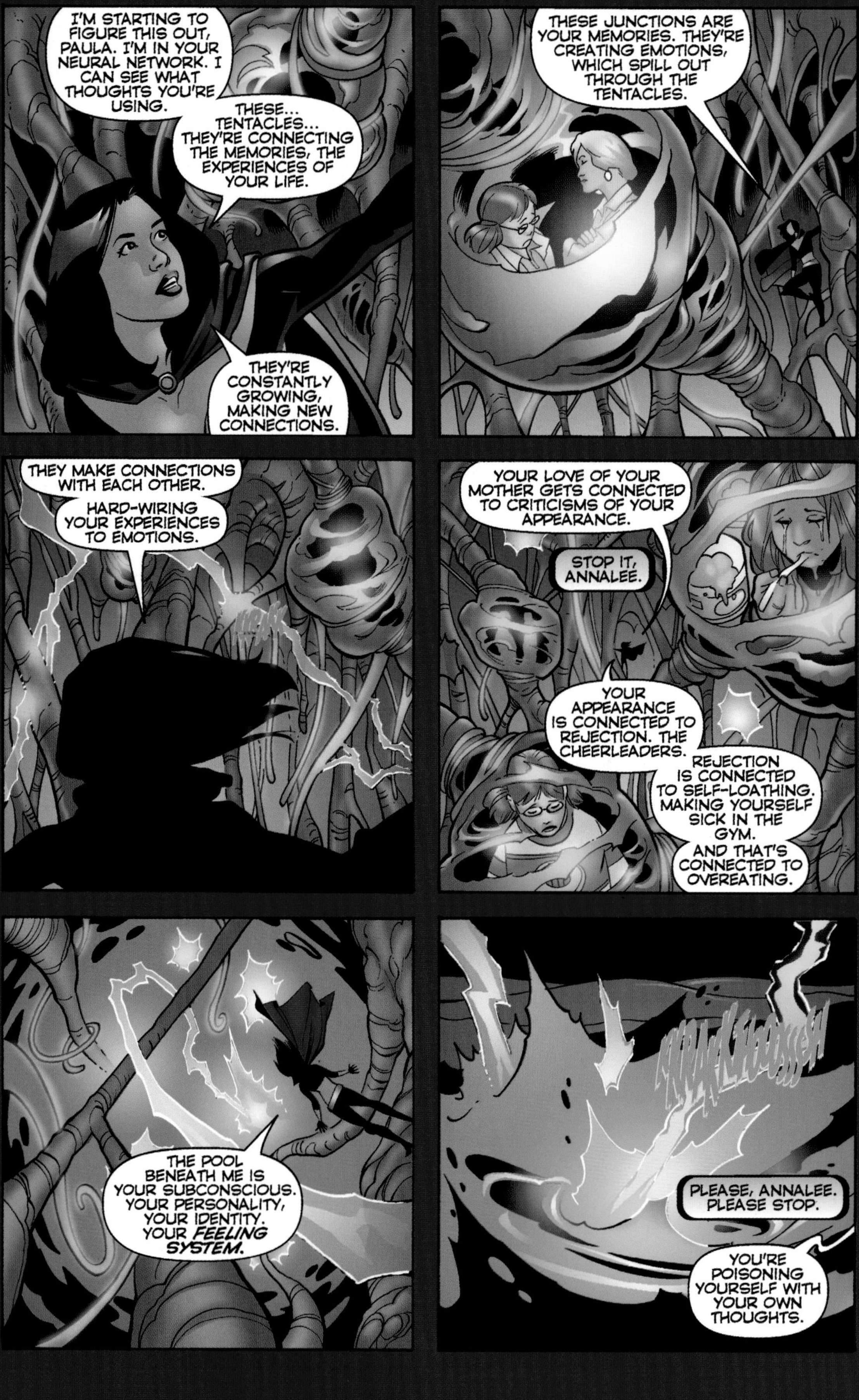
I'M STARTING TO FIGURE THIS OUT, PAULA. I'M IN YOUR NEURAL NETWORK. I CAN SEE WHAT THOUGHTS YOU'RE USING.
THESE... TENTACLES... THEY'RE CONNECTING THE MEMORIES, THE EXPERIENCES OF YOUR LIFE.
THEY'RE CONSTANTLY GROWING, MAKING NEW CONNECTIONS.
THESE JUNCTIONS ARE YOUR MEMORIES. THEY'RE CREATING EMOTIONS, WHICH SPILL OUT THROUGH THE TENTACLES.
THEY MAKE CONNECTIONS WITH EACH OTHER.
HARD-WIRING YOUR EXPERIENCES TO EMOTIONS.
YOUR LOVE OF YOUR MOTHER GETS CONNECTED TO CRITICISMS OF YOUR APPEARANCE.
STOP IT, ANNALEE.
YOUR APPEARANCE IS CONNECTED TO REJECTION. THE CHEERLEADERS.
REJECTION IS CONNECTED TO SELF-LOATHING. MAKING YOURSELF SICK IN THE GYM.
AND THAT'S CONNECTED TO OVEREATING.
THE POOL BENEATH ME IS YOUR SUBCONSCIOUS. YOUR PERSONALITY, YOUR IDENTITY. YOUR *FEELING SYSTEM*.
PLEASE, ANNALEE. PLEASE STOP.
YOU'RE POISONING YOURSELF WITH YOUR OWN THOUGHTS.

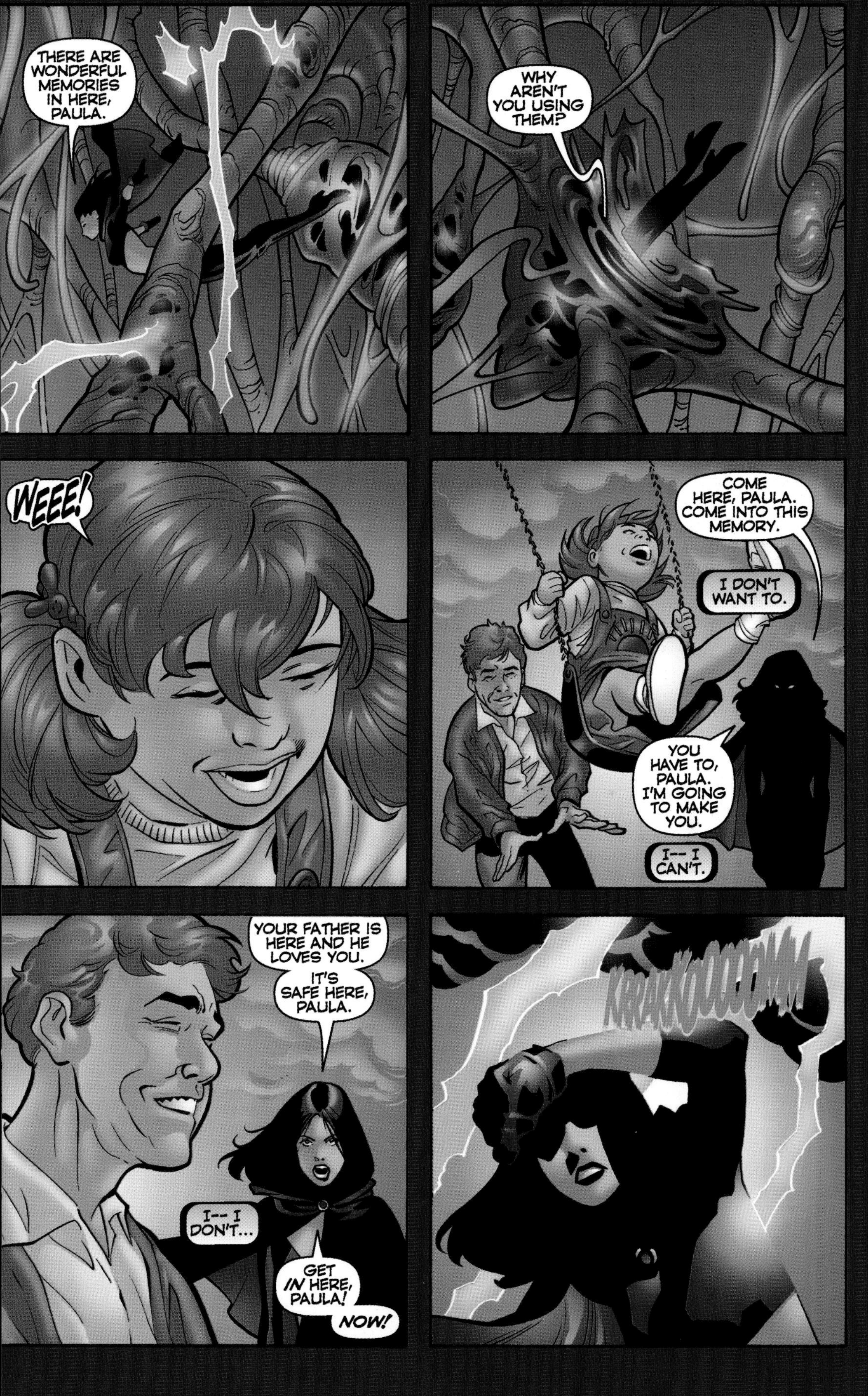
THERE ARE WONDERFUL MEMORIES IN HERE, PAULA.
WHY AREN'T YOU USING THEM?
WEEE!
COME HERE, PAULA. COME INTO THIS MEMORY.
I DON'T WANT TO.
YOU HAVE TO, PAULA. I'M GOING TO MAKE YOU.
I-- I CAN'T.
YOUR FATHER IS HERE AND HE LOVES YOU.
IT'S SAFE HERE, PAULA.
I-- I DON'T...
GET IN HERE, PAULA!
NOW!
KRRAKKOOOOOMM

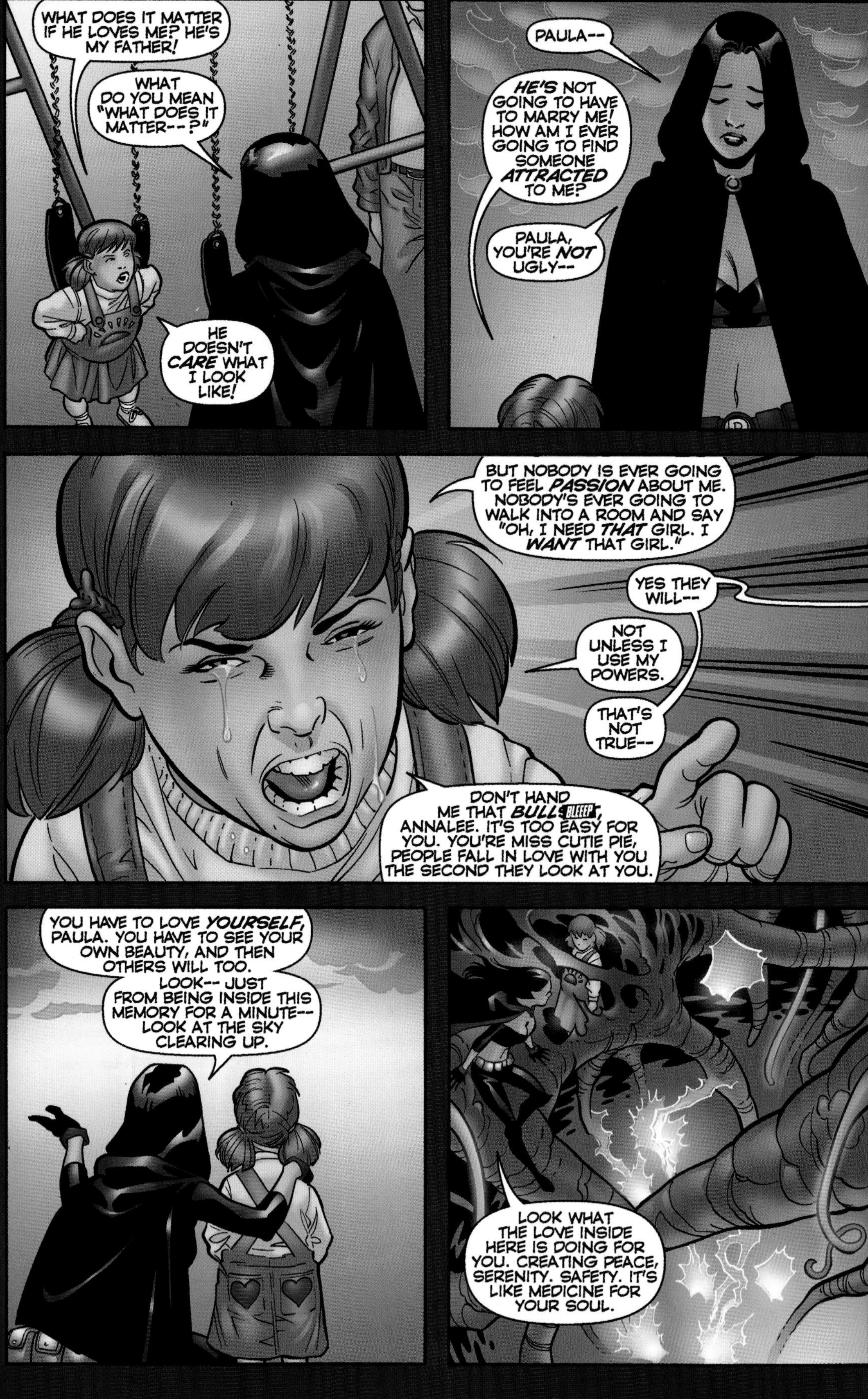
WHAT DOES IT MATTER IF HE LOVES ME? HE'S MY FATHER!
WHAT DO YOU MEAN "WHAT DOES IT MATTER--?"
HE DOESN'T CARE WHAT I LOOK LIKE!
PAULA--
HE'S NOT GOING TO HAVE TO MARRY ME! HOW AM I EVER GOING TO FIND SOMEONE ATTRACTED TO ME?
PAULA, YOU'RE NOT UGLY--
BUT NOBODY IS EVER GOING TO FEEL PASSION ABOUT ME. NOBODY'S EVER GOING TO WALK INTO A ROOM AND SAY "OH, I NEED THAT GIRL. I WANT THAT GIRL."
YES THEY WILL--
NOT UNLESS I USE MY POWERS.
THAT'S NOT TRUE--
DON'T HAND ME THAT BULL BLEEP, ANNALEE. IT'S TOO EASY FOR YOU. YOU'RE MISS CUTIE PIE, PEOPLE FALL IN LOVE WITH YOU THE SECOND THEY LOOK AT YOU.
YOU HAVE TO LOVE YOURSELF, PAULA. YOU HAVE TO SEE YOUR OWN BEAUTY, AND THEN OTHERS WILL TOO.
LOOK-- JUST FROM BEING INSIDE THIS MEMORY FOR A MINUTE-- LOOK AT THE SKY CLEARING UP.
LOOK WHAT THE LOVE INSIDE HERE IS DOING FOR YOU. CREATING PEACE, SERENITY. SAFETY. IT'S LIKE MEDICINE FOR YOUR SOUL.

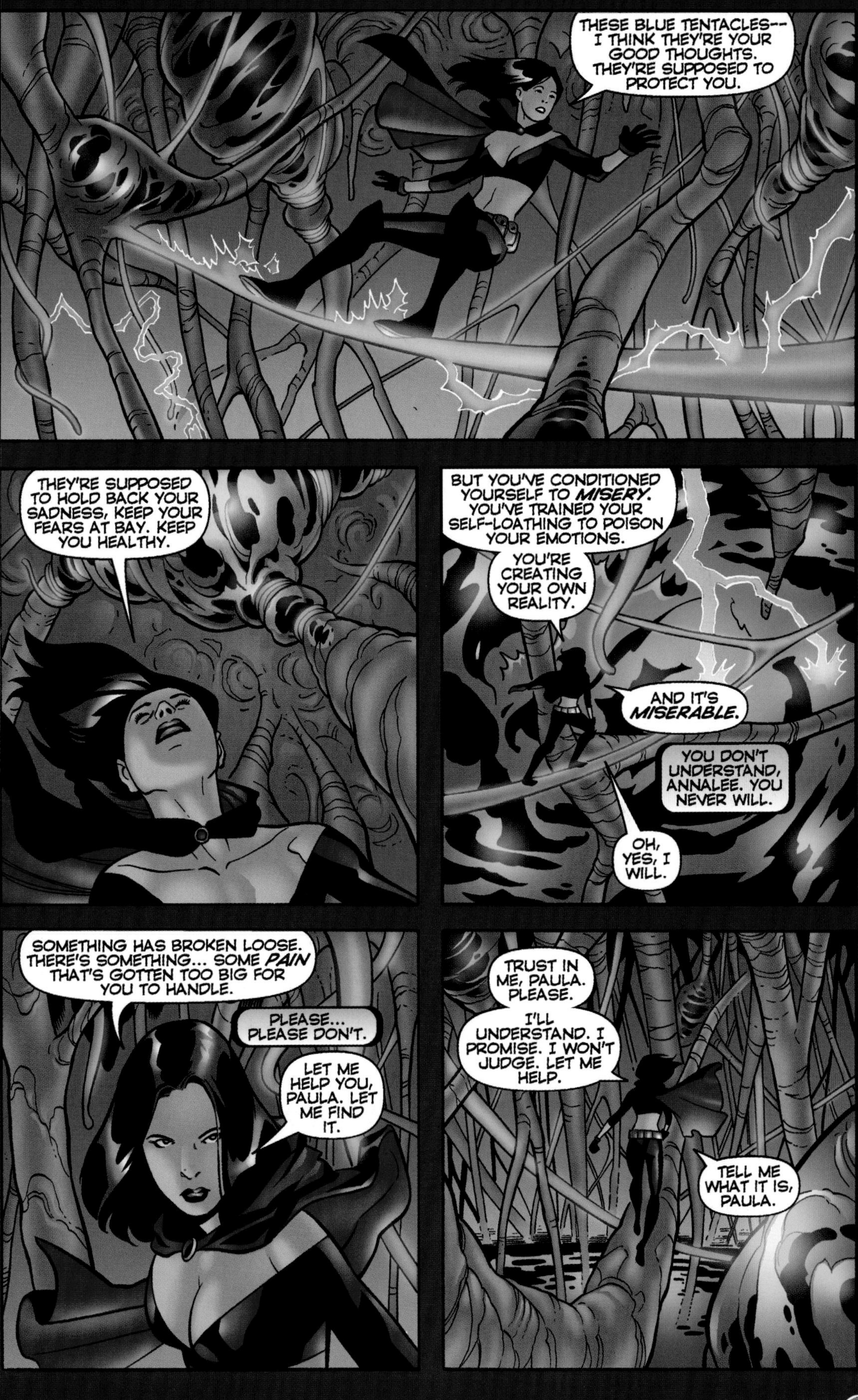
THESE BLUE TENTACLES-- I THINK THEY'RE YOUR GOOD THOUGHTS. THEY'RE SUPPOSED TO PROTECT YOU.
THEY'RE SUPPOSED TO HOLD BACK YOUR SADNESS, KEEP YOUR FEARS AT BAY. KEEP YOU HEALTHY.
BUT YOU'VE CONDITIONED YOURSELF TO MISERY. YOU'VE TRAINED YOUR SELF-LOATHING TO POISON YOUR EMOTIONS.
YOU'RE CREATING YOUR OWN REALITY.
AND IT'S MISERABLE.
YOU DON'T UNDERSTAND, ANNALEE. YOU NEVER WILL.
OH, YES, I WILL.
SOMETHING HAS BROKEN LOOSE. THERE'S SOMETHING... SOME PAIN THAT'S GOTTEN TOO BIG FOR YOU TO HANDLE.
PLEASE... PLEASE DON'T.
LET ME HELP YOU, PAULA. LET ME FIND IT.
TRUST IN ME, PAULA. PLEASE.
I'LL UNDERSTAND. I PROMISE. I WON'T JUDGE. LET ME HELP.
TELL ME WHAT IT IS, PAULA.

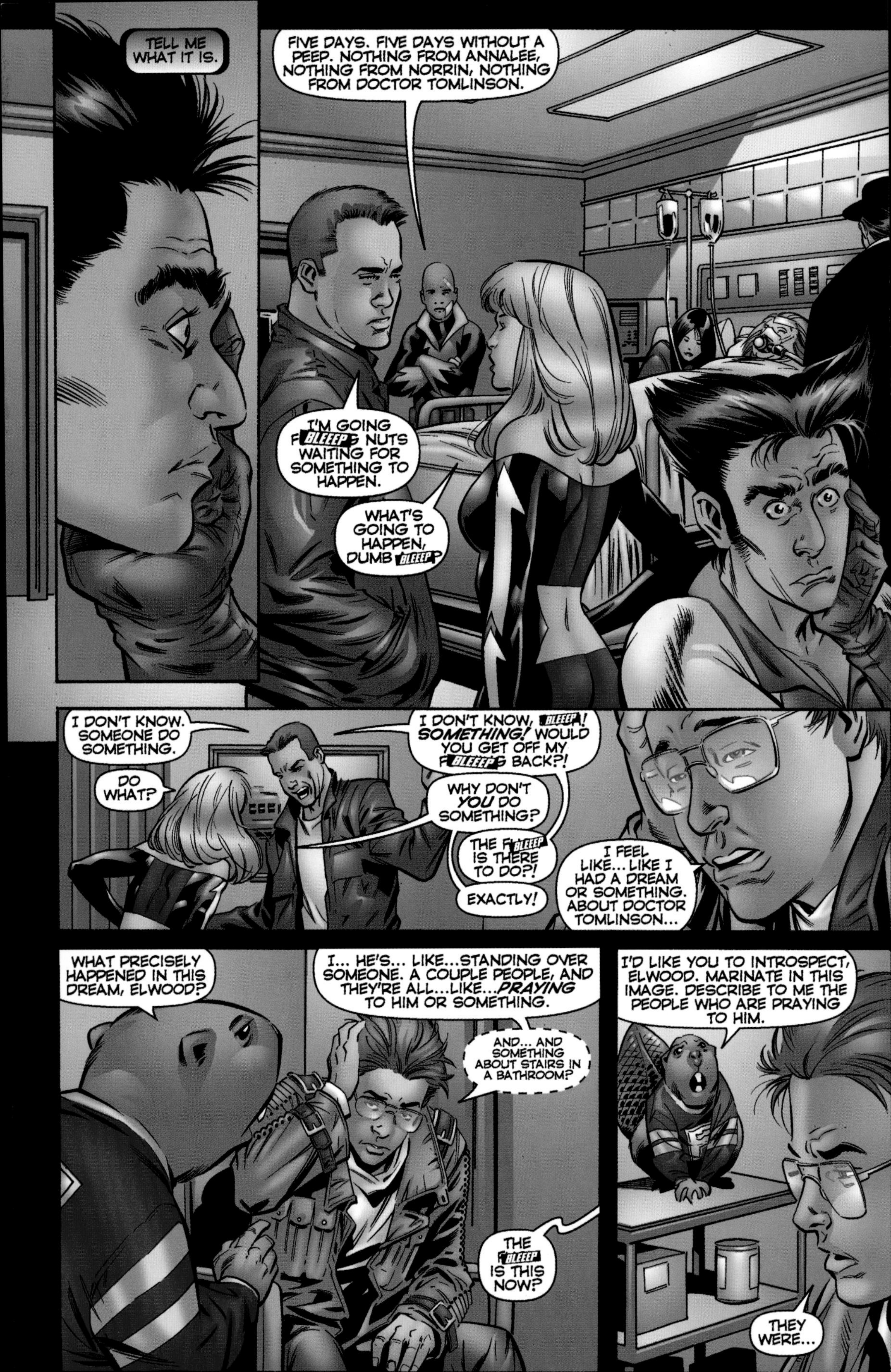
TELL ME WHAT IT IS.
FIVE DAYS. FIVE DAYS WITHOUT A PEEP. NOTHING FROM ANNALEE, NOTHING FROM NORRIN, NOTHING FROM DOCTOR TOMLINSON.
I'M GOING F BLEEEP G NUTS WAITING FOR SOMETHING TO HAPPEN.
WHAT'S GOING TO HAPPEN, DUMB BLEEEP ?
I DON'T KNOW. SOMEONE DO SOMETHING.
DO WHAT?
I DON'T KNOW, BLEEEP ! SOMETHING! WOULD YOU GET OFF MY F BLEEEP G BACK?!
WHY DON'T YOU DO SOMETHING?
THE F BLEEEP IS THERE TO DO?!
EXACTLY!
I FEEL LIKE... LIKE I HAD A DREAM OR SOMETHING. ABOUT DOCTOR TOMLINSON...
WHAT PRECISELY HAPPENED IN THIS DREAM, ELWOOD?
I... HE'S... LIKE...STANDING OVER SOMEONE. A COUPLE PEOPLE, AND THEY'RE ALL...LIKE...PRAYING TO HIM OR SOMETHING.
AND... AND SOMETHING ABOUT STAIRS IN A BATHROOM?
THE F BLEEEP IS THIS NOW?
I'D LIKE YOU TO INTROSPECT, ELWOOD. MARINATE IN THIS IMAGE. DESCRIBE TO ME THE PEOPLE WHO ARE PRAYING TO HIM.
THEY WERE...

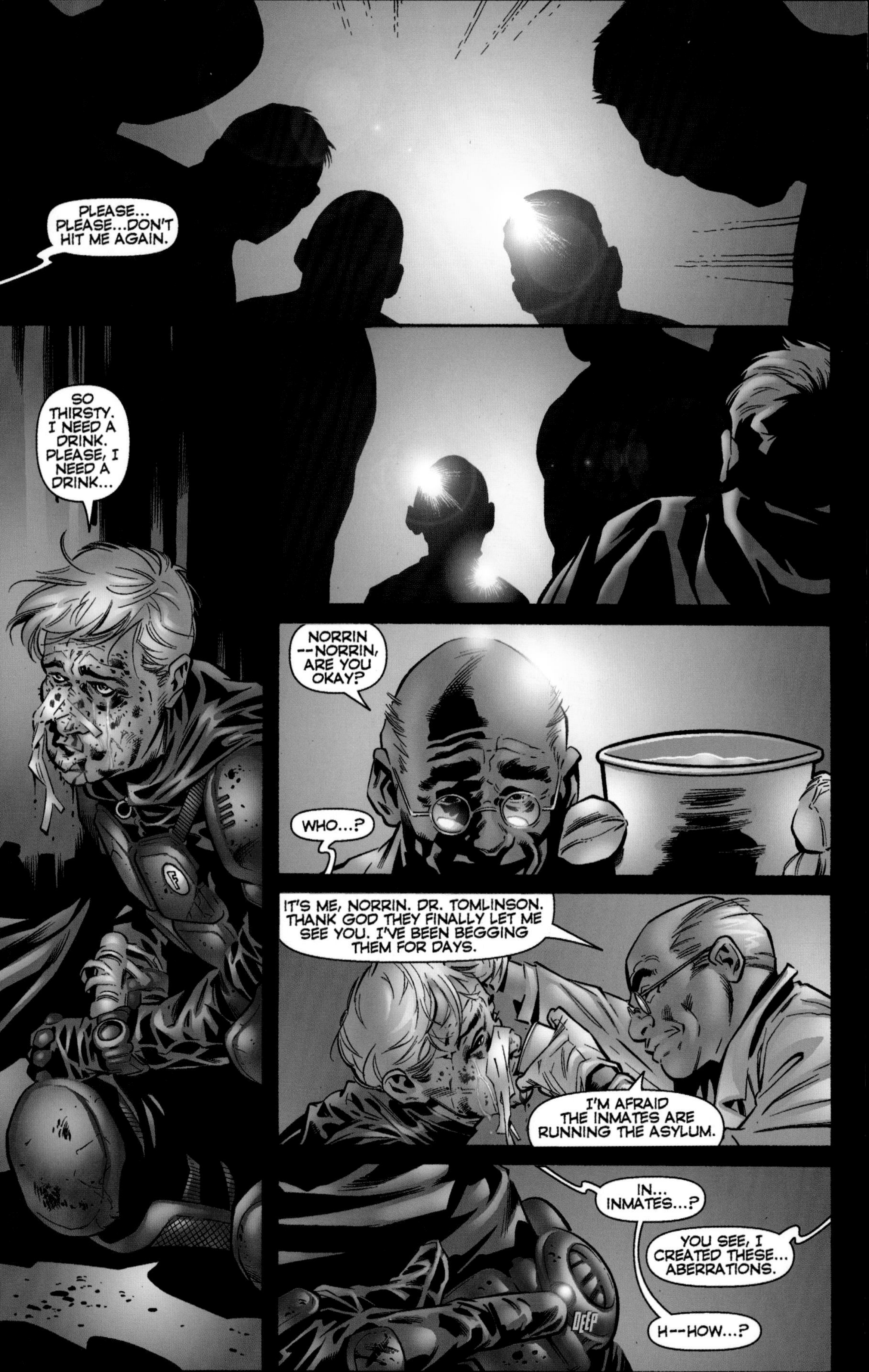
PLEASE... PLEASE...DON'T HIT ME AGAIN.
SO THIRSTY. I NEED A DRINK. PLEASE, I NEED A DRINK...
NORRIN --NORRIN, ARE YOU OKAY?
WHO...?
IT'S ME, NORRIN. DR. TOMLINSON. THANK GOD THEY FINALLY LET ME SEE YOU. I'VE BEEN BEGGING THEM FOR DAYS.
I'M AFRAID THE INMATES ARE RUNNING THE ASYLUM.
IN... INMATES...?
YOU SEE, I CREATED THESE... ABERRATIONS.
H--HOW...?

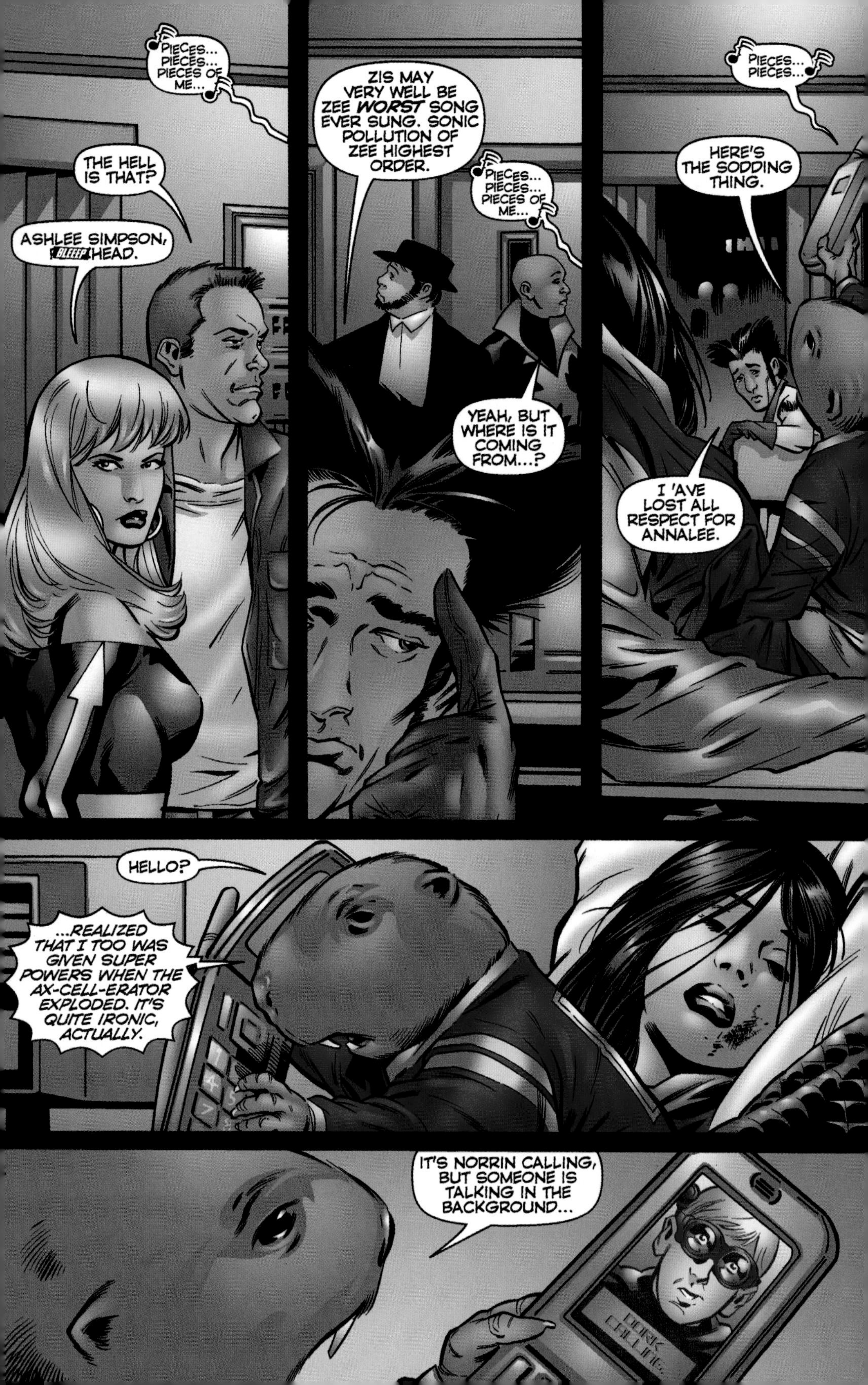
PIECES... PIECES... PIECES OF ME...
THE HELL IS THAT?
ASHLEE SIMPSON, BLEEEP HEAD.
ZIS MAY VERY WELL BE ZEE WORST SONG EVER SUNG. SONIC POLLUTION OF ZEE HIGHEST ORDER.
PIECES... PIECES... PIECES OF ME...
YEAH, BUT WHERE IS IT COMING FROM...?
PIECES... PIECES...
HERE'S THE SODDING THING.
I 'AVE LOST ALL RESPECT FOR ANNALEE.
HELLO?
...REALIZED THAT I TOO WAS GIVEN SUPER POWERS WHEN THE AX-CELL-ERATOR EXPLODED. IT'S QUITE IRONIC, ACTUALLY.
IT'S NORRIN CALLING, BUT SOMEONE IS TALKING IN THE BACKGROUND...
DORK CALLING.

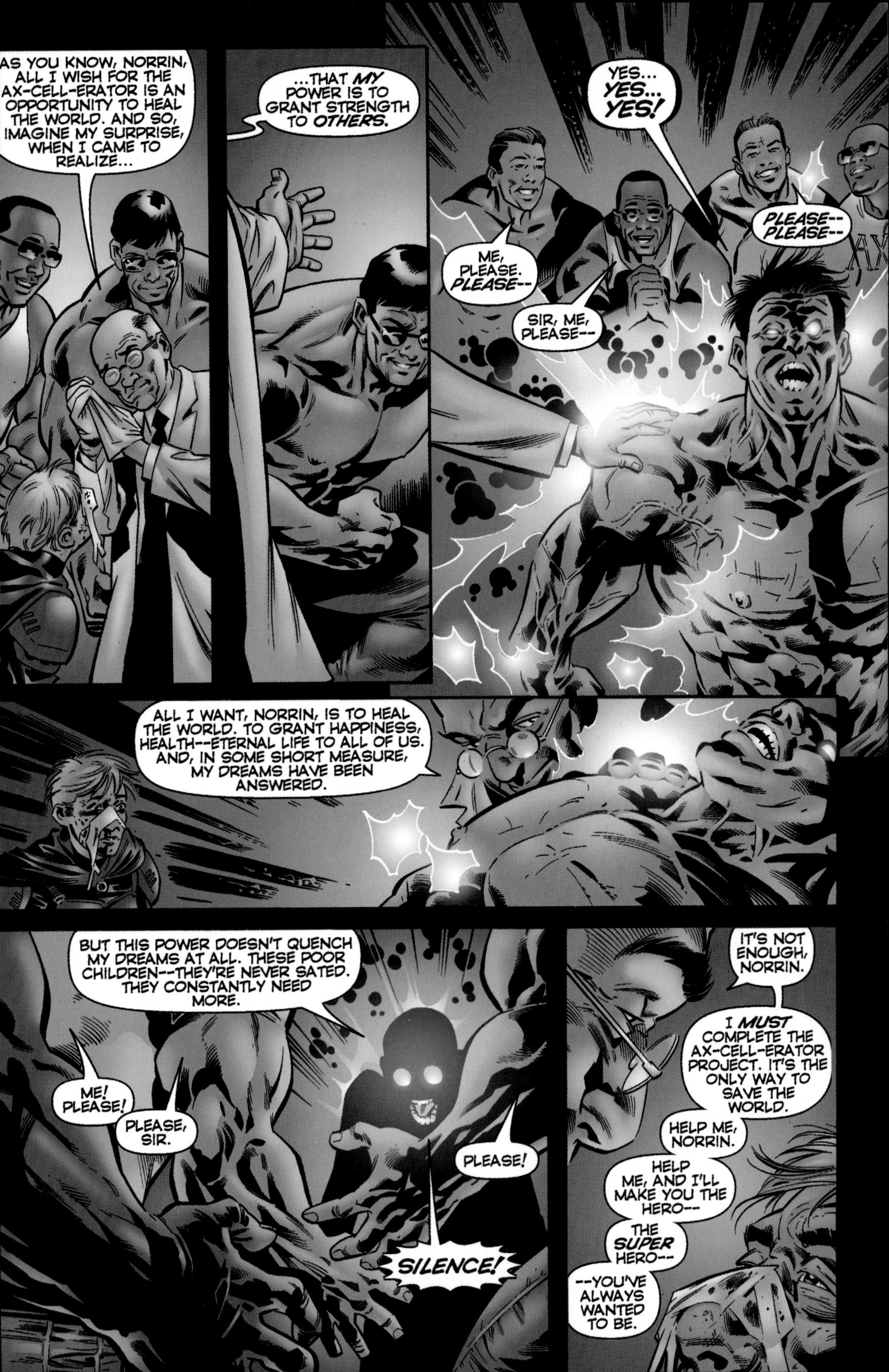
AS YOU KNOW, NORRIN, ALL I WISH FOR THE AX-CELL-ERATOR IS AN OPPORTUNITY TO HEAL THE WORLD. AND SO, IMAGINE MY SURPRISE, WHEN I CAME TO REALIZE...
...THAT MY POWER IS TO GRANT STRENGTH TO OTHERS.
YES... YES... YES!
ME, PLEASE. PLEASE--
SIR, ME, PLEASE--
PLEASE-- PLEASE--
ALL I WANT, NORRIN, IS TO HEAL THE WORLD. TO GRANT HAPPINESS, HEALTH--ETERNAL LIFE TO ALL OF US. AND, IN SOME SHORT MEASURE, MY DREAMS HAVE BEEN ANSWERED.
BUT THIS POWER DOESN'T QUENCH MY DREAMS AT ALL. THESE POOR CHILDREN--THEY'RE NEVER SATED. THEY CONSTANTLY NEED MORE.
ME! PLEASE!
PLEASE, SIR.
PLEASE!
SILENCE!
IT'S NOT ENOUGH, NORRIN.
I MUST COMPLETE THE AX-CELL-ERATOR PROJECT. IT'S THE ONLY WAY TO SAVE THE WORLD.
HELP ME, NORRIN.
HELP ME, AND I'LL MAKE YOU THE HERO--
THE SUPER HERO--
--YOU'VE ALWAYS WANTED TO BE.

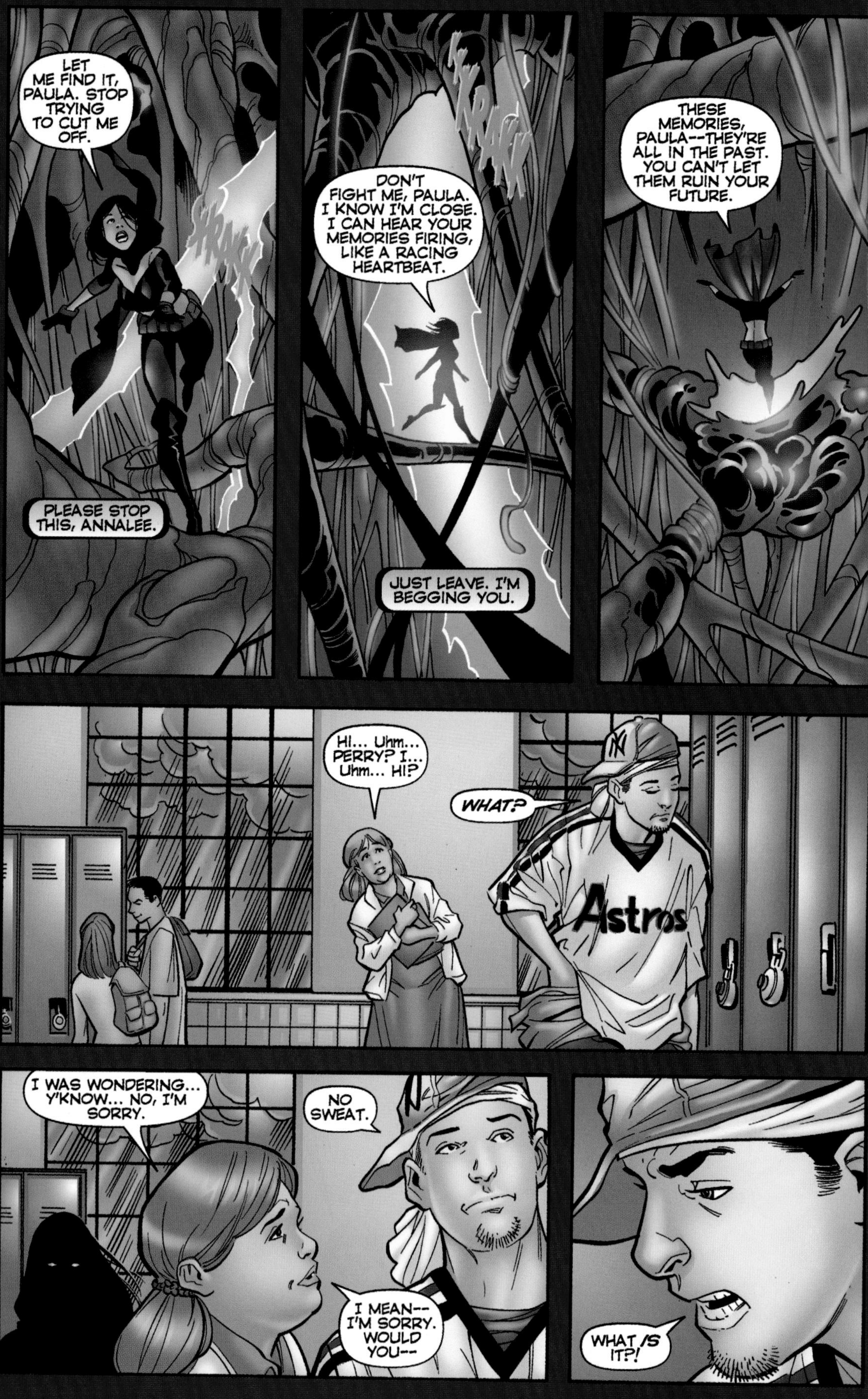
LET ME FIND IT, PAULA. STOP TRYING TO CUT ME OFF.
PLEASE STOP THIS, ANNALEE.
DON'T FIGHT ME, PAULA. I KNOW I'M CLOSE. I CAN HEAR YOUR MEMORIES FIRING, LIKE A RACING HEARTBEAT.
JUST LEAVE. I'M BEGGING YOU.
THESE MEMORIES, PAULA--THEY'RE ALL IN THE PAST. YOU CAN'T LET THEM RUIN YOUR FUTURE.
HI... Uhm... PERRY? I... Uhm... HI?
WHAT?
I WAS WONDERING... Y'KNOW... NO, I'M SORRY.
NO SWEAT.
I MEAN-- I'M SORRY. WOULD YOU--
WHAT IS IT?!

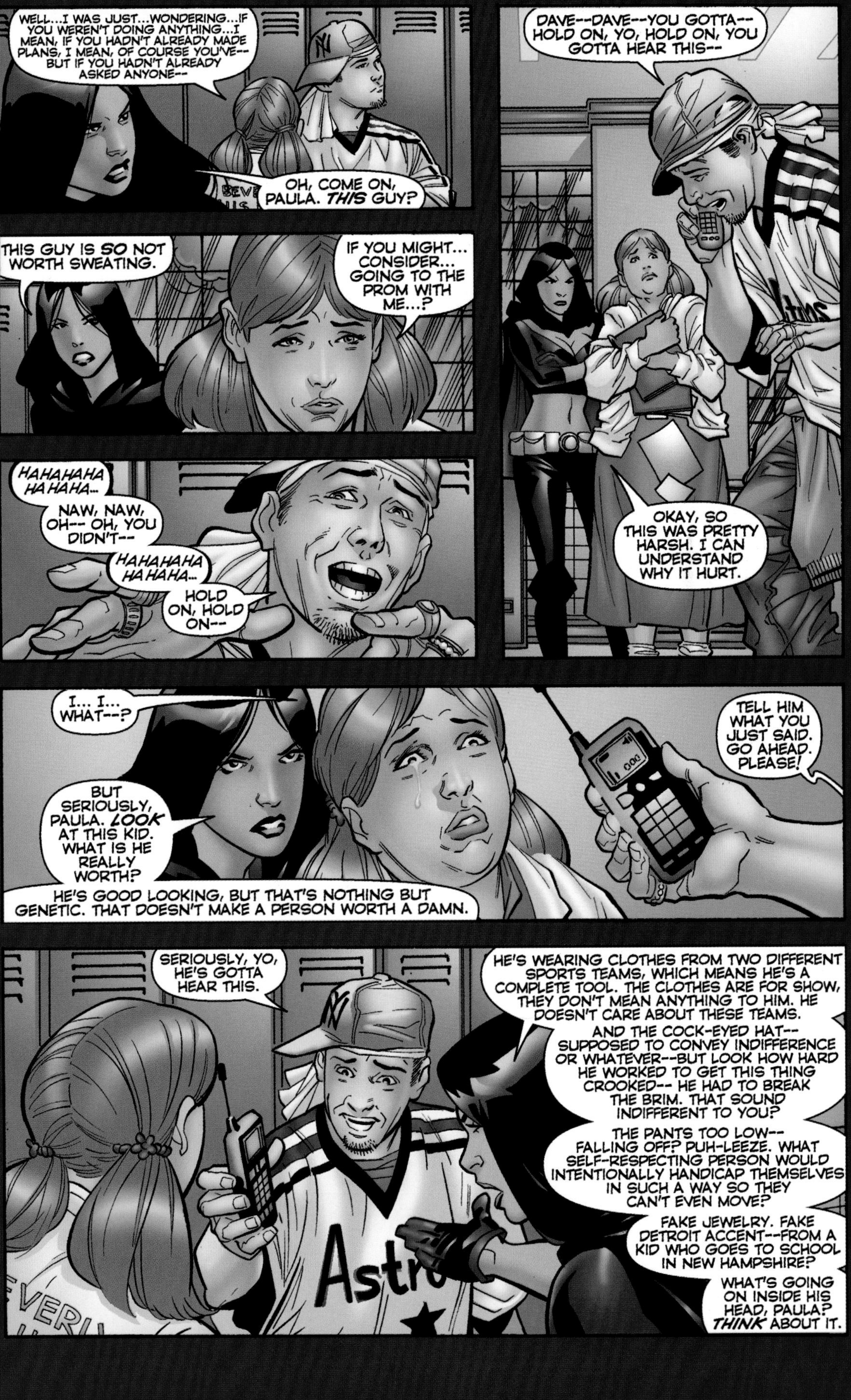

WELL...I WAS JUST...WONDERING...IF YOU WEREN'T DOING ANYTHING...I MEAN, IF YOU HADN'T ALREADY MADE PLANS, I MEAN, OF COURSE YOU'VE-- BUT IF YOU HADN'T ALREADY ASKED ANYONE--
OH, COME ON, PAULA. *THIS* GUY?
THIS GUY IS **SO** NOT WORTH SWEATING.
IF YOU MIGHT... CONSIDER... GOING TO THE PROM WITH ME...?
HAHAHAHA HAHAHA...
NAW, NAW, OH-- OH, YOU DIDN'T--
HAHAHAHA HAHAHA...
HOLD ON, HOLD ON--
DAVE--DAVE--YOU GOTTA-- HOLD ON, YO, HOLD ON, YOU GOTTA HEAR THIS--
OKAY, SO THIS WAS PRETTY HARSH. I CAN UNDERSTAND WHY IT HURT.
I... I... WHAT--?
TELL HIM WHAT YOU JUST SAID. GO AHEAD. PLEASE!
BUT SERIOUSLY, PAULA. *LOOK* AT THIS KID. WHAT IS HE REALLY WORTH?
HE'S GOOD LOOKING, BUT THAT'S NOTHING BUT GENETIC. THAT DOESN'T MAKE A PERSON WORTH A DAMN.
SERIOUSLY, YO, HE'S GOTTA HEAR THIS.
HE'S WEARING CLOTHES FROM TWO DIFFERENT SPORTS TEAMS, WHICH MEANS HE'S A COMPLETE TOOL. THE CLOTHES ARE FOR SHOW, THEY DON'T MEAN ANYTHING TO HIM. HE DOESN'T CARE ABOUT THESE TEAMS.
AND THE COCK-EYED HAT-- SUPPOSED TO CONVEY INDIFFERENCE OR WHATEVER--BUT LOOK HOW HARD HE WORKED TO GET THIS THING CROOKED-- HE HAD TO BREAK THE BRIM. THAT SOUND INDIFFERENT TO YOU?
THE PANTS TOO LOW-- FALLING OFF? PUH-LEEZE. WHAT SELF-RESPECTING PERSON WOULD INTENTIONALLY HANDICAP THEMSELVES IN SUCH A WAY SO THEY CAN'T EVEN MOVE?
FAKE JEWELRY. FAKE DETROIT ACCENT--FROM A KID WHO GOES TO SCHOOL IN NEW HAMPSHIRE?
WHAT'S GOING ON INSIDE HIS HEAD, PAULA? *THINK* ABOUT IT.

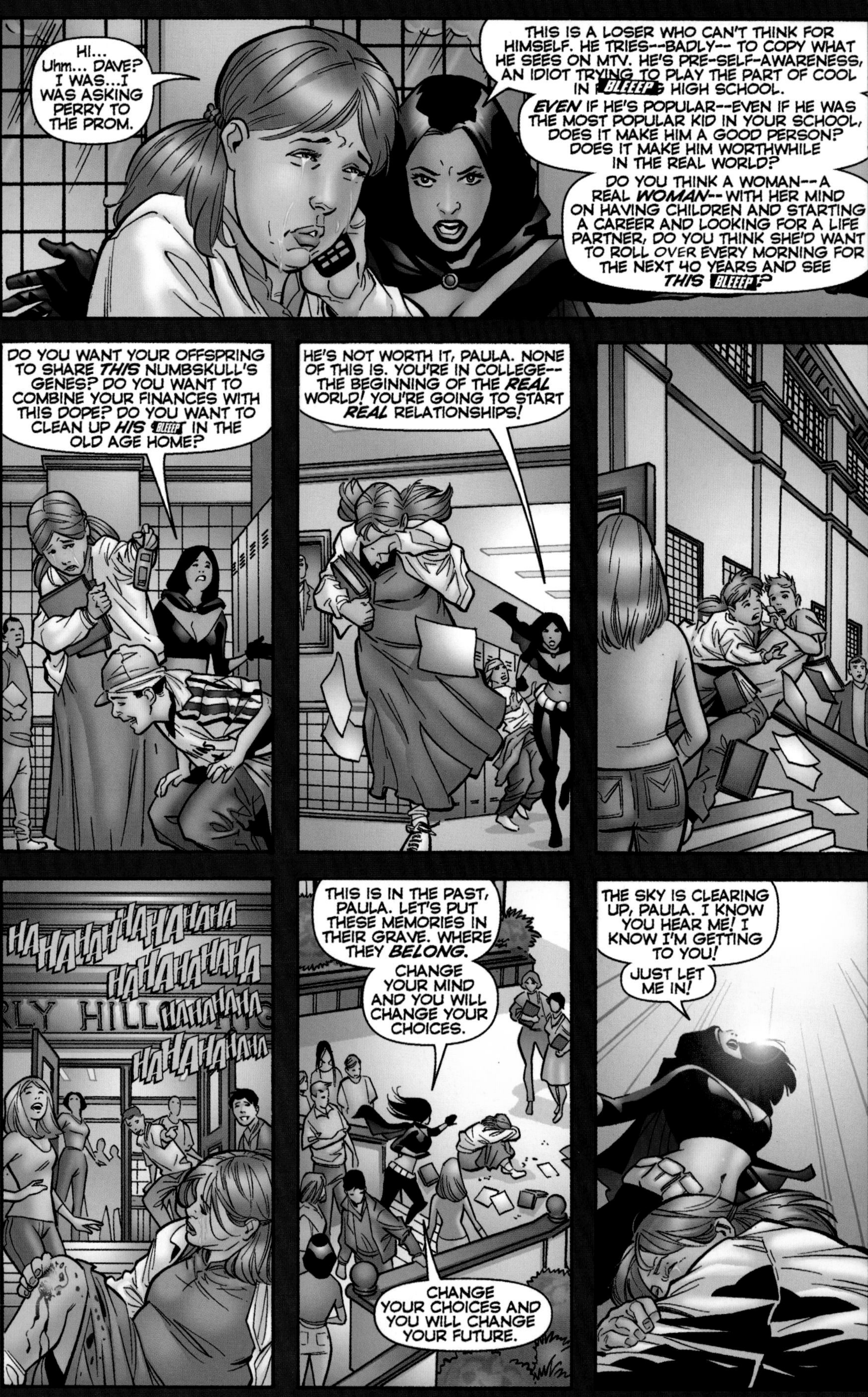
HI... Uhm... DAVE? I WAS...I WAS ASKING PERRY TO THE PROM.
THIS IS A LOSER WHO CAN'T THINK FOR HIMSELF. HE TRIES--BADLY-- TO COPY WHAT HE SEES ON MTV. HE'S PRE-SELF-AWARENESS, AN IDIOT TRYING TO PLAY THE PART OF COOL IN BLEEEP HIGH SCHOOL.
EVEN IF HE'S POPULAR--EVEN IF HE WAS THE MOST POPULAR KID IN YOUR SCHOOL, DOES IT MAKE HIM A GOOD PERSON? DOES IT MAKE HIM WORTHWHILE IN THE REAL WORLD?
DO YOU THINK A WOMAN--A REAL WOMAN--WITH HER MIND ON HAVING CHILDREN AND STARTING A CAREER AND LOOKING FOR A LIFE PARTNER, DO YOU THINK SHE'D WANT TO ROLL OVER EVERY MORNING FOR THE NEXT 40 YEARS AND SEE THIS BLEEEP?
DO YOU WANT YOUR OFFSPRING TO SHARE THIS NUMBSKULL'S GENES? DO YOU WANT TO COMBINE YOUR FINANCES WITH THIS DOPE? DO YOU WANT TO CLEAN UP HIS BLEEEP IN THE OLD AGE HOME?
HE'S NOT WORTH IT, PAULA. NONE OF THIS IS. YOU'RE IN COLLEGE--THE BEGINNING OF THE REAL WORLD! YOU'RE GOING TO START REAL RELATIONSHIPS!
HAHAHAHAHAHAHAHA
HAHAHAHAHAHA
HAHAHAHAHA
HAHAHAHAHAHA
THIS IS IN THE PAST, PAULA. LET'S PUT THESE MEMORIES IN THEIR GRAVE. WHERE THEY BELONG.
CHANGE YOUR MIND AND YOU WILL CHANGE YOUR CHOICES.
CHANGE YOUR CHOICES AND YOU WILL CHANGE YOUR FUTURE.
THE SKY IS CLEARING UP, PAULA. I KNOW YOU HEAR ME! I KNOW I'M GETTING TO YOU!
JUST LET ME IN!

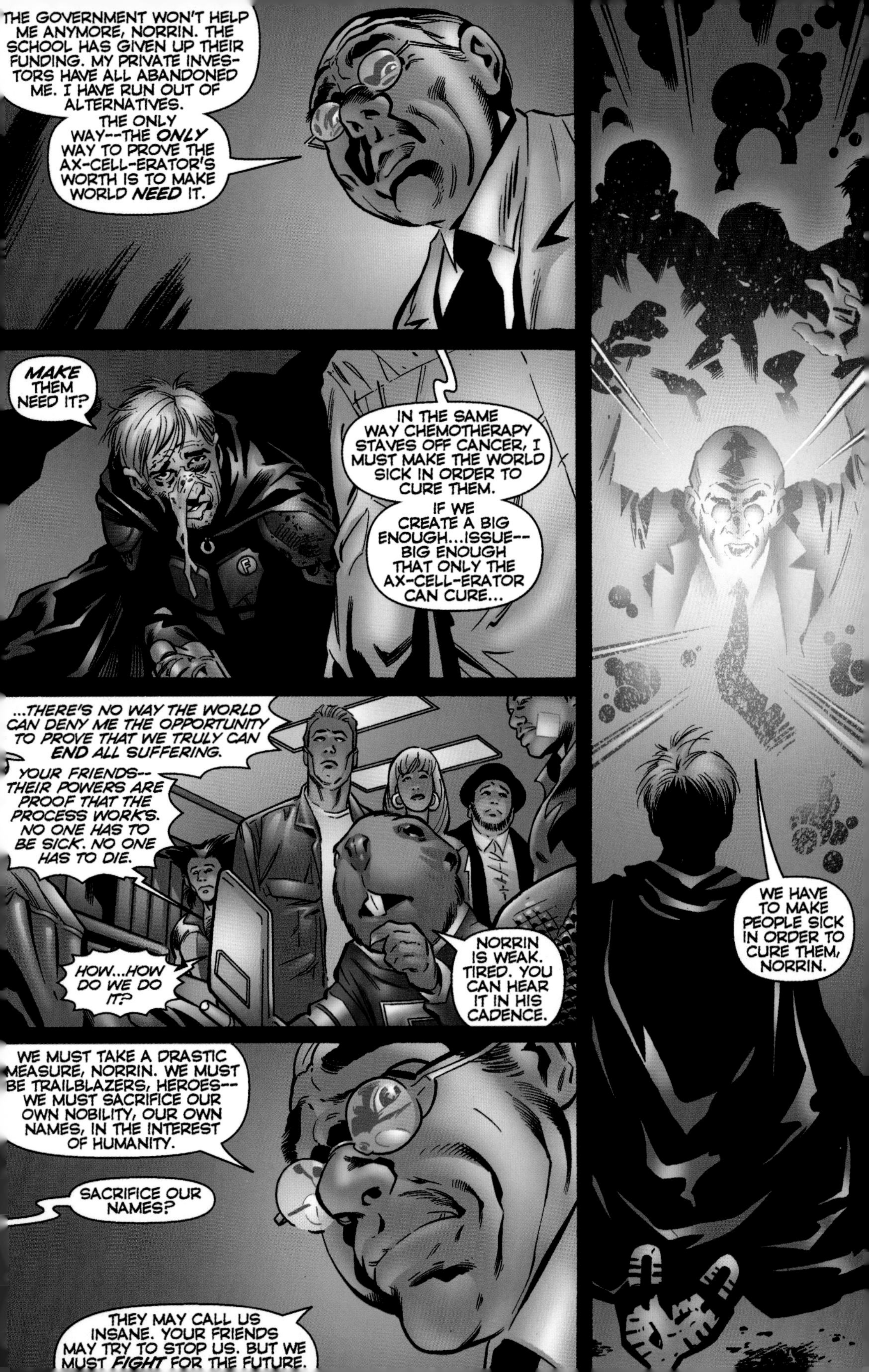
THE GOVERNMENT WON'T HELP ME ANYMORE, NORRIN. THE SCHOOL HAS GIVEN UP THEIR FUNDING. MY PRIVATE INVESTORS HAVE ALL ABANDONED ME. I HAVE RUN OUT OF ALTERNATIVES.
THE ONLY WAY--THE ONLY WAY TO PROVE THE AX-CELL-ERATOR'S WORTH IS TO MAKE WORLD NEED IT.
MAKE THEM NEED IT?
IN THE SAME WAY CHEMOTHERAPY STAVES OFF CANCER, I MUST MAKE THE WORLD SICK IN ORDER TO CURE THEM.
IF WE CREATE A BIG ENOUGH...ISSUE-- BIG ENOUGH THAT ONLY THE AX-CELL-ERATOR CAN CURE...
...THERE'S NO WAY THE WORLD CAN DENY ME THE OPPORTUNITY TO PROVE THAT WE TRULY CAN END ALL SUFFERING.
YOUR FRIENDS-- THEIR POWERS ARE PROOF THAT THE PROCESS WORKS. NO ONE HAS TO BE SICK. NO ONE HAS TO DIE.
HOW...HOW DO WE DO IT?
NORRIN IS WEAK. TIRED. YOU CAN HEAR IT IN HIS CADENCE.
WE MUST TAKE A DRASTIC MEASURE, NORRIN. WE MUST BE TRAILBLAZERS, HEROES-- WE MUST SACRIFICE OUR OWN NOBILITY, OUR OWN NAMES, IN THE INTEREST OF HUMANITY.
SACRIFICE OUR NAMES?
THEY MAY CALL US INSANE. YOUR FRIENDS MAY TRY TO STOP US. BUT WE MUST FIGHT FOR THE FUTURE.
WE HAVE TO MAKE PEOPLE SICK IN ORDER TO CURE THEM, NORRIN.

I... I DON'T THINK...

WE HAVE TO MAKE THEM SICK IN A WAY THAT ONLY THE AX-CELL-ERATOR CAN CURE. IN A WAY THAT WILL GIVE US TIME TO EXPLAIN, TIME TO REASON--

NO. NO WAY--

HEROES TAKE GREAT RISK, NORRIN. YOU KNOW THIS-- NO VICTORY COMES WITHOUT TAKING RISKS.

WE KNOW WE CAN CURE THE WORLD WITH OUR MACHINE. WE JUST HAVE TO FORCE THEM TO LET US.

I... I'M NOT SURE...

A CANCER-CAUSING AGENT, NORRIN. IN THE MILANO/HUFFMAN DAM RESERVOIR. EVEN THE FIRST SIGNS MAY NOT SHOW UP FOR YEARS.

THIS WILL GIVE US MORE THAN AMPLE TIME TO EXPLAIN OURSELVES, TO MAKE THE WORLD SEE THE POWER OF THE AX-CELL-ERATOR. TO MANUFACTURE IT. TO CURE EVERYONE. OF EVERYTHING.

AND WHAT BETTER PROOF THAT THE AX-CELL-ERATOR WILL BE THE CHAMPION OF THE FUTURE? A DISEASE, PERFECTLY BUILT OF RENEGADE, OUT OF CONTROL CELLS THAT MULTIPLY UNTIL THEY KILL THEIR HOST--

ELIMINATED. BY THE INGENUITY OF THE HUMAN MIND.

BY A TEAM OF VANGUARDS. HEROES WHO TOOK A GREAT RISK IN ORDER TO WAKE THE WORLD UP.

LIKE THE TRAILBLAZERS BEFORE US, SACRIFICING THEMSELVES TO TEACH THE WORLD A GREATER TRUTH. THE TRUE HEROES.

WHY...WHY DO YOU NEED MY HELP?

THESE FOOLS...THESE FRAT BOYS...THEY'RE NOT SMART. THEY CAN'T ENSURE THAT THE PLAN WILL BE CARRIED OUT FLAWLESSLY. NO ONE MUST INTERFERE.

MY FRIENDS... THEY WILL TRY TO STOP YOU.

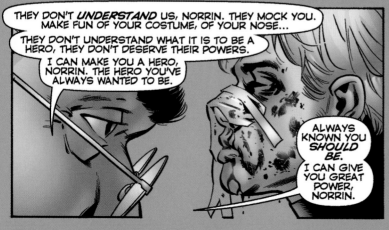

THEY DON'T UNDERSTAND US, NORRIN. THEY MOCK YOU. MAKE FUN OF YOUR COSTUME, OF YOUR NOSE...

THEY DON'T UNDERSTAND WHAT IT IS TO BE A HERO, THEY DON'T DESERVE THEIR POWERS.

I CAN MAKE YOU A HERO, NORRIN. THE HERO YOU'VE ALWAYS WANTED TO BE.

ALWAYS KNOWN YOU SHOULD BE.

I CAN GIVE YOU GREAT POWER, NORRIN.

AND WITH GREAT POWER...

COMES GREAT RESPONSIBILITY.

CLICK

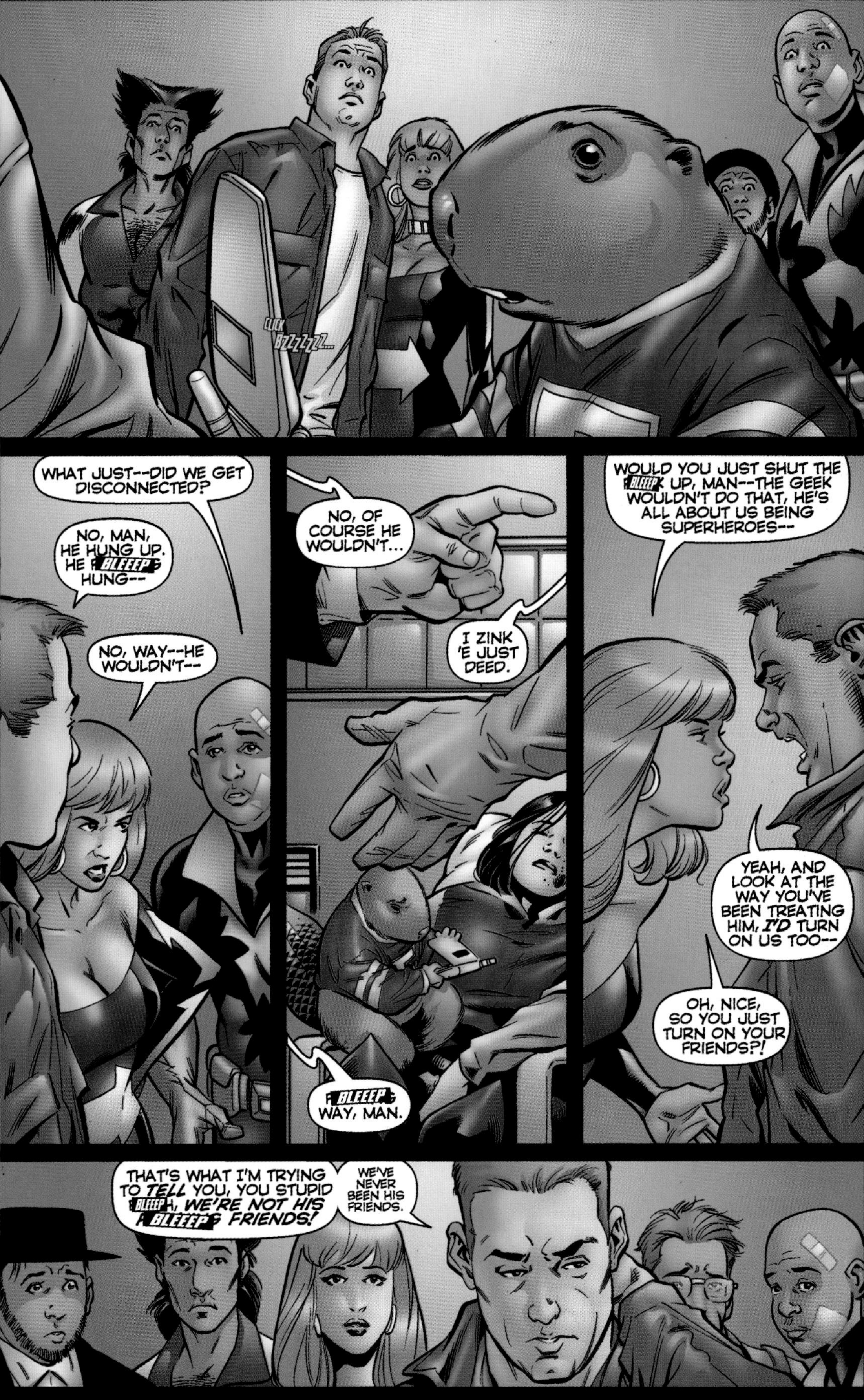
CLICK
BZZZZZZZ...
WHAT JUST--DID WE GET DISCONNECTED?
NO, MAN, HE HUNG UP. HE BLEEEP HUNG--
NO, WAY--HE WOULDN'T--
NO, OF COURSE HE WOULDN'T...
I ZINK 'E JUST DEED.
BLEEEP WAY, MAN.
WOULD YOU JUST SHUT THE BLEEEP UP, MAN--THE GEEK WOULDN'T DO THAT, HE'S ALL ABOUT US BEING SUPERHEROES--
YEAH, AND LOOK AT THE WAY YOU'VE BEEN TREATING HIM, *I'D* TURN ON US TOO--
OH, NICE, SO YOU JUST TURN ON YOUR FRIENDS?!
THAT'S WHAT I'M TRYING TO *TELL* YOU, YOU STUPID BLEEEP, *WE'RE NOT HIS* BLEEEP *FRIENDS!*
WE'VE NEVER BEEN HIS FRIENDS.

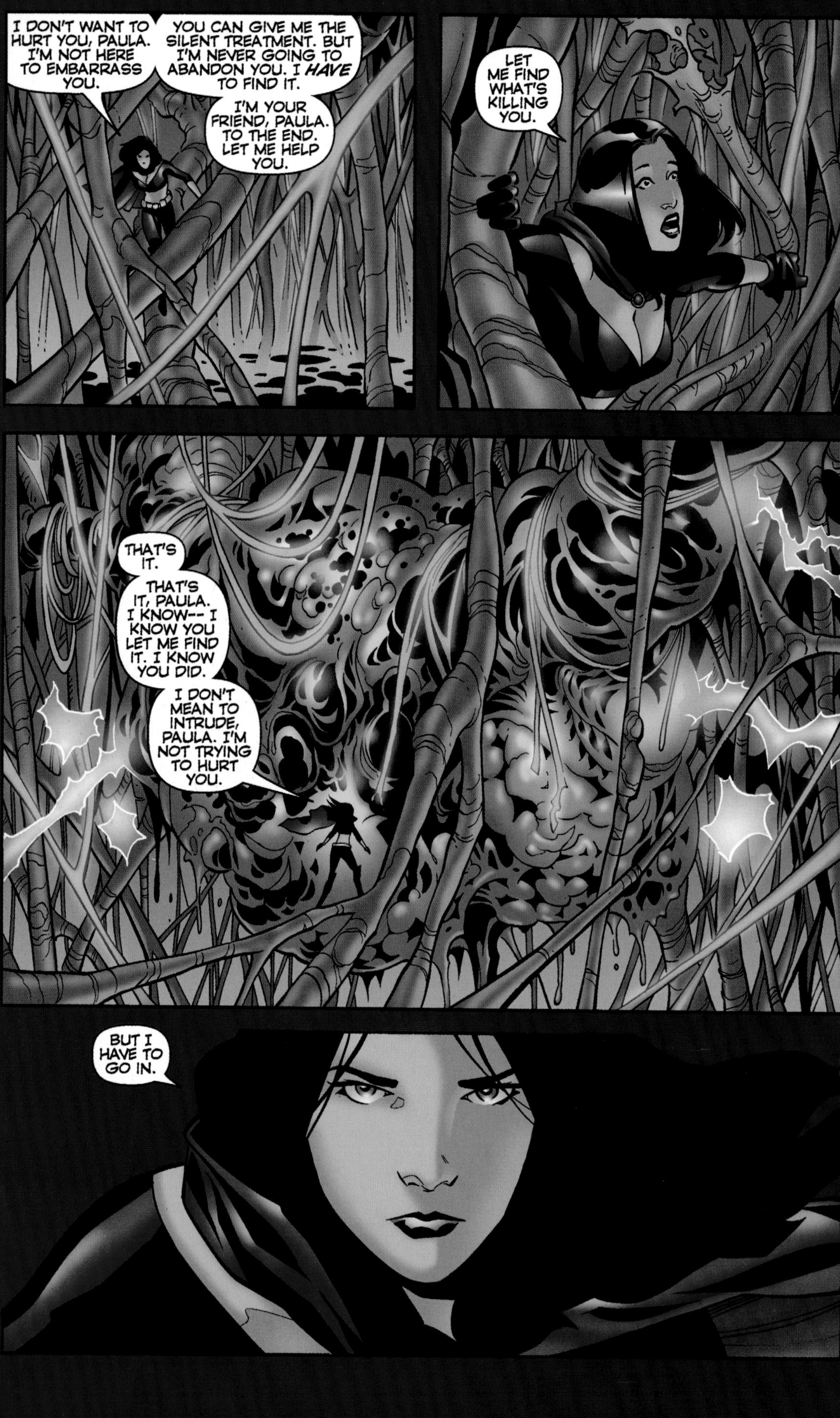
I DON'T WANT TO HURT YOU, PAULA. I'M NOT HERE TO EMBARRASS YOU.
YOU CAN GIVE ME THE SILENT TREATMENT. BUT I'M NEVER GOING TO ABANDON YOU. I *HAVE* TO FIND IT.
I'M YOUR FRIEND, PAULA. TO THE END. LET ME HELP YOU.
LET ME FIND WHAT'S KILLING YOU.
THAT'S IT.
THAT'S IT, PAULA. I KNOW-- I KNOW YOU LET ME FIND IT. I KNOW YOU DID.
I DON'T MEAN TO INTRUDE, PAULA. I'M NOT TRYING TO HURT YOU.
BUT I HAVE TO GO IN.

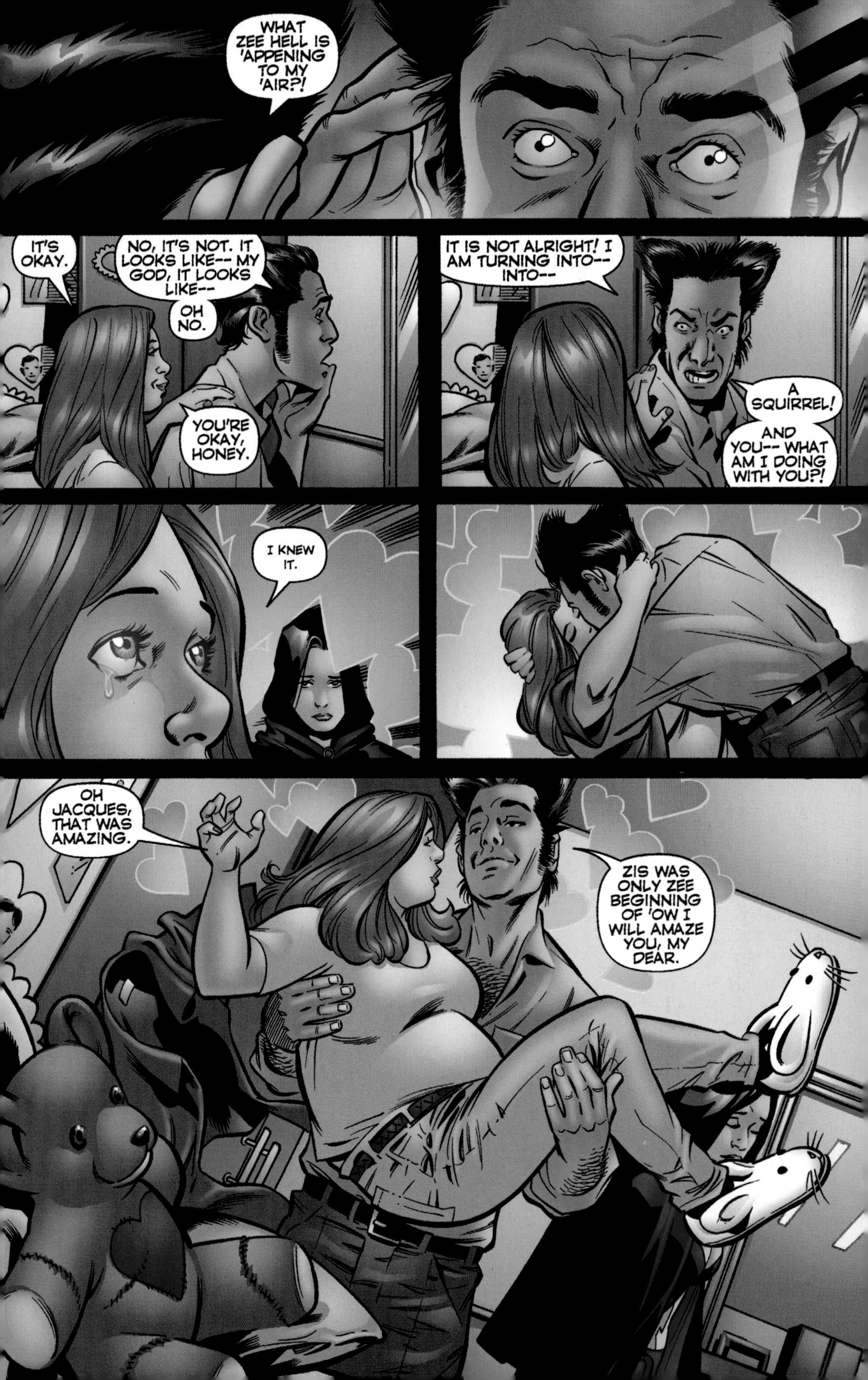
WHAT ZEE HELL IS 'APPENING TO MY 'AIR?!
IT'S OKAY.
NO, IT'S NOT. IT LOOKS LIKE-- MY GOD, IT LOOKS LIKE--
OH NO.
YOU'RE OKAY, HONEY.
IT IS NOT ALRIGHT! I AM TURNING INTO-- INTO--
A SQUIRREL!
AND YOU-- WHAT AM I DOING WITH YOU?!
I KNEW IT.
OH JACQUES, THAT WAS AMAZING.
ZIS WAS ONLY ZEE BEGINNING OF 'OW I WILL AMAZE YOU, MY DEAR.

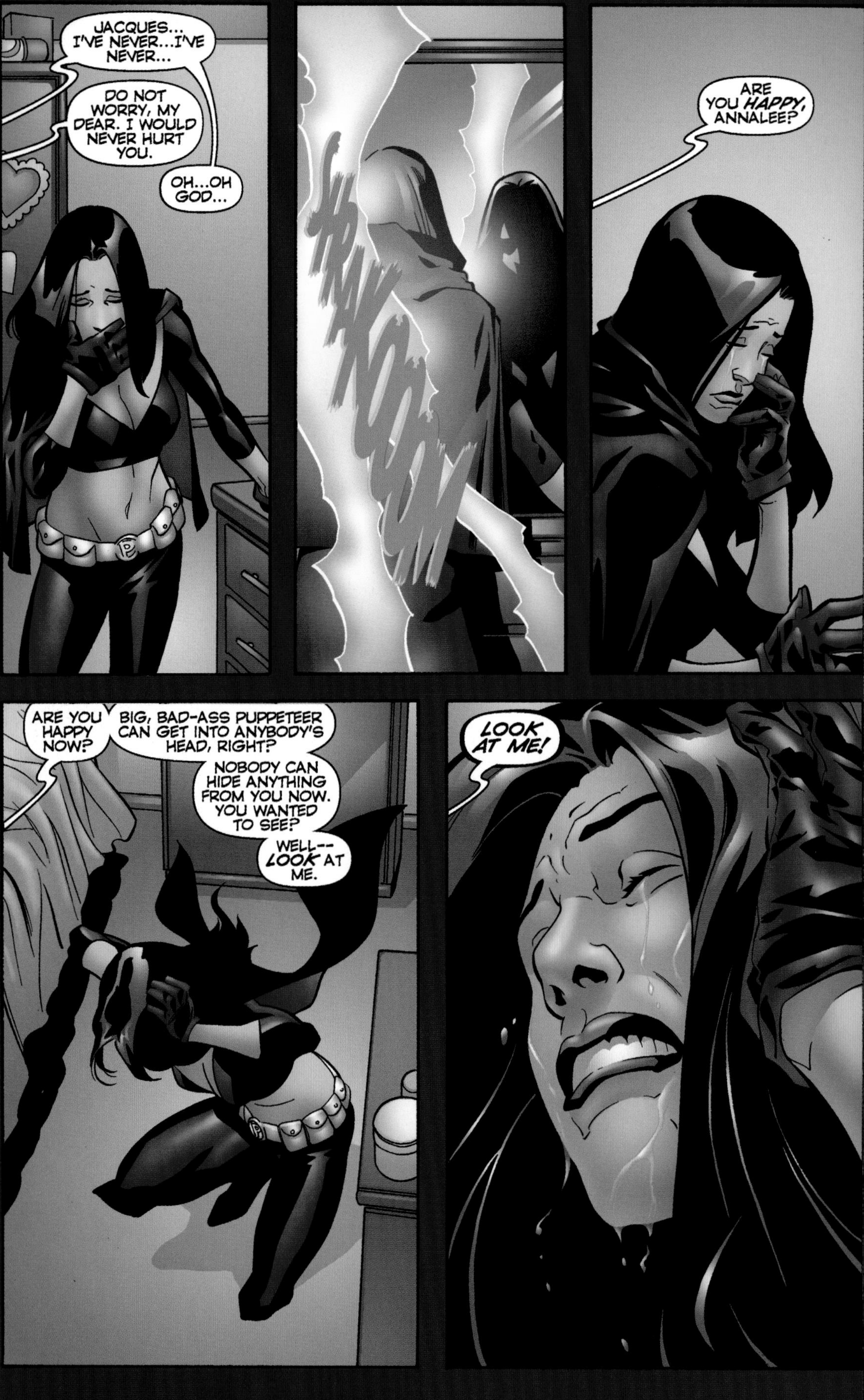
JACQUES... I'VE NEVER...I'VE NEVER...
DO NOT WORRY, MY DEAR. I WOULD NEVER HURT YOU.
OH...OH GOD...
ARE YOU *HAPPY*, ANNALEE?
ARE YOU HAPPY NOW?
BIG, BAD-ASS PUPPETEER CAN GET INTO ANYBODY'S HEAD, RIGHT?
NOBODY CAN HIDE ANYTHING FROM YOU NOW. YOU WANTED TO SEE?
WELL-- *LOOK* AT ME.
LOOK AT ME!

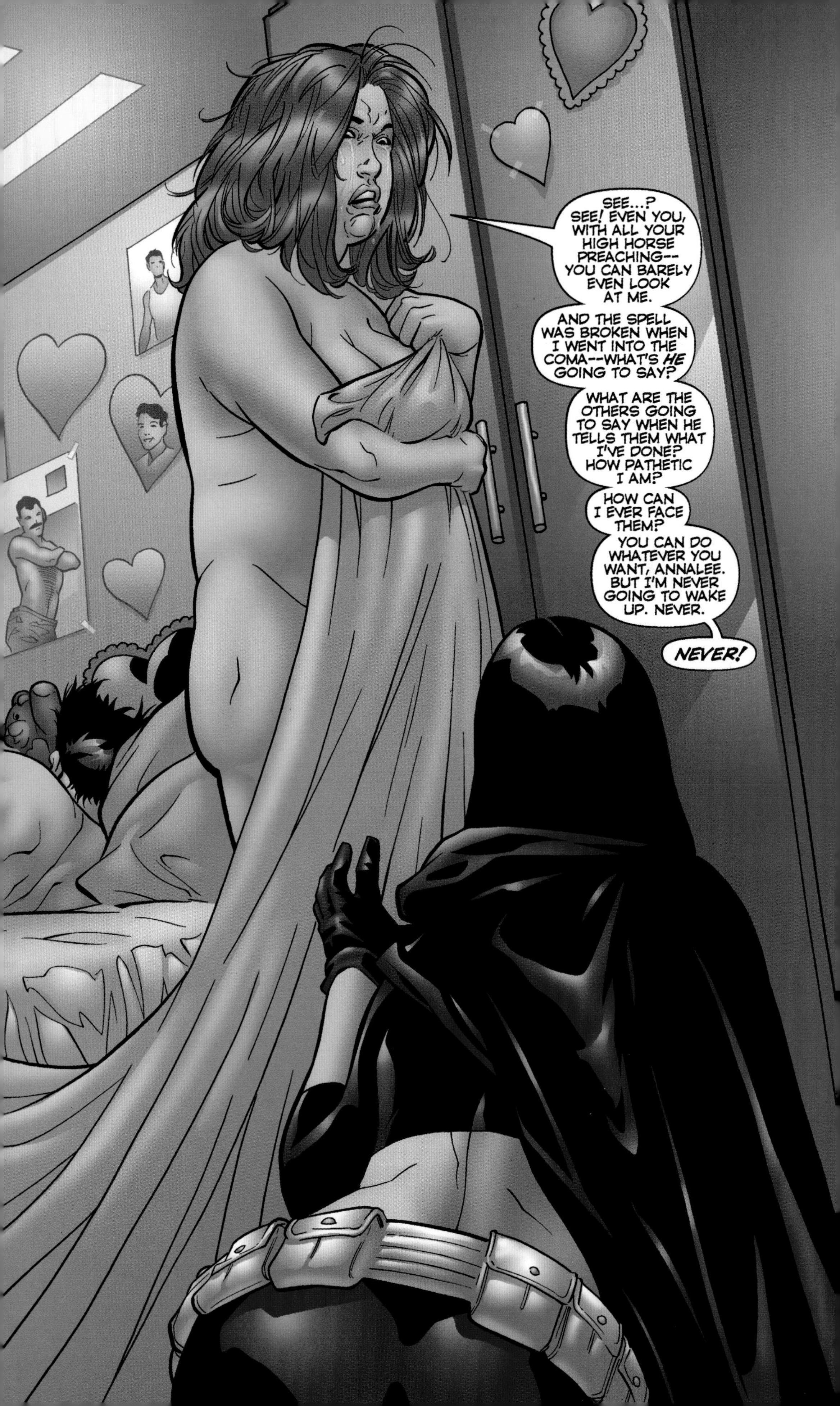

SEE...? SEE! EVEN YOU, WITH ALL YOUR HIGH HORSE PREACHING-- YOU CAN BARELY EVEN LOOK AT ME.
AND THE SPELL WAS BROKEN WHEN I WENT INTO THE COMA--WHAT'S *HE* GOING TO SAY?
WHAT ARE THE OTHERS GOING TO SAY WHEN HE TELLS THEM WHAT I'VE DONE? HOW PATHETIC I AM?
HOW CAN I EVER FACE THEM?
YOU CAN DO WHATEVER YOU WANT, ANNALEE. BUT I'M NEVER GOING TO WAKE UP. NEVER.
NEVER!

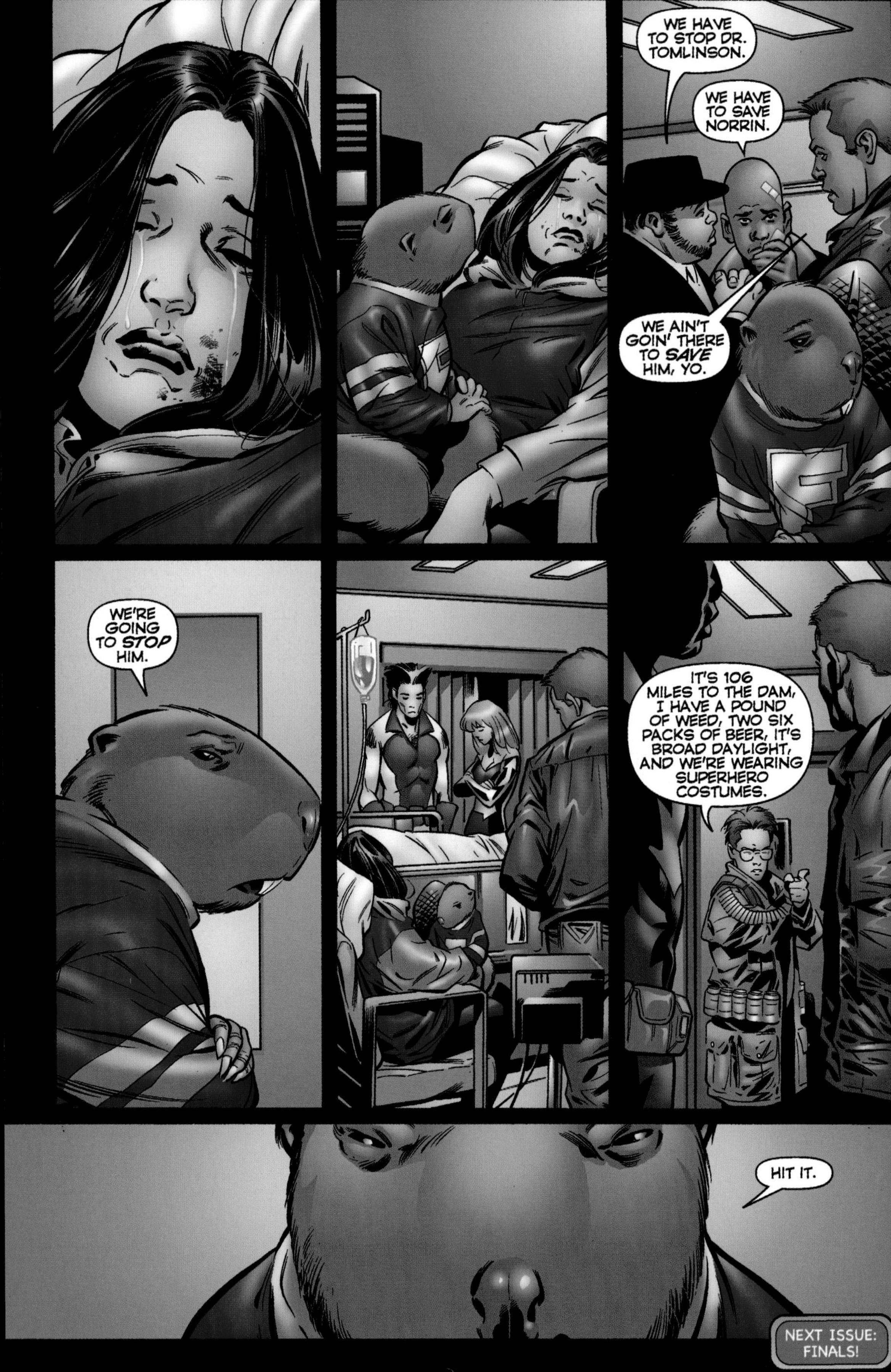
WE HAVE TO STOP DR. TOMLINSON.
WE HAVE TO SAVE NORRIN.
WE AIN'T GOIN' THERE TO SAVE HIM, YO.
WE'RE GOING TO STOP HIM.
IT'S 106 MILES TO THE DAM, I HAVE A POUND OF WEED, TWO SIX PACKS OF BEER, IT'S BROAD DAYLIGHT, AND WE'RE WEARING SUPERHERO COSTUMES.
HIT IT.
NEXT ISSUE: FINALS!

CAST OUT OF THE MAIN DORMS AND FORCED TO LIVE IN TEMPORARY HOUSING IN THE BOUGHL SCIENCE BUILDING, THE FRESHMEN CLASS OF FREESE COLLEGE HAS BEEN IMBUED WITH MIRACULOUS SUPERPOWERS BY THE EXPLOSION OF A MYSTERIOUS DEVICE CALLED THE AX-CELL-ERATOR!

WANNABE-- KENNETH "NORRIN" WEISMEYER, THE WOULD-BE TEAM LEADER AND RESIDENT SUPERHERO GEEK, WHO WENT FOR PIZZA DURING THE PIVOTAL MOMENT AND HAS NO POWERS!

THE PUPPETEER-- ANNALEE ROGERS, WHO CAN JUMP INTO PEOPLE'S MINDS AND VIEW THEIR MEMORIES OR EVEN CONTROL THEM!

THE GREEN THUMB-- CHARLES LEVY, A DEDICATED VEGETARIAN WHO CAN NOW COMMUNICATE WITH PLANTS, LEAVING HIM NOTHING TO EAT!

QUAKER-- LIAM ADAMS, THE AMISH BOY WHO CAN CAUSE EARTHQUAKES BY SHUFFLING HIS BELLY!

THE INTOXICATOR-- ELWOOD JOHNS, FORMER MATH GENIUS WHOSE DRUNKEN BURPS INTOXICATE ANYONE WHO SMELLS THEM!

THE DRAMA TWINS-- RENEE AND BRADY, BICKERING EXES WHO MUST BE IN PHYSICAL CONTACT TO USE THEIR TELEKINESIS!

THE SQUIRREL-- JACQUES LALLEAUX, THE FRENCH EXCHANGE STUDENT WHO COMPULSIVELY HOARDS NUTS!

THE SEDUCTRESS-- PAULA POPHOUSE, THE LOVELORN TEEN WHO CAN MAKE ANYONE FALL IN LOVE WITH HER!

THE BEAVER-- THE SCHOOL MASCOT HAS BEEN IMBUED WITH QUANTUM-BUSTING INTELLIGENCE, BUT CAN'T CONCENTRATE ON ANYTHING BUT BUILDING DAMS!

DR. THEODORE TOMLINSON-- THE SCIENCE PROFESSOR WHO CREATED THE AX-CELL-ERATOR!

PREVIOUSLY IN FRESHMEN:

AFTER DISCOVERING THEIR BIZARRE AND AMAZING POWERS, OUR YOUNG HEROES WERE EMPLOYED BY THE CREATOR OF THE AX-CELL-ERATOR, DR. TOMLINSON, TO HELP REPAIR THE MACHINE THAT COULD CURE ALL DISEASES AND EVEN PREVENT AGING.

IN THE KIDS' FIRST BATTLE WITH THE SUPERPOWERED FRAT GUYS, QUAKER HESITATED TO USE HIS POWERS AND PAULA, THE SEDUCTRESS, WAS INJURED AND REMAINS IN A COMA. THE PUPPETEER JUMPED INTO PAULA'S MIND AND FOUND THAT SHE DOES NOT WANT TO WAKE UP: SHE'S WALLOWING IN SHAME BECAUSE SHE USED HER POWERS TO MAKE EXCHANGE STUDENT JACQUES (THE SQUIRREL) FALL IN LOVE WITH HER.

THE FRAT GUYS HAVE BEEN IMBUED WITH SUPER STRENGTH VIA THE ADDICTIVE TOUCH OF DR. TOMLINSON, WHO WAS ALSO AFFECTED BY THE AX-CELL-ERATOR. DR. TOMLINSON INTENDS TO PROVE HIS INVENTION TO THE WORLD BY RELEASING A CANCER-CAUSING AGENT INTO THE WATER SUPPLY AND USING THE AX-CELL-ERATOR TO CURE HIS VICTIMS.

WANNABE, SCORNED BY HIS PEERS AND HIS UNREQUITED LOVE, ANNALEE, HAS TURNED AGAINST HIS TEAM AND JOINED DR. TOMLINSON IN HIS QUEST TO BECOME A SUPERHERO...

PAULA, NO!

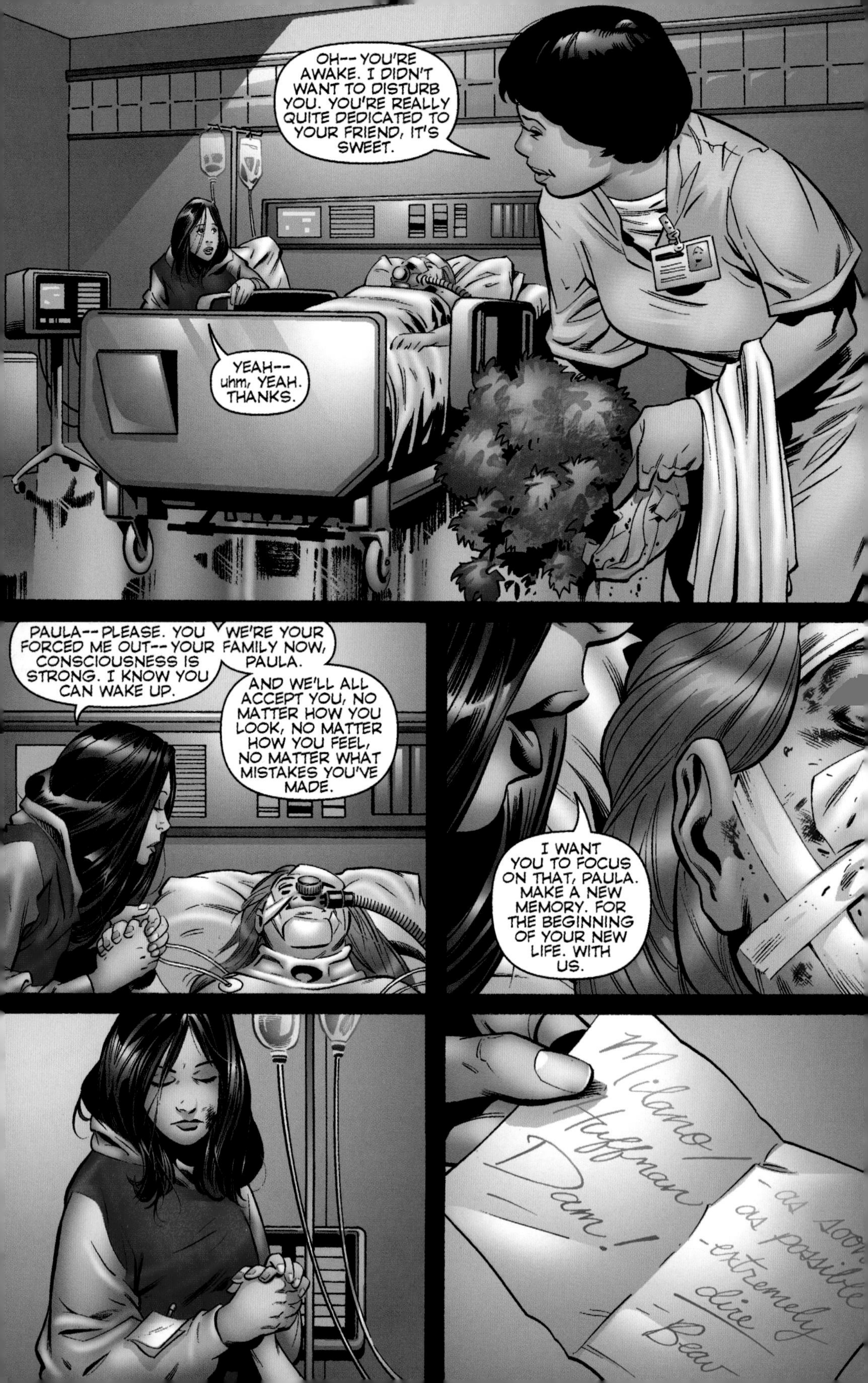
OH-- YOU'RE AWAKE. I DIDN'T WANT TO DISTURB YOU. YOU'RE REALLY QUITE DEDICATED TO YOUR FRIEND, IT'S SWEET.
YEAH-- uhm, YEAH. THANKS.
PAULA-- PLEASE. YOU FORCED ME OUT-- YOUR CONSCIOUSNESS IS STRONG. I KNOW YOU CAN WAKE UP.
WE'RE YOUR FAMILY NOW, PAULA.
AND WE'LL ALL ACCEPT YOU, NO MATTER HOW YOU LOOK, NO MATTER HOW YOU FEEL, NO MATTER WHAT MISTAKES YOU'VE MADE.
I WANT YOU TO FOCUS ON THAT, PAULA. MAKE A NEW MEMORY. FOR THE BEGINNING OF YOUR NEW LIFE. WITH US.
Milano! Huffman Dam!
-as soon as possible
-extremely dire
-Bear

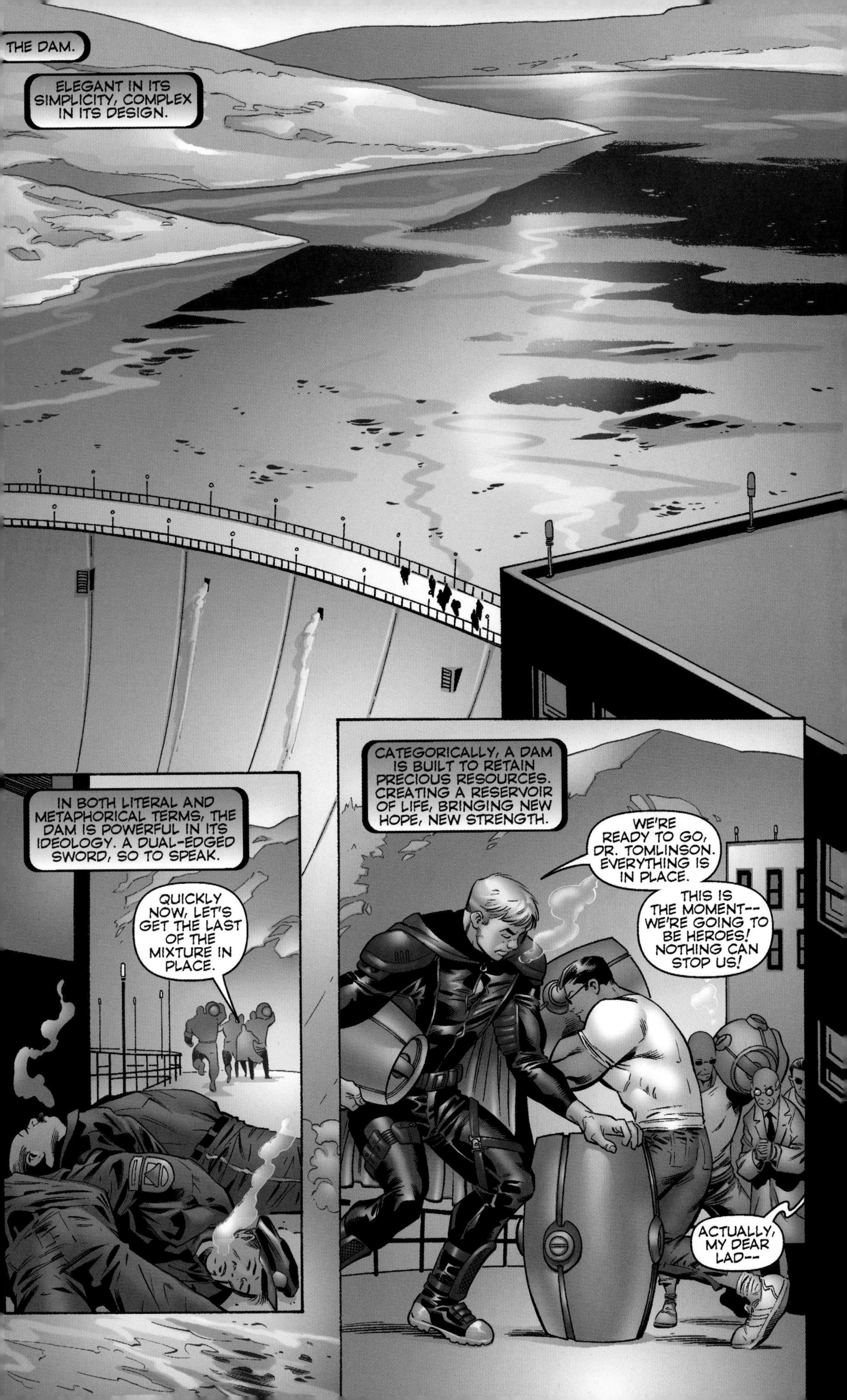
THE DAM.
ELEGANT IN ITS SIMPLICITY, COMPLEX IN ITS DESIGN.
IN BOTH LITERAL AND METAPHORICAL TERMS, THE DAM IS POWERFUL IN ITS IDEOLOGY. A DUAL-EDGED SWORD, SO TO SPEAK.
QUICKLY NOW, LET'S GET THE LAST OF THE MIXTURE IN PLACE.
CATEGORICALLY, A DAM IS BUILT TO RETAIN PRECIOUS RESOURCES. CREATING A RESERVOIR OF LIFE, BRINGING NEW HOPE, NEW STRENGTH.
WE'RE READY TO GO, DR. TOMLINSON. EVERYTHING IS IN PLACE.
THIS IS THE MOMENT-- WE'RE GOING TO BE HEROES! NOTHING CAN STOP US!
ACTUALLY, MY DEAR LAD--

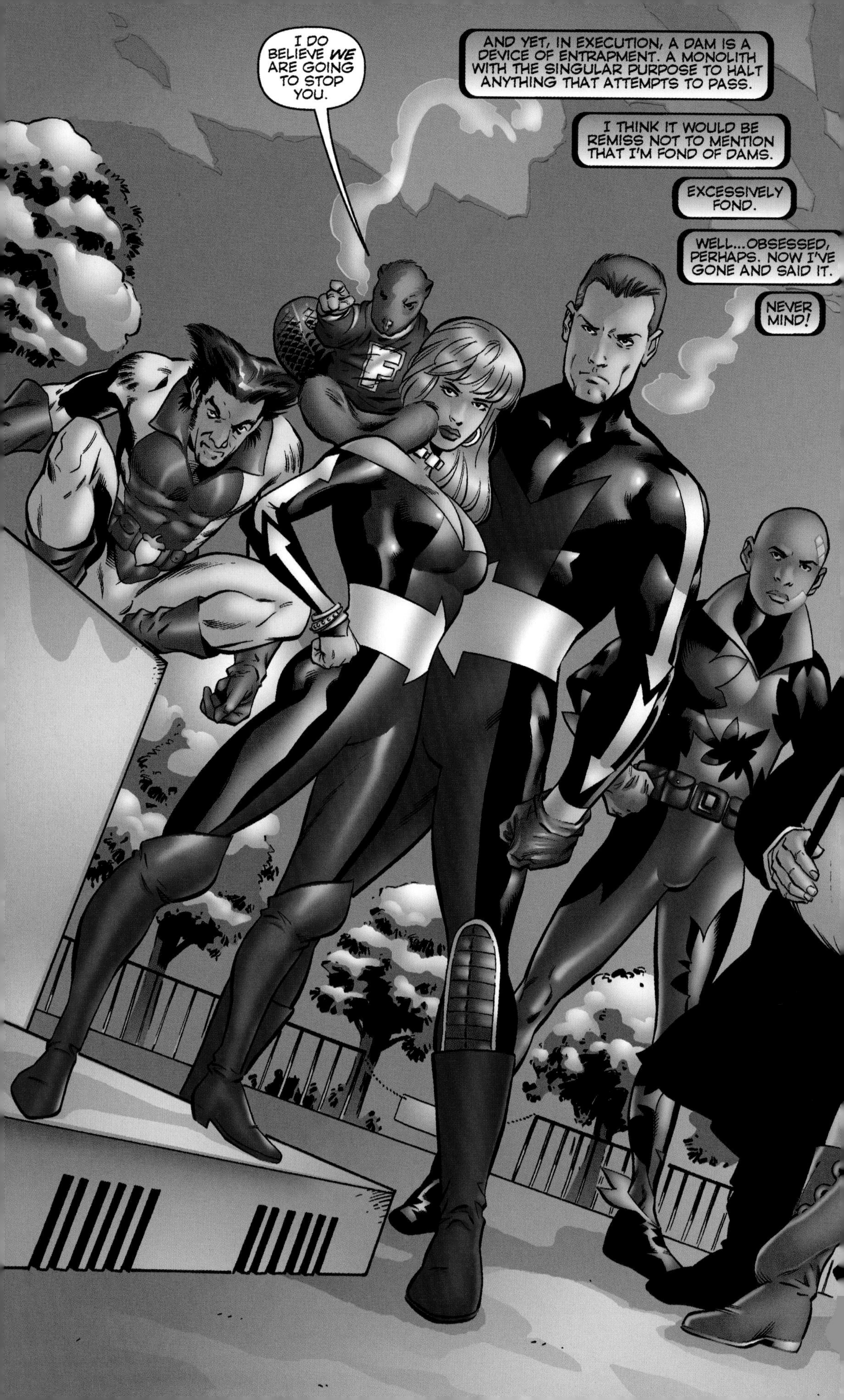

AND YET, IN EXECUTION, A DAM IS A DEVICE OF ENTRAPMENT. A MONOLITH WITH THE SINGULAR PURPOSE TO HALT ANYTHING THAT ATTEMPTS TO PASS.
I DO BELIEVE *WE* ARE GOING TO STOP YOU.
I THINK IT WOULD BE REMISS NOT TO MENTION THAT I'M FOND OF DAMS.
EXCESSIVELY FOND.
WELL...OBSESSED, PERHAPS. NOW I'VE GONE AND SAID IT.
NEVER MIND!

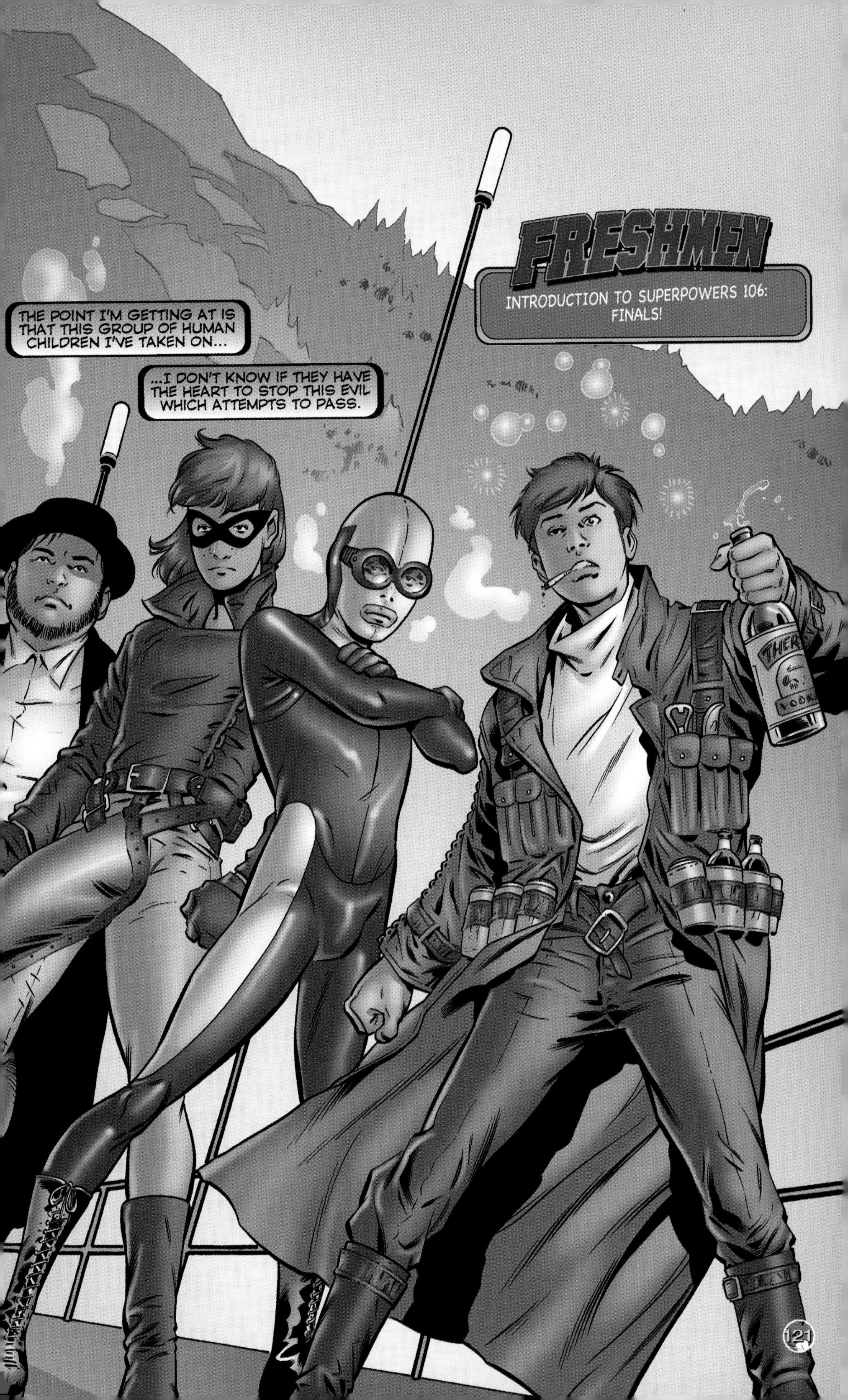
FRESHMEN
INTRODUCTION TO SUPERPOWERS 106: FINALS!
THE POINT I'M GETTING AT IS THAT THIS GROUP OF HUMAN CHILDREN I'VE TAKEN ON...
...I DON'T KNOW IF THEY HAVE THE HEART TO STOP THIS EVIL WHICH ATTEMPTS TO PASS.
VODKA

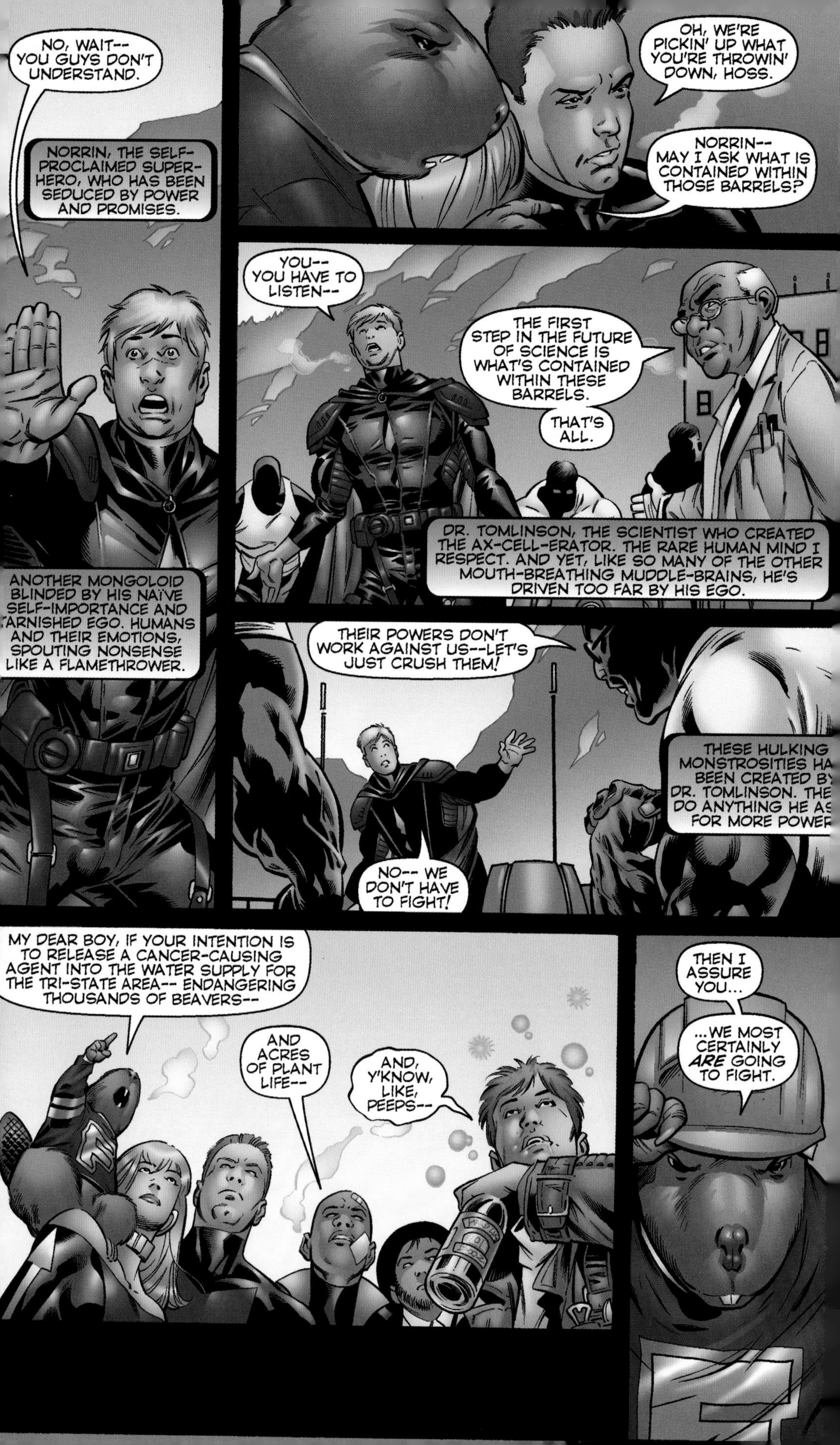
NO, WAIT-- YOU GUYS DON'T UNDERSTAND.
NORRIN, THE SELF-PROCLAIMED SUPER-HERO, WHO HAS BEEN SEDUCED BY POWER AND PROMISES.
OH, WE'RE PICKIN' UP WHAT YOU'RE THROWIN' DOWN, HOSS.
NORRIN-- MAY I ASK WHAT IS CONTAINED WITHIN THOSE BARRELS?
YOU-- YOU HAVE TO LISTEN--
THE FIRST STEP IN THE FUTURE OF SCIENCE IS WHAT'S CONTAINED WITHIN THESE BARRELS.
THAT'S ALL.
DR. TOMLINSON, THE SCIENTIST WHO CREATED THE AX-CELL-ERATOR. THE RARE HUMAN MIND I RESPECT. AND YET, LIKE SO MANY OF THE OTHER MOUTH-BREATHING MUDDLE-BRAINS, HE'S DRIVEN TOO FAR BY HIS EGO.
ANOTHER MONGOLOID BLINDED BY HIS NAÏVE SELF-IMPORTANCE AND TARNISHED EGO. HUMANS AND THEIR EMOTIONS, SPOUTING NONSENSE LIKE A FLAMETHROWER.
THEIR POWERS DON'T WORK AGAINST US--LET'S JUST CRUSH THEM!
THESE HULKING MONSTROSITIES HA BEEN CREATED BY DR. TOMLINSON. THE DO ANYTHING HE AS FOR MORE POWER
NO-- WE DON'T HAVE TO FIGHT!
MY DEAR BOY, IF YOUR INTENTION IS TO RELEASE A CANCER-CAUSING AGENT INTO THE WATER SUPPLY FOR THE TRI-STATE AREA-- ENDANGERING THOUSANDS OF BEAVERS--
AND ACRES OF PLANT LIFE--
AND, Y'KNOW, LIKE, PEEPS--
THEN I ASSURE YOU...
...WE MOST CERTAINLY *ARE* GOING TO FIGHT.

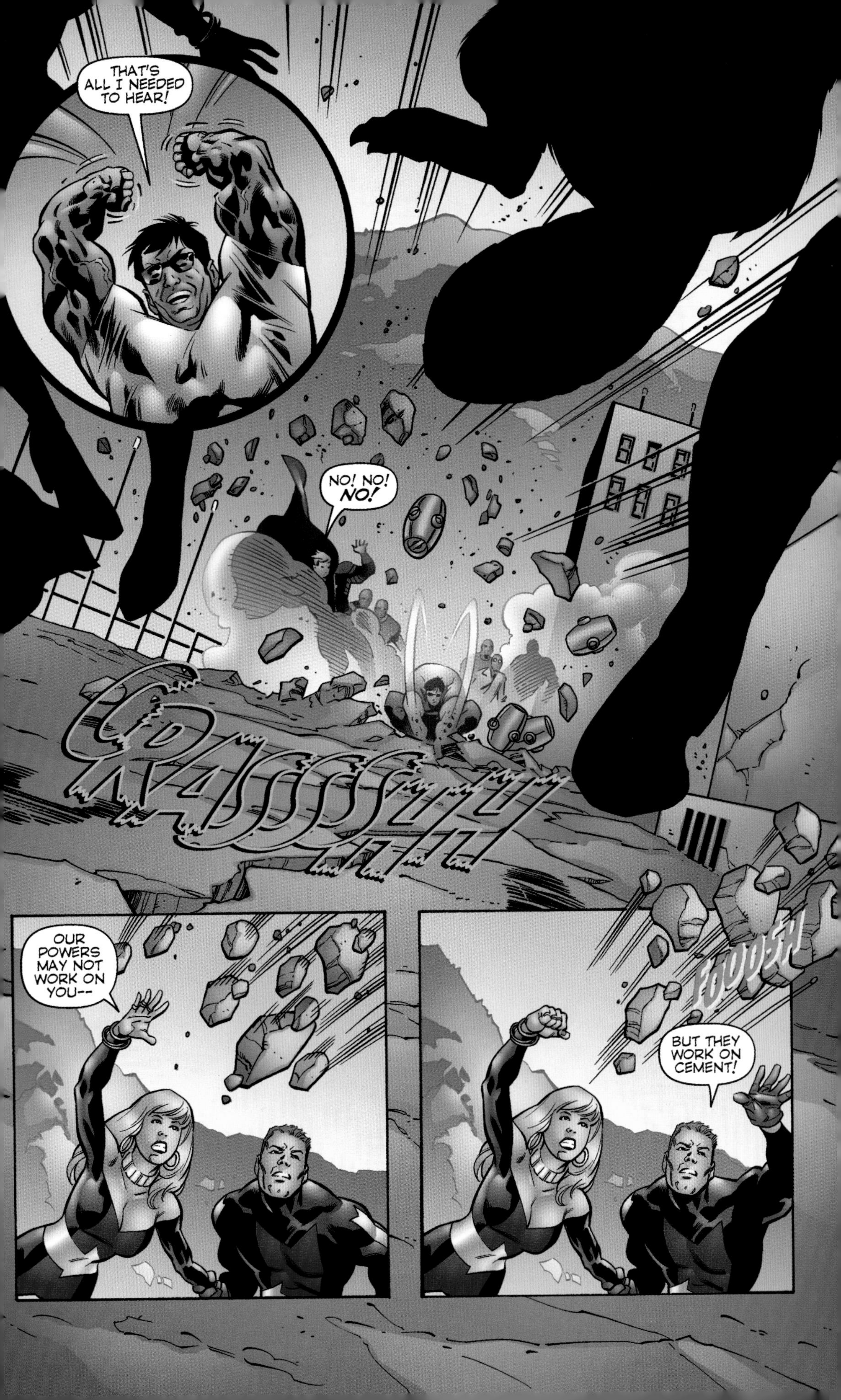

THAT'S ALL I NEEDED TO HEAR!
NO! NO! NO!
CRASSSHH
OUR POWERS MAY NOT WORK ON YOU--
FOOOSH
BUT THEY WORK ON CEMENT!

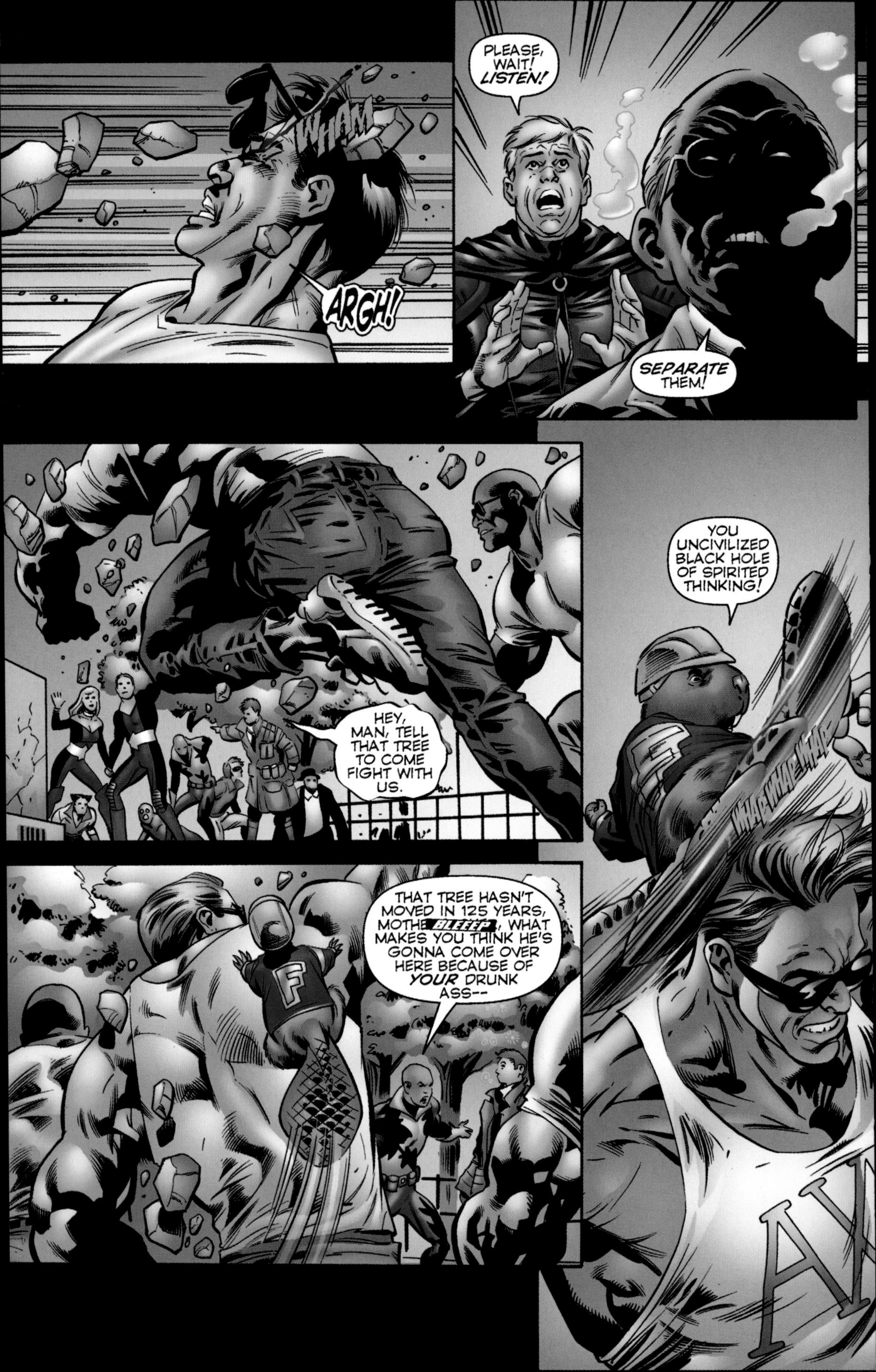
WHAM
ARGH!
PLEASE, WAIT! LISTEN!
SEPARATE THEM!
YOU UNCIVILIZED BLACK HOLE OF SPIRITED THINKING!
HEY, MAN, TELL THAT TREE TO COME FIGHT WITH US.
THAT TREE HASN'T MOVED IN 125 YEARS, MOTHE BLEEEP, WHAT MAKES YOU THINK HE'S GONNA COME OVER HERE BECAUSE OF YOUR DRUNK ASS--
WHAP WHAP WHAP

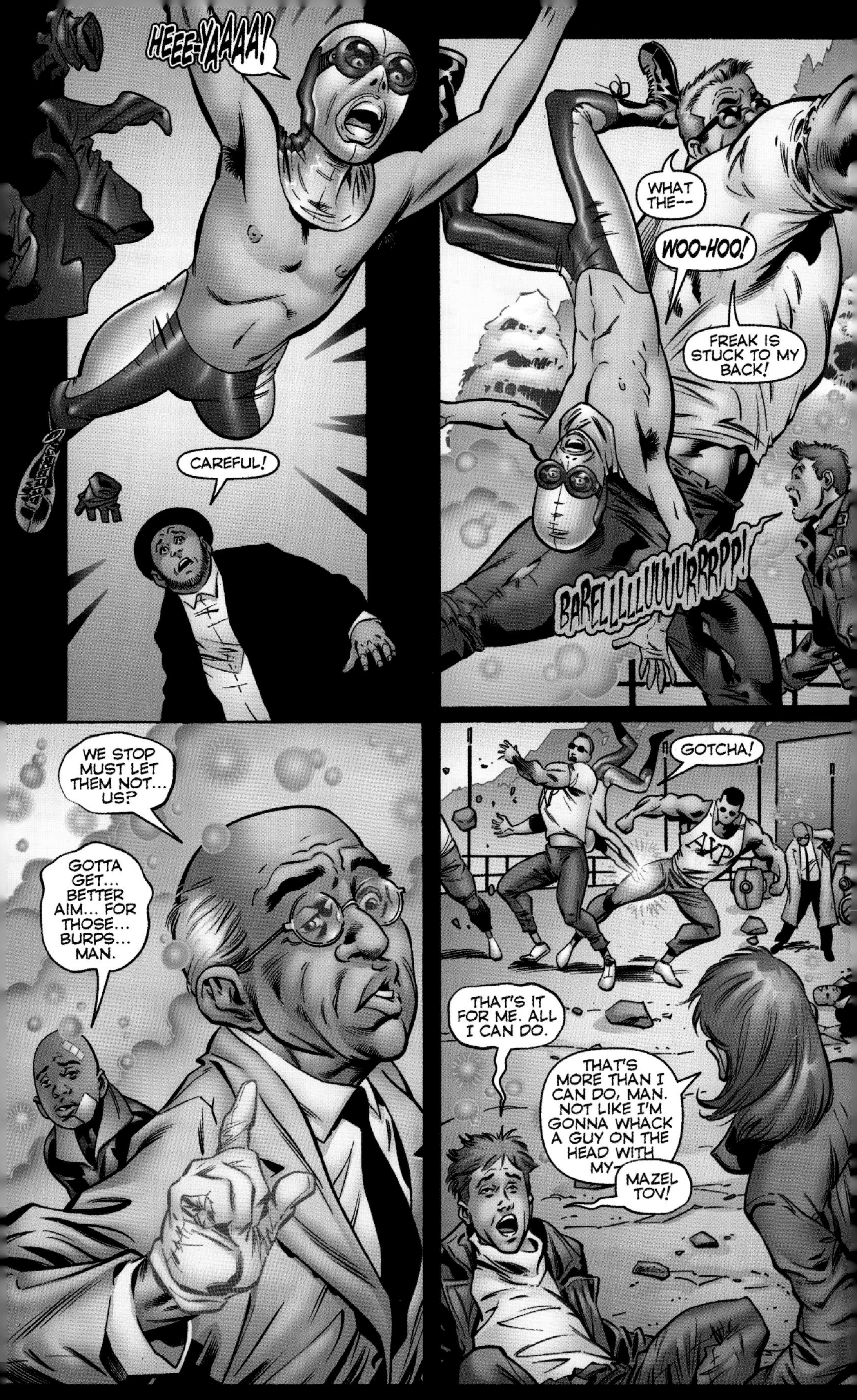
HEEE-YAAAA!
CAREFUL!
WHAT THE--
WOO-HOO!
FREAK IS STUCK TO MY BACK!
BARELLLLLUUUURRRPP!
WE STOP MUST LET THEM NOT... US?
GOTTA GET... BETTER AIM... FOR THOSE... BURPS... MAN.
GOTCHA!
THAT'S IT FOR ME. ALL I CAN DO.
THAT'S MORE THAN I CAN DO, MAN. NOT LIKE I'M GONNA WHACK A GUY ON THE HEAD WITH MY--
MAZEL TOV!

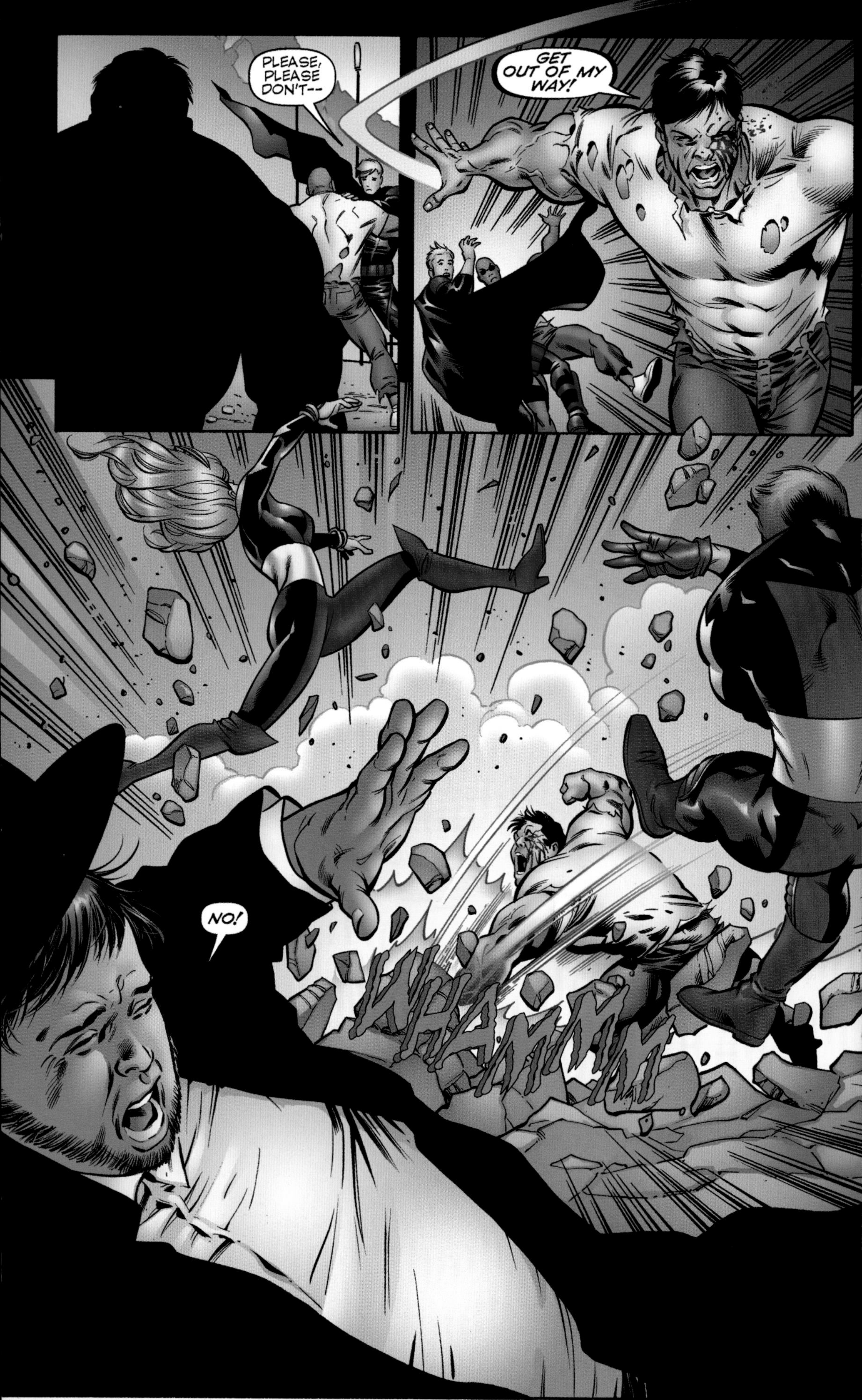
PLEASE, PLEASE DON'T--
GET OUT OF MY WAY!
NO!
WHAMMM

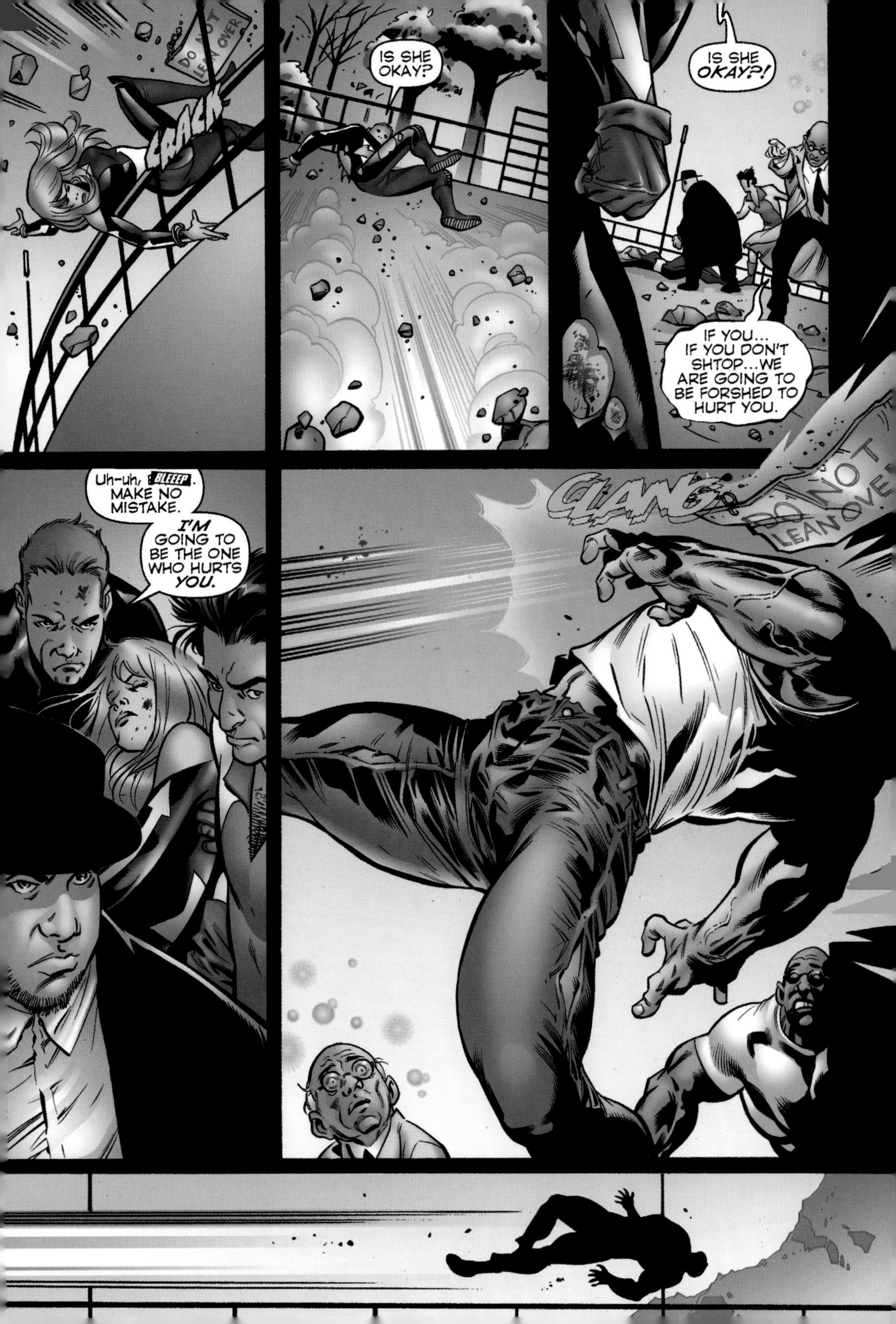
DO NOT LEAN OVER
CRACK
IS SHE OKAY?
IS SHE OKAY?!
IF YOU... IF YOU DON'T SHTOP...WE ARE GOING TO BE FORSHED TO HURT YOU.
Uh-uh, BLEEEP. MAKE NO MISTAKE.
I'M GOING TO BE THE ONE WHO HURTS YOU.
CLANG
DO NOT LEAN OVER

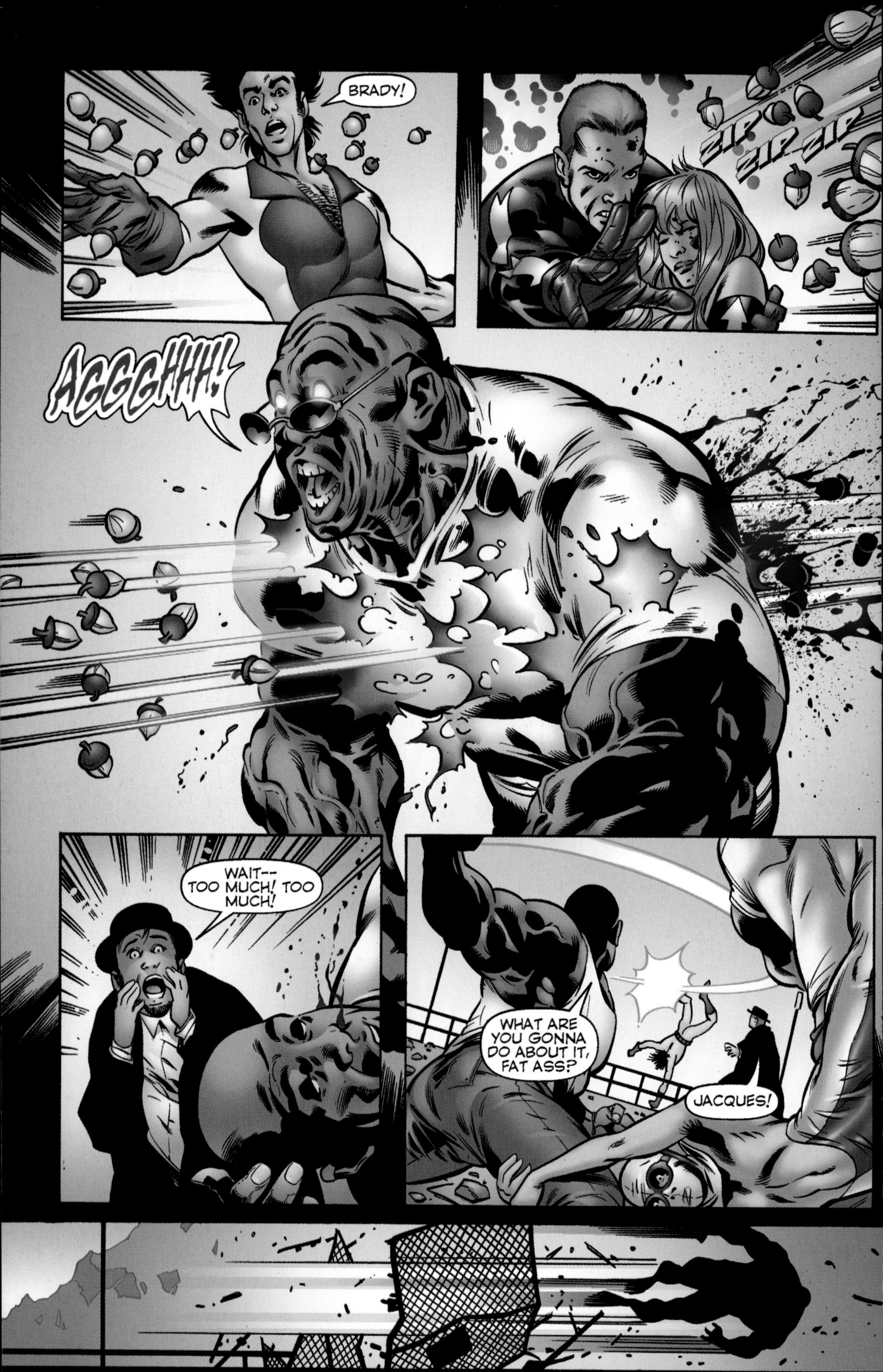
BRADY!
ZIP ZIP ZIP
AGGGHHH!
WAIT-- TOO MUCH! TOO MUCH!
WHAT ARE YOU GONNA DO ABOUT IT, FAT ASS?
JACQUES!

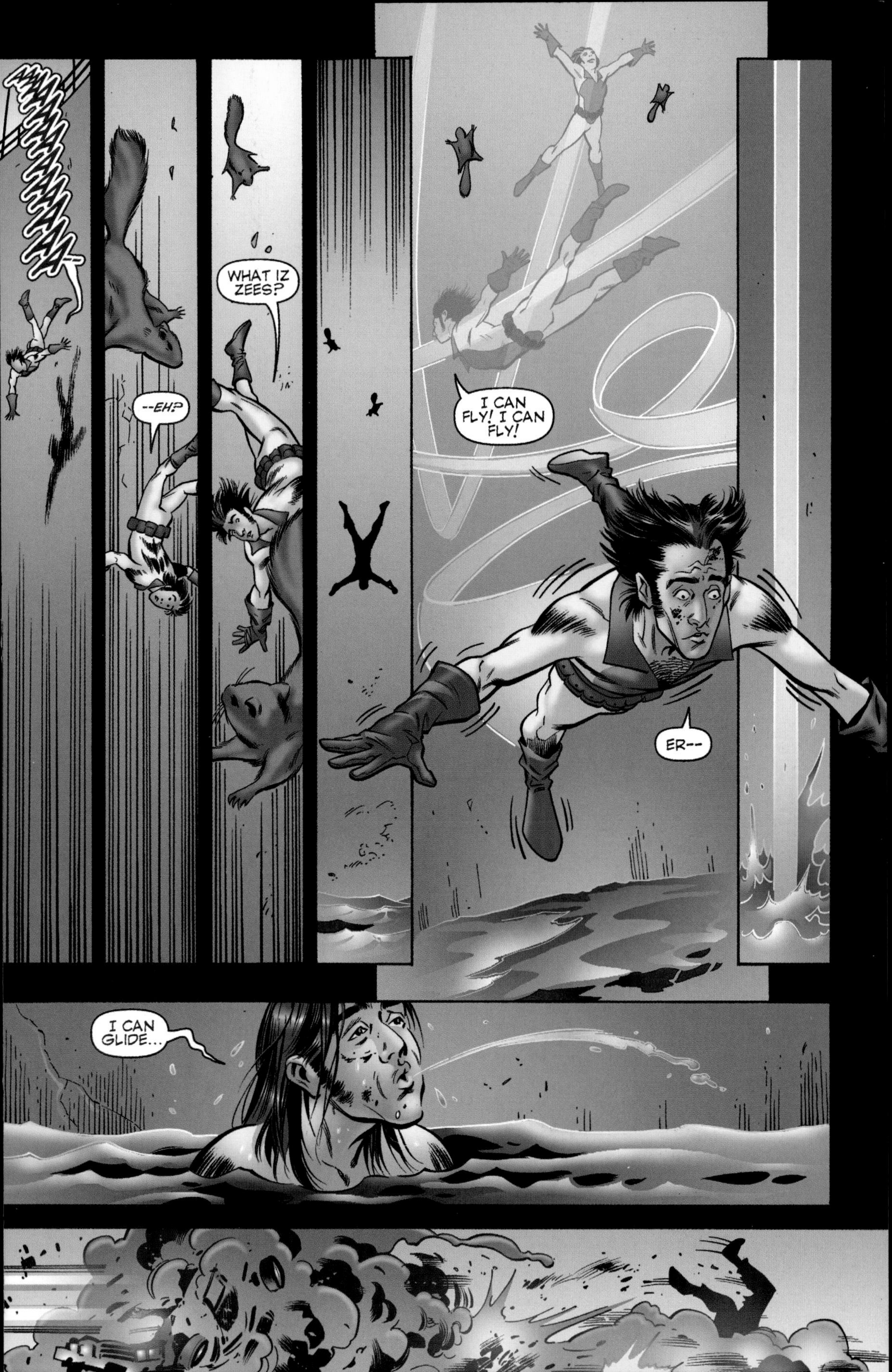
--EH?
WHAT IZ ZEES?
I CAN FLY! I CAN FLY!
ER--
I CAN GLIDE...

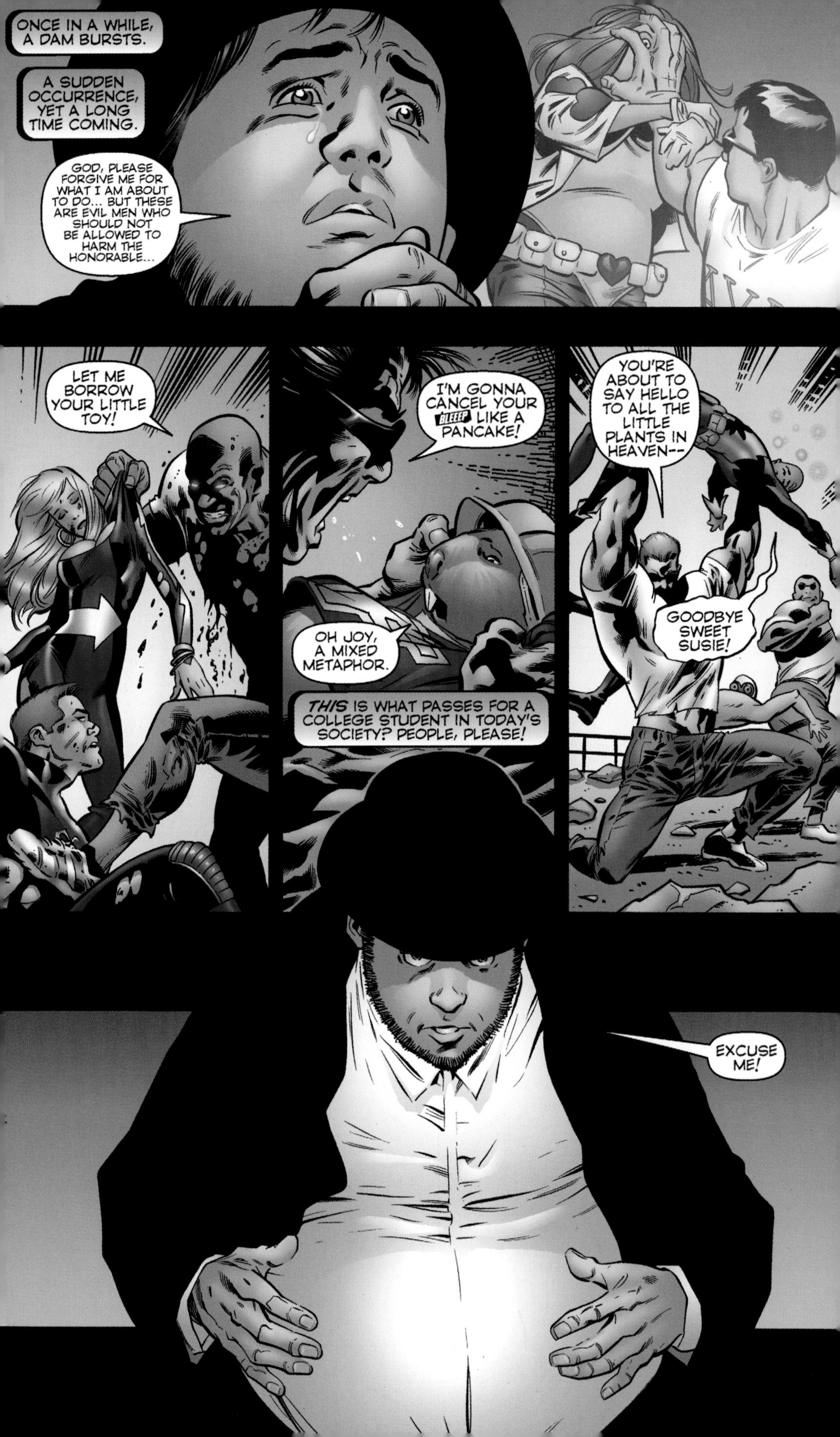
ONCE IN A WHILE, A DAM BURSTS.
A SUDDEN OCCURRENCE, YET A LONG TIME COMING.
GOD, PLEASE FORGIVE ME FOR WHAT I AM ABOUT TO DO... BUT THESE ARE EVIL MEN WHO SHOULD NOT BE ALLOWED TO HARM THE HONORABLE...
LET ME BORROW YOUR LITTLE TOY!
I'M GONNA CANCEL YOUR BLEEEP LIKE A PANCAKE!
OH JOY, A MIXED METAPHOR.
THIS IS WHAT PASSES FOR A COLLEGE STUDENT IN TODAY'S SOCIETY? PEOPLE, PLEASE!
YOU'RE ABOUT TO SAY HELLO TO ALL THE LITTLE PLANTS IN HEAVEN--
GOODBYE SWEET SUSIE!
EXCUSE ME!

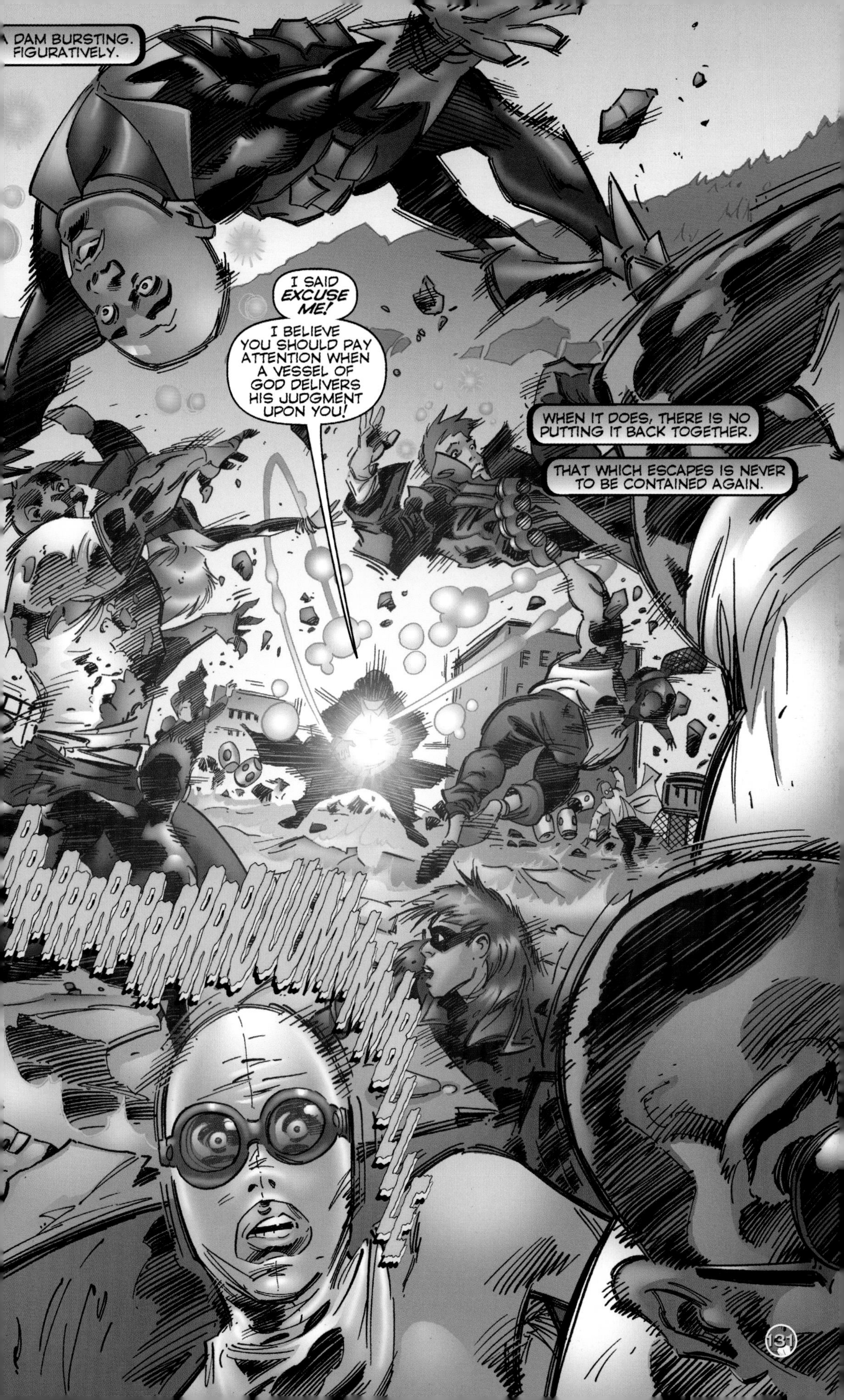
DAM BURSTING. FIGURATIVELY.
I SAID *EXCUSE ME!*
I BELIEVE YOU SHOULD PAY ATTENTION WHEN A VESSEL OF GOD DELIVERS HIS JUDGMENT UPON YOU!
WHEN IT DOES, THERE IS NO PUTTING IT BACK TOGETHER.
THAT WHICH ESCAPES IS NEVER TO BE CONTAINED AGAIN.

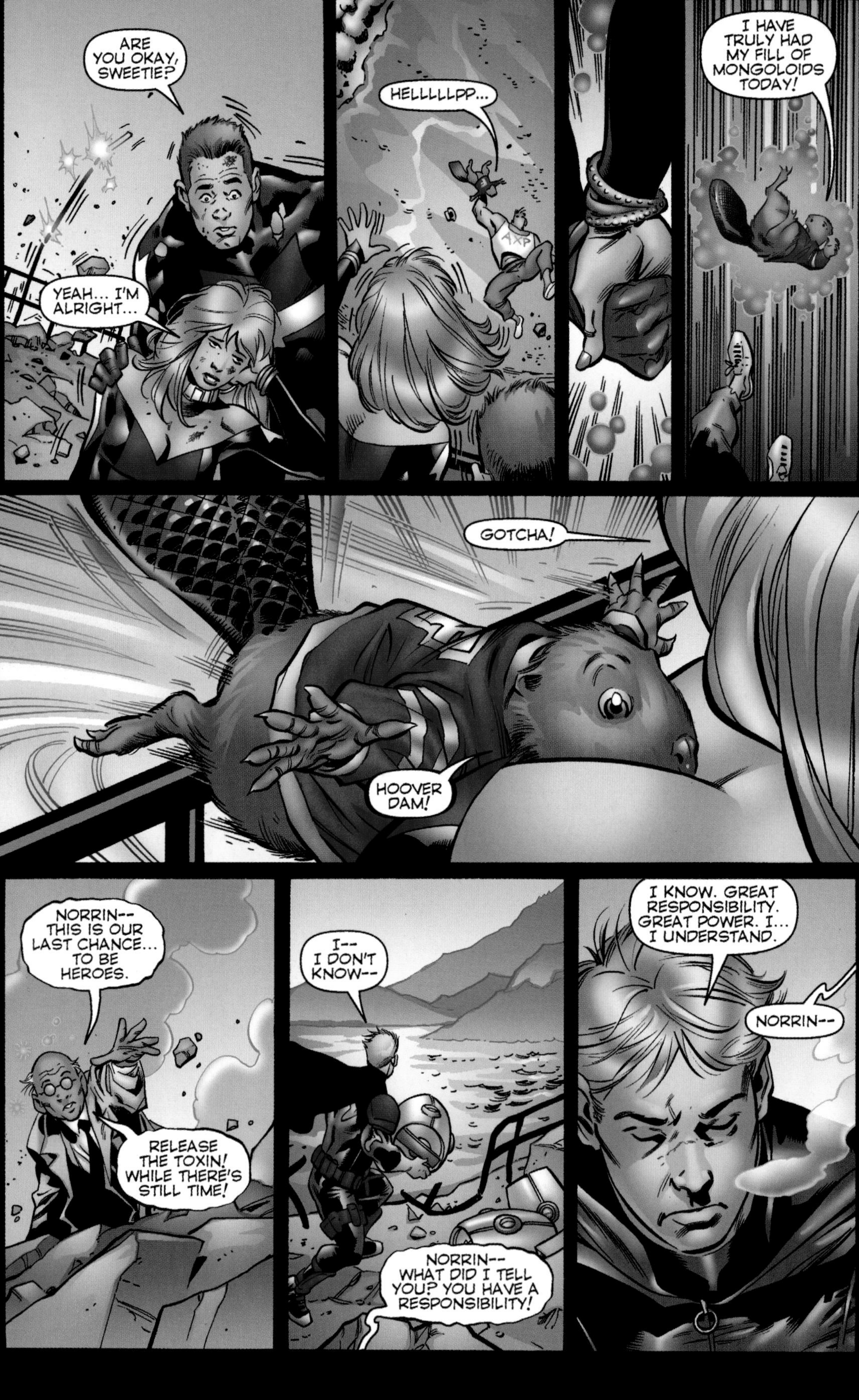
ARE YOU OKAY, SWEETIE?
YEAH... I'M ALRIGHT...
HELLLLLLPP...
I HAVE TRULY HAD MY FILL OF MONGOLOIDS TODAY!
GOTCHA!
HOOVER DAM!
NORRIN-- THIS IS OUR LAST CHANCE... TO BE HEROES.
RELEASE THE TOXIN! WHILE THERE'S STILL TIME!
I-- I DON'T KNOW--
NORRIN-- WHAT DID I TELL YOU? YOU HAVE A RESPONSIBILITY!
I KNOW. GREAT RESPONSIBILITY. GREAT POWER. I... I UNDERSTAND.
NORRIN--

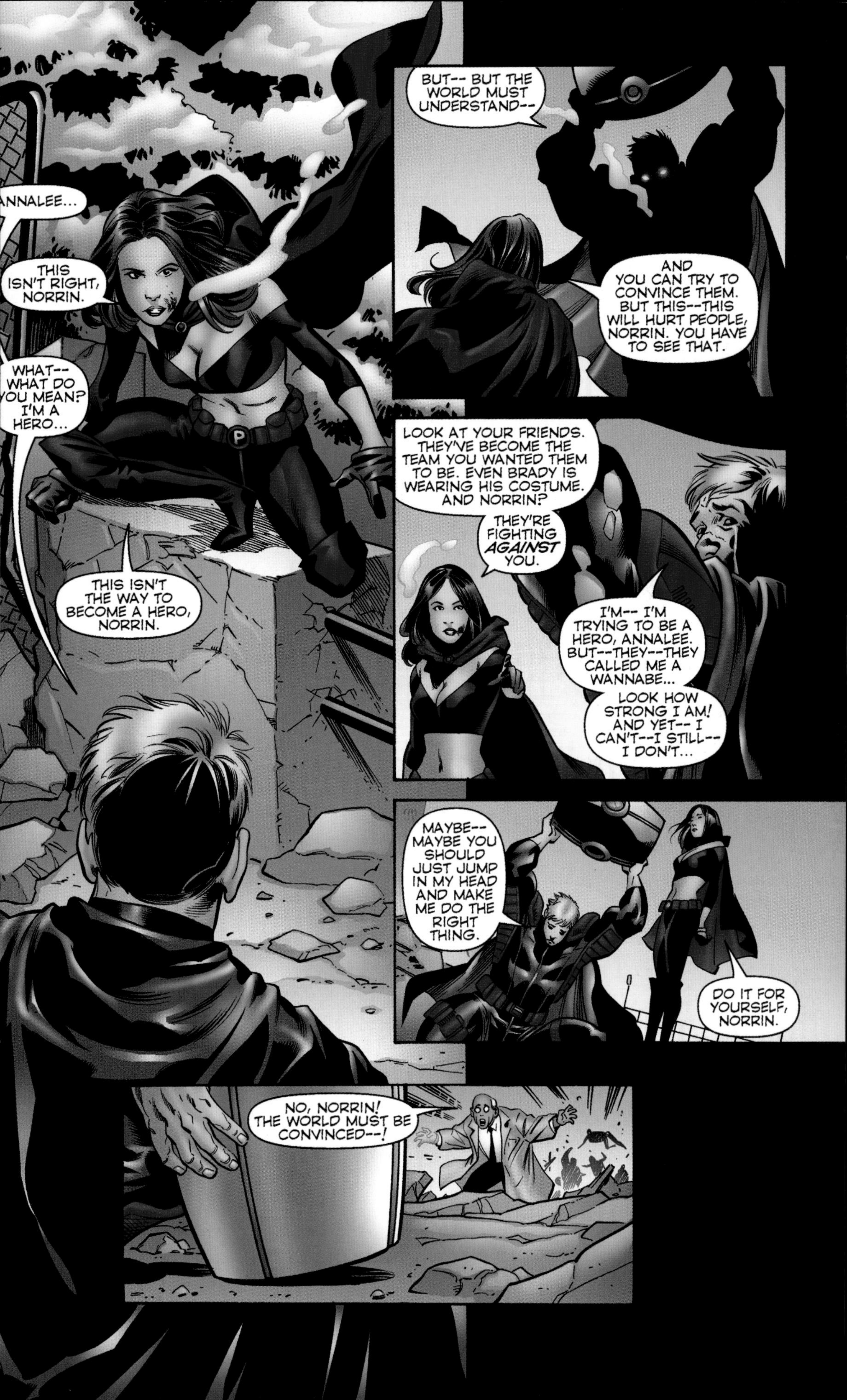
ANNALEE...
THIS ISN'T RIGHT, NORRIN.
WHAT-- WHAT DO YOU MEAN? I'M A HERO...
THIS ISN'T THE WAY TO BECOME A HERO, NORRIN.
BUT-- BUT THE WORLD MUST UNDERSTAND--
AND YOU CAN TRY TO CONVINCE THEM. BUT THIS--THIS WILL HURT PEOPLE, NORRIN. YOU HAVE TO SEE THAT.
LOOK AT YOUR FRIENDS. THEY'VE BECOME THE TEAM YOU WANTED THEM TO BE. EVEN BRADY IS WEARING HIS COSTUME. AND NORRIN?
THEY'RE FIGHTING *AGAINST* YOU.
I'M-- I'M TRYING TO BE A HERO, ANNALEE. BUT--THEY--THEY CALLED ME A WANNABE...
LOOK HOW STRONG I AM! AND YET-- I CAN'T--I STILL-- I DON'T...
MAYBE-- MAYBE YOU SHOULD JUST JUMP IN MY HEAD AND MAKE ME DO THE RIGHT THING.
DO IT FOR YOURSELF, NORRIN.
NO, NORRIN! THE WORLD MUST BE CONVINCED--!

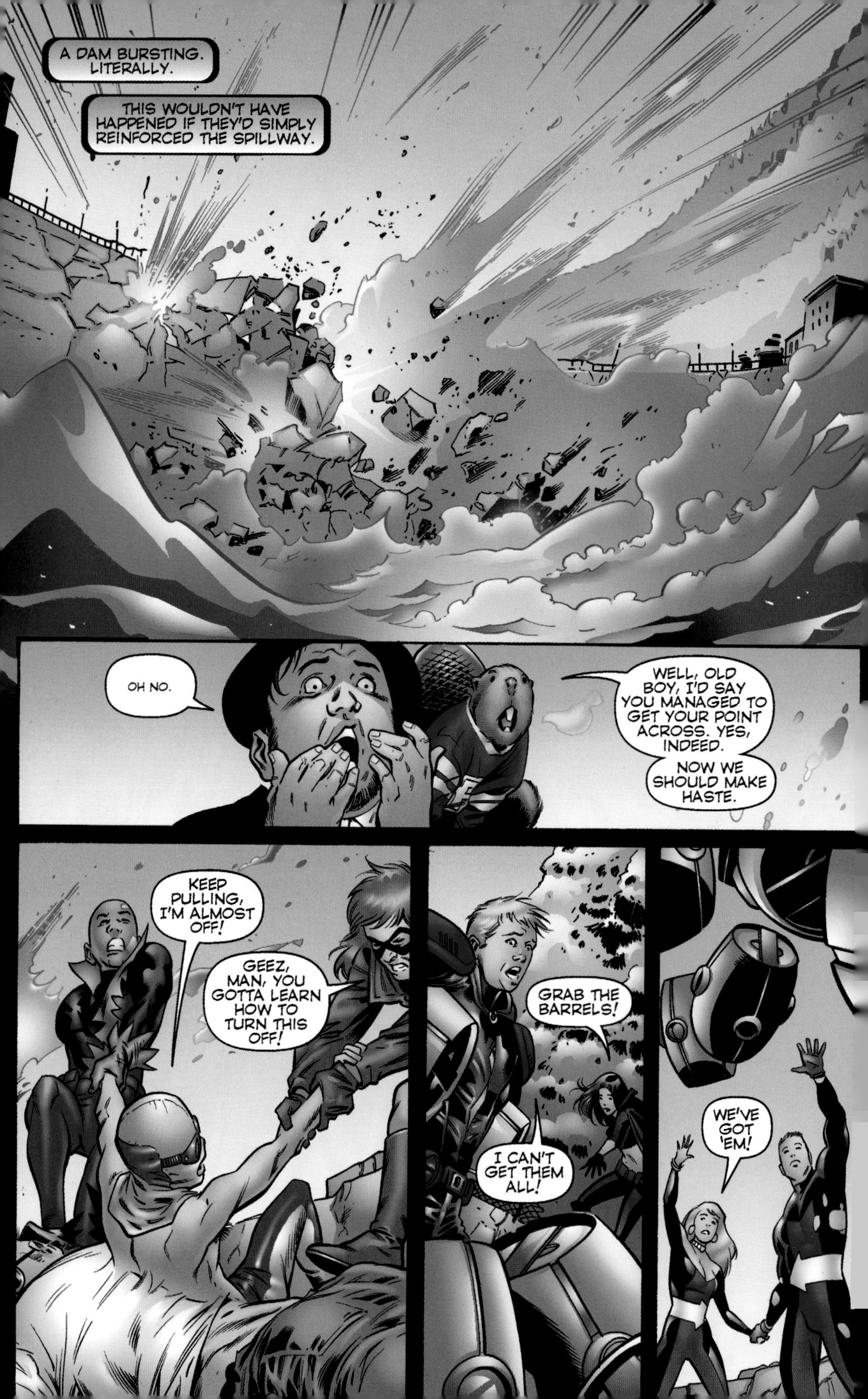
A DAM BURSTING. LITERALLY.
THIS WOULDN'T HAVE HAPPENED IF THEY'D SIMPLY REINFORCED THE SPILLWAY.
OH NO.
WELL, OLD BOY, I'D SAY YOU MANAGED TO GET YOUR POINT ACROSS. YES, INDEED.
NOW WE SHOULD MAKE HASTE.
KEEP PULLING, I'M ALMOST OFF!
GEEZ, MAN, YOU GOTTA LEARN HOW TO TURN THIS OFF!
GRAB THE BARRELS!
I CAN'T GET THEM ALL!
WE'VE GOT 'EM!

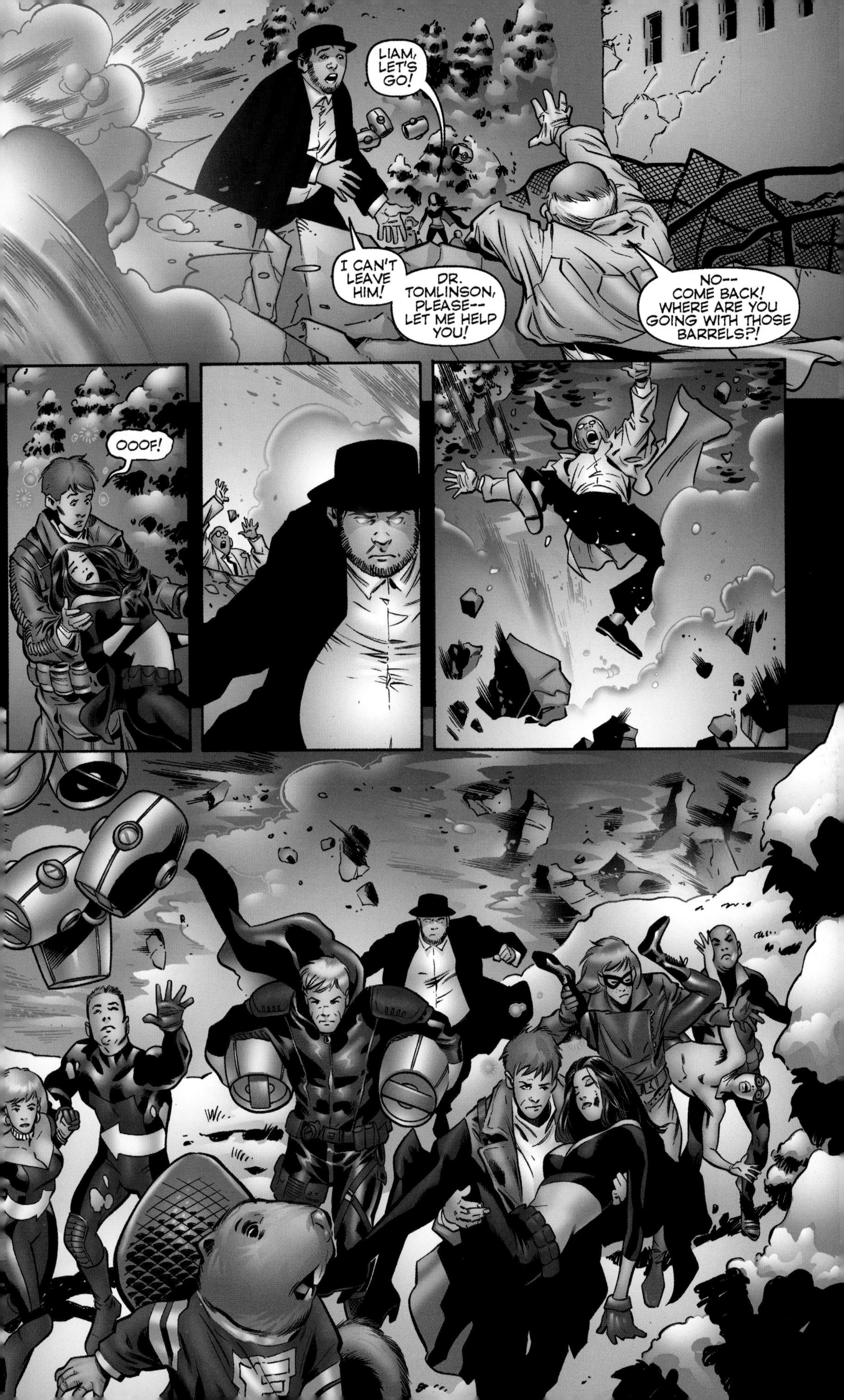
LIAM, LET'S GO!
I CAN'T LEAVE HIM!
DR. TOMLINSON, PLEASE-- LET ME HELP YOU!
NO-- COME BACK! WHERE ARE YOU GOING WITH THOSE BARRELS?!
OOOF!

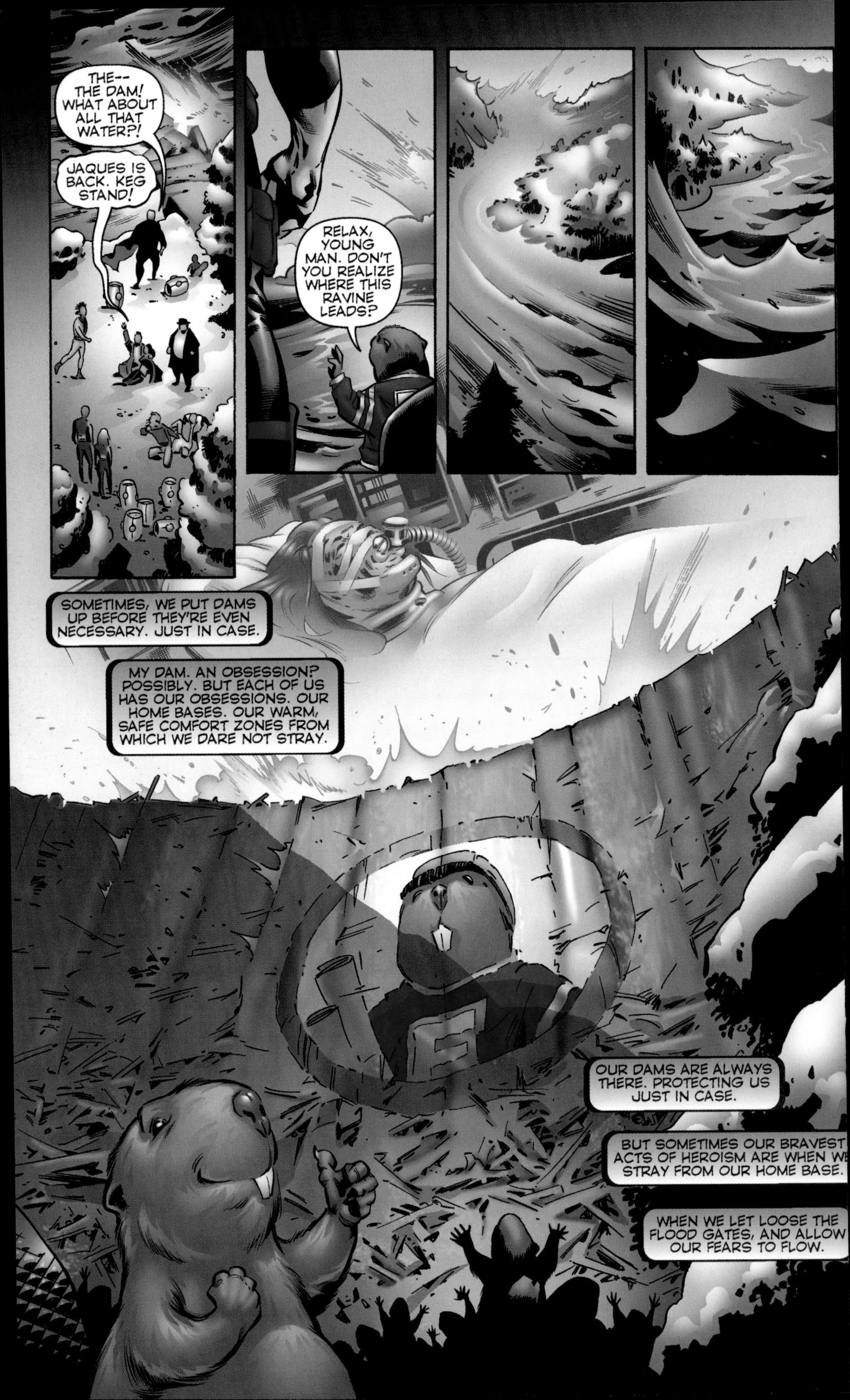
THE-- THE DAM! WHAT ABOUT ALL THAT WATER?!
JAQUES IS BACK. KEG STAND!
RELAX, YOUNG MAN. DON'T YOU REALIZE WHERE THIS RAVINE LEADS?
SOMETIMES, WE PUT DAMS UP BEFORE THEY'RE EVEN NECESSARY. JUST IN CASE.
MY DAM. AN OBSESSION? POSSIBLY. BUT EACH OF US HAS OUR OBSESSIONS. OUR HOME BASES. OUR WARM, SAFE COMFORT ZONES FROM WHICH WE DARE NOT STRAY.
OUR DAMS ARE ALWAYS THERE. PROTECTING US JUST IN CASE.
BUT SOMETIMES OUR BRAVEST ACTS OF HEROISM ARE WHEN WE STRAY FROM OUR HOME BASE.
WHEN WE LET LOOSE THE FLOOD GATES, AND ALLOW OUR FEARS TO FLOW.

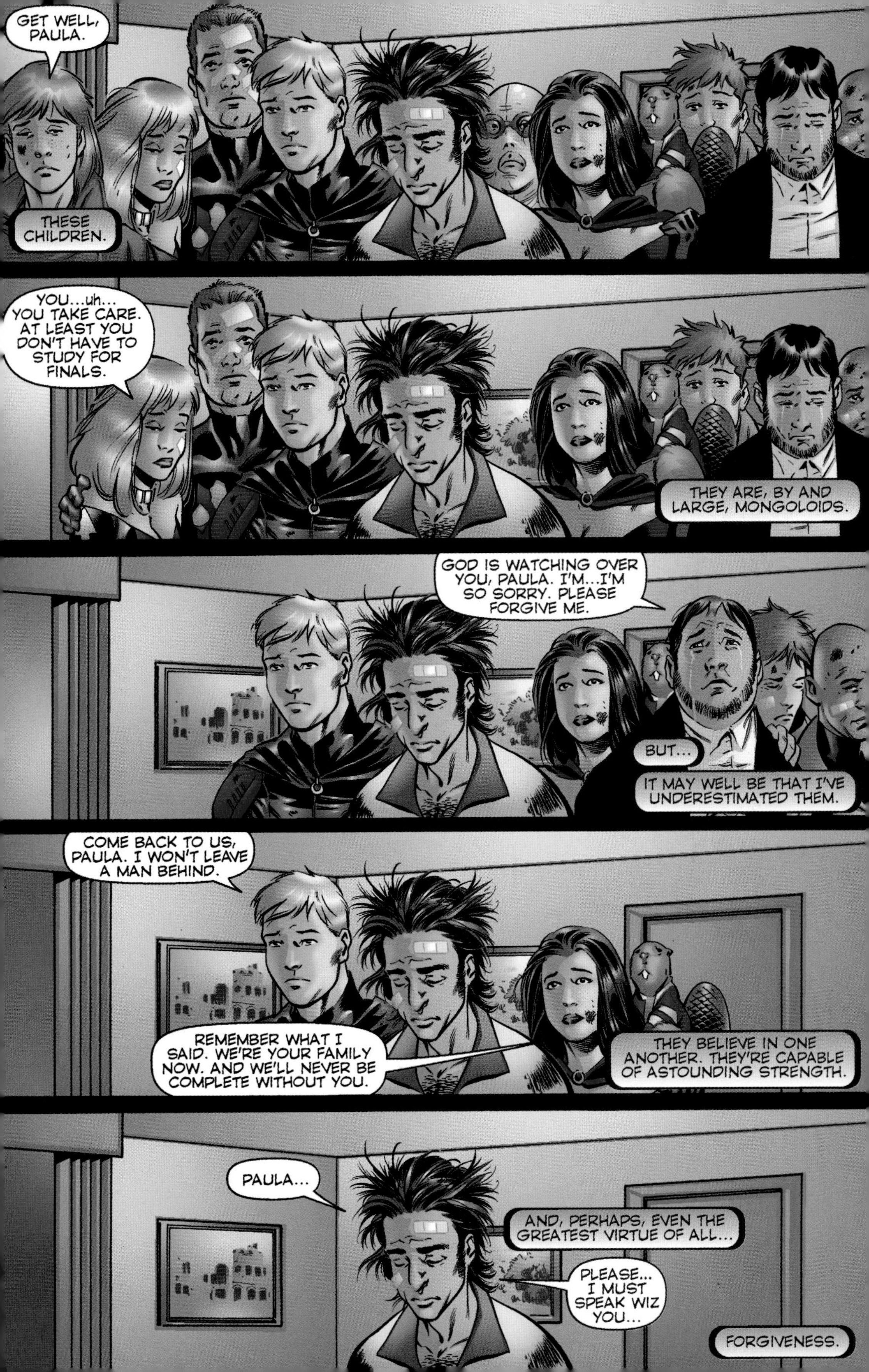
GET WELL, PAULA.
THESE CHILDREN.
YOU...uh... YOU TAKE CARE. AT LEAST YOU DON'T HAVE TO STUDY FOR FINALS.
THEY ARE, BY AND LARGE, MONGOLOIDS.
GOD IS WATCHING OVER YOU, PAULA. I'M...I'M SO SORRY. PLEASE FORGIVE ME.
BUT...
IT MAY WELL BE THAT I'VE UNDERESTIMATED THEM.
COME BACK TO US, PAULA. I WON'T LEAVE A MAN BEHIND.
REMEMBER WHAT I SAID. WE'RE YOUR FAMILY NOW. AND WE'LL NEVER BE COMPLETE WITHOUT YOU.
THEY BELIEVE IN ONE ANOTHER. THEY'RE CAPABLE OF ASTOUNDING STRENGTH.
PAULA...
AND, PERHAPS, EVEN THE GREATEST VIRTUE OF ALL...
PLEASE... I MUST SPEAK WIZ YOU...
FORGIVENESS.

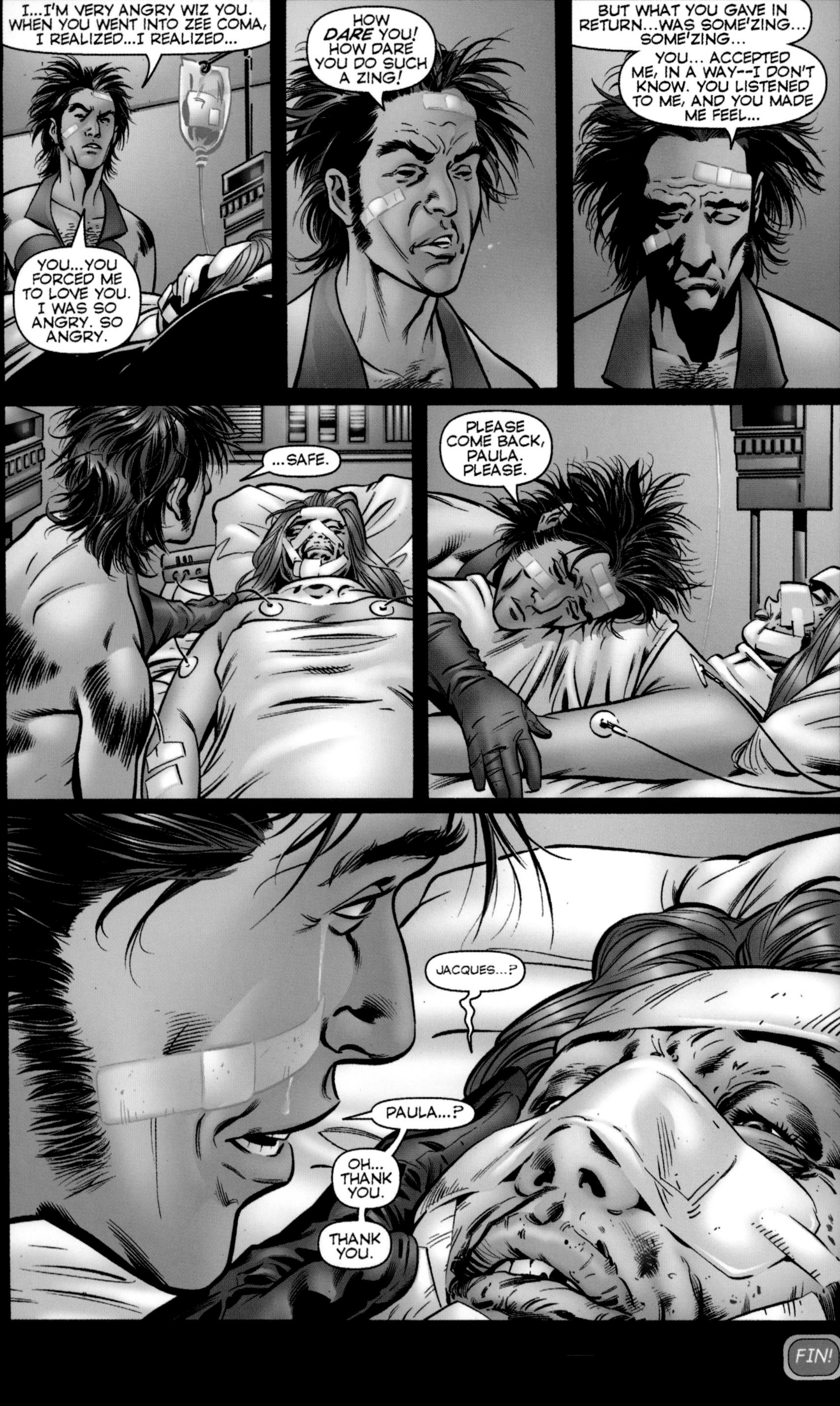
I...I'M VERY ANGRY WIZ YOU. WHEN YOU WENT INTO ZEE COMA, I REALIZED...I REALIZED...
YOU...YOU FORCED ME TO LOVE YOU. I WAS SO ANGRY. SO ANGRY.
HOW DARE YOU! HOW DARE YOU DO SUCH A ZING!
BUT WHAT YOU GAVE IN RETURN...WAS SOME'ZING... SOME'ZING...
YOU... ACCEPTED ME, IN A WAY--I DON'T KNOW. YOU LISTENED TO ME, AND YOU MADE ME FEEL...
...SAFE.
PLEASE COME BACK, PAULA. PLEASE.
JACQUES...?
PAULA...?
OH... THANK YOU.
THANK YOU.
FIN!

Acknowledgements

A lot of my friends rallied to help me on this project. Beside my best friend, there were Dan Milano and Matthew Huffman, who helped us create the characters. Matt Senreich told Top Cow to call me for some good comic ideas. On a separate occasion, Freddie Prinze and Conrad Jackson fearlessly did the same thing. Matt also asked Cartoon Network to air our ads during Robot Chicken, and he and Geoff Johns sat down with me to offer advice about the comic industry. Geoff, Sarah Michelle Gellar, Mila Kunis and Joss Whedon all lent their names to profoundly indifferent cover quotes—Mila even offered her likeness as the Puppeteer, and pimped us to Stuff Magazine. Cat, from DJ's Universal Comics in Studio City, picked me up every time I walked in his store. On the Internet, a host of unbelievably loyal fans welcomed me daily, sometimes with photos of them dressed as our characters. Mark Piccirilli moderated the forum very smoothly. My cousin Ben and my most beloved friend, Derek, both of whom I miss dearly, tirelessly believed in me and left their spirits in my heart. Both this work and my life are dedicated to them. Bill, my most trusted pal, kept me calm. Fat Buddy licked me. My dad, Poppa Sterb, brought our posters to his local comic book stores. And the lovely Lisa, who will be my bride just days after this is printed, is the greatest co-pilot this imaginative guy could imagine.

As represented on the page, the astounding Leonard Kirk created relentlessly brilliant visuals, somehow shoehorning my dense story onto the page. Andrew Pepoy's inks brought him home flawlessly, while the phenomenal Troy Peteri worked overtime to squeeze the Drama Twins' dense dialogue into those unforgiving panels, and Tyson Wengler always kept the Beaver brown. Rodolfo Migliari's covers progressed from jaw-dropping to worthy of weeping. Jim McLauchlin tried (valiantly) to keep my neuroses under control, while Matt Hawkins, Renae Geerlings, Scott Tucker and Annie Pham did all the real work.

And then there's my best friend, who all of you know as the Big Famous Actor. He's the one who everybody asks about, the one who needs security, the one with the busy schedule and the nicknames and the tireless publicist, Brenda, and the awesome manager, Trice. He's the one who was on Buffy, the one who stole The Italian Job, the one you need to ask about Austin Powers 4 or compliment on Party Monster. That's all true. But then there's the guy I know: My internal enemy's worst enemy. My truest true believer. The one who makes me feel like the star. I'd tell you about him, but it's a secret.

-Hugh

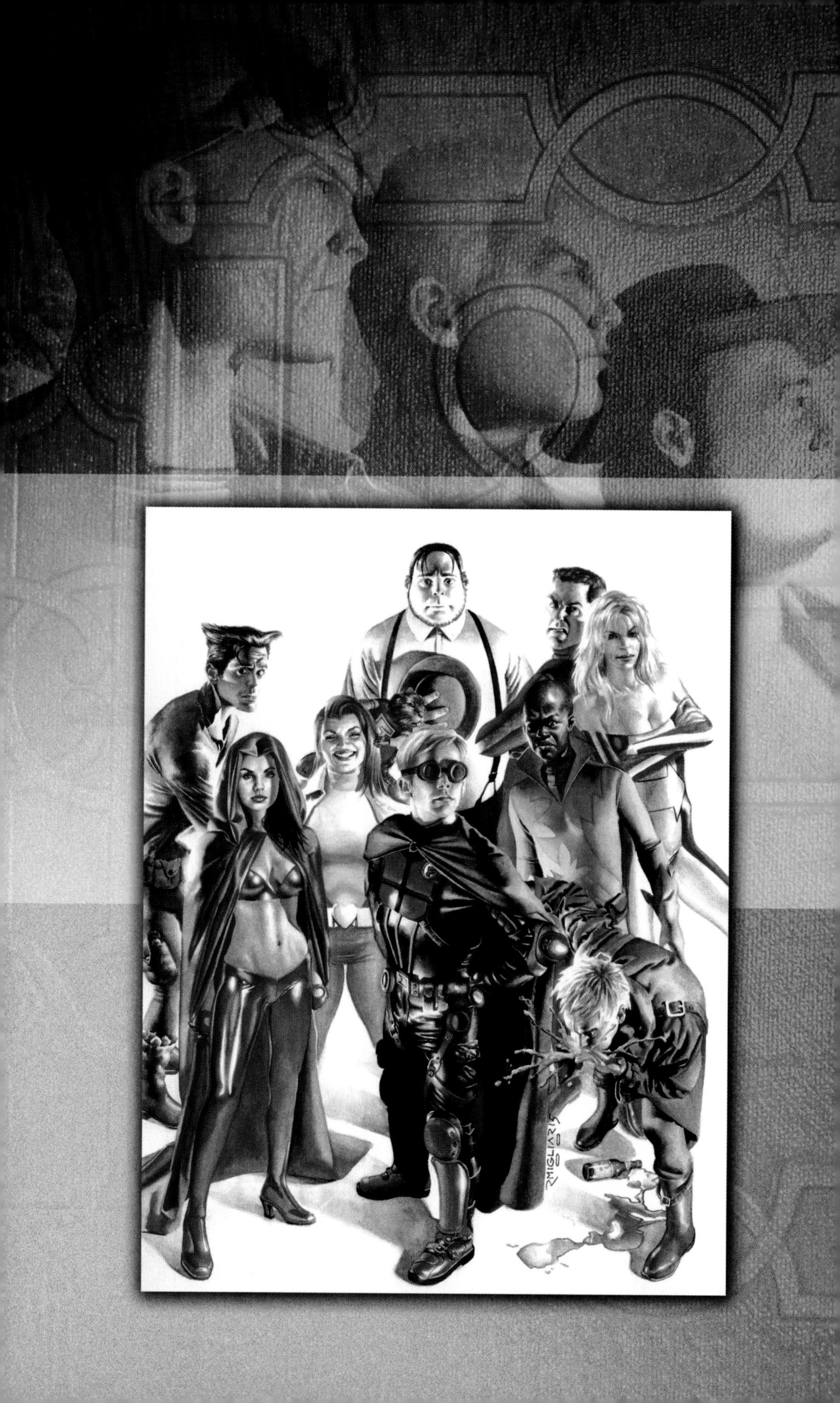

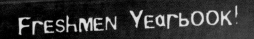

Freshmen Yearbook!

Cacophony by Shawn Dubin and Tyson Wengler
Seductress by J. Michael Linsner and Steve Firchow
Wannabe by Leonard Kirk and Kevin Senft
Puppeteer by Randy Green and Tyson Wengler
Intoxicator by Bill Sienkiewicz and Kevin Senft
The Beaver by Scott Benefiel and Kevin Senft
Drama Twins by Nathan Cabrera
Professor and Frat Guys by Keu Cha
The Squirrel by Tyler Kirkham and Kevin Senft
Green Thumb by Rodolfo Migliari and Kevin Senft
Quaker by Tone Rodriguez and Kevin Senft
Long Dong by Howard Chaykin and Michelle Masden

ADVENTURE, EXCITEMENT. A FRESHMAN CRAVES NOT THESE THINGS.

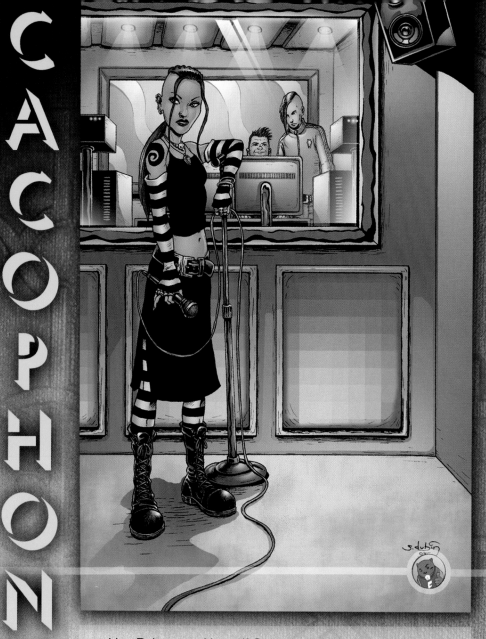

CACOPHONY

Lisa Rohr named herself Cacophony in seventh grade, when she became the lead singer of a punk band she put together with the other kids in her low-income project. "Benny the Hook," as they called themselves, entertained the other kids in the projects playing whatever abandoned musical instruments they could find or make. Eventually, the adults forced them to stop their noise.

As an orphan living with a mentally disturbed aunt who could barely put food on the table, Cacophony became a scrapper and a loner, and most people found her constant glaring off-putting. When she was accepted to D.W. Freese College on a music scholarship, she took the opportunity to attend mostly for assurance that she'd have meals for four years in the dining halls.

When the Ax-Cell-Erator exploded, Cacophony was given the power to recreate any sound with her voice. She can make herself sound like an entire orchestra once she hears their music. She left the school immediately and headed to Los Angeles, where she is competing in a reality TV singing competition and resisting the advances of one of the judges. She has been seen at public events with actor Seth Green, but neither will comment on their relationship.

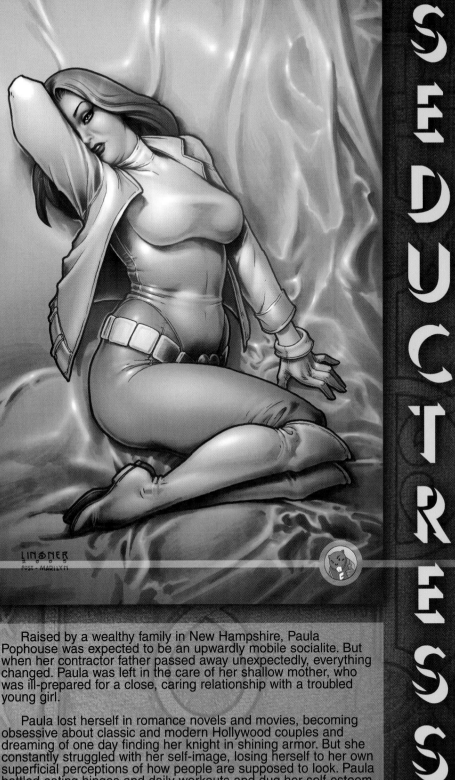

SEDUCTRESS

Raised by a wealthy family in New Hampshire, Paula Pophouse was expected to be an upwardly mobile socialite. But when her contractor father passed away unexpectedly, everything changed. Paula was left in the care of her shallow mother, who was ill-prepared for a close, caring relationship with a troubled young girl.

Paula lost herself in romance novels and movies, becoming obsessive about classic and modern Hollywood couples and dreaming of one day finding her knight in shining armor. But she constantly struggled with her self-image, losing herself to her own superficial perceptions of how people are supposed to look. Paula battled eating binges and daily workouts and dug her self-esteem a very early grave.

As The Seductress, Paula is able to make anyone fall in love with her. It's her lifelong wish come true, but it's also far too easy a power to abuse for such a young, impressionable girl with an unquenchable, lifelong thirst for affection. She has enraptured the exchange student, Jacques. At first, it was revenge for his suggestion that she call herself "Beer Goggles." But now she's falling madly in love with him, despite her fear that this relationship will end terribly if anyone finds out what she's done.

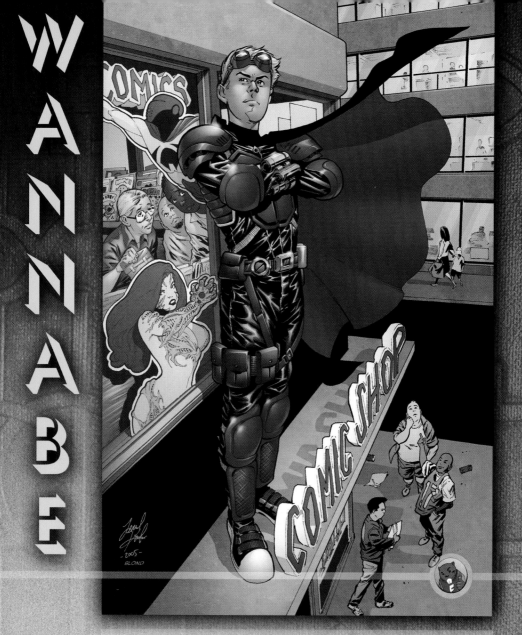

WANNABE

COMICS
COMIC SHOP
2005
BLOND

Kenneth Weismeyer never discovered a love for comic books—it was born with him. His father taught him to read from the classic adventures of the silver age, and soon he was bagging and boarding and trolling a paper route to pay for his weekly addiction. He dubbed himself "Norrin" after his favorite comic book hero, also an outcast, and took to broadcasting his proud geekhood with stickers, T–shirts and hats.

Norrin's middle-class upbringing outside Pittsburgh was frustratingly uneventful. The son of a steelworker and a dog trainer, Norrin dreamed of a bigger future—a calling that would cast him into the role of hero. For a short time he thought he was the target of a secret hoax where he was transplanted to another dimension and everyone around him was an alien performing as his acquaintance. And then there was a month-long excavation in the woods behind his house, where he was sure evil aliens had begun burrowing to the Earth's core.

Older, wiser, but no less a comic fan, Norrin attended Freese College hoping to raise his grades and transfer to USC for film school. He'd put his dreams of adventure behind him, until his fellow students housed in the science building were infused with superpowers upon the explosion of the Ax-Cell-Erator. Finally answering the call of duty, Norrin has taken his self-imposed mantle of leadership very seriously. He has constructed a suit of armor and various comic-inspired weapons, planning to strike fear in the heart of villains everywhere... but one of his first moves was to break his own nose with his grappling hook launcher. He hopes to somehow gain the respect of his hostile teammates, who simply won't take their calling seriously, and his unrequited love, Annalee.

Annalee Rogers was a fun-loving girl until her parents' very ugly divorce during her junior year of high school, when she became introverted and introspective. The constant counseling hasn't helped—in fact, it has hasn't served any purpose other than to make her parents feel like they can wash their hands of guilt. Annalee wasn't against the idea of therapy, she just thought the people her parents hired were low-grade putzes who couldn't really understand her.

As high school progressed and her friends became involved in dramatic and toxic relationships that routinely shattered their emotions and paralyzed their intellect, she became more interested in the subject of counseling and decided to pursue psychology at college. And, again, as soon as she arrived, she was stunned and confused by the way the other kids constructed their own emotional and social roadblocks. And yet, she was still unable to divorce herself from what she considered stupid, childish conventions—like crushes on cute frat guys.

When the Ax-Cell-Erator exploded, Annalee became The Puppeteer. She is able to jump into people's minds for a few minutes at a time—far longer if they're unconscious—and sift through their memories or even control their bodies. Her own body is a completely defenseless shell while she's using her powers, though, and any damage she inflicts on her host body also appears on her own. She's voice of reason on the Freshmen team, and has just begun a journey of discovery that will take her to an understanding of the human condition that no one has ever experienced.

INTOXICATOR

Elwood Johns was a math genius from a long line of math geniuses. His father and mother, both MIT graduates, work in the pharmaceutical research industry. His brother is in Budapest studying ancient cultures on a semester-long break from Harvard. Elwood, more interested in the aerospace industry, hoped to work for NASA. He was also passionate about finance and Wall Street, voraciously reading books on the subject.

And then Elwood took his first alcoholic drink of his life, right at the pivotal moment when the Ax-Cell-Erator exploded. Now, whenever Elwood is under the influence, he produces toxic burps. Upon inhaling these ditties of doom, anyone in Elwood's vicinity becomes as intoxicated as well. His power is even more fearsome when he's hung over, because nothing stops an opponent dead faster than the immediate compulsion to retch. Elwood's personal goal has swiftly gone from working for NASA to going an entire 24 hours without throwing up. In fact, he's failing every single class he's taking.

With the help of Paula, Elwood has assembled his "coat of a thousand highs," which contains all the armament he'll need for even the most massive of battles: Flasks, cans of beers and enough joints to resurrect Miami Vice. Elwood truly is a walking machine of intoxication… but how in the world can you maintain your academic pursuits and prepare for a future in NASA when you're always hung over from being a superhero?

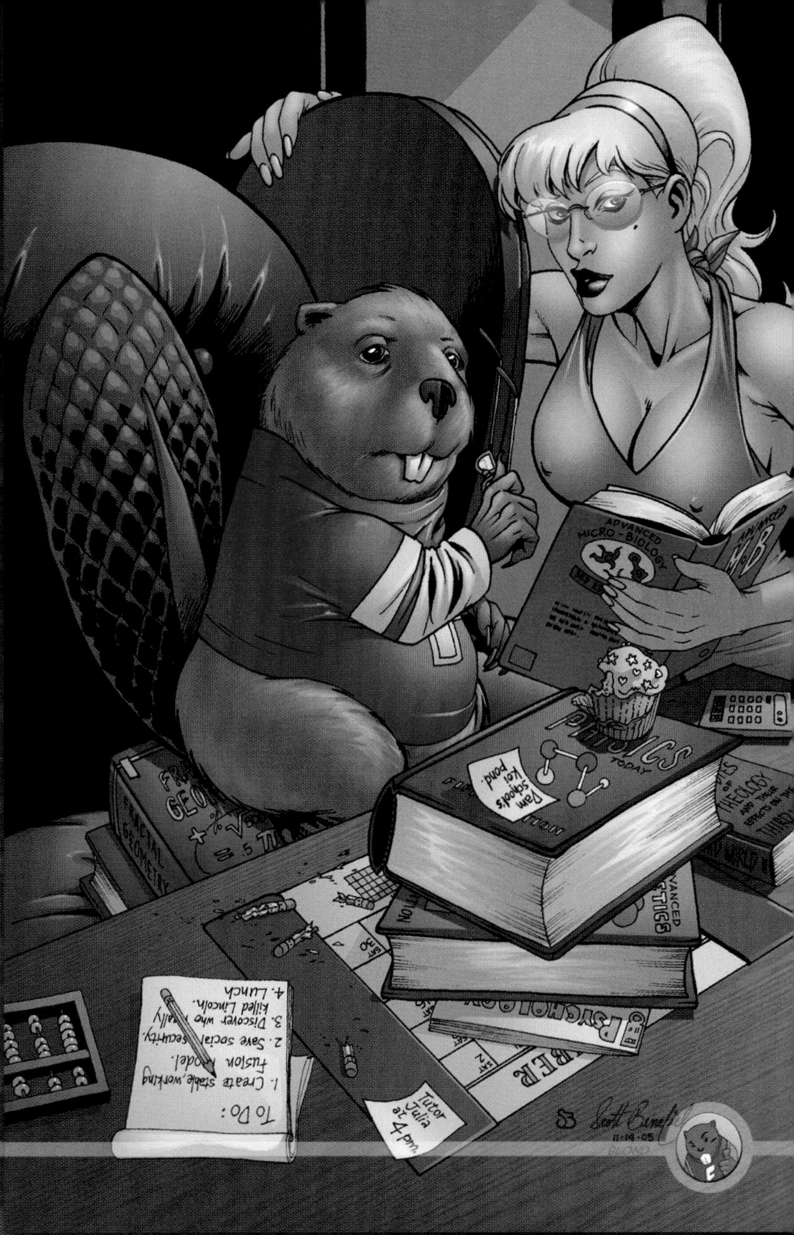
ADVANCED MICRO-BIOLOGY
PHYSICS TODAY
Dam schools koi pond.
FRACTAL GEOMETRY
PSYCHOLOGY
To Do:
1. Create stable, working fusion model.
2. Save social security.
3. Discover who really killed Lincoln.
4. Lunch.
Tutor Julia at 4pm
Scott Benefiel 11-14-05

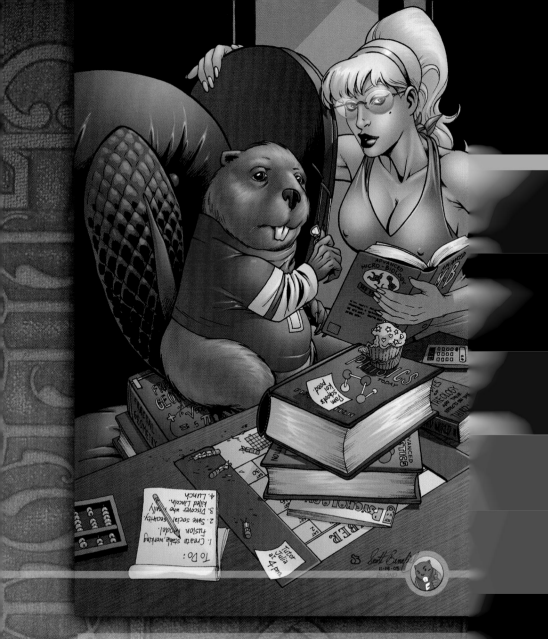

Much mystery surrounds the smallest member of the Freshmen team. Captured at the age of three by a pet store with a special request from D.W. Freese College, the Beaver has spent most of his life in captivity while dreaming of freedom and building dams. He has become institutionalized—comfortable with his school sweatshirt and cushy accommodations, but is still determined to make his mark on the world of dam building.

Before ending up in the Boughl Science Building on the fateful night of the Ax-Cell-Erator's explosion, the Beaver had been captured from his cage in Freese College's athletic department and kept in the Alpha Chi Rho Frat House for six days, sustaining on a strange diet of cupcakes, Ramen Noodles, pizza and beer. He expected the worst when he was left in Paula's closet, and his fears were realized when she started screaming the moment she saw him. As he himself put it later, he was wishing he could convey to each of the kids the "astounding profundity of [their] bankrupt intelligence" when the Ax-Cell-Erator exploded, providing him with off-the-charts intelligence and a snooty English accent that matches his will to insult the students at every opportunity.

The Beaver's first and foremost love, building dams, is always present in his thoughts and dialogue. But now the Beaver leads the Freshmen (or, as he calls them, "the mongoloids") and provides them with an intelligent point of view that is often dismissive but rarely emotional.

DRAMA TWINS

When he turned 14, Brady Lee moved in with his grandmother in New Jersey. He started taking the bus to the local upper-class, snotty junior high school, where he met another outcast, the trash-talking, mafia princess, hurricane slut Renee Bellochio. It was love at first sight, and the two have been inseparable ever since. As a result, Brady has suffered two broken noses, three venereal diseases, two wrecked motorcycles and one trashed science project.

Unable to escape his obsession with this girl, Brady followed Renee to Freese College even though he wasn't enrolled. They had been fighting even more than usual, and Brady gets a pit in his stomach whenever she's out of his sight because she's so prone to cheating on him. The conflict continued once they got to school, but a brief tryst in the girls' dorm room closet during the explosion of the Ax-Cell-Erator led to Renee and Brady sharing telekinetic powers.

When they're in contact, Renee has the ability to psychically pull things toward them, while Brady can push objects away. They must work together to manipulate objects with any degree of precision, but their constant bickering hardly lends itself to cooperation. The situation is bound to reach a boiling point eventually, but for now the entire Freshmen team is trying to handle their volatility.

PROFESSOR AND FRAT GUYS

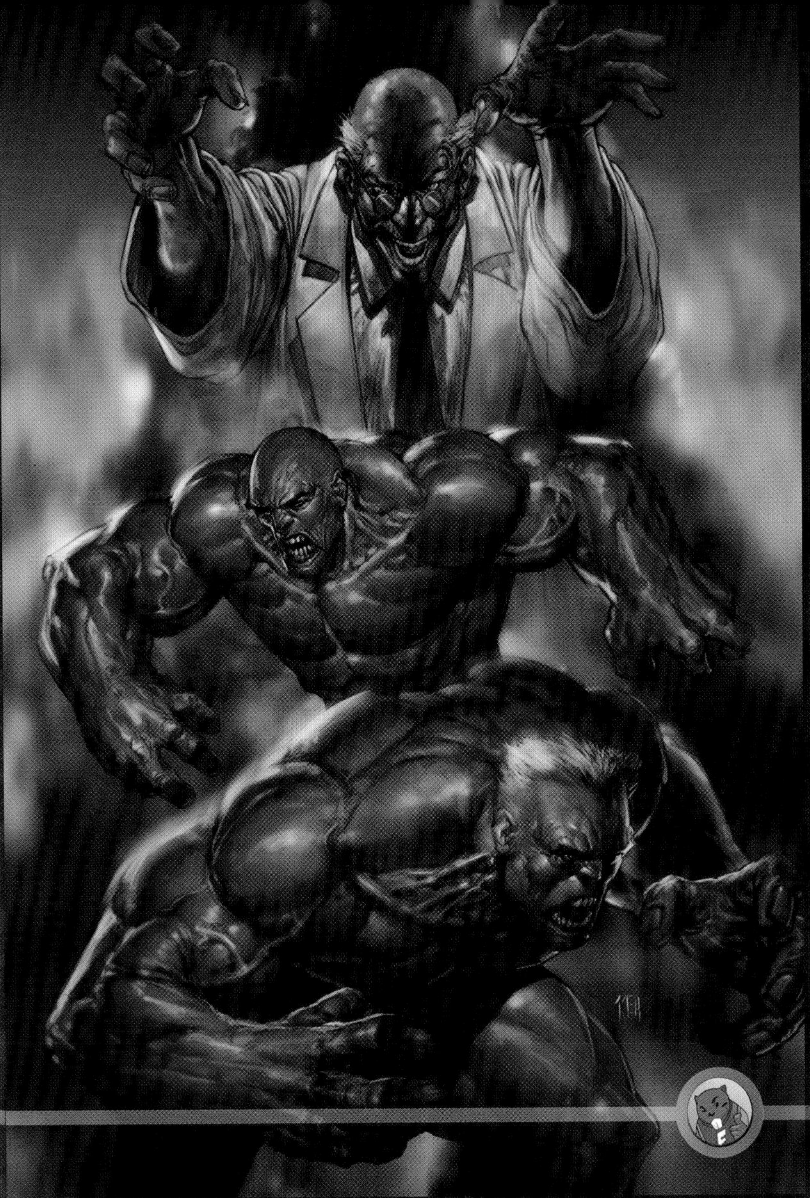

Doctor Theodore Tomlinson has a dream. No, an obsession. A project he has worked on for more than 40 years. And after all this time… all of the failed experiments, the mind-boggling problems, the desperate pleading for funding, the endless research and the brutal determination have paid off: The Ax-Cell-Erator is a reality.

The Ax-Cell-Erator is a breakthrough machine that irradiates cells with new, more intelligent operating instructions: Cure whatever ills them. When the Ax-Cell-Erator, still in Alpha version, exploded in the Boughl Science Building, it infused the Freshmen with superpowers based on whatever they perceived to be their biggest problem at that moment.

The Ax-Cell-Erator was destroyed in the explosion, however, and Dr. Tomlinson's funding has run out. He's determined—at any cost—to prove to the world the value of his life's work. Even if the Freshmen won't help, Dr. Tomlinson cannot allow the Ax-Cell-Erator project to die without being seen.

Meanwhile, Rob, the leader of the Alpha Chi Rho fraternity, and his fellow frat brothers, who terrorized the freshmen when they got to college and sent them into an emotional spiral the evening of the Ax-Cell-Erator's explosion, have mysterious powers as well: Jacked-up strength that seems to have no limits. And Doctor Tomlinson may have a connection with them. Time will tell…

THE SQUIRREL

Jacque Lalleaux was born to a fashion designer mother and jeweler father in the south of France. Raised as elite society from infancy, Jacques has never wanted anything in his life. With an interest in pursuing new sexual conquests in America (he's either had every woman in France or has determined them to be unworthy), Jacques arrived at Freese College and expected to rule the school. At first, everything went according to plan. Jacques bedded his orientation leader in the woman's bathroom of the Physical Therapy building, and then, later that night, a waitress at the local pizza shop. And the stewardess from his flight, also a conquest, was leaving messages on his cell phone.

But the explosion of the Ax-Cell-Erator was ill-timed for Jacques, since it came just at a moment when he was frightened by a squirrel just outside the dorm room window. Since that event, Jacques has been compulsively hoarding acorns, whenever he can get them before the wily squirrels on the Freese campus. His hair has transformed, no matter how much gel he puts into it. And lately he's seen other squirrels staring at him…

After the explosion, Jacques struck up a new relationship. He fell madly in love with Paula Pophouse, despite a complete lack of physical attraction. Since Paula's injury in the battle with the frat guys broke her spell, however, Jacques has realized that Paula used her powers on him and forced him to love her. Now Jacques is trying to come to grips with his humiliating transformation and the realization that his emotions have been manipulated at the deepest level.

Charles Levy became interested in animal protection and environmental activism when he was in sixth grade. His parents, respected Philadelphia lawyers, believed in encouraging their sons' interests and supported him in every way possible. The entire family went vegetarian, and Mr. Levy funded trips to Washington so Charles could participate in important protests. Charles even spoke in front of congress when he was only 12 years old, urging greater legislation for animal rights. This is a young man who takes himself and his work very seriously.

Although Charles has an entire greenhouse full of gorgeous, beloved plants at home in Manayunk, Pennsylvania, he chose to bring only his favorite with him to school: his Ficus Tree, which he calls Susie. He regularly speaks to Susie—a ritual recommended by an herbalist mentor of Chares', who supposes that plants can feel positive and negative reinforcements from our voices through the reverbera-tions—and has come to think of her as the ear of his life's journal. The Ax-Cell-Erator exploded as he was whispering to her, and, when he awoke, he could hear her—and every other plant—talking.

Charles wasn't prepared for the surprisingly abrasive and negative disposition of most plants. Embittered from being displaced and potted, as well as humanity's disregard for the planet's air quality, they're very eager to tell our race's first plant whisperer what they think of us. As a result, Charles finds himself under constant attack. He's also hungry, since now most of his food can beg for mercy. And he's tired, because Susie spends all night with rampaging emotions as she repeatedly declares her love for him, but worries that he's cheating with other plants. Who knows what the future holds for Charles and his tenuous love affair with a Ficus tree…

BLOND

QUAKER

Liam Adams had never left his home in Lancaster, Pennsylvania's Amish Country, before he came to Freese College. He led a very insulated life with his large family, and was quite fulfilled. Then, one night, Liam had a vision. He's unsure whether he was asleep or awake, but a great light outside his window called to him, and he was instilled with a great sensation that he had to explore beyond his hometown. The next morning, he decided that God had compelled him to go forward. Frightened and unsure, and not even completely confident in this vision, he forged ahead, and talked his parents into allowing him to go to an "English" college.

Liam is very naïve, even by Amish standards, but he knows this about himself and tries to keep quiet so he can observe rather than seem foolish. But the outrageous and often confusing machines of the outside world overwhelm and amuse him to no end.

Overweight since he was very young due to a medical condition, Liam was considering his weight when the Ax-Cell-Erator exploded. Soon after, he discovered he could make the ground shake with a roll of his ample belly. But what purpose would this serve in God's eyes? How would he be judged? How can he use this ability to serve God? Liam continues to struggle with these questions as he internalizes his guilt over Paula's injury, which he did nothing to stop out of fear for hurting Rob and the Frat Guys. More than any of the other Freshmen, Liam is alone and confused, and hoping to find a direction for himself and his new powers.

Ray McFarland has always had self-esteem problems. He was a fourth-stringer on the high school baseball team, cut from the junior varsity bowling team, reject-ed from the school newspaper and couldn't get a date to the senior prom. Determined to reinvent himself, Ray spent the summer between high school and college delving into pop culture, immersing himself in whatever was important to people, trying to become more viable in a college conversation. Leaving home in South Carolina for the distant Freese College, with no familiar faces to betray his life as an outcast, Ray was sure this was his big chance to change his life.

Ray already knew which fraternity he'd pledge at Freese: Alpha Chi Rho. It's where he wanted to be, with the cool kids. When he was invited to a party at their house, he jumped at the opportunity to meet some of the brothers, so they'd remember him next semester when he could pledge. He thought he was doing well, chatting up a couple of the guys, when someone suddenly grabbed and gagged him, then ripped down his pants and slung him over the balcony. Ending his dreams of being one of the cool kids. Again.

Ray was humiliated even further when some of the laughing partygoers point-ed out his humble private part. Trying to figure out where he stood if five inches was indeed average, Ray was measuring himself when the Ax-Cell-Erator explod-ed.

Now it's fifteen feet long. And, as Ray is soon to find out, indestructible.

Watch out, world. Be on guard, ladies. Long Dong is here.

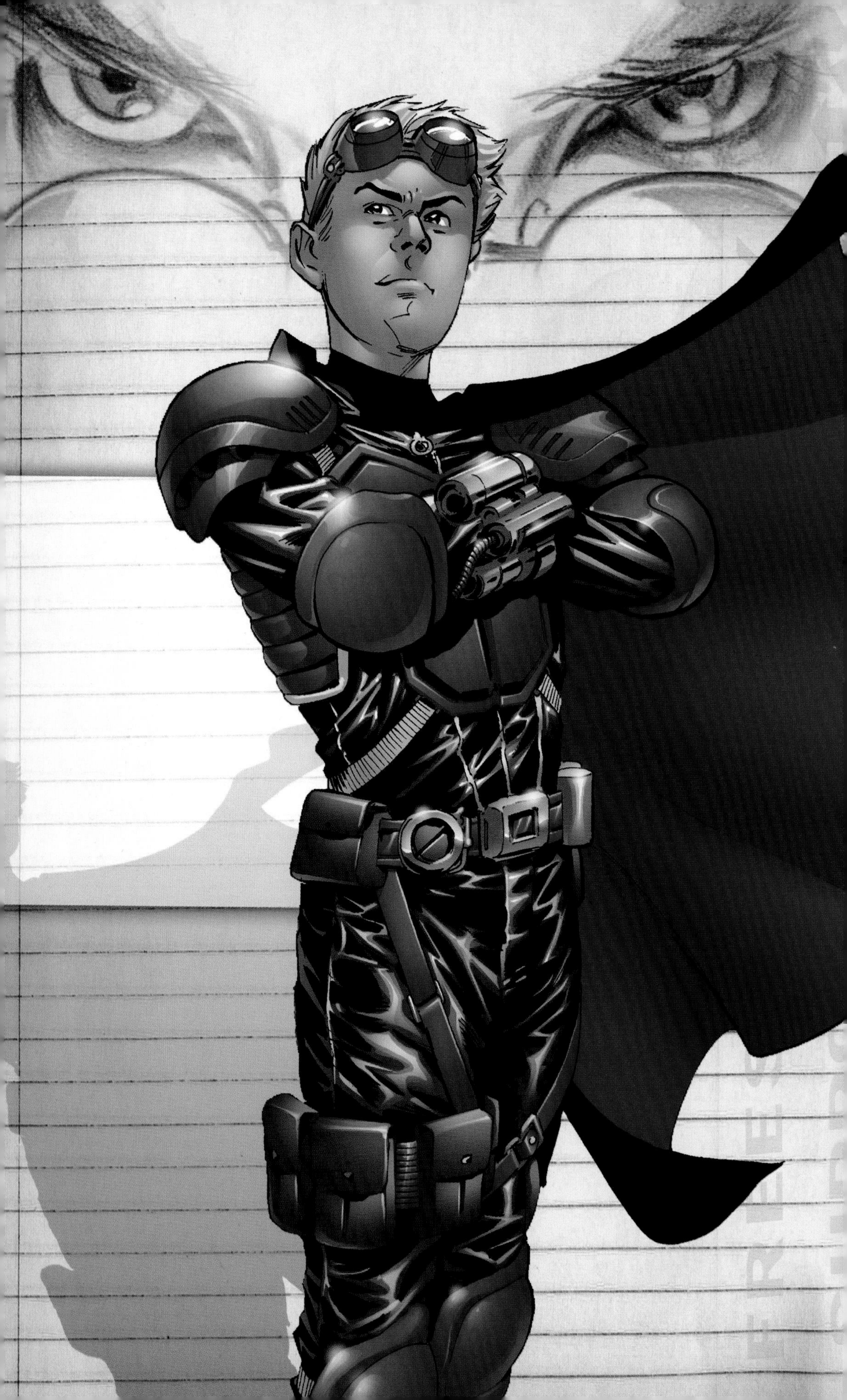

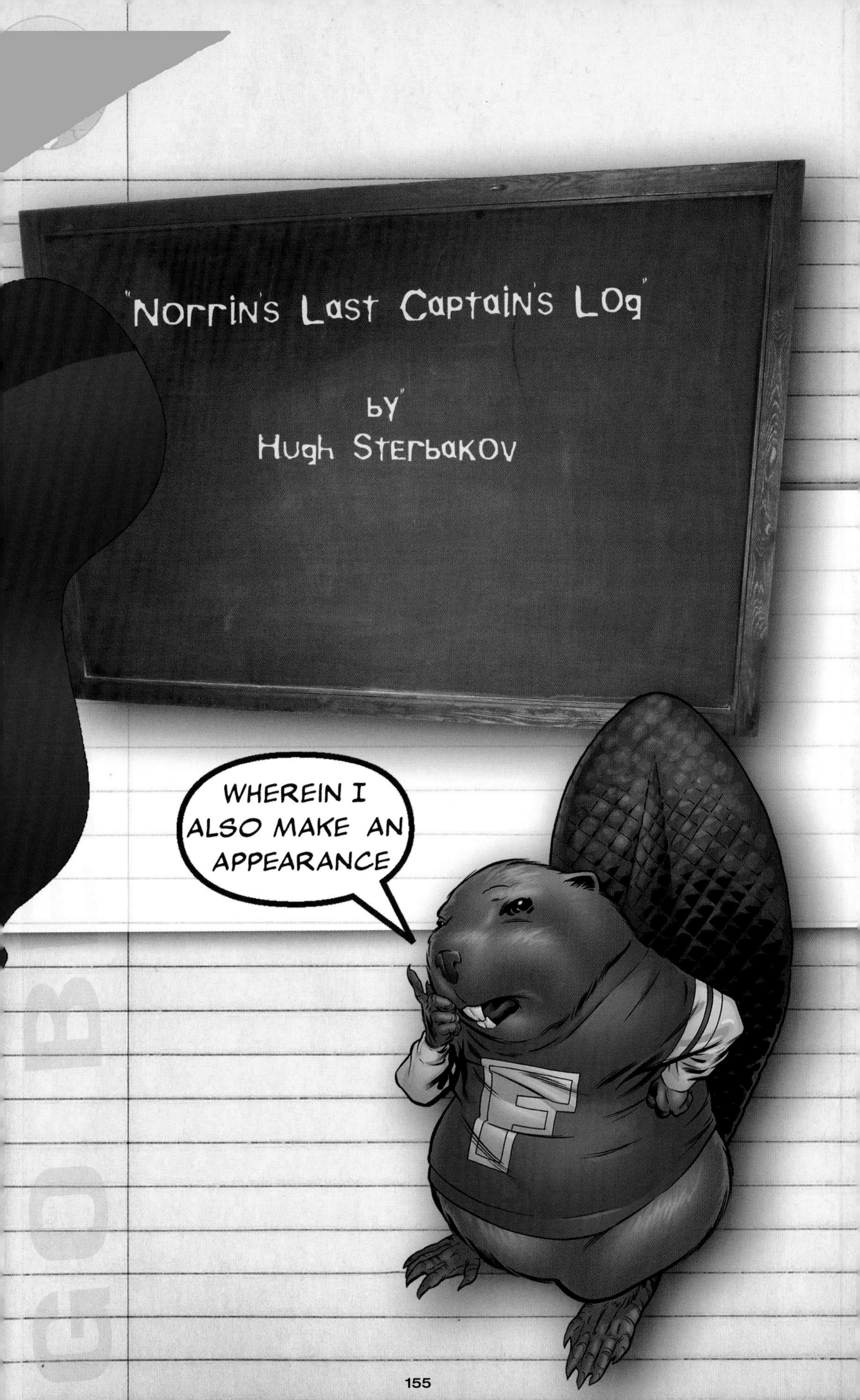
"Norrin's Last Captain's Log"
by"
Hugh Sterbakov
WHEREIN I ALSO MAKE AN APPEARANCE

Captain's Log: The Journal of Norrin Weismeyer

Stardate: December 19th – 2pm

LAST DAY OF SCHOOL

I got B's in Intro to Film and History of Photography, A's in Creative Writing and Basic Drawing, and an A- in Sociology 101. Poor Elwood failed two of his classes. They told him he's on academic probation. If he doesn't get a 3.0 next semester, he'll be kicked out. I won't let that happen, though.

It's been a week since Paula woke up, and most of it was taken up by cramming for finals. I'm glad it's over. The week was tense. Nobody is mad at me—at least, they're not showing it if they are—but I'm mad at myself. Looking back on it, I don't know exactly where I went wrong. I may never know. But I have to learn to evaluate myself better. I have to act more like a Patrick Stewart character.

The Beaver is coming home with me for Christmas vacation—he said he needs a place to stay and wants to see Pittsburgh, but I think he wants to keep an eye on me. I hate being patronized.

The powers that Dr. Tomlinson gave me faded quickly, but they left behind an intense craving—maybe a physical addiction. I had a rough couple days getting over them, and I just wasn't up for keeping my journal. It hurt. A lot.

But it got my head in the right place. I'm turning over a new leaf. I'm becoming what I promised myself I could be. When we get back next semester, I'm going to show everybody why I should be the team's leader. And I'm going to start right now.

Mom is here to pick me up. It's an eight-hour drive to Pittsburgh (the Beaver will have to stay in a cage), and I'm going to hear all about her dog training and dad's gripes at the steel mill. And they said something about Vickie having a new boyfriend. Yuck.

Stardate: December 19th — 6pm

Mom keeps talking to the other cars. Why wouldn't they let me fly? I hate country music. Looks like the Beaver hates it even more—he's been whimpering. I need a code name—still haven't been able to come up with anything that sounds authoritative and regal. Maybe The Authority? This trip is taking forever.

Stardate: December 20th -- 12:09 am

The Beaver said something about hating humanity and disappeared into the woods, so I'm going to sleep. Mom has like 20 dogs downstairs from her boarding business. It sounds like a zoo. It smells like one of them got in my bedroom and pissed somewhere. And I think Vickie went through some of my action figures. But it's nice to have my own room to myself. In some ways, college seems like a dream that I just woke up from. Did it all really happen?

Code names: Vector? Valor? Anything other than Wannabe,
that's awful. What would Stan Lee think of a hero called
Wannabe?

Stardate: December 20th – 11:30 am

Weird dreams, and I slept later than I intended. Today is
my first day of training. I'm going to become an idea, a
legend. I'm going to strike fear into the hearts of my enemies,
and inspire others to change their lives. Maybe The Captain?

Stardate: December 20th – 2:45 pm

I'm up to 25 push-ups at a time now, and I've done 1,000
crunches today. I have to go online to get some meditation
training exercises, but Vickie is on the computer (she's talking
on the phone, but pretending to use the computer just so I can't
have it). I called and the next Tae Kwan Do class is Thursday
night.

Stardate: December 20th – 7:30 pm

I have to find my Center, my Inner Self. My Northern Star.

Stardate: December 21st – 3:28 pm

I THINK MY SISTER IS DATING A SUPERVILLAIN!!!!!!

Vickie has this new boyfriend—Stang is his name (!), and
apparently he's been hanging around the house a lot. Mom and
Dad really like him. But Dad always said he doesn't want Vickie

to date until she's 19! And Mom cooked brisket for him—she never cooks brisket when I ask for it! Something is going on, this guy has totally mesmerized my family. I felt like he was staring at me, too—trying to make eye contact or something. I kept my gaze averted, and my spirit alert.

Stardate: December 23 – 4:52 pm

Haven't written in a while, been busy. Stang (it's short for Mustang, his father is a car freak) was over again and, yet again, my family's disposition totally changed with him around. I excused myself from the dinner table—said I wasn't feeling well—and suited up. It felt good to wear the costume again, it felt right. I wonder if that's what righteous means. Anyway—

I followed Stang to his house. His family is really rich. I don't know what they do, but their property is huge. It had that weird smell, too, that smell I noticed behind the house last year when we were visited by aliens (yeah, I've started to think it was real again, I'll write more about it later).

I took notes in my pocket recorder as I looked around the house. I'll transcribe them and do analysis later. Nothing overtly diabolical to the naked eye, but that doesn't really mean anything. Stang is up to no good—he has some sort of preternatural control over my family, and I'll get to the heart of it.

Stardate: December 24th – 2:30

More weird dreams. I'm a little kid in them. Really strange. Dad went to DJ's Comics and picked up all of my pull books from the whole semester!! I forgot to tell him I found a store near school—now I have some doubles, but it's still cool. It was nice of him, because he has the truck all day and by the time he gets home, they're closed. I've been dying to read these.

Stardate: December 25th – 8 am
MERRY CHRISTMAS!!!

I got a new laptop computer! I have to get some serious security protocols going if this is going to be the keeper of the team's important data. First up: Villain profiling. Stang is coming over for "brunch." More on that later. Man, the name thing is kicking my ass. It seems like all the good names are taken. I thought about "Hardwired" now that I have a new computer. I've done 1,000 sit-ups every day, and I'm now up to 30 consecutive push-ups. I have to learn stealth.

Stardate: December 27th – 3:21 am
DISASTER!!!

I am SO PISSED OFF RIGHT NOW!!!! Stang came over for lunch and I saw him mesmerize my mom right in front of me. She completely changed her entire disposition just because he gave her this casual sideways glance. So I went upstairs and listened, and waited for him to leave.

I followed him home—which was really hard to do because he has a car and I was on my bike, and (of course) that's the minute the Beaver picks to show back up. He said he was building a dam—I don't even wanna know where he built it or whether it's gonna cause any irrigation problems in the woods (Irrigation? Right word?). So he wants to know what I'm doing, and I tell him, and he flips out and tells me I'm being a mongoloid. We had this huge fight, which was really frustrating because I don't understand half the things he says, and I got angry and left for Stang's house. I took the shortcut through McGready's farm (turns out he's not really a Chupacabra after all—gotta write more about that).

So I get to Stang's house and find his garage door slightly open. I knew it was the perfect opportunity for an entrance, so I slid under. I ripped my cape a little bit, but I got in undetected. His house is huge! They have Xbox 360! Stang and his older brother sat down to play Call of Duty, so I used my stealth skills to sneak into his room. He has pictures of girls all over the walls—Vickie won't like it when she sees that. I heard someone coming, so I hid in his closet. There was plenty of room in there, and I covered up with some stuff on the floor. I practiced my meditation, having the forethought to know I might be stuck there until morning. The door opened, and I reached into my Inner Self to slow my heartbeat and breathing, making myself undetectable—

--and it was the Beaver!!!

(I recorded this dialogue on my gauntlet's digital voice recorder, for future reference in case he tries to misrepresent this moment).

"Norrin, have you completely lost your woefully precarious grasp on sanity?"

"What? No—shut up, I'm on a stakeout!"

"You're concealed in this dimwitted club foot's closet, buried beneath mounds of soiled clothing—wearing a cape, no less—and—"

"Shut up! They're going to hear you!"

"Perhaps you should seek psychological counseling, Norrin. You're simply too prone to overblown speculations which lead to flights of absurd extravagance."

"He has mesmerized my family!"

The Beaver stared at me for a moment, mouth agape, moving his nose up and down. Those stupid teeth seemed to be mocking me.

"Have you gone completely and utterly off the proverbial deep end? What are you doing for the future of your race? What possible asset are you to society?"

I'd had enough. "If he has a mind control device, I have to find out about it!"

"A mind... control... device? On the shoulders of your forefathers, under the weight of their blood, sweat and tears, you mount this declaration of intellectual nihilism?"

And then the door opened.

And the Beaver and I looked up at Stang. Blankly and dumbly.

I would have thought of this, but the Beaver kicked on my ultrabright headlight, temporarily blinding Stang. He pushed me out of the closet and we raced down the stairs. Stang's parents must have been sleeping, because I heard them respond to his yelling. The brother never put down the Xbox 360 controller.

We got out of the house and now I'm home. I catalogued all the details I could remember about Stang's house and his room into the Villain Database, but I don't have enough raw data to run a composite just yet. The Beaver has been lecturing me nonstop. I'm trying to make him understand that it's better to be safe than sorry—that if we'd done our homework on Dr. Tomlinson, we would have known not to help him reassemble the Ax-Cell-Erator, and it's likely that Paula would never have gotten hurt (by the way, the Beaver called Annalee and it turns out that Paula has movement in her arms and legs, she's going to be fine).

Stardate: December 27th - 4:11 am

The Beaver still hasn't stopped talking. He just compared me to Napoleon, James Cameron and Charles Lindbergh.

Stardate: December 30th – 2:45 pm

The Beaver won't let me out of his sight. Even when I try to leave him behind, he just follows. Mom thinks he's adorable. I'm up to 35 push-ups at a time. I've definitely put on some muscle. Tae Kwon Do class went great. More weird dreams, by the way—could someone in the area have a dream control device?

Stardate: January 3rd, 4:25 pm

Stang was just over and the Beaver observed him. He says he's a "charmer." He says humans act silly and stupid around people they like, and my family likes Stang. I know what a charmer is, I just don't find Stang all that charming. Sounds fishy to me. Still, though, I understand what he's saying. I keep wondering how Annalee's vacation is going.

Stang doesn't seem to remember what happened, or at least he hasn't said anything about it to us. There's no way he could have known it was me, the costume and goggles conceal my identity very nicely.

45 push-ups a day now, and 2,000 sit-ups. I've started weightlifting on days when I don't have Tae Kwon Do, and it's going really well. The Beaver is watching my every move. He's driving me nuts. Only 10 more days until I go back to Freese.

Stardate: January 4th – 4:38 am

The Beaver is cuddled up on one of my sister's stuffed bears—it really doesn't look right. I've seen him have some really intense sessions with Paula's bunny slippers at school, too. I think he needs a girl.

Anyway, I got woken up by that dream again and I wanted to write it down while I remembered it. I've been seeing this guy who looked really familiar, and it just struck me.

His name is Mr. Fiddlesticks, and he's from this children's book I had when I was a little kid—"Mr. Fiddlesticks goes to Africa." It was a whole series, but I didn't have any of the other books. At first I could just sort of hear him talking in my dream. Then I saw him a couple times, sort of really weird, like he was kind of there and kind of not there. It's hard to explain. Tonight was really different, though—I felt like he was talking to me. I actually felt like he was really here. He's very tall and thin, and annoyingly polite and proper—like a friendly version of the Beaver. He always knew all of the customs in other countries, and he'd teach them to kids in his books. He warned me that danger is coming, and I need to be prepared for it.

Like I didn't know that!

Something else happened, though, more importantly! Right when I woke up, it hit me, just like I knew it would—perfectly square in the gut. An answer out of the blue, like a calling from above: My code name! Henceforth, I shall be known as The Scarlet Knight! And I shall cast fear into the heart of villains with my Scarlet Armory. And track them with my Scarlet Computer!

The ~~dawn~~ dusk of the Scarlet Knight is upon us!

Man, the Beaver really should get a room with that stuffed bear.

That's all for this journal. Tomorrow, I'll begin The Chronicles of the Scarlet Knight! Excelsior!

FRESHMEN

Cover Gallery

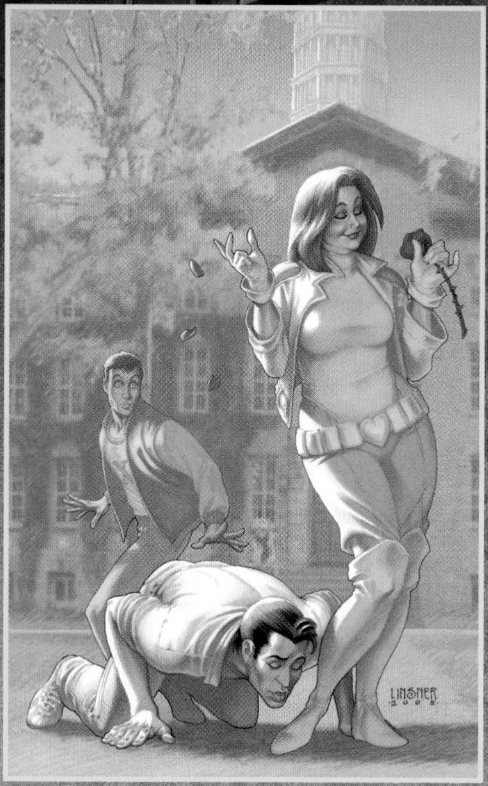

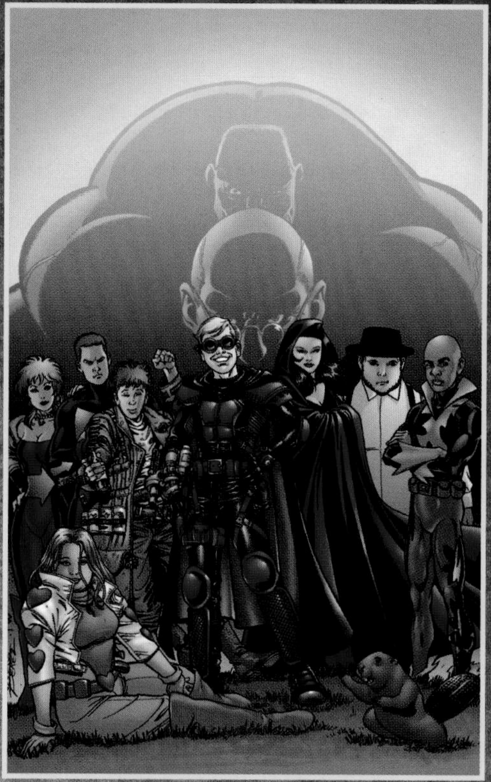

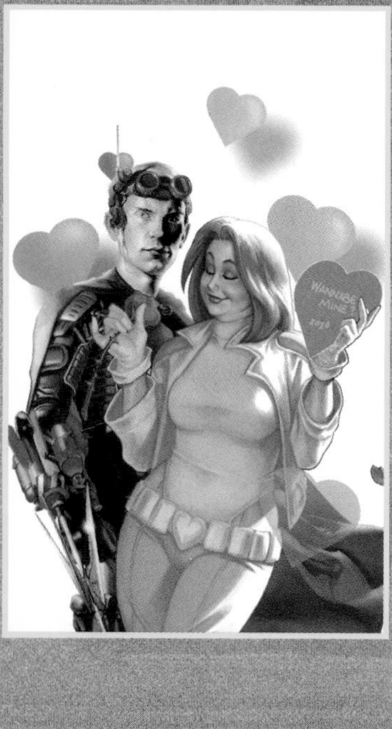
WANNABE MINE

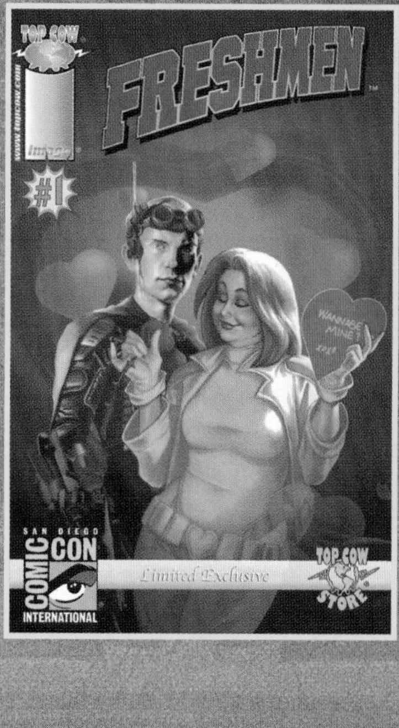
TOP COW
FRESHMEN
#1
WANNABE MINE
SAN DIEGO COMIC CON INTERNATIONAL
Limited Exclusive
TOP COW STORE

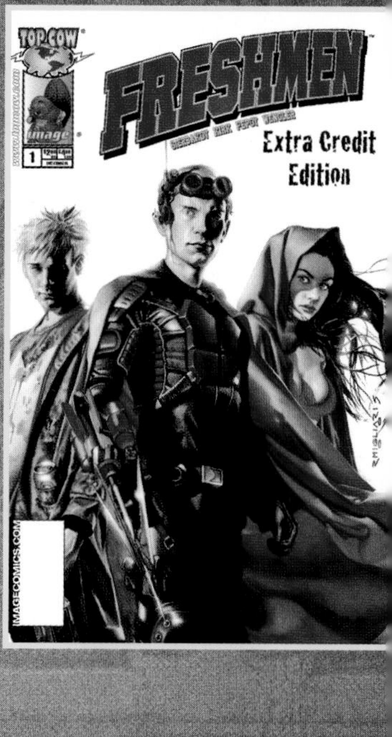
TOP COW
FRESHMEN
Extra Credit Edition
IMAGECOMICS.COM

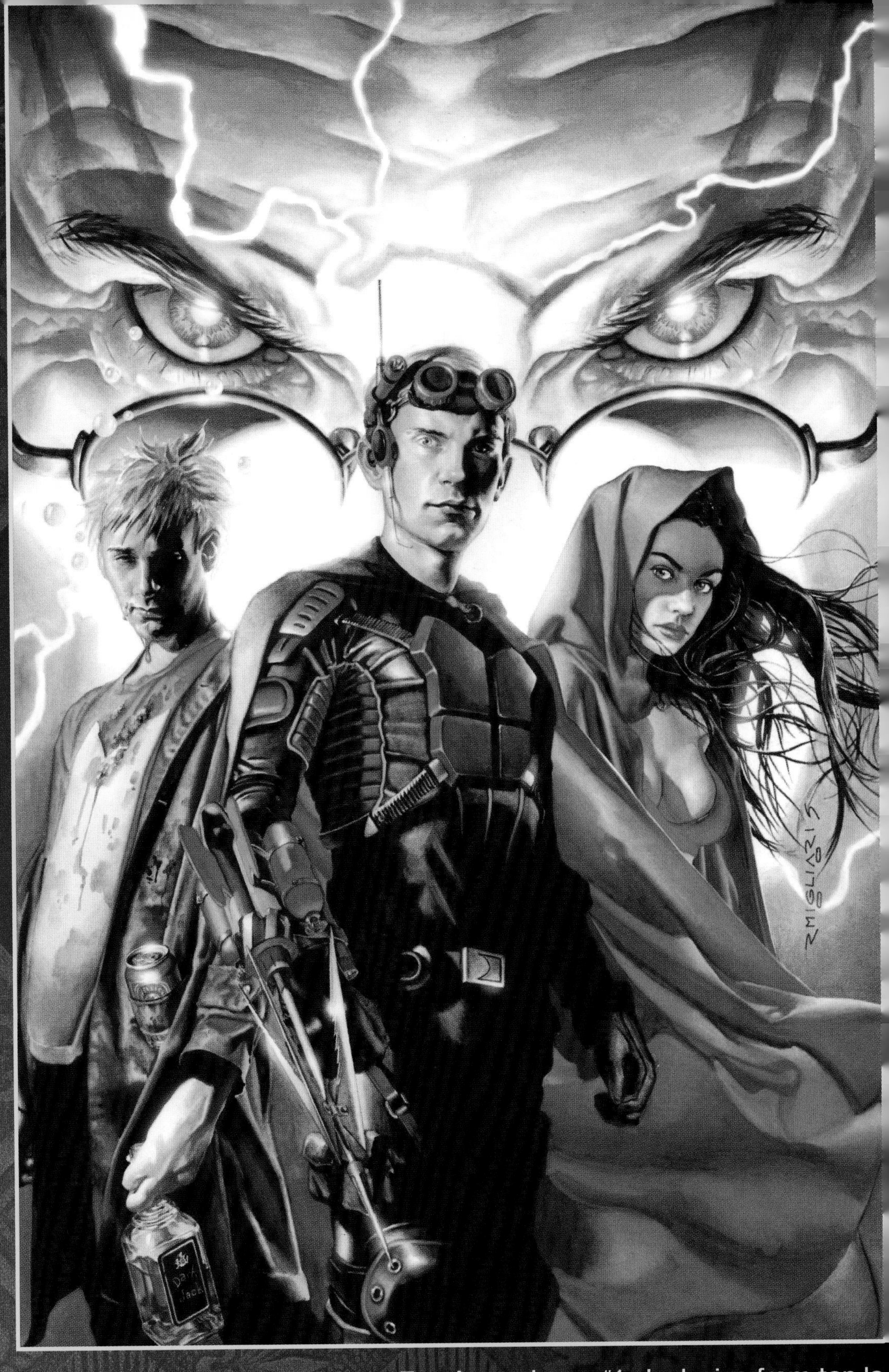

Freshmen issue #1 clockwise from top le
art by: Joseph Michael Linsne
art by: George Perez and Tyson Wengle
(above and to the left) art by: Rodolfo Migliari, the pride of Argentin

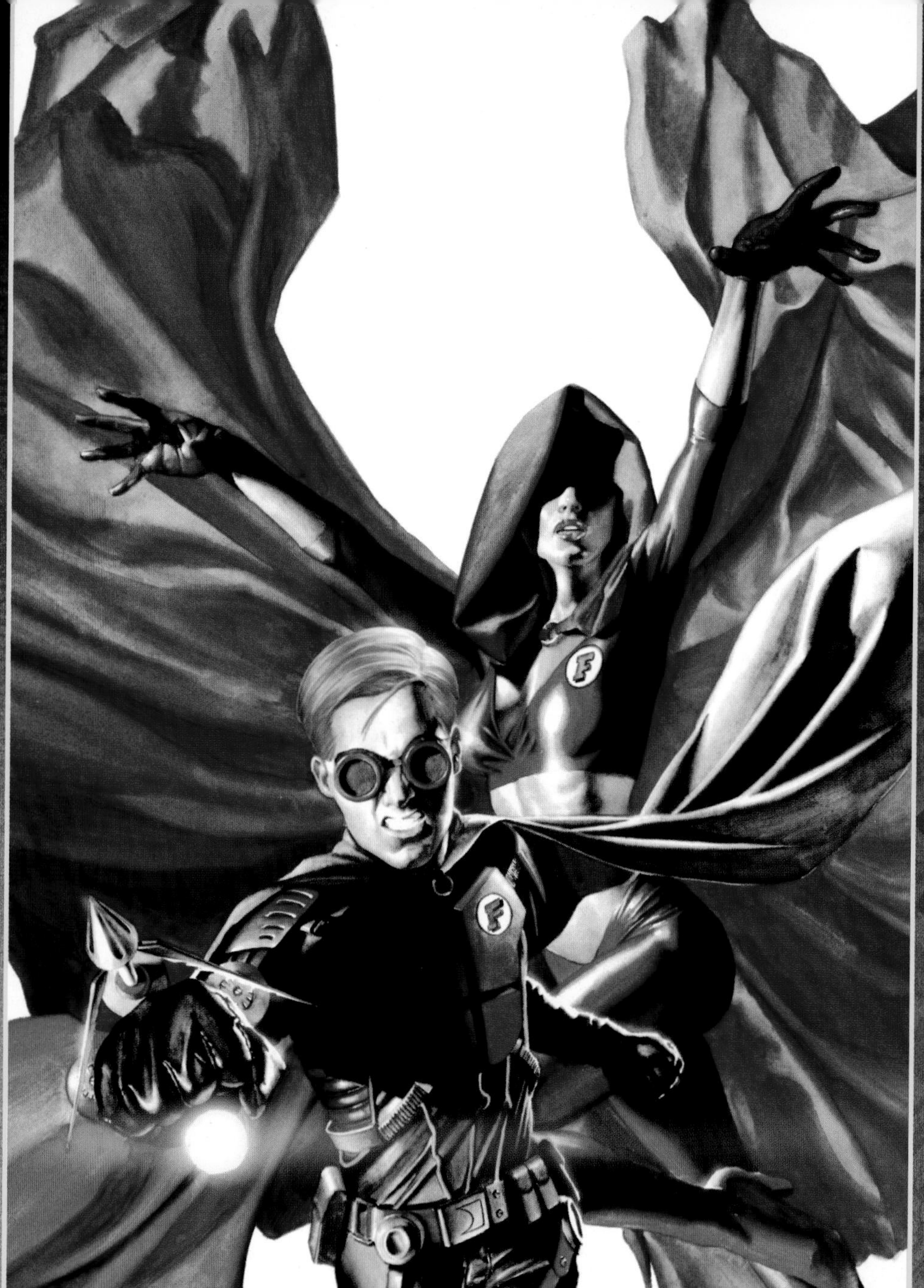

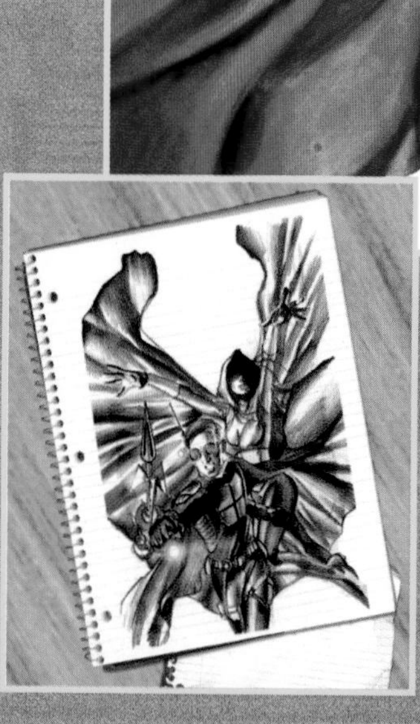

Freshmen issue #2
art by: Rodolfo Migliari

concept art shown left

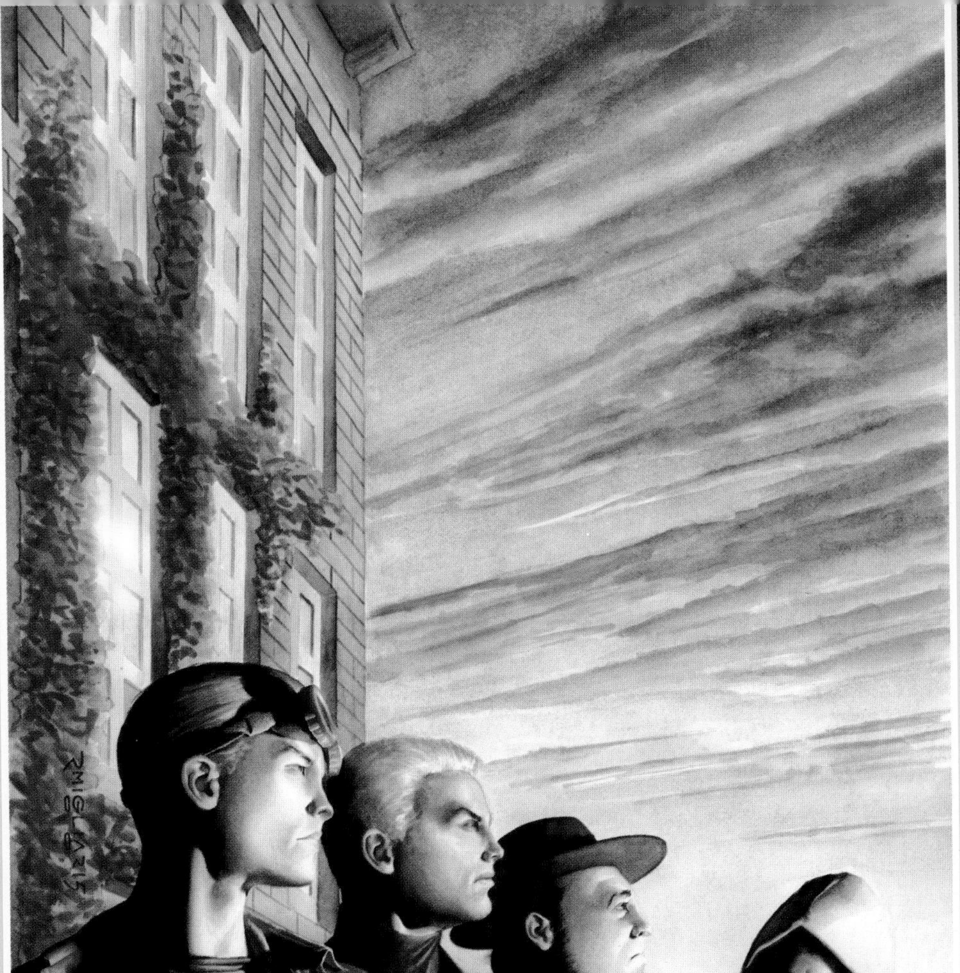

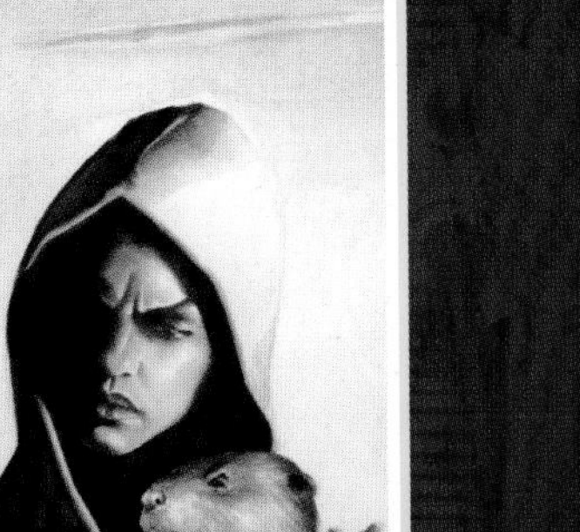

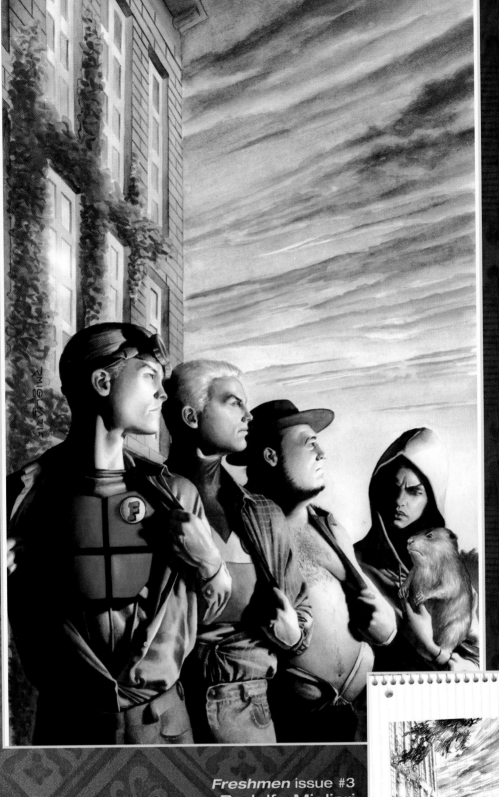

Freshmen issue #3
art by: Rodolfo Migliari

concept art shown right

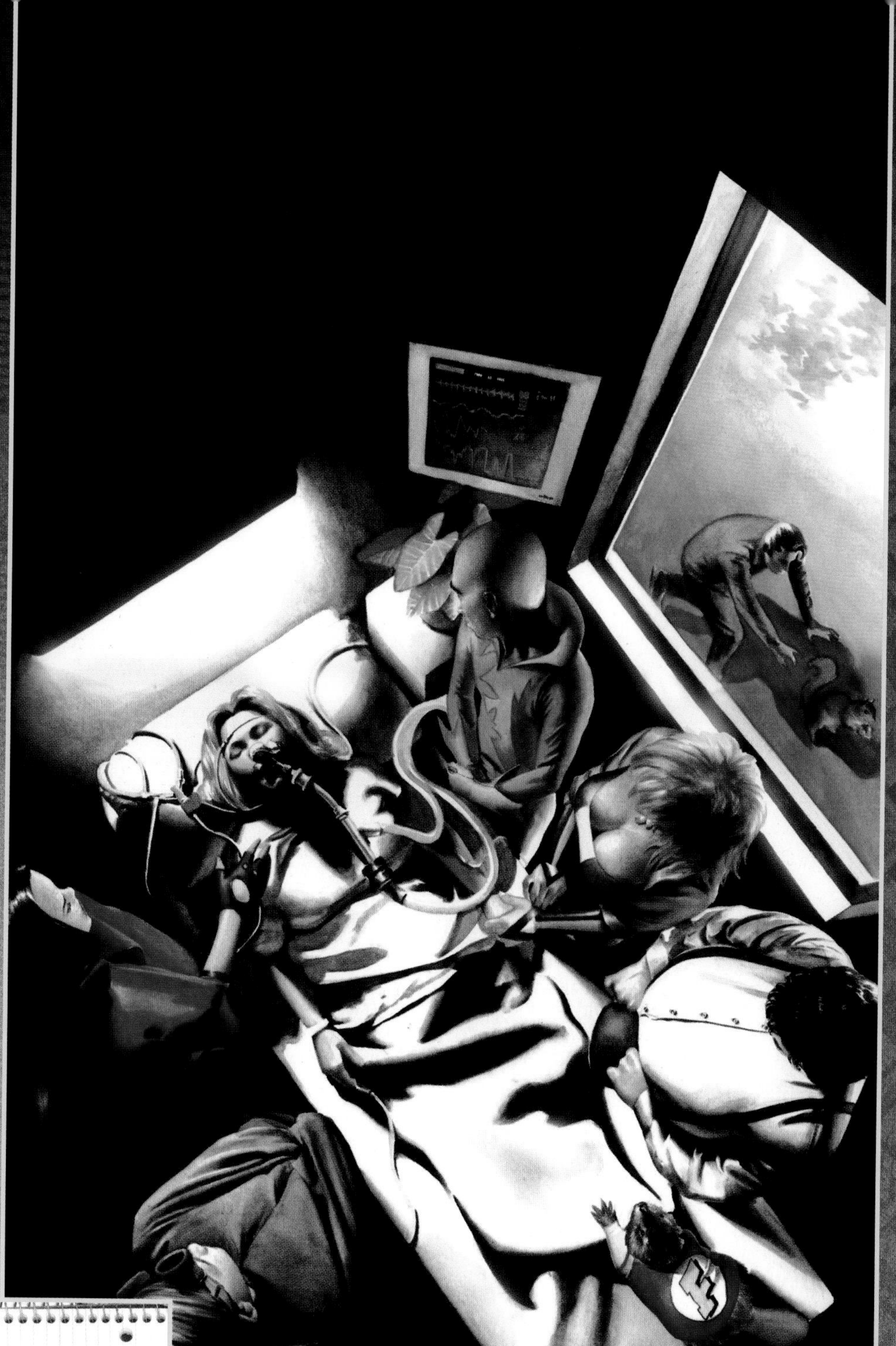

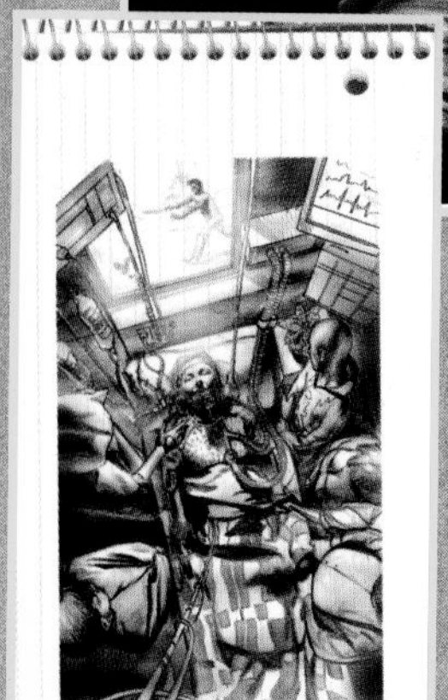

Freshmen issue #4
art by: Rodolfo Migliari

concept art shown left

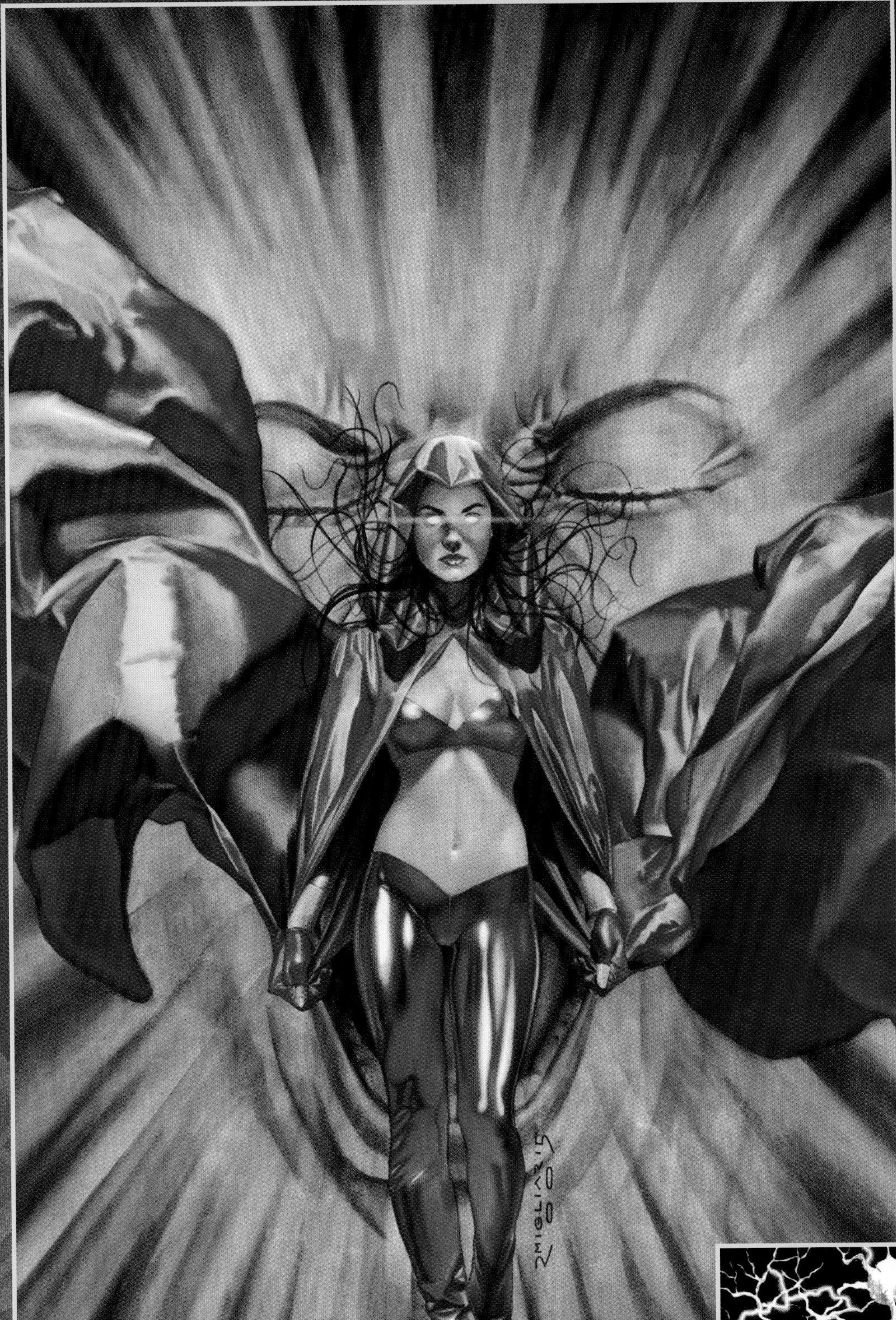

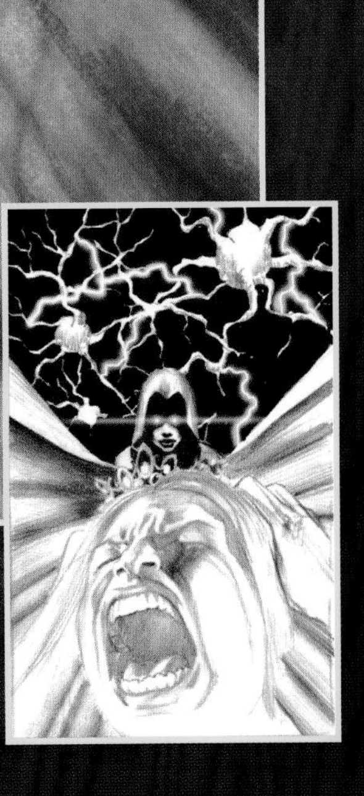

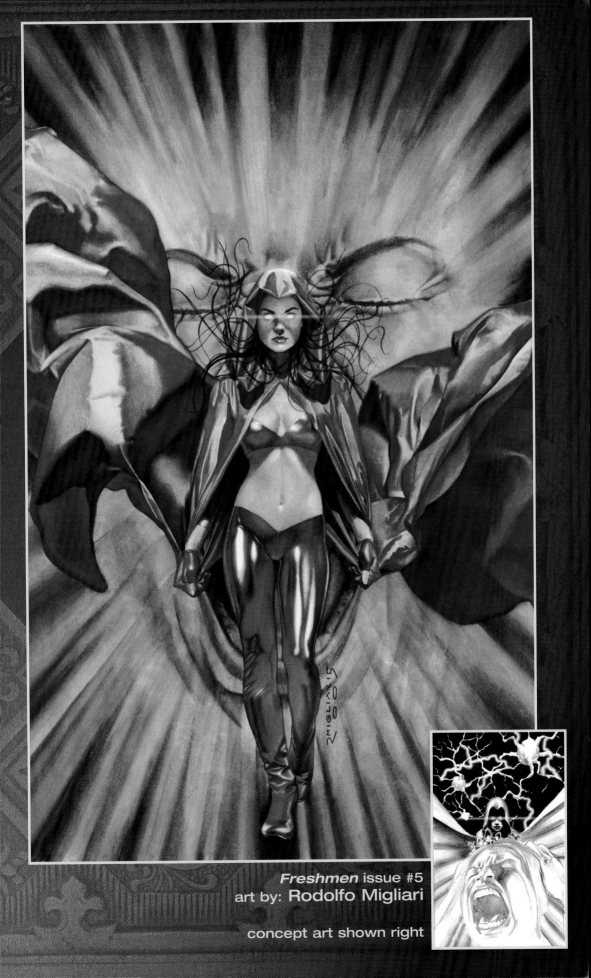

Freshmen issue #5
art by: Rodolfo Migliari

concept art shown right

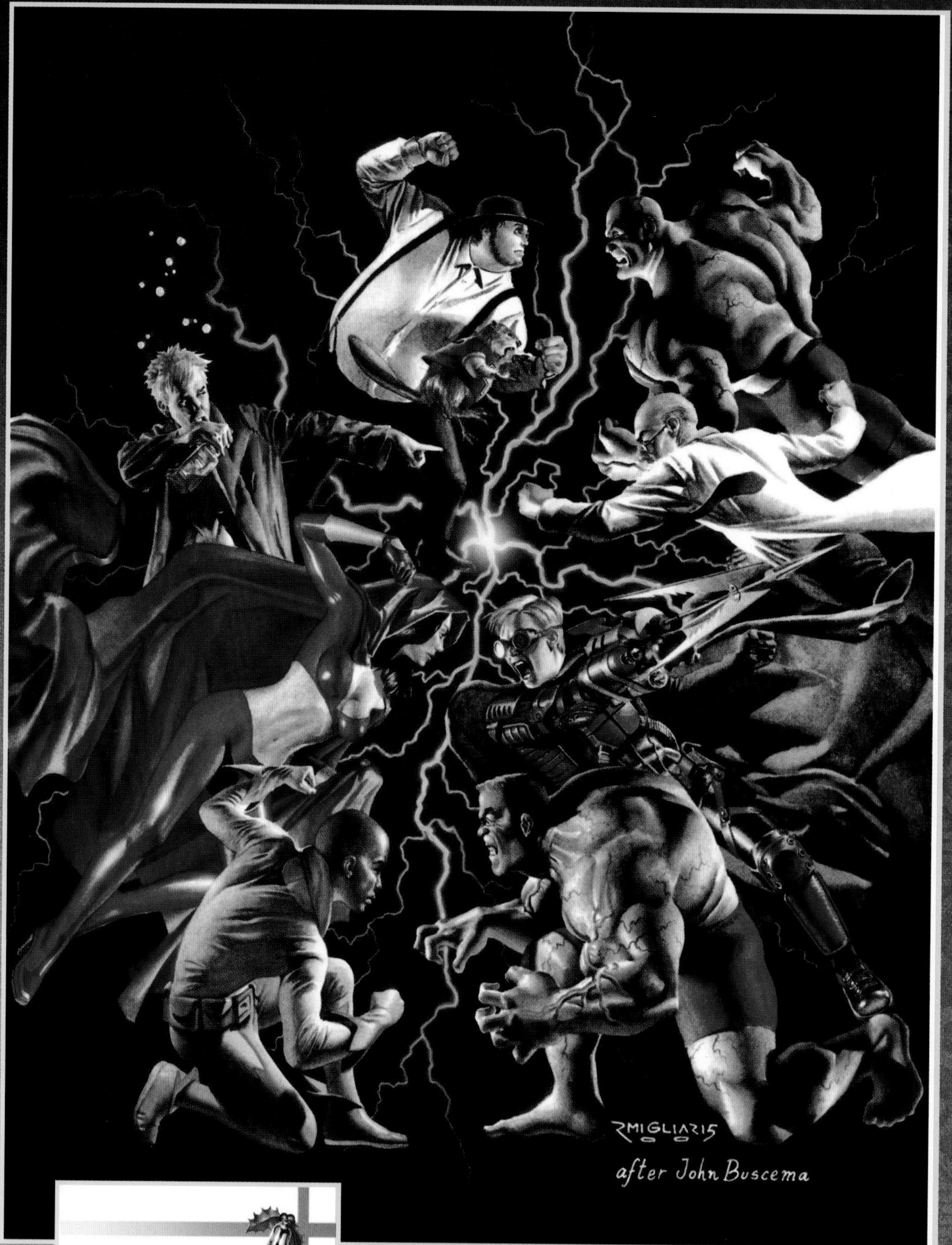
RMIGLIARIS
after John Buscema

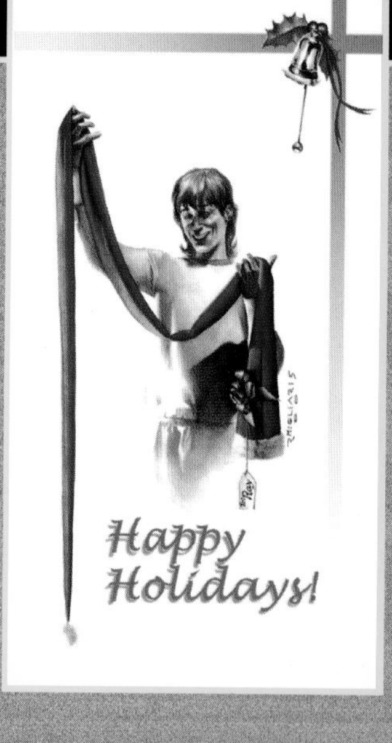
Happy
Holidays!

Shown above

Freshmen issue #6
art by: Rodolfo Migliari

facing page top

Freshmen: Yearbook
art by: Rodolfo Migliari
art by: Leonard Kirk and Kevin Senft with design by Zach Matheny

Freshmen Holiday Card
art by: Rodolfo Migliari

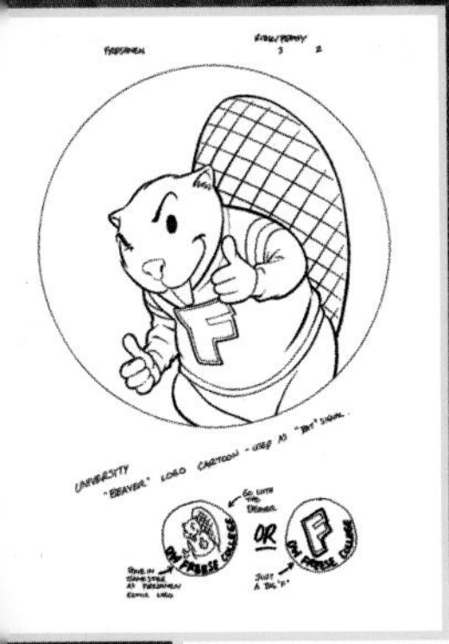

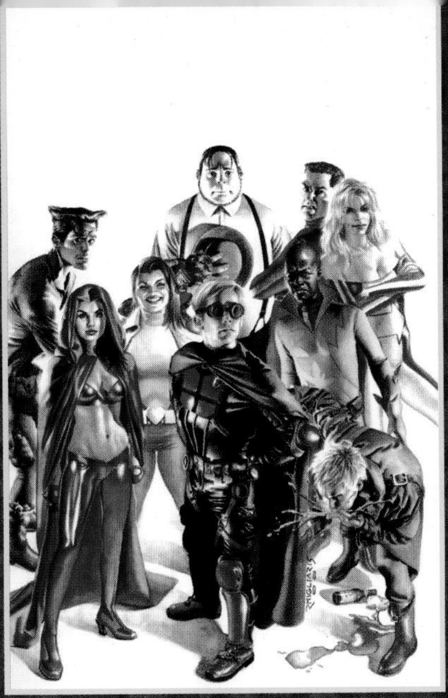

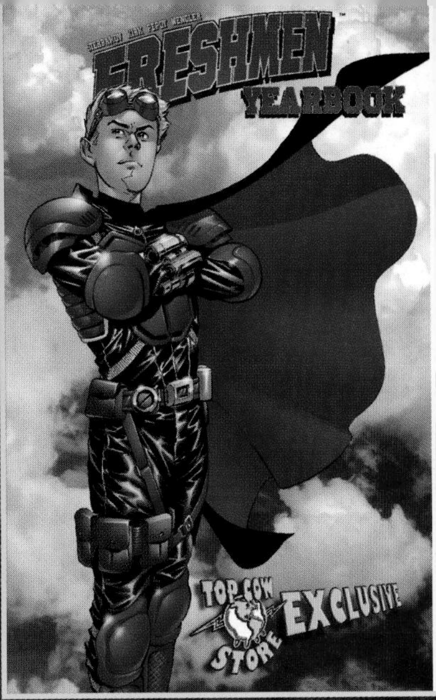

FRESHMEN
YEARBOOK
TOP COW STORE EXCLUSIVE

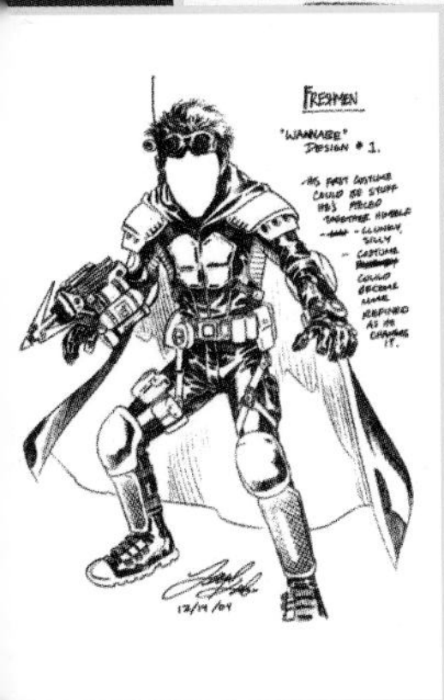

FRESHMEN
"WANNABE" DESIGN #1.

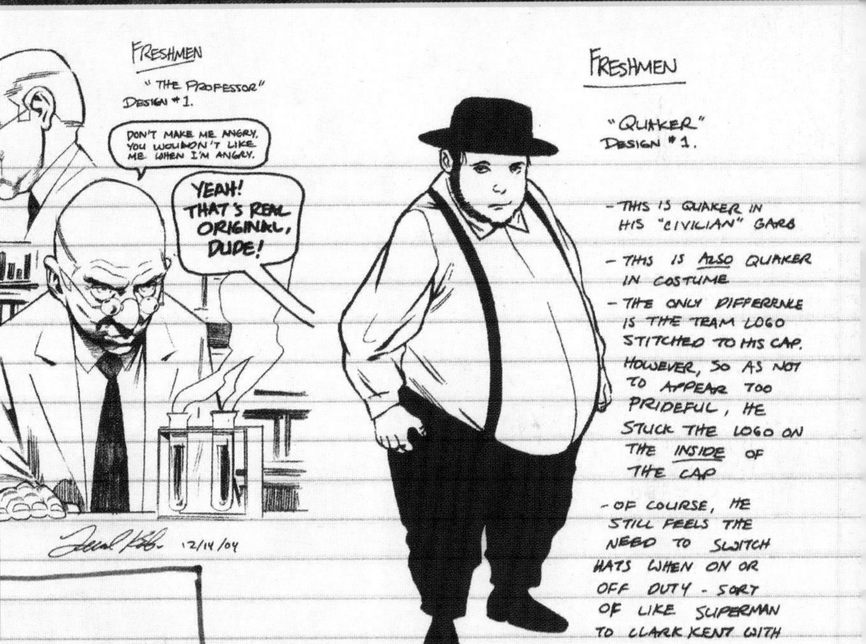

FRESHMEN
"THE PROFESSOR" DESIGN #1.
DON'T MAKE ME ANGRY. YOU WOULDN'T LIKE ME WHEN I'M ANGRY.
YEAH! THAT'S REAL ORIGINAL, DUDE!
12/14/04
FRESHMEN
"QUAKER" DESIGN #1.
- THIS IS QUAKER IN HIS "CIVILIAN" GARB
- THIS IS ALSO QUAKER IN COSTUME
- THE ONLY DIFFERENCE IS THE TEAM LOGO STITCHED TO HIS CAP. HOWEVER, SO AS NOT TO APPEAR TOO PRIDEFUL, HE STUCK THE LOGO ON THE INSIDE OF THE CAP
- OF COURSE, HE STILL FEELS THE NEED TO SWITCH HATS WHEN ON OR OFF DUTY - SORT OF LIKE SUPERMAN TO CLARK KENT WITH THE GLASSES

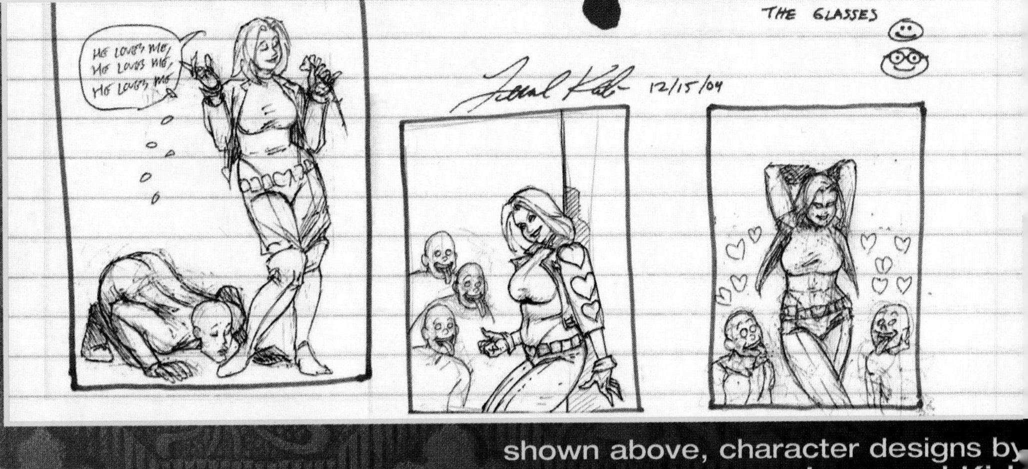

12/15/04
HE LOVES ME, HE LOVES ME, HE LOVES ME

shown above, character designs by
Leonard Kirk

and below, cover concepts for *Freshmen* issue #1 variants by
Joseph Michael Linsner

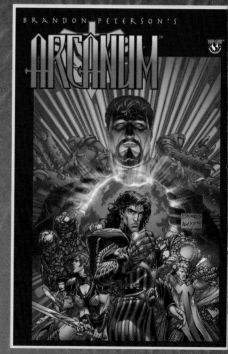

COMMON GROUNDS
"Endearing, moving and painfully human..." — Guillermo del Toro, director, Hellboy and Blade II

Common Grounds

written by: Troy Hickman with ar
Dan Jurgens, George Perez
Ethan van Sciver and more!

(ISBN: 1-58240-436-4) US $14.9

"Endearing, moving and painfully human, COMMON GROUNDS is as uncommon as it gets. Enjoy."

-Guillermo del Toro, *Blade II, Hellb* director

PIN-UP BY
STAN SAKAI (USAGI YOJIMBO)
INTRODUCTION BY
J. MICHAEL STRACZYNSKI
(RISING STARS, AMAZING SPIDER-MAN)
No Honor
FIONA KAI AVERY · CLAYTON CRAIN
JONATHAN GLAPION · MATT NELSON

No Honor

written by: Fiona Kai Avery with art by Clayton Crain, Jonathan Glapion and Matt Nelson

(ISBN: 1-58240-321-x) US $12.99

"There is something acutely powerful about Avery's handling of action sequences, which seem to explode with color and emotion."

-Daniel E. Blackston, SFReader.com, Firebrand Fiction Reviews

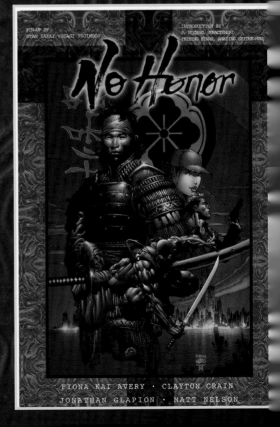

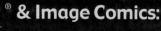